Quattro Pro® 4 QuickStart

Don Roche Jr.

Publisher: Lloyd J. Short

Associate Publisher: Rick Ranucci

Product Development Manager: Thomas H. Bennett

Book Designer: Scott Cook

Production Team: Claudia Bell, Christine Cook, Jerry Ellis, Dennis Clay Hager, Phil Kitchel, Bob LaRoche, Linda Quigley, Linda Seifert, Dennis Sheehan, Louise Shinault, Susan VandeWalle, Johnna VanHoose, Mary Beth Wakefield, Lisa Wilson

Product Director
Kathie-Jo Arnoff

Aquisitions Editor
Tim Ryan

Production Editor
Barbara K. Koenig

Editors
Karen Grooms
Julie McLaughlin Foster

Technical Editor
Mark Silvia

*Composed in ITC Garamond
and MCPdigital by Que Corporation.*

Dedication

This book is dedicated to my beautiful wife, Kathy, for always understanding and believing; and to the memory of my mother, who would
have liked to have seen my name on the inside cover of a book.

About the Author

Don Roche Jr. is currently a software trainer and consultant in Austin, Texas. He spent the past two years as a senior trainer and curriculum developer for JWP Business Land. Prior to joining JWP, Don worked for Lotus Development Corporation for seven years. He is the author of *Excel 4 for Windows Quick Reference* and a contributing author to Que's *Using 1-2-3 for Windows*, *1-2-3 Power Macros*, and *Using 1-2-3 Release 2.4*, Special Edition. He also has served as technical editor on 15 books for four publishers, including Que.

Trademark Acknowledgments

Que Corporation has made every effort to supply trademark information about company names, products, and services mentioned in this book. Trademarks indicated below were derived from various sources. Que Corporation cannot attest to the accuracy of this information.

1-2-3, Lotus, Symphony, and VisiCalc are registered trademarks and Allways is a trademark of Lotus Development Corporation.

Bitstream is a registered trademark of Bitstream Inc.

CompuServe is a registered trademark of CompuServe Incorporated.

dBASE, dBASE II, dBASE III, and dBASE IV are registered trademarks and dBASE III PLUS is a trademark of Ashton-Tate Corporation.

EPSON is a registered trademark of Epson Corporation.

Harvard Graphics is a registered trademark of Software Publishing Corporation.

IBM and PS/2 are registered trademarks and XT is a trademark of International Business Machines Corporation.

MS-DOS and MultiPlan are registered trademarks and Windows is a trademark of Microsoft Corporation.

Paradox and Quattro are registered trademarks and Reflex is a trademark of Borland International, Inc.

PostScript is a registered trademark of Adobe Systems Incorporated.

WordPerfect is a registered trademark of WordPerfect Corporation.

Acknowledgments

Tim Ryan, for his confidence and direction, and for putting together a terrific team for this project.

Kathie-Jo Arnoff, for her contributions to developing the structure of the book, her valuable insights on book content, and for understanding the needs of the readers of this book.

Barbara Koenig, for her superb edit of the book, her insightful questions, her dedication to ensuring high quality in the final manuscript, and for keeping a sense of humor with Appendix A.

Mark Silvia, for his excellent technical edit and valuable content recommendations for this book.

Contents at a Glance

Introduction 1

1 An Overview of Quattro Pro 7

2 Getting Started 27

3 Introducing Spreadsheet Basics 55

4 Working with Blocks 103

5 Building A Spreadsheet 125

6 Modifying a Spreadsheet 159

7 Formatting a Spreadsheet 201

8 Using @Functions 225

9 Printing Reports 255

10 Managing Files 295

11 Creating and Printing Graphs 329

12 Managing Data 383

13 Understanding Macros 445

14 Customizing the SpeedBar 475

A Installing Quattro Pro 4 489

B Summary of Quattro Pro Commands 497

Index 515

Table of Contents

Introduction 1

What Does This Book Contain? 1

Who Should Use This Book? 3

What Do You Need To Run Quattro Pro? 3

What Is New in Quattro Pro 4? 4

Where To Find More Help 5

Conventions Used in This Book 5

1   An Overview of Quattro Pro 7

What Is a Spreadsheet? 9

The Quattro Pro Electronic Spreadsheet 11

The Size of Quattro Pro's Spreadsheet 13

The Spreadsheet Window 15

Cells 16

Formulas 16

What-If Analyses 17

@Functions 19

Commands 19

The SpeedBar 20

Quattro Pro Graphics 20

Quattro Pro Database Management 23

Macros and Macro Commands 24

Summary 25

2   Getting Started 27

Starting Quattro Pro 28

WYSIWYG Mode versus Text Mode 29

Suspending and Exiting Quattro Pro 30

Using /File Utilities DOS Shell To Suspend Quattro Pro 31

Using /File Exit To Exit Quattro Pro 34

Learning the Keyboard 35

The Alphanumeric Keys 37

The Numeric Keypad and Direction Keys 39

The Function Keys 39

Ctrl-Key Shortcuts 41

Understanding the Quattro Pro Screen 42

The Pull-Down Menu Bar 43

The Input Line 44

The Spreadsheet Area 44

The Status Line 45

The SpeedBar 45

The Quattro Pro Indicators 47

Accessing the Quattro Pro Help System 50

Summary 53

3   Introducing Spreadsheet Basics **55**

Moving around the Spreadsheet 56

Using the Basic Direction Keys 60

Scrolling the Spreadsheet 60

Using the Home and End Keys 63

Using the GoTo (F5) Key 66

Selecting Commands from Menus 67

Highlighting Method 68

Typing Method 69

Mouse Method 69

Entering Data into the Spreadsheet 71

Entering Labels 71

Entering Numbers 76

Entering Formulas 76

Using Mathematical Operators in Formulas 79

Editing Data in the Spreadsheet 86

Using the Undo Feature 88

Activating Undo 89

What Cannot Be Undone? 90

Naming, Saving, and Retrieving Files 90

Naming Files 90

Saving Files 92

Retrieving Files 95

Summary 100

4   Working with Blocks **103**

What Is a Block? 104

Designating a Block 105

Typing a Block Address 105

Highlighting a Block 106

Typing a Block Name 108

Naming Blocks 108
    Naming a Single Cell or a Group of Cells 111
    Naming a Series of Single Cells 112
    Changing the Cell Addresses of a Block Name 114
Deleting Block Names 114
Erasing Blocks 116
Listing Block Names 117
Creating a Table of Block Names 119
Attaching a Note to a Block Name 120
Summary 122

5   Building a Spreadsheet 125
Setting Column Widths 126
    Setting the Width of a Single Column 127
    Setting the Widths of All Columns at Once 128
    Setting the Width of Contiguous Columns 129
Hiding Columns 131
Splitting the Screen 133
Locking Titles On-Screen 137
Inserting Columns and Rows 141
Deleting Columns and Rows 143
Suppressing the Display of Zeros 146
Recalculating the Spreadsheet 148
Protecting the Spreadsheet 150
    Protecting the Entire Spreadsheet 150
    Protecting a Block in the Spreadsheet 151
    Protecting Formulas in a Spreadsheet 153
Summary 156

6   Modifying a Spreadsheet 159
Moving the Contents of Cells 160
Copying the Contents of Cells 163
    Copying Only the Contents of a Cell 169
    Copying Only the Format of a Cell 171
    Addressing Cells 174
    Transposing Rows and Columns 186
    Converting Formulas to Values 188
    Tips for Copying 190

Searching for and Replacing Cell Contents 191
   Searching for a String 191
   Replacing One String with Another String 194
   Tips for Using the Search-and-Replace Feature 197
Summary.. 198

7   **Formatting a Spreadsheet** **201**

Formatting Cell Contents 202
   Setting Block and Spreadsheet Formats 204
   Controlling the International Formats 209
Changing the Font in a Block 210
   Changing the Font Color in a Block 212
   Using Prearranged Fonts 214
Setting a Border and Shading for a Block 215
   Setting a Border for a Block 216
   Setting Shading for a Block 218
Defining and Using Styles 220
Summary.. 222

8   **Using @Functions** **225**

Entering a Quattro Pro @Function 226
Using Mathematical Functions 227
   Computing Integers with @INT 228
   Rounding Numbers with @ROUND 229
Using Date and Time Functions 230
   Converting Date Values to Serial Numbers with @DATE 231
   Converting Date Strings to Serial Numbers
      with @DATEVALUE 232
   Finding the Current Date and Time with @NOW 233
Using Financial Functions 234
   Calculating Loan Payment Amounts with @PAYMT 236
   Calculating Present and Future Values
      with @PVAL and @FVAL 237
Using Statistical Functions... 238
   Computing the Arithmetic Mean with @AVG 239
   Counting Cell Entries with @COUNT 239
   Finding Maximum and Minimum Values
      with @MAX and @MIN 240
Using Database Statistical Functions 241

Using Logical Functions 243
    Creating Conditional Tests with @IF 244
    Checking for Errors with @TRUE and @FALSE 246
Using String Functions 246
    Converting the Case of Strings with @LOWER, @UPPER,
    and @PROPER 248
    Repeating Strings with @REPEAT 249
Using Miscellaneous Functions 249
    Trapping Errors with @ERR and @NA 251
    Finding Table Entries with @HLOOKUP
    and @VLOOKUP 251
Summary 252

9   Printing Reports **255**
Selecting a Print Option 256
Printing Draft-Quality Reports 258
    Printing a Full Screen of Data 258
    Printing a One-Page Report 259
    Printing Two or More Pages with Headings 262
Excluding Segments within a Print Block 266
    Excluding Columns 267
    Excluding Rows 269
    Excluding Blocks 272
Controlling Paper Movement 274
    Using the Skip Line, Form Feed, and Align Options 275
    Setting Page Breaks within the Spreadsheet 276
Enhancing Reports with Print Options 278
    Adding Headers and Footers 278
    Changing the Page Layout 282
Previewing a Printed Report 284
Printing a Listing of Cell Contents 286
Resetting the Print Options 288
Preparing Output for Other Programs 289
Summary 292

10 Managing Files **295**
Erasing a File from Memory 296
Protecting Files with Passwords 297
    Creating a Password 298
    Retrieving a Password-Protected File 300

Deleting a Password 300

Changing a Password 301

Saving and Retrieving Partial Files 302

Extracting Data 302

Combining Files 305

Linking Cells between Files 312

Establishing a Link 312

Refreshing Links 315

Specifying a Drive and Directory 317

Deleting Files 320

Importing Files into Quattro Pro 322

Importing ASCII Text Files 322

Importing and Exporting Files from Other Programs 325

Summary.. 326

11 Creating and Printing Graphs 329

Creating a Graph: An Overview 330

Hardware Requirements 331

The Graph Creation Process 331

Creating a Basic Graph with Fast Graph 336

Selecting a Graph Type 339

Specifying a Data Series Block 348

Defining One Data Block at a Time 349

Defining All Data Blocks at Once 354

Enhancing the Appearance of a Graph 356

Using the Text Option 357

Entering Labels within a Graph 360

Using the Legends Option 363

Setting a Background Grid...................................... 366

Annotating Graphs 368

Zooming and Panning a Graph 373

Saving Graph Settings 375

Placing a Graph in a Spreadsheet 377

Printing Graphs 379

Summary... 381

12 Managing Data 383

What Is a Database? 384

Using Quattro Pro as a Database 386

Understanding the Database Menu 387

Planning and Building a Database 388
    Determining Required Output 388
    Positioning the Database 390
    Entering Data 390
    Restricting Data Entry Movement to a Particular Block 393
Modifying a Database 395
    Inserting and Deleting Records 396
    Inserting and Deleting Fields 398
Sorting Database Records 400
    A One-Key Row Sort 402
    A Two-Key Row Sort 405
    A One-Key Column Sort 408
    Tips for Sorting Database Records 411
Searching for Records 414
    Minimum Search Requirements 415
    Searching for Specific Records 416
    Listing All Specified Records 423
    Creating More Complex Critcria Tables 429
    Performing Other Types of Searches 437
    Using the Query (F7) Key 441
Summary 441

13 Understanding Macros **445**

What Is a Macro? 446
    The Elements of Macros 448
    Macro Key Names and Special Keys 449
Planning Macros 453
Positioning Macros in the Spreadsheet 454
Documenting Macros 455
Naming Macros 456
Using the Record Feature To Record Keystrokes 459
Executing Macros 463
Using an Automatic Macro 464
Debugging and Editing Macros 465
    Common Errors in Macros 466
    Undoing Macros 466
    Using DEBUG Mode To Debug Macros 467
    Editing Macros 469

Creating a Macro Library 470
   A Macro That Prints a Specified Block 471
   A Macro That Enters Text 472
   A Macro That Sets the Widths of a Block of Columns 472
   A Macro That Saves a File 472
   A Macro That Sums a Specified Block 472
   Summary 473

14 Customizing the SpeedBar **475**

Customizing the READY Mode SpeedBar 476
   Modifying a Button on the READY Mode SpeedBar 476
   Adding a New Button to the READY Mode SpeedBar 481
Customizing the EDIT Mode SpeedBar 484
   Modifying a Button on the EDIT Mode SpeedBar 484
   Adding a New Button to the EDIT Mode SpeedBar 486
Summary 488

A Installing Quattro Pro 4 .... **489**

The Quattro Pro Diskettes 490
Installing the Program 490
   Starting the Installation 491
   Selecting a Monitor Type 491
   Entering Purchase Information 492
   Selecting To Install on a Server 492
   Selecting a Printer 492
   Selecting the Display Mode 492
   Selecting To Install for Windows 493
   Selecting Bitstream Fonts 493
   Completing the Installation 493
Loading and Quitting Quattro Pro 494
Reconfiguring and Enhancing Quattro Pro 494
Upgrading from Version 3.0 to Version 4.0 494

B Summary of Quattro Pro Commands **497**

Index **515**

Introduction

If you are new to Quattro Pro and have access to Version 4 of the program, this book is for you. *Quattro Pro 4 QuickStart* helps you grasp the basics of using Quattro Pro, enabling you to begin creating your own spreadsheets (or modify existing spreadsheets created by others) with minimal effort. You don't even need to be familiar with computers; you learn keyboard basics and, if you haven't already installed the program, how to install Quattro Pro on your computer.

Quattro Pro 4 QuickStart uses a tutorial approach, taking you step-by-step through important concepts, describing all the fundamentals you need to know about the program. The text supplies essential information and provides comments on what you see. The book's numerous illustrations help guide you through procedures and clarify difficult concepts.

Learning any new program can be an intimidating experience. *Quattro Pro 4 QuickStart* is designed to help shorten your learning curve by enabling you to learn basic concepts quickly. Whether you are new to Quattro Pro or have tried unsuccessfully to learn the program, you will find *Quattro Pro 4 QuickStart* a quick way to learn the fundamentals of Quattro Pro.

What Does This Book Contain?

The chapters in *Quattro Pro 4 QuickStart* are organized to take you from basic information to more sophisticated tasks, including printing reports and creating graphs.

Chapter 1, "An Overview of Quattro Pro," shows you the wide range of Quattro Pro's capabilities. You explore how you can use Quattro Pro for spreadsheet, graphics, and database applications.

Chapter 2, "Getting Started," explains how to start and leave Quattro Pro and teaches you the basics about the keyboard, the screen, and Quattro Pro's Help features.

Chapter 3, "Introducing Spreadsheet Basics," teaches you about the fundamental tasks of using a spreadsheet. In this chapter, you discover how to enter and edit data, move around in the spreadsheet, select commands from pulldown menus, and save and retrieve files.

Chapters 4, 5, 6, and 7 cover all the basic tasks you need to create a spreadsheet. Chapter 4, "Working with Blocks," teaches you how to use blocks and commands associated with block commands. Chapter 5, "Building a Spreadsheet," shows you how to use spreadsheet commands to enhance the appearance of your spreadsheets. Chapter 6, "Modifying a Spreadsheet," explains how to modify your spreadsheet by moving and copying cell contents, and finding and replacing cell contents. Chapter 7, "Formatting a Spreadsheet," shows you step-by-step how to perform formatting tasks.

Chapter 8, "Using @Functions," introduces you to Quattro Pro's selection of built-in @functions for performing a variety of calculations. Among the functions illustrated are those for performing mathematical, statistical, and logical calculations.

Chapter 9, "Printing Reports," shows you how to set print specifications and organize your data for printing. You also learn to hide columns and rows, control paper movement, enhance a report by adding headers and footers, and change the page layout.

Chapter 10, "Managing Files," describes how to erase files from memory, how to use passwords to protect your spreadsheets, how to save and retrieve parts of files, and how to link cells between different files. This chapter also explains how to delete your files and import files from other software programs into Quattro Pro.

Chapter 11, "Creating and Printing Graphs," teaches you how to produce graphs with Quattro Pro, from selecting graph types to creating basic graphs. The chapter also teaches you how to enhance a basic graph with titles and legends. In addition, you learn how to insert a graph into a spreadsheet.

Chapter 12, "Managing Data," explains how to use Quattro Pro for data management. You learn to create and modify a database, and sort and search for specific records.

Chapter 13, "Understanding Macros," gives you an introduction to the concept of simple keystroke macros. The chapter teaches you to plan, position, create, name, and edit simple macros. The chapter also includes macros you can use to start your own macro library.

Chapter 14, "Customizing the SpeedBar," shows you how to customize both the READY mode and EDIT mode SpeedBars. You learn how to modify a SpeedBar button, how to completely change a SpeedBar button, and how to add a button to the SpeedBar.

The book concludes with two appendixes and an index. Appendix A shows you how to install Quattro Pro 4. Appendix B provides a reference to Quattro Pro's commands.

As you notice from the index, each topic is referenced in only one or two places. This apparent "lack" of cross-referencing actually means that this book does its job well; most information about a particular topic is contained in one section—or chapter—of this book.

Who Should Use This Book?

Quattro Pro 4 QuickStart is designed to be a quick guide for new Quattro Pro users. Whether you are sitting down with Quattro Pro for the first time or are trying—for the umpteenth time—to learn enough about Quattro Pro to use it efficiently, *Quattro Pro 4 QuickStart* gives you enough information to get you going quickly. The book highlights important concepts and takes you through important information by providing steps and explanations interwoven with examples and illustrations.

What Do You Need To Run Quattro Pro?

There are no prerequisites to using this book or, for that matter, to using Quattro Pro. This text assumes, of course, that you have the software, the hardware, and a desire to learn to use the program.

The following hardware is required to run Quattro Pro:

- An IBM XT, AT, PS/2 or compatible computer with a hard disk drive (6M) and a single floppy disk drive
- DOS 2.0 or later (3.2 or later is recommended)
- At least 512K of RAM (640K is recommended)

- A monochrome or color monitor (to use WYSIWYG, you must have an EGA card with a minimum of 256K, or a VGA card)
- A printer (optional, but recommended)
- A mouse (optional, but highly recommended)

What Is New in Quattro Pro 4?

This book discusses the most commonly used and new features available with Quattro Pro 4. This version of Quattro Pro has been enhanced with the following additional options:

Spreadsheet Enhancements

- The SpeedBar, which is a row of buttons at the top of the screen (or to the right of the screen if you are in Text mode) that enables you to perform spreadsheet tasks quickly by clicking a button.
- Dialog boxes rather than menus in some areas, which makes setting multiple options easier and quicker.
- The capability to copy only the format of a cell or block or only the contents of a cell or block.
- The capability to protect only cells that contain formulas in a spreadsheet.
- A selection remains selected after you perform an operation, enabling you to perform multiple operations quickly on the selected block.
- The capability to sort by columns, which enables you to sort your data regardless of the database's structure.
- Additional file list box buttons, which enable you to retrieve your data quickly and easily from different drives or directories.
- Enhanced Lotus 1-2-3 compatibility, enabling you to retrieve 1-2-3 Release 3.1 files, 1-2-3 Release 2.2 files using Allways formats, and 1-2-3 Release 2.3 files using Impress and WYSIWYG publishing formats.
- The capability to create your own styles and then save them to use with other spreadsheets. You also can create your own numeric formats to use with any spreadsheet.

Graph Enhancements

- The capability to zoom in on a specific part of a graph and then pan across the graph.

4

- The capability to use bubble graphs to show not only the position of the data on the graph, but the relationship of the data to each other.

When comparing Version 4 to previous versions of Quattro Pro (Versions 2 and 3), you may find slight differences in the wording of the menu items. In this book, the illustrations and text reflect Version 4.

Where To Find More Help

After you learn the fundamentals presented in this book, you may want to learn more advanced applications of Quattro Pro. Que Corporation has a full line of Quattro Pro books you can use. Among these are *Using Quattro Pro 4*, Special Edition, and *Quattro Pro 4 Quick Reference*. For more information on how to use DOS commands, new computer users will benefit from reading Que's *MS-DOS 5 QuickStart*.

You can use Quattro Pro's Help feature to answer some of your questions while working with Quattro Pro. Using Help is explained and illustrated in Chapter 2, "Getting Started."

Should all else fail, contact your computer dealer, or call Borland International Product Support at (408) 438-5300. If you subscribe to the CompuServe information service, you can send messages to Borland's technical support staff at the Borland forum.

Conventions Used in This Book

Quattro Pro 4 QuickStart uses a number of conventions to help you learn the program. One example of each convention is provided to help you distinguish the different elements in Quattro Pro.

References to keys are presented as they appear on the keyboard of the IBM Personal Computer and most compatibles. For example, the Enter key appears as ⏎Enter. In Quattro Pro, you use the function keys, F1 through F10, for special situations, and each of these keys is named according to its function. In the text, the key name is followed by the function key in parentheses, such as Graph (F10).

Direct quotations of words that appear on-screen are spelled as they appear on-screen and are printed in a special typeface. Information you are asked to type is printed in a **bold blue typeface**. One letter (usually the first) in each Quattro Pro menu command, such as Numeric Format, also appears in a bold blue typeface. This letter indicates the key you press to select that command.

Elements printed in uppercase include block names (SALES), functions (@PAYMT), and cell references (A1..G5).

Conventions that pertain to macros deserve special mention here:

- Single-character macro names appear as a backslash (\) followed by a lowercase single-character. For example, \a indicates that you press and hold down Alt and then press A.
- In a macro line, Quattro Pro menu keystrokes appear in lowercase, such as /enc.
- Block names within macros appear in uppercase, such as /encTEST.
- In macros, representations of direction keys, such as {DOWN}; function keys, such as {CALC}; and editing keys, such as {DEL}, appear in uppercase letters and are surrounded by braces.
- The Enter key appears as a tilde (~).

When two keys are separated by a hyphen, such as Ctrl-Break or Alt-F10, you press and hold down the first key and then press the second key.

In the illustrations, blue lines emphasize the most important areas of the screen figures. Note that most of the illustrations in this book assume the following:

- Display mode is WYSIWYG
- Mouse and mouse driver are installed
- Undo is enabled
- Grid is turned off
- Quattro Pro menu tree is displayed (not the Lotus 1-2-3 menu tree)
- Dialog boxes are turned on (select /Options Startup Use Dialog Boxes Yes)
- Protection and Formula Protect are disabled

An Overview of Quattro Pro

Before you put your fingers on the keyboard to start using Quattro Pro, you need to know the range of capabilities of this software package. If you are inheriting a spreadsheet created by someone else, coming up to speed with Quattro Pro may require little more than simply entering data. On the other hand, if someone hands you the Quattro Pro package and says, "Prepare a sales forecast for product A," your task may seem a bit intimidating. Whether you are an experienced or new spreadsheet user, this chapter shows you some of the many features of Quattro Pro and describes how they can fit into your day-to-day tasks.

As you read through this chapter, ask yourself which of the Quattro Pro features you will use most often. Will you maintain an accounts receivable spreadsheet? Perhaps your department is in charge of setting up a database to track inventory. Will you be responsible for printing reports and graphs? Whatever the application, read the appropriate overview sections closely, and look for chapter references at the ends of these sections for chapters in this book that deal more specifically with that topic.

What is a spreadsheet?

The Quattro Pro electronic spreadsheet

Quattro Pro graphics

Quattro Pro database management

Macros and macro commands

1

Key Terms in This Chapter

Electronic spreadsheet	The Quattro Pro spreadsheet (or *worksheet*) is known as the electronic replacement for the accountant's pad.
Direction keys	The keys that enable you to move within the Quattro Pro spreadsheet—including PgUp, PgDn, Home, End, Tab, ←, →, ↑, and ↓.
Mouse	A pointing device, separate from your computer's keyboard, that enables you to move within the Quattro Pro spreadsheet and select commands and functions.
Cell	The intersection of a row and column in the Quattro Pro spreadsheet.
Cell selector	The highlighted bar that enables you to enter data within the spreadsheet area.
Formula	An action performed on a specified cell or group of cells. For example, +A1+B1 sums the contents of cells A1 and B1.
@Function	A shorthand method of using formulas. For example, instead of typing the formula +A1+B1+C1+D1+E1, you can use the @SUM function @SUM(A1..E1).
Command	A menu selection you use to carry out an operation within the spreadsheet.

Whether you are an experienced computer user who is new to the Quattro Pro program or you are using a computer for the first time, you will find that you can quickly grasp the fundamentals of Quattro Pro. If you start by learning the most basic concepts of Quattro Pro and then gradually build on your knowledge and experience, you will be amazed by how easily you learn the program. If, however, you jump right in and immediately start using string functions or macros, you may find yourself running into snags. This book uses an easy, step-by-step approach to demonstrate the fundamental tasks you can perform with Quattro Pro.

What Is a Spreadsheet?

Sometimes known as a ledger sheet or accountant's pad, a *spreadsheet* is a specialized piece of paper on which you record information in columns and rows. Spreadsheets usually contain a mixture of descriptive text and accompanying numbers and calculations. Typical business applications include balance sheets, income statements, inventory sheets, and sales reports.

Although you may be unfamiliar with business applications for spreadsheets, you already use a rudimentary spreadsheet if you keep a checkbook. Similar to an accountant's pad, a checkbook register is a paper grid divided by lines into rows and columns. Within this grid, you record the check number, the date, a transaction description, the check amount, any deposits, and a running balance.

NUMBER	DATE	DESCRIPTION OF TRANSACTION	PAYMENT/DEBT (−)	✓	FEE (IF ANY) (−)	DEPOSIT/CREDIT (+)	BALANCE $1000 00	
1001	9/3/89	Department Store Credit	51 03				948 97	
1002	9/13/89	Electric	95 12				853 85	
1003	9/14/89	Grocery	74 25				779 60	
1004	9/15/89	Class Supplies	354 57				425 03	
	9/16/89	Deposit				250 00	675 03	
1005	9/21/89	Telephone	49 43				625 60	

This example shows a manual checkbook register.

What happens when you make an invalid entry in your checkbook register or when you have to void an entry? Such procedures are messy because you have to erase or cross out entries, rewrite them, and recalculate everything. The limitations of manual spreadsheets are apparent, even with this simple example of a checkbook register.

For complex business applications, the dynamic quality of an electronic spreadsheet such as Quattro Pro is indispensable. You can change one number and recalculate the entire spreadsheet in an instant. Entering new values is nearly effortless. Performing calculations on a column or row of numbers is accomplished with formulas—usually the same type of formulas that calculators use.

1

Compare the manual checkbook register to the following electronic one. Notice that the electronic checkbook register is set up with columns and rows. Columns are marked by letters across the top of the spreadsheet; rows are numbered along the side. Each transaction is recorded in a row, the same way you record data in a manual checkbook.

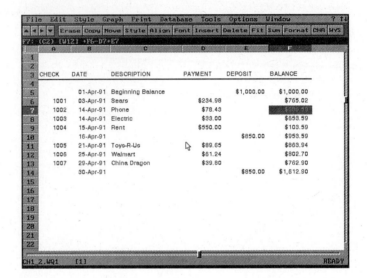

This example shows an electronic checkbook register.

Assigning column letters and row numbers lends itself well to creating formulas. Note the following formula in the upper left corner of the electronic checkbook:

    +F6–D7+E7

To Quattro Pro, these instructions translate to

    Previous BALANCE minus PAYMENT plus DEPOSIT

As you can see from this simple example, formulas enable you to establish mathematical relationships between values stored in certain places on your spreadsheet. Formulas enable you to make changes to a spreadsheet easily, and you can quickly see the results. In the electronic checkbook, if you delete an entire transaction (row), the spreadsheet automatically recalculates itself. You also can change an amount and not worry about recalculating your figures, because the electronic spreadsheet updates all balances.

If you forget to record a check or deposit in Quattro Pro, you can insert a new row at the location of the omitted transaction and enter the information. Subsequent entries move down one row, and the new balance is automatically calculated. Inserting new columns is just as easy. Indicate where you want the new column to go, and Quattro Pro inserts a blank column at that point, moving existing information to the right of that column.

What if you want to know how much you have spent at the local department store since the beginning of the year? With a manual checkbook, you have to look for each check written to the store and total the amounts. Not only does this task take considerable time, but you may overlook some of the checks. An electronic checkbook can sort your checks by description so that all similar transactions are together. You then create a formula that totals all the checks written to the department store.

This simple checkbook example demonstrates how valuable an electronic spreadsheet is for maintaining financial data. Although you may not want to use Quattro Pro to balance your personal checkbook, an electronic spreadsheet is an indispensable tool in today's modern office.

The Quattro Pro Electronic Spreadsheet

Quattro Pro has a number of capabilities, but the foundation of the program is the electronic spreadsheet. The framework of this spreadsheet contains the graphics and data management elements of the program. You produce graphics with spreadsheet commands. Data management occurs in the standard row and column spreadsheet layout.

The importance of the spreadsheet as the basis for Quattro Pro cannot be overemphasized. All the commands for the related features of Quattro Pro are initiated from the same main menu as the spreadsheet commands, and all the commands have the same format. For example, all the commands for graphics display refer to data in the spreadsheet, and they use this data to draw graphs on-screen. For easy data management, the database is composed of records that are actually rows of cell entries in a spreadsheet.

Quattro Pro's integrated electronic spreadsheet replaces traditional financial modeling tools, reducing the time and effort needed to perform sophisticated accounting tasks.

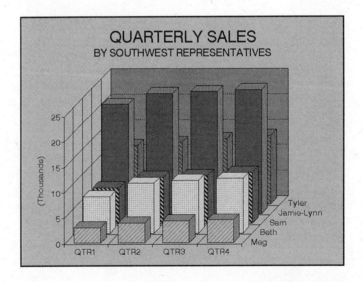

For example, Quattro Pro enables you to calculate monthly payments on a loan.

Also, with Quattro Pro's graphics capabilities, you can create 11 different types of two-dimensional graphs and 4 different types of three-dimensional graphs.

For example, this 3-D bar graph shows the sales dollars each salesperson contributed quarterly.

Finally, Quattro Pro's database commands and statistical functions help you manage and manipulate data.

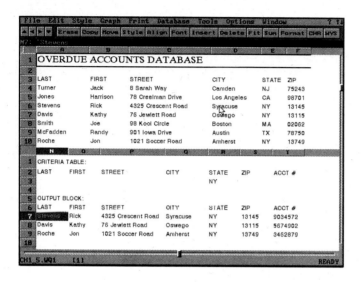

For example, from a database of overdue accounts, you can extract a list of the customers from New York, as displayed in the bottom half of this spreadsheet.

The Size of Quattro Pro's Spreadsheet

With 256 columns and 8,192 rows, the Quattro Pro spreadsheet contains more than 2,000,000 cells. The columns are lettered from A to Z, AA to AZ, BA to BZ, and so on, to IV for the last column. The rows are sequentially numbered from 1 to 8,192.

13

1

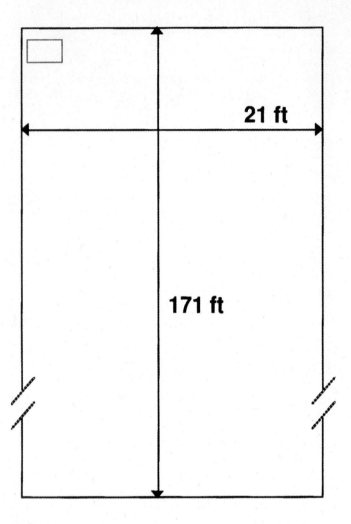

To visualize the spreadsheet (or *worksheet*), imagine a giant sheet of grid paper approximately 21 feet wide and 171 feet high—the approximate dimensions of Quattro Pro's spreadsheet. The small box in the upper left corner of this illustration represents the approximate size of your screen.

Although the Quattro Pro spreadsheet contains many columns and rows, using the entire sheet presents some limitations. If you imagine storing just one character in each of the 2,097,152 available cells, you end up with a spreadsheet that is far larger than the 640K maximum random-access memory (RAM) of an IBM PC.

For Quattro Pro 4, the program alone requires 512K of RAM, though 640K is recommended. Quattro Pro needs this amount of RAM because the program keeps in its memory all cell formats, spreadsheet and command blocks, print options, and graph settings.

The Spreadsheet Window

Because the Quattro Pro grid is so large, you cannot view the entire spreadsheet on-screen at one time. The screen thus serves as a *window* to a small section of the spreadsheet. To view other parts of the spreadsheet, you can use the *direction keys* ([Tab⇄], [PgUp], [PgDn], [Home], [End], [←], [→], [↑], and [↓]) or a mouse to move the cell selector around the spreadsheet. When the cell selector reaches the edge of the current window, the window shifts to follow the cell selector across and up (or down) the spreadsheet.

To illustrate the window concept, imagine cutting a one-inch square hole in a piece of cardboard. If you place the cardboard over this page, you can see only a one-inch square piece of text. The rest of the text is still on the page, but it's hidden from view. When you move the cardboard around the page (the same way that the window moves as you press the direction keys), different parts of the page become visible.

By default, a Quattro Pro spreadsheet displays 9 columns—each 9 characters wide—and 22 rows (if WYSIWYG display mode was selected as the default setting during installation).

You can change the default number of columns that are displayed by narrowing or widening one or more of the columns.

1

Cells

Each row in a Quattro Pro spreadsheet is assigned a number; each column is assigned a letter. The intersections of the rows and columns are called *cells*. Cells are identified by their row and column coordinates. The cell located at the intersection of column A and row 15, for example, is called A15. The cell at the intersection of column X and row 55 is called X55. You can fill cells with two types of information: labels, which are text entries; or values, which consist of numbers or formulas, or both.

A *cell selector* enables you to enter information into the current cell. In Quattro Pro, as in most spreadsheets, the cell selector looks like a highlighted rectangle on-screen. The cell selector typically is one row high and one column wide.

In this example, the cell selector is highlighting cell D10, which contains a numeric value.

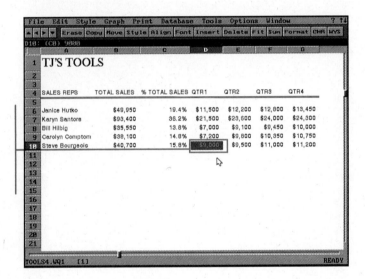

Formulas

Electronic spreadsheets enable you to create mathematical relationships between cells by referring to the cell addresses and using the appropriate operators (+, −, /, and *). Suppose, for example, that cell C1 contains the formula

    +A1+B1

Cell C1 then displays the sum of the contents of cells A1 and B1. (The + sign before A1 tells Quattro Pro that what you have entered into this cell is a formula, not text.) The cell references serve as variables in the equation. Each time you modify the contents of cell A1 or B1, the sum in cell C1 automatically reflects these changes.

Although you see only values in the spreadsheet cells, Quattro Pro stores all the data, formulas, and formats in memory. A simple Quattro Pro spreadsheet displays values, not the formulas "behind" them.

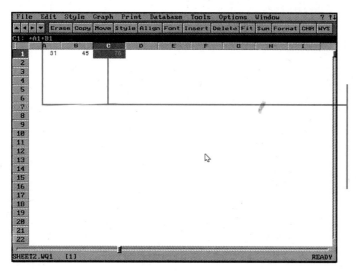

In this example, the cell selector is positioned on C1, and its formula is displayed at the top left of the screen.

What-If Analyses

With Quattro Pro, you can play "what if " with your spreadsheet data. After you have built a set of formulas into Quattro Pro's spreadsheet, you can modify and recalculate the spreadsheet with amazing speed, using several sets of assumptions. Working with a variety of assumptions—each using different data—enables you to build different what-if scenarios. If you use only paper, a pencil, and a calculator to build your spreadsheet data, every change re-quires manual recalculation of each formula. If the model has 100 formulas and you change the first one, you must make 100 manual calculations so that the change flows through the entire model. If you use a Quattro Pro spread-sheet, however, the same change requires pressing only a few keys—the program does the rest. This capability enables you to perform extensive what-if analyses.

Suppose, for example, that you want to establish the taxes paid by employees. You can quickly figure the tax amount paid for different tax rates using the Quattro Pro spreadsheet.

If you enter **8.5%** into D4 as the tax rate, Quattro Pro calculates the tax amount in column D.

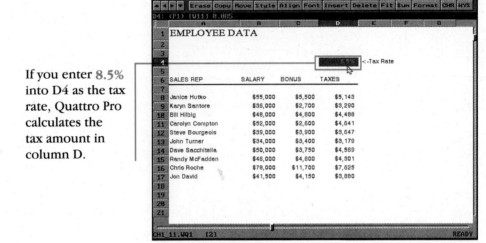

If you change the tax rate from 8.5% to 10%, Quattro Pro automatically recalculates the new tax figures.

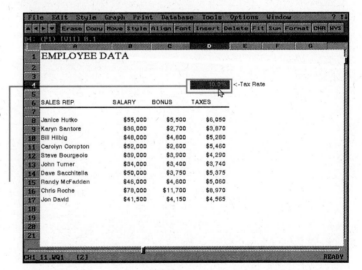

With Quattro Pro's Undo feature, you have even greater flexibility in playing the what-if game with your spreadsheet. By inserting a new value, you can see the implications throughout the spreadsheet. If the results are unsatisfactory, use the Undo feature (press Alt-F5) to return the spreadsheet to its previous condition. (Note that you must enable the Undo feature before you can use it.)

@Functions

With Quattro Pro, you can create complex formulas by using *@functions*, which are shortcuts that help you make common mathematical computations with a minimum of typing. @Functions are like abbreviations for long and cumbersome formulas. The @ symbol signals Quattro Pro that an expression is a function. For instance, you can use the shorter @SUM function @SUM(A1..E1) instead of typing the formula +A1+B1+C1+D1+E1.

Building applications would be difficult without Quattro Pro's capacity for calculating mathematical, statistical, logical, financial, and other types of formulas. Quattro Pro comes with many functions that enable you to create complex formulas for a wide range of applications, including business, scientific, and engineering applications. (You learn more about Quattro Pro's functions in Chapter 8, "Using @Functions.")

Commands

Quattro Pro has many commands that help you perform a number of tasks in the spreadsheet. You use these commands at every phase of building and using a spreadsheet application. To issue a command, you press the slash (/) key and select a menu, or click a menu name with the mouse. This action displays a menu of commands, from which you choose the command you want.

Commands are available to format spreadsheets; name blocks; erase, copy, and move data; perform calculations; store files; protect spreadsheet cells; protect files with passwords; print spreadsheets; create graphs; retrieve files; and much more. (In Chapter 3, you learn how to select commands, and Chapter 4 begins a discussion of specific commands.)

1

The SpeedBar

The Quattro Pro SpeedBar is a row of buttons that appears at the top of the spreadsheet if you are in WYSIWYG mode or to the right of the spreadsheet if you are in Text mode. The SpeedBar offers an alternative method for invoking spreadsheet commands.

Click a SpeedBar button to invoke a command within the spreadsheet, such as a command to format a block of cells or delete a row.

Quattro Pro uses two SpeedBars, one for general spreadsheet work and another specifically designed for formulas.

Quattro Pro displays this SpeedBar in EDIT mode.

The general, or READY mode, SpeedBar is available whenever you are not editing a cell or entering a formula. The EDIT mode SpeedBar appears whenever you are editing a cell or entering a value or formula. To display the EDIT mode SpeedBar, press Edit (F2) or click the mouse pointer on the input line at the top of the screen.

Quattro Pro Graphics

The spreadsheet alone makes Quattro Pro a powerful program with all the functions many users need. The addition of graphics features, which accompany the spreadsheet, makes Quattro Pro a tool you can use to present data visually and to conduct graphic what-if analyses.

Quattro Pro has eleven basic graph types: stacked bar, bar, line, XY (scatter), pie, area, rotated bar, column, high-low, text, and bubble. You also have four 3-D graph choices: bar, ribbon, area, and step. You have an exceptional amount of flexibility in your choices of graph formats, colors, shading, labels, titles, and subtitles.

You can represent up to six blocks of data on a single graph (except for pie graphs, XY graphs, and bubble graphs). For example, you can create a line graph with six different lines.

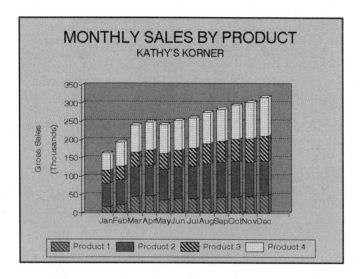

The stacked bar graph is the default graph type for Quattro Pro. That is, if you do not specify a particular type, Quattro Pro displays the data as a stacked bar graph.

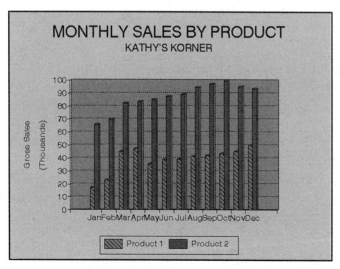

The bar graph, typically used to show the trend of numeric data across time, often compares two or more data items.

1

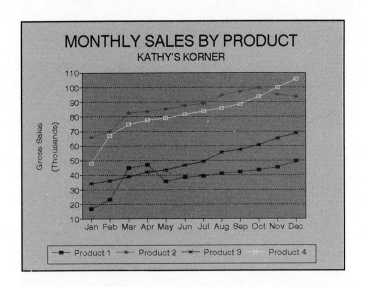

The line graph
also shows the
trend of numeric
data across time.

The XY (scatter)
graph compares
one numeric data
series to another,
determining
whether one set
of values appears
to depend on the
other.

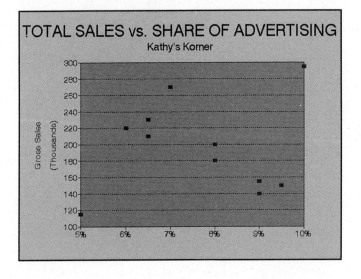

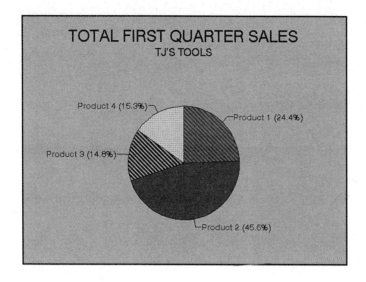

TOTAL FIRST QUARTER SALES
TJ'S TOOLS

Product 4 (15.3%)
Product 1 (24.4%)
Product 3 (14.8%)
Product 2 (45.6%)

The pie graph shows only one data series, in which the parts total 100 percent of a specific numeric category.

Quattro Pro Database Management

The row and column structure used to store data in a spreadsheet program is similar to the structure of a relational database. When you use Quattro Pro's true database management commands and functions, you can sort, query, extract, and perform statistical analyses on data in up to 8,191 records (with up to 256 fields of information).

One important advantage of a Quattro Pro database over independent database programs is that its database commands are similar to the other commands used in the Quattro Pro program. This similarity enables you to learn the Quattro Pro database manager and the rest of the Quattro Pro program simultaneously.

A row in Quattro Pro is equal to a record in a conventional database. In that record, you might store a client's name, address, and phone number.

1

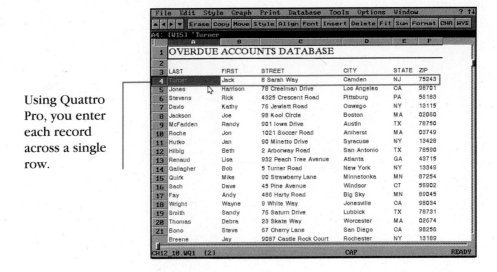

Using Quattro Pro, you enter each record across a single row.

Quattro Pro has sophisticated facilities for performing sort and search operations. You can sort the database on any number of items and by numerous criteria, and you can find a particular record with a few simple keystrokes.

Macros and Macro Commands

Two other features—macros and macro commands—make Quattro Pro one of the most powerful and popular integrated spreadsheet, graphics, and database programs. When you use Quattro Pro's macros and macro commands, you can automate and customize Quattro Pro for your particular applications.

By using Quattro Pro macros, you can reduce multiple keystrokes to a two-keystroke operation. Simply press two keys, and Quattro Pro does the rest, whether you're formatting a block of cells, creating a graph, or printing a spreadsheet.

You can create a macro, for example, to move the cell selector to a specific part of the spreadsheet. Suppose that you have positioned a database section in the block of cells at R23..Z100. Because Quattro Pro is first displayed with the cell selector at A1, you have to use several keystrokes to get to cell R23 when you want to work with the database. You can create a macro that records the keystrokes you need to get to cell R23. After you assign a macro name and save the macro, you can access that part of the spreadsheet simply by typing the macro name.

1

Think of simple keystroke macros as the building blocks for macro command programs. When you begin to add macro commands to simple keystroke macros, you control and automate many of the actions required to build, modify, and update Quattro Pro models. At the most sophisticated level, Quattro Pro's macro commands are used as a full-fledged programming language for developing custom business applications.

When you use Quattro Pro's macro commands, you see what kind of power is available for your Quattro Pro applications. For the applications developer, the set of advanced macro commands is much like a programming language (such as BASIC), but the programming process is significantly simplified by all the powerful features of Quattro Pro's spreadsheet, database, and graphics commands. Quattro Pro offers more than 90 "invisible" commands—the macro commands that give you a greater range of control over your Quattro Pro applications. (You learn about macros in Chapter 13, "Understanding Macros.")

Summary

In this overview chapter, you saw how one of the simplest examples of a spreadsheet—a checkbook register—becomes easier to use in electronic form. You were introduced to the features of Quattro Pro's spreadsheet, such as its size, window, and cells. You learned how Quattro Pro spreadsheets are designated and can be recalculated for what-if analyses. And you learned about Quattro Pro's powerful commands and functions, with which you can build formulas for a wide variety of applications.

The chapter gave you a glimpse of Quattro Pro's flexible graphics capabilities. You had a quick view of Quattro Pro's database and its power for managing and reporting on stored data. The chapter touched on macros and the macro commands, which enable you to automate and customize your use of Quattro Pro and its graphics and database capabilities.

Specifically, you learned the following key information about Quattro Pro:

■ The Quattro Pro spreadsheet contains 8,192 rows and 256 columns. All rows on the Quattro Pro spreadsheet are assigned numbers. All columns on the Quattro Pro spreadsheet are assigned letters.

■ A *cell* is the intersection of a column and a row. Cells are identified by their column and row coordinates, such as A2, B4, and G10.

■ The *cell selector* is the highlighted rectangle that enables you to enter data into the spreadsheet.

■ You can use formulas in Quattro Pro to create mathematical relationships between cells.

■ Quattro Pro's *@functions* are built-in formulas that automatically perform complex operations.

■ Quattro Pro has two SpeedBars, the READY mode SpeedBar and the EDIT mode SpeedBar. The READY mode SpeedBar offers an alternative method for invoking spreadsheet commands. The EDIT mode SpeedBar appears in EDIT mode—or when you are entering a value or formula—and it contains buttons specific to using formulas and functions in Quattro Pro.

■ You issue a command by pressing the slash key (⟋), selecting a menu, and selecting the command you want. You also can issue a command by using your mouse to point to and click the menu name and then the command you want. Using Quattro Pro's menu system, you can perform many common spreadsheet tasks.

■ Quattro Pro's graphics capability enables you to create ten types of graphs from spreadsheet data. Many options are available for enhancing the appearance of these graphs.

■ Each row of a Quattro Pro database corresponds to a database record. With the database features available in Quattro Pro, you can perform complex operations, such as sorting and searching records.

■ Macros and macro commands deliver exceptional power to Quattro Pro by automating both simple and complex tasks into two-keystroke operations.

The power of Quattro Pro is best realized by actually using the program. The next chapter shows you how to get started.

Getting Started

This chapter will help you get started using Quattro Pro. Before you begin, be sure that Quattro Pro is installed on your computer system. Follow the instructions in Appendix A, "Installing Quattro Pro 4," to complete the installation. Even if you have already installed Quattro Pro, you may want to check the appendix to make sure that you haven't overlooked any important details.

The information in this chapter will be useful if you have little familiarity with computers or with Quattro Pro. If you find this introductory material too basic and want to begin using the Quattro Pro spreadsheet immediately, skip to Chapter 3, "Introducing Spreadsheet Basics."

2

Starting Quattro Pro

WYSIWYG mode versus Text mode

Suspending and exiting Quattro Pro

Learning the keyboard

Understanding the Quattro Pro screen

Accessing the Quattro Pro Help system

2

Key Terms in This Chapter

Alphanumeric keys

The keys in the center section of most computer keyboards. Most of these keys resemble those on a typewriter keyboard.

Numeric keypad

The keys on the right side of the IBM PC, PC AT, and enhanced keyboards. You use this keypad for entering and calculating numbers, moving the cell selector in the spreadsheet area, moving the cursor in the input line, and selecting commands from the command menu.

Function keys

The 10 keys on the left side of the PC and PC AT keyboards or the 12 keys at the top of the enhanced keyboard. You use these keys for special Quattro Pro functions, such as accessing help, editing cells, and recalculating the spreadsheet.

SpeedBar

The area at the top of the Quattro Pro display. The SpeedBar enables you to perform certain Quattro Pro tasks if you have a mouse and mouse driver software loaded in your computer's memory at the beginning of a Quattro Pro session. You can select commands and functions and move around the spreadsheet if you use a mouse with Quattro Pro.

Starting Quattro Pro

Starting Quattro Pro is quite easy. To start Quattro Pro, follow these steps:

1. With the system prompt (usually C:\>) displayed on-screen, change to the Quattro Pro directory by typing **CD \QPRO** (or the name of your Quattro Pro subdirectory) and pressing ⏎Enter.

2. Start Quattro Pro by typing **Q** and pressing ⏎Enter.

   After a few seconds, the Quattro Pro logo appears. The logo remains on-screen for a few seconds, and then the spreadsheet is displayed. You are now ready to use Quattro Pro.

WYSIWYG Mode versus Text Mode

Two different display modes are available in Quattro Pro: *WYSIWYG mode* and *Text mode*. WYSIWYG stands for "What You See Is What You Get." Use this display mode if you are concerned with presentation-quality spreadsheets.

2

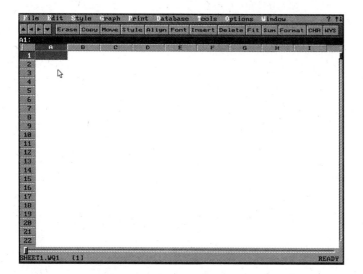

This screen display is in WYSIWYG mode.

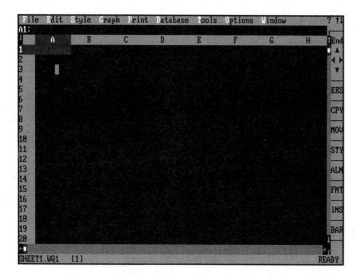

This screen display is in Text mode.

2

In WYSIWYG display mode, the mouse pointer looks different than when in Text mode. In WYSIWYG mode, the mouse pointer is an arrow; in Text mode, the mouse pointer is a rectangle. The SpeedBar (the buttons directly under the menu options) appears at the top of the screen in WYSIWYG display mode, but it appears at the right side of the screen in Text mode.

In WYSIWYG mode, you can switch to Text mode by selecting /Options Display Mode A:80x25 or by clicking the CHR button on the SpeedBar. In Text mode, you can switch to WYSIWYG mode by selecting /Options Display Mode B:WYSIWYG or by clicking the WYS button on the SpeedBar (in Text mode, the WYS button is not visible until you first click the BAR button).

You can change between WYSIWYG and Text mode using the /Options Display Mode menu.

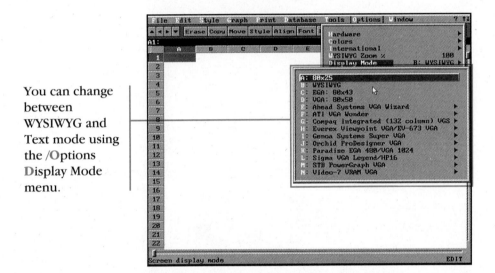

Suspending and Exiting Quattro Pro

To leave the Quattro Pro program and return to DOS, you can either use the /File Utilities DOS Shell command to *suspend* Quattro Pro and return to DOS, or use the /File Exit command to *leave* Quattro Pro and return to DOS. Both commands are accessible from Quattro Pro's main menu. To access the main menu, press the slash key (/) or click the menu name with the mouse. The Utilities and Exit commands are listed among the options on the File menu.

Using /File Utilities DOS Shell To Suspend Quattro Pro

The /File Utilities DOS Shell command returns you to the DOS system prompt, but you do not exit the Quattro Pro program. Your departure is only temporary.

To leave Quattro Pro temporarily, follow these steps:

1. Press /.

2. To select File, press F or press ↵Enter or click the menu name.

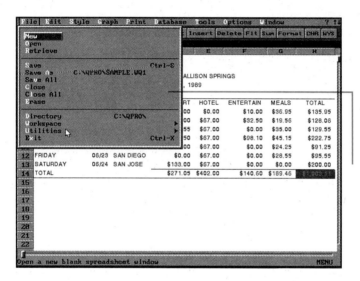

The Quattro Pro File menu appears.

3. To select Utilities, press U, or highlight the command and press ↵Enter, or click the command.

2

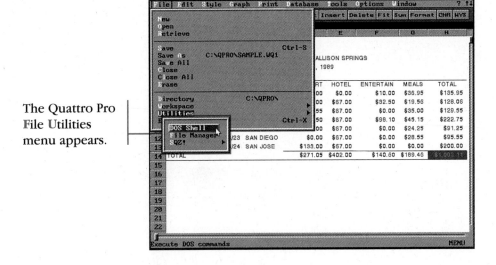

The Quattro Pro File Utilities menu appears.

4. To select **DOS Shell**, press D, or highlight the command and press ←Enter, or click the command.

5. Press ←Enter to access DOS.

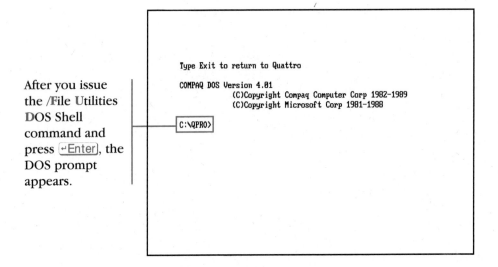

After you issue the /File Utilities **DOS Shell** command and press ←Enter, the DOS prompt appears.

6. While at the DOS level, perform the desired system operation (such as listing the files in a directory, copying files, or formatting a new diskette).

7. To return to the Quattro Pro spreadsheet, type **EXIT** and press
   ⏎Enter.

You return to the current spreadsheet, in the exact place where you issued the
/**File** Utilities **D**OS Shell command.

2

The Advantages of Using /File Utilities DOS Shell

/**File** Utilities **D**OS Shell is a very useful command because it enables you to
perform a DOS operation without exiting Quattro Pro. /**File** Utilities **D**OS
Shell saves you the trouble of having to quit the Quattro Pro program, issue
the appropriate DOS commands, and then get back into the spreadsheet.

The /**File** Utilities **D**OS Shell command is particularly useful for accessing
your system's file-handling commands. For example, if you want to save your
spreadsheet, but your data diskette is full, you can use the /**File** Utilities **D**OS
Shell command to suspend Quattro Pro while you prepare a new diskette
using the DOS FORMAT command. After you type **EXIT** and press ⏎Enter to
return to Quattro Pro, you can save your spreadsheet to the new diskette with
the /**File** **S**ave command.

The Limitations of Using /File Utilities DOS Shell

You should be aware of two potential limitations in using the /**File** Utilities
DOS Shell command. First, if you have a large spreadsheet that takes up much
memory, the /**File** Utilities **D**OS Shell command may fail because not enough
memory is available to suspend Quattro Pro and access DOS. If the
/**File** Utilities **D**OS Shell command fails, Quattro Pro displays the error message `Cannot Invoke DOS`, and the ERROR indicator appears in the lower right
corner of the screen.

The second problem is that certain terminate-and-stay resident (TSR) programs you run from Quattro Pro using the /**File** Utilities **D**OS Shell command
may cause Quattro Pro to abort when you try to return by typing **EXIT** and
pressing ⏎Enter. You can safely invoke from Quattro Pro the DOS file-
management commands—such as FORMAT, COPY, DELETE, DIR, and
DISKCOPY. Starting one of the many memory-resident utility programs,
however, may cause Quattro Pro to abort when you type **EXIT** and press
⏎Enter. Before trying to use the /**File** Utilities **D**OS Shell command during an
important Quattro Pro session, take a few minutes to experiment with the
programs you want to use.

2

Using /File Exit To Exit Quattro Pro

The /File Exit command from Quattro Pro's main menu enables you to exit both the spreadsheet and the Quattro Pro program. If you have changed any open file but have not saved it, you are asked to verify this command choice before you exit Quattro Pro; this prevents your changes from being lost. Note that a shortcut for the /File Exit command is Ctrl-X.

To exit Quattro Pro, follow these steps:

1. Press / to access the Quattro Pro menu.
2. Press X to select Exit, or highlight the command and press ↵Enter.

In this example, the Exit command is highlighted.

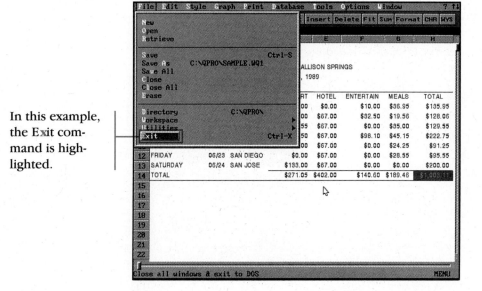

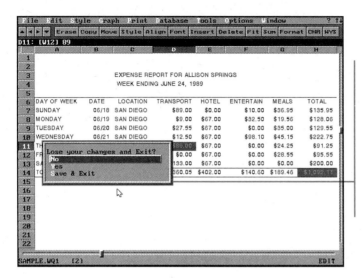

2

If you have made changes in your current spreadsheet but have not saved them with /File Save, Quattro Pro displays a reminder when you try to exit.

3. If you have made changes to the file since you last saved it and you want to abandon these changes, press Y (or highlight **Y**es and press ↵Enter) to override the warning message and exit from Quattro Pro.

   Otherwise, if you need to save the file before exiting Quattro Pro, press S (or highlight **S**ave & Exit and press ↵Enter) to save your file before you exit Quattro Pro.

   Note: You can avoid the Quattro Pro reminder by using the /File Save command (or pressing Ctrl-S) before you exit. Next, for a new file, enter the file name and press ↵Enter. For a previously saved file, press R (for **R**eplace) to update the current file. The process of saving files is explained in more detail in the next chapter.

Learning the Keyboard

Before you begin learning Quattro Pro, you need to get to know your keyboard. Each of the three most popular keyboards consists of these sections: the alphanumeric keys in the center, the numeric keypad with direction keys on the right, and the function-key section on the left or across the top. The enhanced keyboard, the standard keyboard for all new IBM personal computers and most compatibles, also has a separate set of direction keys.

2

The following keyboard is the original IBM PC keyboard:

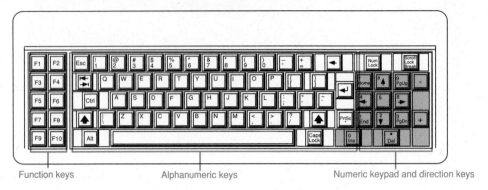

Function keys   Alphanumeric keys   Numeric keypad and direction keys

The following keyboard is the original IBM PC AT keyboard:

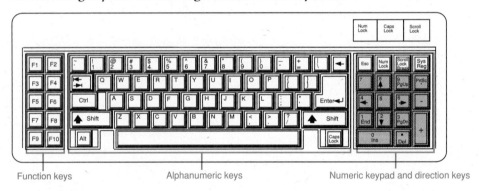

Function keys   Alphanumeric keys   Numeric keypad and direction keys

The following keyboard is the IBM Enhanced keyboard:

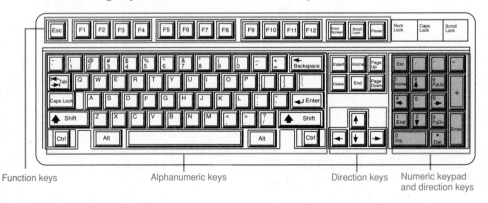

Function keys   Alphanumeric keys   Direction keys   Numeric keypad and direction keys

2

The Alphanumeric Keys

Most of the alphanumeric keys on the computer keyboard perform the same actions as those on a typewriter. In Quattro Pro, several of the keys have special functions. For example, the slash key (/) accesses the Quattro Pro menu, and the period key (.) defines a block of cells. Table 2.1 highlights each of these important keys.

Table 2.1
The Special Keys

Key	Action
Esc	Returns to the previous menu; erases the current entry during editing; erases the block or command specification; exits a Help screen; clears error messages from the screen.
Tab	Moves the cell selector one screen to the right. Shift-Tab moves the cell selector one screen to the left.
Caps Lock	Activates capitalization of all alphabetic characters when you press the keys for those characters. Displays the CAP indicator in the status line when active. Remains in effect until you press this key again (acts as a toggle).
Shift	Changes lowercase letters and characters to uppercase. When not in NUM mode, enables you to type numbers with the numeric keypad. Performs specific tasks or initiates commands when you use it with certain function keys.
Ctrl	When used with ← or →, respectively, moves the cell selector one screen to the left or right in READY mode, or moves the cursor five characters to the left or right in EDIT mode; when used with Break, returns Quattro Pro to READY mode or halts execution of a macro. When used with F10, switches from Paradox to Quattro Pro (in Paradox Access).
Alt	Invokes macros when you use it with other keys; performs specific tasks or initiates commands when you use it with certain function keys.

continues

37

2

Table 2.1 *(Continued)*

Key	Action
Space bar	Inserts a space within a cell entry; moves the menu selector to the right one item when selecting a menu from the main menu, or down one item when selecting an option from a menu.
⬅Backspace	Erases the previous character in a cell during cell definition; erases the character to the left of the cursor during editing.
↵Enter	Accepts an entry into a cell; selects a highlighted menu command.
.	Moves the active cell from corner to corner within a block of cells; anchors a cell address during pointing; functions as a decimal point.
/	Accesses Quattro Pro's main menu; functions as a division sign.
\	Repeats the character or characters typed directly after the backslash across the width of the cell. When you use it with a letter to name a macro, you can then run that macro by pressing Alt and the assigned letter.
Scroll Lock	Scrolls the entire screen one row or column when you move the cell selector. Displays the SCR indicator in the status line when active. Acts as a toggle.
Num Lock	Activates the numeric representation of keys in the numeric keypad. Displays the NUM indicator in the status line when active. Acts as a toggle.
Ins	Changes Quattro Pro from Insert mode to Overtype mode during editing. When pressed, turns on Overtype mode, displays the OVR indicator in the status line, and enables you to overwrite existing text with new characters. Acts as a toggle.
Del	Deletes the character at the cursor during the editing process; deletes entire cell contents in READY mode.

The Numeric Keypad and Direction Keys

You use the keys in the numeric keypad mainly for data entry and to move the cell selector or cursor. The enhanced keyboard has separate direction keys for this movement function.

To use the numeric keypad for entering numbers rather than positioning the cell selector or cursor, either press [Num Lock] before and after you enter the numbers and then move to the next cell, or hold down [⇧Shift] when you press the number keys.

Neither method is ideal because you have to switch between functions. If you have an enhanced keyboard, you don't have this problem because your keyboard has a special set of direction keys that has no other purpose. If you don't have an enhanced keyboard, you can create a simple macro that enables you to enter numbers and move to the next cell without having to press [⇧Shift] or [Num Lock].

The Function Keys

The function keys [F1] through [F10] are for special tasks, such as accessing help, editing cells, and recalculating the spreadsheet. Certain function keys also perform special tasks when you use them with [⇧Shift], [Alt], or [Ctrl]. Although the enhanced keyboards have 12 function keys ([F1] through [F12]), Quattro Pro uses only the first 10 of these. A plastic function-key template that describes each key's function on the enhanced keyboard is provided with Quattro Pro. Another version of the template is provided for users with PC, AT, or compatible keyboards. Table 2.2 explains the operations of the function keys.

Table 2.2
The Function Keys

Key	Name	Action
[F1]	Help	Accesses Quattro Pro's on-line Help facility.
[F2]	Edit	Shifts Quattro Pro to EDIT mode.
[⇧Shift]-[F2]	Debug	Shifts Quattro Pro to Macro DEBUG mode.
[Alt]-[F2]	Macro Menu	Displays the Macro menu.

continues

39

2

Table 2.2 *(Continued)*

Key	Name	Action
F3	Choices	Displays a list of named blocks in POINT and VALUE modes.
Shift-F3	Macro List	Displays a list of macro commands.
Alt-F3	Functions	Displays a list of @functions.
F4	Abs	Changes a relative cell address to an absolute or a mixed cell address during cell definition.
F5	GoTo	Moves the cell selector to the specified cell coordinates (or block name).
Shift-F5	Pick Window	Displays a list of the open windows.
Alt-F5	Undo	Reverses the last action performed.
F6	Pane	Moves the cell selector from an active window to an inactive window.
Shift-F6	Next Window	Moves the cell selector to the next window.
Alt-F6	Zoom	Expands or shrinks the active window.
F7	Query	Repeats the most recent /Database Query operation.
Shift-F7	Select	Selects an item in a list.
Alt-F7	Select All	Selects all the items in a list.
F8	Table	Repeats the most recent /Tools What-If command.
Shift-F8	Move	Removes selected files (in the File Manager).
F9	Calc	Recalculates all formulas in the spreadsheet.
Shift-F9	Copy	Copies selected files (in the File Manager).
F10	Graph	Displays the current graph on-screen.

Key	Name	Action
⇧Shift-F10	Paste	Inserts files stored in the Clipboard.
Ctrl-F10	Paradox	Switches from Paradox to Quattro Pro (in Paradox access).

Ctrl-Key Shortcuts

Several Quattro Pro menus offer Ctrl-key shortcuts that enable you to execute a command quickly. Ctrl-key shortcuts replace all of the steps required to execute a command from the pull-down menus. To use a Ctrl-key shortcut, you press and hold down Ctrl and press the appropriate letter. Table 2.3 displays the list of Quattro Pro's Ctrl-key shortcuts.

Table 2.3
Ctrl-Key Shortcuts

Shortcut Key	Equivalent Menu Command
Ctrl-A	/Style Alignment
Ctrl-C	/Edit Copy
Ctrl-D	Date entry
Ctrl-E	/Edit Erase Block
Ctrl-F	/Style Numeric Format
Ctrl-G	/Graph Fast Graph
Ctrl-I	/Edit Insert
Ctrl-M	/Edit Move
Ctrl-N	/Edit Search & Replace Next
Ctrl-P	/Edit Search & Replace Previous
Ctrl-R	/Window Move/Size (available only in Text mode)
Ctrl-S	/File Save
Ctrl-T	/Window Tile
Ctrl-W	/Style Column Width
Ctrl-X	/File Exit

Understanding the Quattro Pro Screen

The main Quattro Pro screen is divided into five parts: the *pull-down menu bar* and *input line* at the top of the screen, the *spreadsheet area*, the *SpeedBar* just below the pull-down menu bar, and the *status line* at the bottom of the screen. A reverse-video border separates the input line from the spreadsheet area. This border contains the letters and numbers that mark the columns and rows of the spreadsheet area. The sections that follow describe each of these areas in more detail.

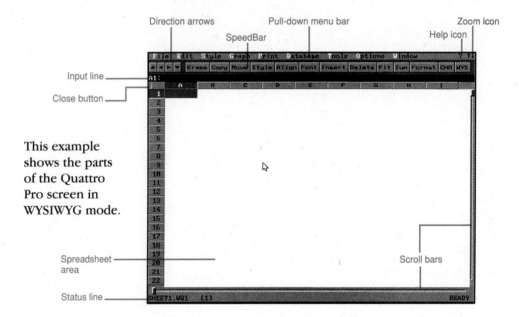

This example shows the parts of the Quattro Pro screen in WYSIWYG mode.

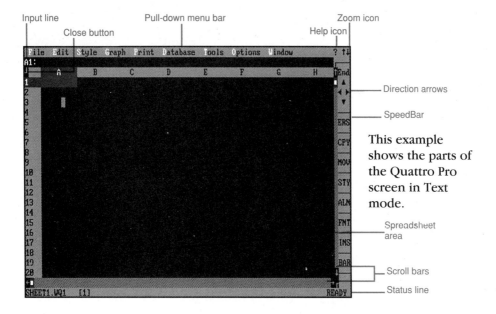

This example shows the parts of the Quattro Pro screen in Text mode.

2

The Pull-Down Menu Bar

Nine options are available on the pull-down menu bar: File, Edit, Style, Graph, Print, Database, Tools, Options, and Window. Each of these options has a different function. The File option, for example, calls up a menu from which you can perform file operations. To create a file, retrieve an existing file, save and close a file, or accomplish other file activities, you use the commands from the File menu.

At the right end of the menu bar are two icons you can click with the mouse:

Icon	Name	Description
?	Help	Invokes the Help screen.
↑↓	Zoom	Shrinks or enlarges the active window (available only in Text mode).

Using the mouse, click the Zoom icon once to shrink the active spreadsheet; click the icon a second time to enlarge the spreadsheet so that it again fills the screen. Using the keyboard, you can press F1 to access the Help screen, or select /Window Zoom to shrink or enlarge your spreadsheet.

The Input Line

The input line is located directly below the SpeedBar.

2

The input line
displays the
contents of and
information about
the current cell
(the cell high-
lighted by the
cell selector).

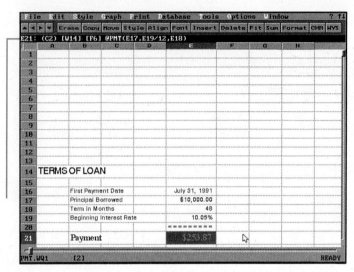

In this example, the input line displays

```
E21: (C2) [W14] [F6] @PMT(E17,E19/12,E18)
```

This line shows the address of the cell (E21), followed by the display format
(C2, or Currency with two decimal places), the column width (14 characters),
the font format (font #6), and the contents of the cell (in this case, an @for-
mula). This line may also show the protection status of the cell.

The Spreadsheet Area

The largest part of the Quattro Pro screen is the spreadsheet area. As described in Chapter 1, the Quattro Pro spreadsheet is bordered across the top
horizontally by 256 lettered columns and bordered down the left side of the
screen by 8,192 numbered rows. The right and bottom sides of the spreadsheet area are bordered respectively by horizontal and vertical scroll bars. If
you use a mouse with Quattro Pro, you can use the scroll box within the scroll
bars to move the cell selector.

You enter information into the spreadsheet through the cell selector, and
the information is stored in a cell—the intersection of a column and a row.

2

Remember that only a portion of the spreadsheet is displayed on-screen at any time.

The Status Line

The status line is the bottom line of the Quattro Pro screen. This line normally displays the current file name and window number in the lower left corner, and the READY status indicator in the lower right corner. When certain types of errors occur, however, the status line displays the appropriate error messages. This line also contains any status or key indicators, which are described in the section, "The Quattro Pro Indicators," further in this chapter.

The SpeedBar

The SpeedBar is the series of button choices displayed on-screen if you have connected a mouse to your computer and have loaded the mouse driver software into your computer's memory. When you are in WYSIWYG mode, the SpeedBar appears directly below the pull-down menu bar. When you are in Text mode, the SpeedBar appears along the right side of your screen.

When Quattro Pro is in READY mode, the buttons on the SpeedBar enable you to reproduce commonly used menu choices and keyboard keystrokes with one click of the mouse. The READY mode buttons are described in table 2.4. When Quattro Pro is in EDIT mode, the program displays a SpeedBar with specific buttons for editing your spreadsheet. The Edit mode buttons are described in table 2.5.

Table 2.4
READY Mode SpeedBar Buttons

Button	Description
▲ ◄ ► ▼	Move the cell selector around the spreadsheet.
Erase	Erases data from a cell or a range.
Copy	Copies data from one cell or range to another cell or range.
Move	Moves data from a cell or range to another cell or range.

continues

45

2

Table 2.4 *(Continued)*

Button	Description
Style	Displays the Style Use Style list.
Align	Displays the Style Alignment list.
Font	Displays the Style Font list.
Insert	Displays the Edit Insert menu.
Delete	Displays the Edit Delete menu.
Fit	Applies the Style Block Size Auto Width command.
Sum	Uses @SUM to total rows, columns, or both.
Format	Displays the Style Numeric Format menu.
CHR	Switches to Text mode.
WYS	Switches to WYSIWYG mode.
BAR	Displays more buttons (available only when all buttons don't fit on-screen).

Table 2.5
EDIT Mode SpeedBar Buttons

Button	Description
▲ ◄ ► ▼	Move the cell selector around the spreadsheet.
Name	Displays a list of named blocks (equivalent to pressing F3).

Button	Description
Abs	Toggles cell coordinates between absolute and relative (equivalent to pressing F4).
Calc	Calculates the formula on the input line (equivalent to pressing F9).
Macro	Displays a list of menu-equivalent macro categories (equivalent to pressing Shift-F3).
@	Displays a list of @functions (equivalent to pressing Alt-F3).
+	Enters a plus sign.
−	Enters a minus sign.
*	Enters a multiplication sign.
/	Enters a division sign.
(	Enters an open parenthesis.
,	Enters a comma, which is an argument separator.
)	Enters a close parenthesis.
BAR	Displays more buttons (available only when all buttons don't fit on-screen).

The Quattro Pro Indicators

The Quattro Pro screen may display three different types of indicators; *mode*, *status*, and *key* indicators appear in the status line in the lower right corner. The next few sections explain each of these types of Quattro Pro indicators.

The Mode Indicators

Quattro Pro is always in a specific mode, depending on what you are doing. The mode indicator appears in the status line (the mode indicators are summarized in table 2.6). For example, the mode indicator READY appears in the status line whenever Quattro Pro is "ready" for you to enter data into the spreadsheet or invoke the menu. VALUE appears as the mode indicator when you enter numbers or formulas; and LABEL appears when you enter letters, such as in a title or label. You see the EDIT indicator after you press Edit (F2) to edit a formula or label on the input line.

Table 2.6
Quattro Pro Mode Indicators

Indicator	Description
DEBUG	A macro is executing, one step at a time, to find macro execution problems.
EDIT	A cell entry is being edited.
ERROR	An error has occurred, and Quattro Pro is waiting for you to press Esc or ↵Enter to show the error, or to press F1 to access information about the cause and possible correction.
FIND	Quattro Pro is searching for a match to a search string specified in a /Database Query operation.
FRMT	A format line is being edited during a /Tools Parse operation.
HELP	Quattro Pro is displaying a Help screen.
LABEL	A label is being entered.
MACRO	Quattro Pro is executing a macro.
MENU	A menu is activated.
OVLY	Quattro Pro is loading an overlay file.
POINT	A block is being highlighted.
READY	Quattro Pro is waiting for a command or cell entry.
REC	The macro recorder is active and is recording your keystrokes and mouse clicks.

Indicator	Description
REP	The value you enter in a menu command replaces the existing value.
VALUE	A number or formula is being entered.
WAIT	Quattro Pro is in the middle of a command and cannot respond to other commands. WAIT flashes on and off.

The Status Indicators

Other indicators report the status of the spreadsheet. They include general message indicators, such as CALC and OVR, and warnings, such as CIRC and ERROR. These indicators also appear in the status line. Note that when an error occurs, Quattro Pro displays message in the lower left corner of the status line. To clear the error and get back to READY mode, press Esc or ↵Enter. Quattro Pro's status indicators are summarized in the following table:

Indicator	Description
CALC	The spreadsheet has not been recalculated since your last change to the spreadsheet.
CIRC	A circular reference (a formula that refers to itself) has been found.
EXT	You have pressed ⇧Shift-F7 to extend a block. This status is unavailable when the END indicator is displayed.

The Key Indicators

The key indicators NUM, CAPS, and SCR represent the keyboard's Num Lock, Caps Lock, and Scroll Lock keys, respectively. These keys are "lock" keys because they can temporarily lock the keyboard into a certain function. When a lock key is active, Quattro Pro displays the key's indicator in the lower right corner of the screen. Many keyboards also use a light to show when a particular lock key is active. Each lock key is a toggle, which means that repeatedly pressing the key turns its function alternately on and off. Therefore, to turn off a lock key that is on, you simply press it again.

2

Two other key indicators used within Quattro Pro are OVR for the Ins key and END for the End key. When OVR appears at the bottom of the screen, Quattro Pro is in Overtype mode—the characters you type will replace existing characters. Quattro Pro's key indicators are summarized in the following table:

Indicator	Description
OVR	[Ins] has been pressed, and Quattro Pro is in Overtype mode.
NUM	[Num Lock] has been pressed and is active.
CAP	[Caps Lock] has been pressed and is active.
SCR	[Scroll Lock] has been pressed and is active.
END	[End] has been pressed and is active.

Accessing the Quattro Pro Help System

One of the best features of Quattro Pro is its user-friendliness. Borland created a spreadsheet program that is easy to learn and use. The program includes a Help system you can access at any time during your Quattro Pro session.

Quattro Pro has a context-sensitive Help system. In other words, when you need clarification on a particular topic, you can press Help ([F1]) and select the topic you need from the displayed list. Suppose, for example, that you want to access the Help screen for the financial function @PMT. You can display the Help screen directly from your spreadsheet. While in EDIT mode, press Help ([F1]) to display a context-sensitive screen about moving around in EDIT mode.

2

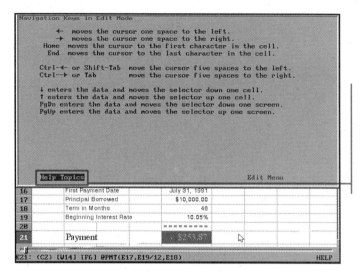

To access the Help index, highlight Help Topics at the bottom of the screen and press ↵Enter.

From the list of Help topics, you can choose many different topics. To access the Help screen for functions, select Formulas and then @Function Topics.

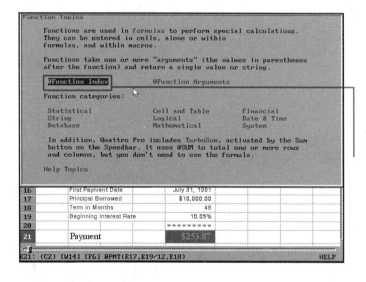

Then select @Function Index.

2

Press PgDn
to display the
second screen of
the list of func-
tions; choose
@PMT to learn
more about that
function.

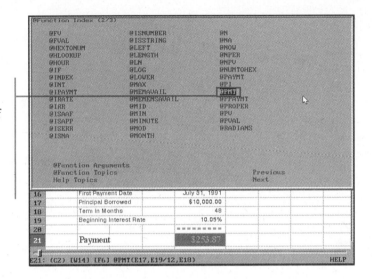

Within the
explanation of
@PMT is informa-
tion about related
functions.

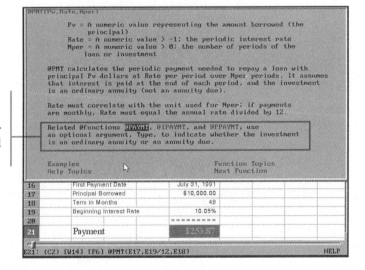

Press `◆Backspace` to redisplay the preceding Help screen. Repeatedly pressing `◆Backspace` takes you back to previous Help screens. Press `Esc` at any time to return to your spreadsheet.

2

Summary

In this chapter, you learned that you invoke Quattro Pro directly from the DOS prompt. You can leave Quattro Pro temporarily to perform DOS commands, or you can exit Quattro Pro entirely after verifying your intention to leave the program.

You were introduced to the different sections of the keyboard and learned how various keys of these sections are important to Quattro Pro. The chapter also called attention to the parts of Quattro Pro's screen. Information about each indicator was provided in tables, which you can refer to as you learn more about Quattro Pro. Finally, the chapter acquainted you with a feature designed especially to make Quattro Pro user-friendly: the Help system.

Specifically, you learned the following key information about Quattro Pro:

- You can start Quattro Pro directly from DOS by typing Q and pressing `⏎Enter` from the Quattro Pro directory.
- Quattro Pro has two display modes: WYSIWYG and Text. Use Text mode if you are not concerned with the presentation quality of your spreadsheets.
- The /File Utilities DOS Shell command enables you to leave Quattro Pro temporarily so that you can perform DOS commands. To return to the current Quattro Pro spreadsheet, type **EXIT** and press `⏎Enter` from DOS.
- Use the /File Exit command to exit the spreadsheet and the Quattro Pro program. Quattro Pro enables you to cancel this choice if you have made changes to your spreadsheet since you last saved it.
- Most keyboards contain alphanumeric keys in the center of the keyboard, a numeric keypad and direction keys on the right side, and function keys on the left side or across the top.
- The Quattro Pro screen consists of five areas: the pull-down menu bar, the SpeedBar (which displays only if you have the appropriate hardware and software), the input line, the spreadsheet area, and the status line.

53

2

■ The mode indicator is always displayed in the lower right corner of the status line. The status and key indicators appear in the status line, according to what you are doing.

■ Quattro Pro provides a context-sensitive Help system you can access by pressing Help (F1) during a Quattro Pro session. You also can access an index that provides several options from which you can choose a particular topic.

Now that you are familiar with the Quattro Pro environment, you are ready to begin using Quattro Pro by entering data and formulas.

Introducing Spreadsheet Basics

3

In Chapter 1, you learned that Quattro Pro is an integrated program that can do much more than make spreadsheet calculations. Depending on your business needs or assigned tasks, you can use Quattro Pro to create spreadsheets, generate reports, develop simple or complex databases, and produce graphics that illustrate spreadsheet data.

This chapter explores some of the most elementary operations in Quattro Pro: moving around the spreadsheet; selecting commands from menus; entering and editing data; using formulas and @functions; and naming, saving, and retrieving files. If you have used Lotus 1-2-3 or other spreadsheet programs, you may be familiar with some of the procedures discussed in this chapter. If this is your first experience with spreadsheets, however, you will find the basics discussed in this chapter informative and helpful.

Moving around the spreadsheet

Selecting commands from menus

Entering data into the spreadsheet

Editing data in the spreadsheet

Using the Undo feature

Naming, saving, and retrieving files

3

Key Terms in This Chapter

Cursor	In WYSIWYG and Text modes, the block that appears in the input line in EDIT mode. In Text mode, also the blinking underscore that appears inside the cell selector in READY mode.
Block name	An alphanumeric name given to a cell or a rectangular group of cells.
Menu selector	The rectangular bar that highlights menu commands.
Data	Labels or values you enter in a spreadsheet cell.
Label	A text entry you enter in the spreadsheet.
Value	A number or formula you enter in the spreadsheet.
Label prefix	A single character you type before a label for alignment purposes.
Operator	A mathematical or logical symbol that specifies an action to be performed on data.
Order of precedence	The order in which an equation or formula is executed; determines which operators are acted on first.
Wild card	A character, such as an asterisk or question mark, that represents any other character or characters that may appear in the same place.

Moving around the Spreadsheet

After you start entering data in your spreadsheet, you need some easy ways to move the cell selector quickly and accurately. Remember that the Quattro Pro spreadsheet is immense—it contains 8,192 rows, 256 columns, and more than 2,000,000 cells. You may have data blocks in widely separated parts of the spreadsheet. The program provides several ways to move the cell selector quickly to any location in the spreadsheet.

Remember that the cell selector and the cursor are not the same. The *cell selector* is the bright rectangle that highlights a cell in the spreadsheet area. The highlighted cell is the active cell. In Text mode the cell selector contains a blinking underscore; whenever you move the cell selector, the cursor—inside the selector—moves with it. The *cursor* is the block that appears in the input line when you enter or edit data.

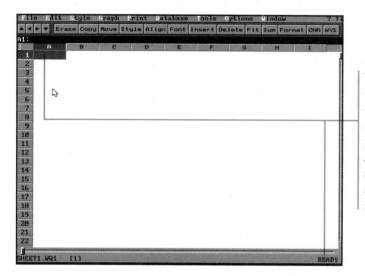

When you start Quattro Pro, the cell selector is automatically positioned in cell A1 of the spreadsheet, and READY appears as the mode indicator.

When Quattro Pro is in READY mode, the program is ready for you to enter data in the highlighted cell. To enter data in a different cell, first use the direction keys to move the cell selector to the desired location, and then enter the data.

When you begin to enter data, the READY mode indicator changes to LABEL or VALUE, depending on whether you are entering text or numbers.

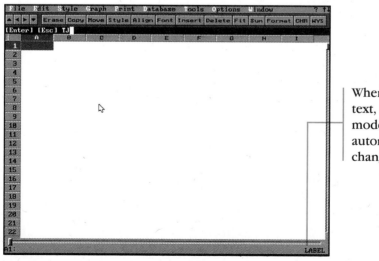

When you enter text, the READY mode indicator automatically changes to LABEL.

57

The POINT mode indicator signifies that you can position or expand (or both) the cell selector to highlight a block in your spreadsheet.

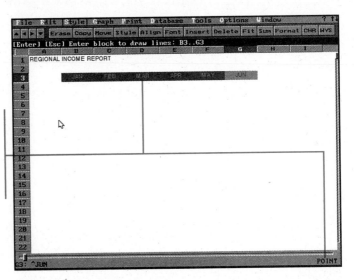

When Quattro Pro is in POINT mode, you can use the direction keys to highlight a block.

In EDIT mode, the direction keys move the cursor one character to the left or right or, in a multiple-line edit, one line up or down.

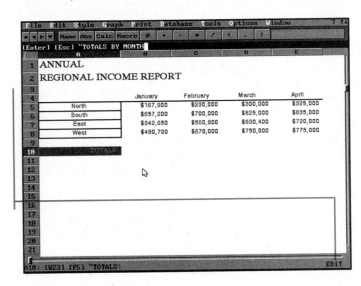

The actions of the direction keys in EDIT mode are described in table 3.1.

Table 3.1
Direction Keys

Key	Action
←	Moves the cell selector one column to the left in the spreadsheet. In the input line, moves the cursor one character to the left in EDIT mode, or moves the menu selector one item to the left in Menu mode.
→	Moves the cell selector one column to the right in the spreadsheet. In the input line, moves the cursor one character to the right in EDIT mode, or moves the menu selector one item to the right in MENU mode.
↑	Moves the cell selector up one row.
↓	Moves the cell selector down one row.
Tab⇄ or Ctrl-→	Moves the cell selector one screen to the right in the spreadsheet. In the input line, moves the cursor five characters to the right in EDIT mode.
⇧Shift-Tab⇄ or Ctrl-←	Moves the cell selector one screen to the left in the spreadsheet. In the input line, moves the cursor five characters to the left in EDIT mode.
PgUp	Moves the cell selector up one screen.
PgDn	Moves the cell selector down one screen.
Home	Returns the cell selector to cell A1 from any location in the spreadsheet.
End	When used before any arrow key, moves the cell selector (in the direction of the arrow key) to the intersection of the next blank cell and a cell containing data. When you press Home after you press End, moves the cell selector to the last cell that contains data or the lower right corner of the current spreadsheet.
F5 (GoTo)	Moves the cell selector to the cell coordinates (or block name) you specify.

To use the mouse to move the cell selector to a specific cell, move the mouse pointer to that cell and then click.

Using the Basic Direction Keys

The arrow keys on the numeric keypad (or on the separate keypad of the enhanced keyboard) are the basic keys for moving the cell selector. Depending on which arrow key you use, the cell selector moves one column or one row each time you press the key. If you hold down the arrow key, the cell selector moves in the direction of the arrow until you let go of the key. When you reach the edge of the screen, the spreadsheet continues scrolling in the direction of the arrow.

Scrolling the Spreadsheet

You can press Tab⇄ to scroll the spreadsheet to the right, one screen at a time, and press ⇧Shift-Tab⇄ (hold down ⇧Shift while you press Tab⇄) to scroll to the left. You also can press Ctrl-→ and Ctrl-← to scroll the spreadsheet to the right and left, respectively, one screen at a time. You can press PgUp and PgDn to move up or down, respectively, one screen at a time. These scrolling methods enable you to page through the spreadsheet quickly.

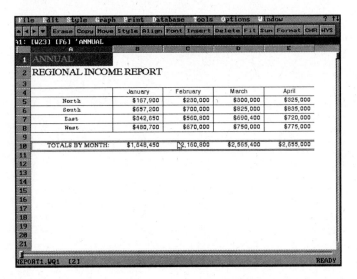

In this income spreadsheet, the cell selector is in cell A1, and columns A through E are displayed.

60

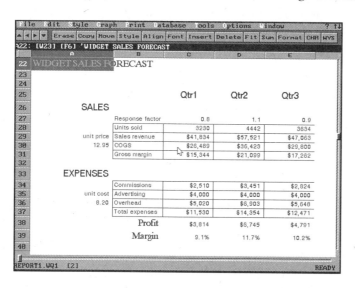

When you press Tab↹, the spreadsheet scrolls one screen to the right. The cell selector now appears in cell F1, and columns F through K are displayed.

If you then press ⬆Shift-Tab↹, the spreadsheet scrolls one screen to the left. In this example, the cell selector returns to its original location at cell A1.

When you press PgDn, the spreadsheet scrolls down one screen. The cell selector now appears in cell A22, and rows 22 through 40 are displayed.

If you then press PgUp, the spreadsheet scrolls up one screen, and in this example, the cell selector returns to its original location at cell A1.

Pressing [Scroll Lock] to turn on the scroll function makes the spreadsheet appear to move in the opposite direction of the arrow key you press—no matter where the cell selector is positioned on-screen. Learning Quattro Pro is usually easier if you turn off the scroll function.

With the cell selector positioned at cell A1, press [Scroll Lock]. The SCR indicator appears at the bottom of the screen, indicating that Scroll Lock is on.

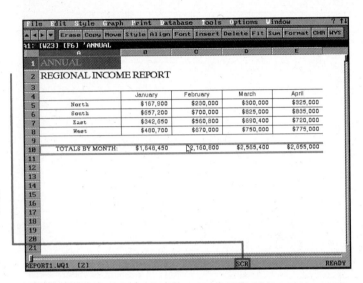

When you press [→] with Scroll Lock enabled, the entire spreadsheet, not just the cell selector, moves one column to the right.

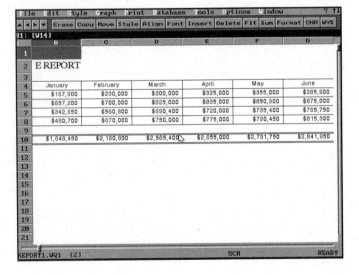

Using the Home and End Keys

The Home key provides a quick way to return to the beginning of the spreadsheet when Quattro Pro is in READY or POINT mode. Pressing [Home] makes the cell selector return to cell A1 from anywhere in the spreadsheet. Pressing [Home] in POINT mode is a handy and quick way to highlight a block of data you want to print.

Note: As you learn later in this chapter, some keys, such as [Home] and [End], have different actions in EDIT mode; for example, pressing [Home] moves the cursor in the input line.

When you press [Home] in POINT mode, the cell selector highlights a rectangle from the original position of the cell selector to cell A1.

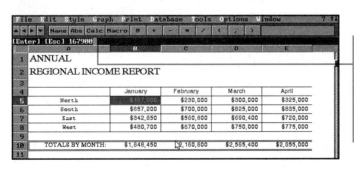

When you press Edit ([F2]), the cursor appears in the input line after the last character of your cell entry.

3

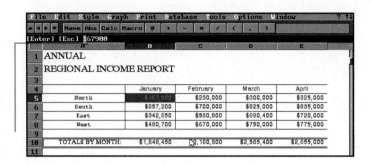

When you press
Home in EDIT
mode, the cursor
moves to the first
character in the
cell entry.

Quattro Pro uses the End key in a unique way. When you press an arrow key after you have pressed and released End, the cell selector moves in the direction of the arrow key to the next intersection of a blank cell and a cell containing data. The End key is very useful for moving the cell selector between blocks of data that are far apart; pressing End moves the cell selector directly to the next data block, because that data block would be the next intersection of a blank cell and one containing data.

As the following example illustrates, you can use the End key with the arrow keys to reach the borders of the spreadsheet area quickly in a new (blank) spreadsheet.

To learn how the End key works with the arrow keys, start with a blank spreadsheet and follow these steps:

1. If the cell selector is not in cell A1, press Home. Then move the cell section to cell A5.

This example
shows an income
report spread-
sheet with the cell
selector in cell A5.

File Edit Style Graph Print Database Tools Options Window	? ↑↓

	A	B	C	D	E
1	ANNUAL				
2	REGIONAL INCOME REPORT				
3					
4		January	February	March	April
5	North	$167,900	$230,000	$300,000	$325,000
6	South	$657,200	$700,000	$825,000	$835,000
7	East	$342,650	$560,800	$690,400	$720,000
8	West	$480,700	$670,000	$750,000	$775,000
9					
10	TOTALS BY MONTH:	$1,648,450	$2,160,800	$2,565,400	$2,655,000
11					
12					

2. Press End and then press →

The cell selector jumps to the right to cell N5, the rightmost data cell before a blank cell.

3. Press `End` and then press `↓`.

The cell selector jumps down to cell N8, the bottommost data cell before a blank cell.

4. Press `End` and then press `←`.

The cell selector jumps to cell A8, the left boundary of the spreadsheet. Because no intersection of a blank and non-blank cell exists to the left, the cell selector jumps to column A, the left boundary column.

Using the GoTo (F5) Key

The GoTo (F5) key enables you to move the cell selector directly to a cell location. To move the cell selector to any cell in the spreadsheet, press F5

3

When you press GoTo (F5), Quattro Pro prompts you for the new cell address.

In response to the prompt, type the desired cell address and press ⏎Enter The cell selector jumps to the specified cell. When you work on a large spreadsheet, you may forget the cell addresses for specific parts of the spreadsheet and therefore have difficulty using the GoTo (F5) key. You can, however, use block names with the GoTo (F5) key so that you don't have to remember cell addresses.

You can assign a block name to a cell or a rectangular group of cells. After you press the GoTo (F5) key, you can type the block name instead of the cell address, and then press ⏎Enter When the block name refers to more than one cell, the cell selector moves to the upper left corner of the block. (Blocks and block names are discussed in detail in Chapter 4, "Working with Blocks.")

In this example, JANSALES (a block that begins in cell B5) is specified as the location to go to.

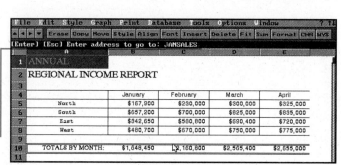

Selecting Commands from Menus

If commands are the tools for performing Quattro Pro tasks, menus are the toolboxes. The menus display the available commands. If you select the wrong command, you can press ⌷Esc⌷ at any time to return to the preceding menu.

You first have to press the slash key (⌷/⌷) to access Quattro Pro's main menu. When you want to access the main menu to select a command, make certain that Quattro Pro is in READY mode and then press ⌷/⌷.

3

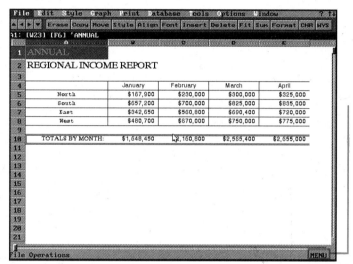

As soon as you press ⌷/⌷, the mode indicator changes to MENU.

The *menu selector*, the rectangular bar you use to highlight menu selections, is positioned on the File menu name.

A very convenient feature of the menu system is found on the left side of the status line: a brief explanation of the highlighted command. As you move the menu selector to highlight different commands, a new explanation appears for each command. This handy assistance is displayed at all levels of menus.

A helpful aspect of menus is the ease with which you can use them to invoke commands. You can *highlight* the command you want and press ⌷←Enter⌷; you can *type* the first letter of the command name; or you can *click* the command. Although the three methods of selecting commands from menus are discussed in this section, *the examples throughout the remainder of this book emphasize the typing method of selecting commands.*

Highlighting Method

When you are in MENU mode, press ⬅ or ➡ to highlight a menu name on Quattro Pro's main menu. You can interchangeably press ➡ or space bar to move the menu selector to the menu name you want. After you highlight the desired menu name, press ↵Enter to display that menu.

If you highlight the rightmost menu name, Window, and then press ➡ again, the menu selector reappears on the first main menu choice, File. Note that you can press End to move the menu selector to the rightmost menu name, or press Home to move it to the leftmost menu name.

To use the highlighting method to select a command, follow these steps:

1. Press / to access Quattro Pro's main menu.

2. Press ➡ or ⬅ to move the menu selector to the desired menu name.

3. Press ↵Enter.

In this example, Quattro Pro displays the pull-down Edit menu.

4. Press ⬆ or ⬇ to highlight the command you want from the displayed menu.

5. Press ↵Enter.

68

Typing Method

Another way to select a command from a menu is to type its boldfaced letter. After you become familiar with the commands in Quattro Pro's various menus, you probably will prefer to use the typing method because it is faster than the highlighting method.

To use the typing method to select a command, follow these steps:

1. Press ⌐/⌐ to access Quattro Pro's main menu.

2. Type the boldfaced letter of the menu you want to select.

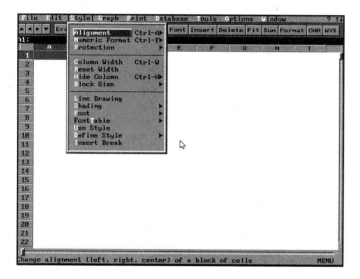

If you press ⌐S⌐, for example, you select the **S**tyle pull-down menu from Quattro Pro's main menu.

3. Type the boldfaced letter of the command you want to select.

Mouse Method

You also can use the mouse to select menus and commands by clicking the menu name and then the command you want to invoke. Note that if you are using WYSIWYG mode, the mouse pointer is an arrow; if you are using Text mode, it is a small rectangular block.

To use the mouse method to select a command, follow these steps:

1. Move the mouse pointer to the name of the menu you want.

3

Here, the mouse pointer points to the Database menu name in WYSIWYG mode.

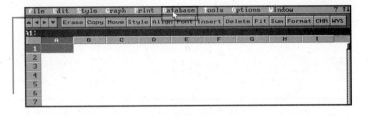

Here, the mouse pointer points to the Database menu name in Text mode.

2. Click the menu name to display that menu.

If you click the Database command, for example, Quattro Pro displays the pull-down Database menu.

3. Move the mouse pointer to the command you want to invoke from the menu.

4. Click the command.

Note: If you make the wrong command selection, you can press Esc at any time to return to the previous menu. For instance, if you realize that you should have selected Insert, not Delete, from the Edit menu, press Esc to return to the Edit menu. You can press Esc as many times as necessary to return to any location in the series of menus or to leave MENU mode completely.

Entering Data into the Spreadsheet

You can enter data into a cell by highlighting the cell with the cell selector and then typing the entry. To complete the entry, press ⏎Enter or any of the direction keys discussed in this chapter. You also can enter data into a cell by clicking the cell to move the cell selector to that cell, typing the entry, and then clicking the spreadsheet or pressing ⏎Enter.

3

If you enter data into a cell that already contains information, the new data replaces the previous information. This method is one way to change data in a cell; another method involves the Edit (F2) key and is explained in "Editing Data in the Spreadsheet," further in this chapter.

Quattro Pro has two types of cell entries: *labels* and *values*. Labels are text entries, and values are either numbers or formulas (including @functions, which Quattro Pro treats as built-in formulas). Quattro Pro uses the first character you enter to determine whether the entry is a label or a value. Your entry is treated as a value (a number or a formula) if your first character is one of the following:

    0 1 2 3 4 5 6 7 8 9 + − . (@ $

When you begin your entry with a character other than one of the preceding, Quattro Pro treats your entry as a label.

You can use a value—whether a number, formula, or @function—for computation purposes. A label is a collection of characters and would not logically be used in a calculation.

Entering Labels

Labels are commonly used in Quattro Pro for row and column headings, and they play an important role in spreadsheet development. For example, *you* might know that column B in your spreadsheet contains January data and that row 10 shows the monthly totals, but unless your spreadsheet has labels, how would someone unfamiliar with the spreadsheet know?

3

Labels make values more evident in a spreadsheet and help you find information quickly.

File	Edit	Style	Graph	Print	Database	Tools	Options	Window		? ↑↓

| ▲ | ◄ | ► | ▼ | Erase | Copy | Move | Style | Align | Font | Insert | Delete | Fit | Sum | Format | CHR | WYS |

A1: [W23] [F6] 'ANNUAL

	A	B	C	D	E
1	ANNUAL				
2	REGIONAL INCOME REPORT				
3					
4		January	February	March	April
5	North	$167,900	$230,000	$300,000	$325,000
6	South	$657,200	$700,000	$825,000	$835,000
7	East	$342,650	$560,800	$690,400	$720,000
8	West	$480,700	$670,000	$750,000	$775,000
9					
10	TOTALS BY MONTH:	$1,648,450	$2,160,800	$2,565,400	$2,655,000
11					

A label can be up to 254 characters long and can contain any string of characters and numbers. A label that is too long for the width of a cell continues (for display purposes) across the cells to the right, as long as the neighboring cells contain no other entries.

When you make an entry into a cell and the first character does not indicate a value entry, Quattro Pro assumes that you are entering a label. After you type the first character, Quattro Pro shifts to LABEL mode.

You can control how labels are displayed in the cell. By preceding a text entry with a label prefix, you can tell Quattro Pro to left-justify ('), center (^), right-justify ("), or repeat (\) a label when it is displayed.

Because the default position for displaying labels is left-justified, you don't have to type the label prefix when entering most labels; Quattro Pro automatically supplies it for you. When you enter numbers followed by text (as in addresses), you must use a label prefix before Quattro Pro will accept the entry into a cell.

When you enter a number as a label—for example, the year 1992—Quattro Pro assumes that you are entering a value. To signal that you want the program to treat this numeric entry as text, you can use one of the label prefixes. In this case, you can enter 1992 as a centered label by typing ^1992.

Aligning Labels

To align labels as you enter them into the spreadsheet, you must first type a label prefix. (Remember that you don't need to type a prefix for left-aligned labels because Quattro Pro left-justifies labels by default). Use the following prefixes for label alignment:

Type	To
'	Left-justify a label
"	Right-justify a label
^	Center a label

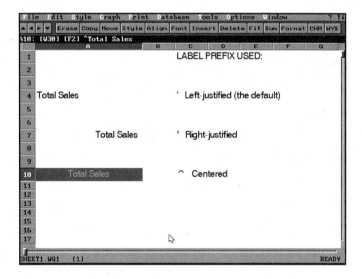

You can use label prefixes to align labels three different ways, as shown in column A of this spreadsheet.

Repeating Label Characters

An additional label prefix—the backslash (\)—is available for repeating one or more characters in a single cell. For example, you can use the backslash, or *repeat character*, to create a separator line that fills an entire cell. You use this feature primarily in Quattro Pro's Text mode. In WYSIWYG mode, you can use the /Style Line Drawing command to draw separator lines.

To repeat characters within a single cell, follow these steps:

1. Switch to Text mode: either select the /Options Display Mode A: 80x25 command or click the CHR button on the SpeedBar.

2. Highlight the cell in which you want to place the repeating label.

   In this example, highlight cell A2.

3. Type \ and then type the character or series of characters you want to repeat within the highlighted cell.

In this example, type \= to fill cell A2 with equal signs that will form a separator line.

4. Press ⏎Enter to enter the label into the highlighted cell.

In this example, Quattro Pro fills cell A2 with equal signs when you press ⏎Enter.

3

You can repeat these steps in the cells that adjoin A2 to form the remainder of the separator line, as shown in this example.

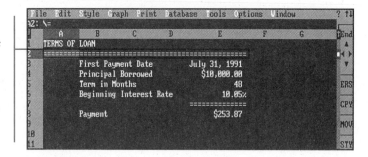

Controlling Label Prefixes

You can control label prefixes either before or after you enter the labels. To change the alignment of a block of labels *after* you have entered the labels, you can use the /Style Alignment command, or in place of this command, you can use the Ctrl-A shortcut key combination.

Suppose that you enter several left-justified labels and then decide that you want to center them. Using the /Style Alignment command, you can change the block of labels from left-justified to centered. (You learn more about blocks in the following chapter, "Working with Blocks.")

To change the alignment of a block of labels, follow these steps:

1. Press / to access Quattro Pro's main menu.

2. Press S to select Style.

3. Press A to select Alignment.

4. Select one of the following alignment choices: General, Left, Right, or Center (press G, L, R, or C, respectively). General changes the alignment to the default alignment.

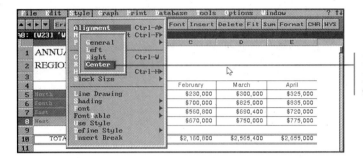

In this example, press C to select Center.

5. Specify the block of cells you want to align (by highlighting or typing) and press ꜱEnter.

   In this example, type **A5..A8** and press ꜱEnter.

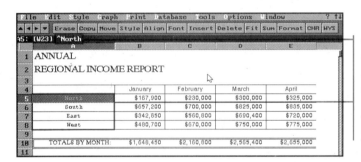

Quattro Pro centers the labels in cells A5..A8 and inserts a caret (^) at the beginning of each label in the block.

To set the alignment of an entire spreadsheet to the left, right, or center before you enter labels, you can use the /Options Formats Align Labels command. This command does not change the alignment of existing labels. (You must use the /Style Alignment command, as discussed in the preceding section, or the Edit key, F2, to change the alignment of existing labels.)

To set the alignment of labels for the entire spreadsheet, follow these steps:

1. Press / to access Quattro Pro's main menu.

2. Press O to select **O**ptions.

3. Press F to select **F**ormats.

4. Press A to select **A**lign Label.

5. Select one of the following alignment choices: **L**eft, **R**ight, or **C**enter (press L, R, or C, respectively).

75

3

Entering Numbers

As you know, values in Quattro Pro consist of numbers and formulas. Numbers are used frequently in Quattro Pro spreadsheets for many different types of applications, especially applications involving data entry tasks.

The rules for entering numbers follow:

- A number entry must begin with one of the following characters: a number from 0 to 9, a decimal point (.), a minus sign (–), a dollar sign ($), a plus sign (+), or parentheses. (Note, however, that a plus sign or parentheses at the beginning of a number entry will not appear in the cell.)

- Ending a number with a percent sign (%) causes Quattro Pro to divide the number preceding the sign by 100.

- A number cannot have more than one decimal point.

- You can enter a number in scientific notation, such as 1.234E+06.

- You cannot enter spaces between numbers.

- Do not start a number entry with a space (or spaces). If you do, Quattro Pro treats the entry as a label. The beginning space does not cause an immediate error, but Quattro Pro treats the cell contents as *zero* the next time the number is used in a formula.

If you do not follow these rules, Quattro Pro beeps when you press `⏎Enter`, displays an error message box stating `Invalid cell or block address`, and shifts to EDIT mode so that you can correct the error.

Entering Formulas

In addition to simple numbers, you can enter formulas into cells. Enter formulas either by *typing* the formula into the cell or by *highlighting*, which involves moving the cell selector so that Quattro Pro enters the cell addresses for you.

Suppose that you want to create a formula that adds a row of numbers. For example, you want to add the amounts in cells B6, B7, B8, and B9, and place the result in cell B13. Using the *typing* method, you type +B6+B7+B8+B9+B10 in cell B13. The plus sign at the beginning of the formula indicates that you are entering a formula, not a label. Quattro Pro then switches to VALUE mode, the appropriate mode for entering numbers and formulas.

To use the *highlighting* method to enter a formula that contains cell addresses, follow these steps:

1. Highlight the cell in which you want to place the formula.

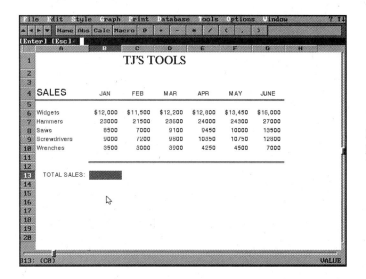

In this example, highlight cell B13.

2. Press ⊕ and highlight the cell of the first cell address in the formula.

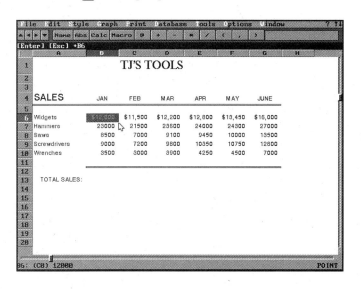

In this example, press ⊕ and highlight cell B6.

The mode indicator in the lower right corner of the screen shifts from VALUE to POINT as you move the cell selector to cell B6. Notice that the address for the cell appears after the plus sign in the input line—in this case, +B6.

3. Press ⊕ and highlight the cell of the next cell address in the formula.

    When you press ⊕, the cell selector immediately moves back to the previous cell—in this example, from cell B6 to cell B13. The mode indicator also shifts back to VALUE.

3

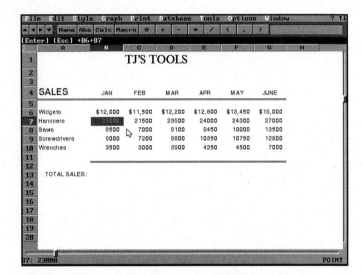

In this example, press ⊕ and highlight cell B7.

4. Continue pressing ⊕ and highlighting cells until you complete the formula.

    In this example, press ⊕ and highlight cell B8; press ⊕ and highlight cell B9; and then press ⊕ and highlight cell B10.

5. Press ⏎Enter to complete the operation.

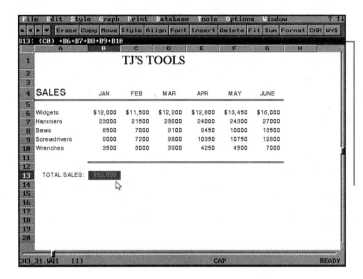

Your final formula should be +B6 +B7+B8+B9+ B10, as shown in the input line of this example.

3

Note: You also can use a combination of typing and highlighting to enter a formula that contains one or more cell addresses. Use the method that works best for you. When the cells in a formula are close to the cell you are defining, highlighting cell addresses is easier than typing them. When the formula cells are far away from the one you are defining, typing is easier. You get the same results with either method.

Using Mathematical Operators in Formulas

Operators are symbols that indicate arithmetic operations in formulas, and they are either logical or mathematical. Logical operators are discussed in Chapter 12, "Managing Data." The mathematical operators are the following:

Operator	Meaning
^	Exponentiation
+, –	Positive, negative
*, /	Multiplication, division
+, –	Addition, subtraction

This list indicates, from the top down, the *order of precedence*—that is, the order in which Quattro Pro evaluates these operators. For example,

3

exponentiation takes place before multiplication, and division occurs before subtraction. Quattro Pro always evaluates operations inside parentheses first and evaluates operators at the same level of precedence in order from left to right.

Consider the following formula:

* tells Quattro Pro to multiply the values from F4 and C6

+ indicates a positive value

– subtracts the second element (G2^C7) from the first (F4*C6)

^ indicates exponentiation

The first operator that Quattro Pro evaluates in a formula is exponentiation—the power of a number. In the formula $8+2\char`^3$, for example, Quattro Pro evaluates $2\char`^3$ (2 to the power of 3) before the addition. The answer is 16 (8+8), not 1000 (10 to the power of 3).

The next set of operators that Quattro Pro evaluates is the sign of a value; that is, whether it is positive or negative. Notice the difference between a + or – sign that indicates a positive or negative value and a + or – sign that indicates addition or subtraction. When you use these signs to indicate positive or negative values, Quattro Pro evaluates these operators before multiplying or dividing; when you use them to indicate addition and subtraction, the program evaluates them after multiplying or dividing. For example, Quattro Pro evaluates 5+4/–2 as 5+(–2), returning the answer 3. The – sign indicates that 2 is negative, then 4 is divided by –2, and finally 5 is added to –2, resulting in the answer 3.

You always can use parentheses to override the order of precedence. Consider the order of precedence in the following formulas, in which cell B3 contains the value 2, C3 contains the value 3, and D3 contains the value 4. Notice how parentheses affect the order of precedence and the results in the first two formulas.

Formula	Evaluation	Result
+C3–D3/B3	3–(4/2)	1
(C3–D3)/B3	(3–4)/2	–0.5
+D3*C3–B3 ^ C3	(4*3)–(2 ^ 3)	4
+D3*C3*B3/B3 ^ C3–25/5	((4*3*2)/(2 ^ 3)–(25/5))	–2

Correcting Errors in Formulas

Making errors when you enter formulas is easy. The more complex the formula, the more likely you are to encounter a problem creating it. Quattro Pro, however, provides ways to help you discover and correct these sometimes inevitable errors.

If you try to enter a formula that contains a logical or mathematical error, the program will beep and display an error message box indicating the error that has occurred. After you press ↵Enter to acknowledge the error, Quattro Pro automatically shifts to EDIT mode and moves the cursor to the section of the formula where the problem most likely exists.

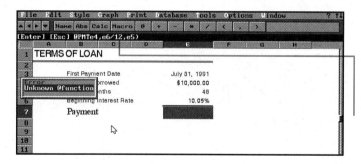

The formula shown in this input line contains an error.

If you don't know what the problem is, you can give yourself some time to think by converting the formula to a label. While in EDIT mode, follow these steps:

1. Press Home, type ', and then press ↵Enter to convert the formula to a label.

3

The formula shown in the input line has been converted to a label.

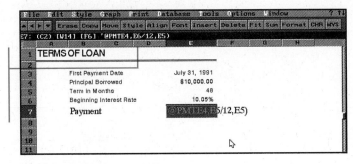

2. Correct the formula and then press $\boxed{\text{Home}}$, $\boxed{\text{Del}}$ (while in EDIT mode), and $\boxed{\leftarrow\text{Enter}}$ to delete the apostrophe.

The corrected formula is shown in the input line (the opening parenthesis was missing).

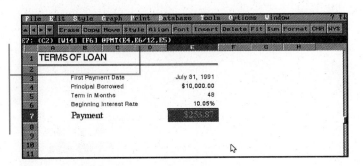

If your formula is long and complex, break it down into logical segments and test each segment separately. Using small segments helps you debug the formula.

Common errors include open parentheses and commas that are missing from built-in formulas (@functions). What appears to be a logical error may be only a missing punctuation mark. For instance, if you forget a right parenthesis, Quattro Pro beeps to indicate a formula error and displays an error message box indicating `Missing right parenthesis`. Check the formula and add the missing parenthesis to correct the formula.

Formulas should not contain spaces. Quattro Pro makes adjustments for spaces in some circumstances, but the potential for a formula error is strong if a formula contains spaces.

Quattro Pro provides two commands to help you examine and analyze your formulas. The /Print Format Cell-Formulas command (discussed in Chapter 9) prints a list of all the formulas in your spreadsheet. The /Style Numeric Format command (discussed in Chapter 4) displays existing formulas in their spreadsheet locations.

Using @Functions in Formulas

Like any electronic spreadsheet, Quattro Pro includes built-in functions. These functions, called @*functions*, fall into eight basic categories: mathematical, date and time, financial, statistical, database statistical, logical, string, and miscellaneous. Some of Quattro Pro's @functions are described in the text that follows. You can learn more about Quattro Pro's @functions in Chapter 8, "Using @Functions."

The *mathematical* functions perform standard arithmetic operations such as computing absolute values (@ABS) or square roots (@SQRT), rounding numbers (@ROUND), and computing sines (@SIN), cosines (@COS), and tangents (@TAN).

The *date* and *time* functions, such as @DATE and @TIME, convert dates and times to serial numbers. The serial numbers enable you to perform date and time arithmetic or to document your spreadsheets and reports.

The *financial* functions calculate returns on investments (@IRR and @IRATE), loan payments (@PAYMT), present values (@NPV and @PVAL), future values (@FVAL), and compound growth periods (@NPER).

The *statistical* functions perform standard calculations on lists, such as summing values (@SUM), calculating averages (@AVG), finding minimum and maximum values (@MIN and @MAX), and computing standard deviations and variances (@STD and @VAR).

The *database statistical* functions perform statistical calculations on a field of a database, based on certain criteria. These functions, such as @DSUM and @DAVG, have names and purposes similar to statistical functions.

The *logical* functions, such as @IF, @TRUE, and @FALSE, enable you to perform conditional tests. You can use these functions to test whether a condition is true or false.

The *string* functions help you manipulate text. You can use string functions to repeat text characters (@REPEAT), to convert letters to uppercase or lowercase (@UPPER or @LOWER), and to change strings to numbers and numbers to strings (@VALUE and @STRING).

The *miscellaneous* functions perform a variety of tasks. For example, @CELL and @CELLPOINTER can return as many as ten different characteristics of a cell, including its width, format, type of address, and prefix.

3

Entering a Quattro Pro @Function

Quattro Pro's @functions perform many different tasks—from simple arithmetic to complex statistical analysis and depreciation calculations. @Func-
tions consist of three parts: the @ sign, the function name, and the argument
or block. Note that *block* refers to the block of cells that the @function will
use.

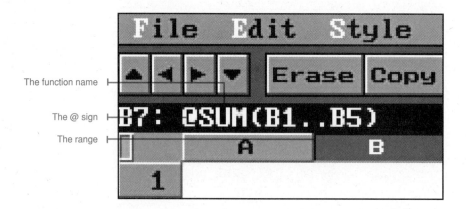

The function name
The @ sign
The range

In this example, the function in cell B7 computes the total of the block of five
cells from B1 through B5. The @ sign signals that the entry is a function. SUM
is the name of the @function in this example. You can enter @function names
with upper- or lowercase letters; this book uses uppercase letters to denote
Quattro Pro @functions. The statement (B1..B5) is the argument—in this case,
a block. An @function's arguments, always enclosed in parentheses, specify
the cell or block of cells on which the function will act. This @function tells
Quattro Pro to compute the sum of the numbers in cells B1, B2, B3, B4, and
B5 and to display the result in cell B7.

Some @functions can be quite complex. For example, you can combine
several @functions in a single cell by having one @function use other @func-
tions as its arguments. The length of an argument, however, is limited—
@functions, like formulas, can contain only 254 characters per cell.

Entering Formulas Containing @Functions

When you enter a formula containing an @function that requires a cell
address, you can enter the address by typing or highlighting.

To enter the formula @SUM(B8..B5), for example, follow this procedure:

1. Move the cell selector to the cell in which you want to place the formula (B10 in this example), and type **@SUM(**.

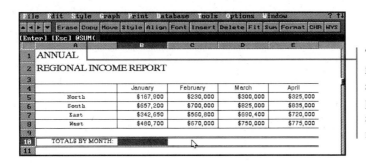

The @ sign, function name, and opening parenthesis appear in the input line.

2. Move the cell selector to B8 and press ⌐.⌐.

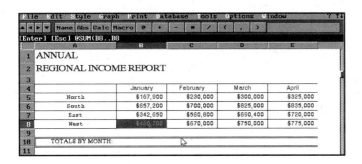

Pressing ⌐.⌐ anchors the cell selector at B8.

3. Press ↑ three times.

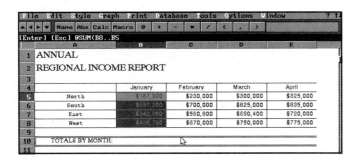

This procedure highlights the block of cells between B8 and B5.

4. Type) as the closing parenthesis and press ⏎Enter.

85

3

In cell B10,
Quattro Pro
enters the sum of
cells B5, B6, B7,
and B8.

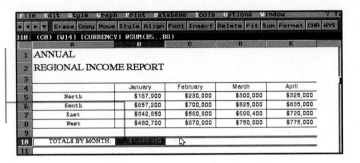

Editing Data in the Spreadsheet

One of the first things you need to be able to do is to modify the contents of
cells without retyping the complete entry, and in Quattro Pro, this procedure
is quite easy to accomplish. Begin by moving the cell selector to the appropriate cell and pressing the Edit (F2) key. (If you have a mouse, you can click
the input line to invoke EDIT mode.)

After you press Edit (F2), the mode indicator in the lower right corner of the
screen changes to EDIT. The cell's contents are duplicated in the input line,
the cursor appears at the end of the entry (unless you used the mouse to
invoke EDIT mode, in which case the cursor appears at the beginning of the
entry), and you are ready to edit.

When you first press Edit (F2), Quattro Pro is in *Insert mode*. Any new
characters you type are inserted at the cursor, and any characters on the right
side of the cursor are pushed to the right. If you activate *Overtype mode*—
press Ins on the numeric keypad—any new character you type replaces the
character directly above the cursor, and the cursor moves one position to the
right. When Quattro Pro is in Overtype mode, the indicator OVR appears at the
bottom of the screen. Pressing Ins a second time switches Quattro Pro back to
Insert mode.

To edit the contents of a cell, follow these steps:

1. Highlight the cell you want to edit (A10 in this example), and press
   F2 (Edit).

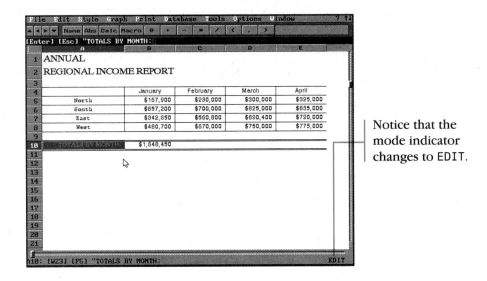

Notice that the mode indicator changes to EDIT.

3

2. Press → or ← to move the cursor to the part of the entry you want to edit.

3. Use one or more of the editing keys (see table 3.2) to modify the cell's contents.

4. Press ⏎Enter to complete the edit and return the spreadsheet to READY mode.

You also can use EDIT mode when you are entering data into a cell for the first time. If you make a mistake while you are entering the data, press F2 and move the cursor to correct the error.

Table 3.2
EDIT Mode Keys

Key	Action
→	Moves the cursor one character to the right.
←	Moves the cursor one character to the left.
Tab⇄ or Ctrl-→	Moves the cursor five characters to the right.
⇧Shift-Tab⇄ or Ctrl-←	Moves the cursor five characters to the left.
Home	Moves the cursor to the first character in the entry.

continues

3

Table 3.2 *(Continued)*

Key	Action
End	Moves the cursor one character to the right of the last character in the entry.
◆Backspace	Deletes the character to the left of the cursor.
Ins	Toggles between Insert and Overtype modes.
Del	Deletes the character above the cursor.
Esc	Clears the input line in EDIT mode. When pressed again, abandons your changes and leaves EDIT mode.
Ctrl-◆Backspace	Erases contents in the input line.
Ctrl-\	Deletes contents to the right of the cursor in the input line.

Using the Undo Feature

When you use an electronic spreadsheet, you can destroy hours of work by using the wrong commands. You may easily confuse the command to delete rows or columns with the command to erase a block, or accidentally delete a row or column while intending merely to erase data. The results may be difficult to recover from, particularly when formulas depend on those deleted rows or columns.

The Undo feature, which you can activate with the /Edit Undo command or by pressing Alt-F5, returns the spreadsheet to its previous appearance and condition. You can undo only the last command, and if you change your mind about what you just undid, you can use Undo again to "reverse the undo." By default, the Undo feature is disabled; you must enable it to use the command.

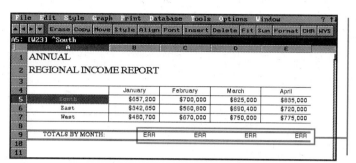

Accidentally deleting a row containing cells referenced by formulas can cause many cells in the spreadsheet to display ERR.

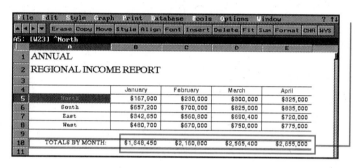

Press the Undo (Alt-F5) key to undo the last command and return the original contents to the deleted row of cells.

Using the command that resets (clears) *all* block names (/Edit Names Reset), instead of the command that deletes *individual* block names (/Edit Names Delete), is another common mistake that can create much frustration—especially when your spreadsheet contains many block names. Undo is a quick solution for recovering lost block names. You must, however, catch errors immediately, because the only command you can reverse is the one you last issued.

The Undo feature also has other uses. Every user is sometimes apprehensive about using certain commands because of the possibility of unexpected results or potential disasters. With Undo you can proceed with a command, having confidence that if you don't like the results you can reverse them.

Activating Undo

When you enter Quattro Pro, the Undo feature is disabled because, when enabled, Undo uses enough memory to result in a minor loss in Quattro Pro's operating speed. To activate Undo during a Quattro Pro session, follow these steps:

1. Press ⃞/ to access the Quattro Pro menu.
2. Press ⃞O to select **O**ptions.
3. Press ⃞O to select **O**ther.
4. Press ⃞U to select **U**ndo.
5. Press ⃞E to select **E**nable.
6. Press ⃞Q to select **Q**uit and return to the spreadsheet.

3

This command makes the Undo feature available only for your current Quattro Pro session. To make Undo available at the beginning of every Quattro Pro session, issue the /Options Update command before selecting Quit.

What Cannot Be Undone?

Certain commands cannot be undone. You cannot "unerase," "unsave," or "unextract" a disk file, for example; nor can you "unprint" your last printed output.

You can undo most other commands, however, including the entire sequence of commands associated with creating graphs, setting up blocks for data query commands, and all "undoable" steps embedded within a macro.

Naming, Saving, and Retrieving Files

The sections that follow explain file operations that beginning Quattro Pro users need most often: naming, saving, and retrieving files. See Chapter 10, "Managing Files," for information about other file operations, such as deleting and listing files, protecting files with passwords, and combining, linking, and transferring files.

Naming Files

Quattro Pro file names can be up to eight characters long with a three-character extension.

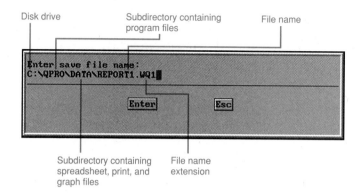

The basic rules for naming files are the following:

- File names may include the characters A through Z, 0 through 9, and the underscore (_). Depending on your system, you may be able to use other special characters, but Quattro Pro does not accept the characters <, >, or *. Although Quattro Pro separates the file name from the three-letter extension with a period (.), the program does not accept the period *within* the file name. The following file names are illegal:

    CH<15>.WQ1

    TOM*BBS.PRN

    SALES.91.WQ1

- File names may not contain blank spaces. For example, you cannot use the file name SALES RPT.WQ1.

- Quattro Pro automatically converts lowercase letters to uppercase letters in file names.

Although you determine the eight-character file name, Quattro Pro automatically creates the extension according to the file format you use. The basic file extensions are

- WQ1, which is added to names of spreadsheet files you save with the /File Save, /File Save As, or /File Save All commands (old versions of Quattro Pro use the extension WKQ).

- PRN, which is added to names of files you save in print (ASCII) format with the /Print Destination File command. You can print PRN files and import them into Quattro Pro and other programs.

3

Remember to be descriptive when naming a file. Choose a file name that indicates the contents of the file. This method will prevent confusion after you have created several files and need to access one of them quickly. The following list provides examples of file names that describe the contents of the files:

File name	Description
INV_JUN	Inventory spreadsheet for June
PRO_REST	*Pro forma* spreadsheet for a planned restaurant
EMPLSTDP	Employee list for the Data Processing department

If you work with many different spreadsheets that contain basically the same information, you should use similar file names to name them. If you name a spreadsheet SALES92 for your 1992 sales, for example, you can follow this naming scheme to name the sales spreadsheets for 1993 and 1994, respectively naming the files SALES93 and SALES94. This naming technique will help you recall file names later.

Saving Files

Computerized spreadsheets have one danger that isn't as common with manual worksheets. If you keep track of your business accounts manually, you simply can get up from your desk and walk away when you decide to quit working. You don't have to "exit" anything, turn off anything (except, perhaps, a calculator), or worry about anything that might cause your work to vanish from your desk. Unless you misplace or accidentally throw away the materials you use in a manual accounting system, they remain safely on your desk until morning.

With electronic spreadsheets—and with computer files in general—the risks of power outages or human errors can be costly in terms of data and time loss. If you exit Quattro Pro without saving your file, you lose any work you have done since the last time you saved the file. You can recover the data only by retyping it into the spreadsheet. You should make an effort, therefore, to save your files frequently—at least once every half hour to one hour (depending on how often you make changes).

To save an existing or new file, follow these steps:

1. Press ⌐/⌐ to access the Quattro Pro menu.

2. Press ⸤F⸥ to select **F**ile.

3. Press ⸤S⸥ to select **S**ave.

4. If you are saving a new file, type a file name at the prompt in the dialog box and press ⸤↵Enter⸥.

If you are saving the file under a file name that already exists, another menu appears, with the options **C**ancel, **R**eplace, and **B**ackup.

To update the current file on-disk, press ⸤R⸥ to select **R**eplace; alternatively, press ⸤B⸥ to select the **B**ackup option, save the changes to the file, and retain the old version of the file as a backup copy with the extension BAK.

Backup is an alternative to the **C**ancel and **R**eplace options of /**F**ile **S**ave. **B**ackup renames the older version of your file—using the same file name—and adds BAK as the file extension. The current version of your file is then saved with the extension WQ1. If you use this process, your two most recent spreadsheet versions will always be available.

Note that you also can use the ⸤Ctrl⸥-⸤S⸥ shortcut key combination in place of the /**F**ile **S**ave command.

To save an existing file under a *new* name, use the /**F**ile **S**ave **A**s command in place of the /**F**ile **S**ave command. Quattro Pro automatically supplies a list box of the spreadsheet files on the current drive and directory. Press Choices (⸤F3⸥) to view a full-screen list of spreadsheet file names. Highlight the name under which you would like to save the file and press ⸤↵Enter⸥, or type a new file name and press ⸤↵Enter⸥.

Saving to the Hard Disk or a Floppy Diskette

You may want to save a spreadsheet to your hard disk or a floppy diskette. To save your spreadsheet to the hard disk, follow these steps:

1. Press ⸤/⸥⸤F⸥⸤A⸥ to select /**F**ile **S**ave **A**s.

3

2. Type the file name after the hard disk drive and directory prompt.

3. Press ⏎Enter .

   Note: If you are saving a file that you have already saved, highlight (or type) the file name, press ⏎Enter , and press R to select **R**eplace.

To save your spreadsheet to a floppy diskette, follow these steps:

1. Press / F A to select /File Save **A**s.

2. Press Esc one or more times, until the dialog box prompt Enter save file name is all that remains.

3. Type the disk drive designation, such as **A:**, and then the file name.

For example, type **A:INCOME91**.

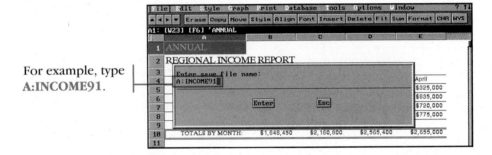

4. Press ⏎Enter .

Checking Disk Space

As you use Quattro Pro, you soon will have several spreadsheet files that take up significant disk space. You need to monitor the amount of remaining disk space your files use, whether you save your spreadsheets to your hard disk or to floppy diskettes. Nothing is worse than getting the message Disk full after you have worked on an important spreadsheet and are attempting to save it.

With Quattro Pro's /File Utilities DOS Shell command, you can avoid this problem. In READY mode, whenever you press / F U D and then ⏎Enter , Quattro Pro "steps aside" and enables you to enter a DOS command.

At the DOS prompt, type **CHKDSK** and press ⏎Enter to see how much space is available on your hard disk.

```
  Type Exit to return to Quattro

  COMPAQ DOS Version 4.01
            (C)Copyright Compaq Computer Corp 1982-1989
            (C)Copyright Microsoft Corp 1981-1988

  C:\QPRO>CHKDSK A:

      1213952 bytes total disk space
       827392 bytes in 18 user files
       386560 bytes available on disk

          512 bytes in each allocation unit
         2371 total allocation units on disk
          755 available allocation units on disk

       655360 total bytes memory
        79552 bytes free

  C:\QPRO>
```

To check a floppy diskette, you must follow the CHKDSK command with the disk drive designation, such as **CHKDSK A:**.

3

You also can use the FORMAT command within DOS to format a new diskette (see your DOS manual or Que's *Using MS-DOS 5*).

If your hard disk is almost full, you can erase some of the old files before saving the new files. (First make sure that you have a proper backup of the old files.)

When you finish the DOS operations, type **exit** and press ↵Enter to return to the Quattro Pro spreadsheet. Now you can save the working model.

Note: When you use /File Utilities DOS Shell to exit to DOS, do *not* start any program from DOS that will alter memory, such as a memory-resident program. If you do, you won't be able to return to the Quattro Pro spreadsheet, and you will lose any work you have not saved.

Retrieving Files

To recall a file from disk into memory, you can use the /File Retrieve command, which replaces the current file with the new file. If you are just starting Quattro Pro, this command brings a new file into memory.

To retrieve a file, follow these steps:

1. Press / to access the Quattro Pro menu.
2. Press F to select File.
3. Press R to select Retrieve.

3

Quattro Pro
displays a list box
of files in the
current drive and
directory.

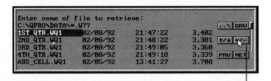

If you want to list
your file names
with the date and
time the files
were created and
their sizes, you
can click the +/–
button in the
dialog box.

Quattro Pro 4.0 spreadsheet files have the extension WQ1. Also listed
are any WKQ files from older versions of Quattro Pro and any file
names with extensions that begin with *W*.

If you don't see the file name you want, press F3 (Choices). You also
can click the ↑/↓ button in the dialog box to get a partial-screen list of
file names.

Quattro Pro
displays a partial-
screen list of the
files in the
current drive and
directory.

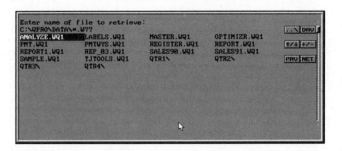

4. Highlight or type the name of the file you want to retrieve, and then
   press ↵Enter. You also can click the file name to retrieve that file.

   You can click the PRV button in the dialog box to list the last nine files
   you have opened, which means you can quickly choose a file you work
   with frequently.

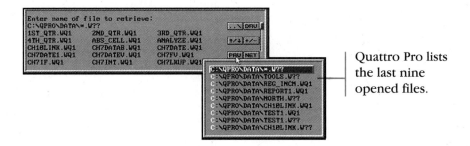

Quattro Pro lists the last nine opened files.

3

Select a file name from the list by highlighting it and pressing ⏎Enter, or click the file name to retrieve that file.

Opening Files

Like the /File Retrieve command, the /File Open command also recalls a file from disk into memory. The /File Open command, however, does not replace the current file in memory; it retrieves the file into memory along with the current file. This feature enables you to have multiple files in memory at the same time.

To open a file, follow these steps:

1. Press / to access the Quattro Pro menu.

2. Press F to select File.

3. Press O to select Open.

   Quattro Pro displays a list box of files in the current drive and directory.

4. Highlight or type the name of the file you want to open, and then press ⏎Enter. You also can click the file name to retrieve that file.

Using Wild Cards to Retrieve Files

You can use wild cards to retrieve files with Quattro Pro. *Wild cards*—the asterisk (*) and the question mark (?)—are helpful when you need to limit the number of files displayed on-screen, or when you are unsure of the exact spelling of the file you want to retrieve.

If you want to display only those file names that begin or end with a certain character or characters, use the asterisk (*). For example, you could type **S*** and press ⏎Enter at the Enter name of file to retrieve prompt.

Quattro Pro
displays all the
file names that
begin with the
letter S.

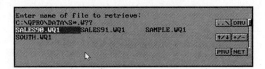

3

You can use the asterisk (*) wild card in place of any combination of characters; the question mark (?) wild card stands for any one character. You can use the asterisk by itself or following other characters. According to these rules, SALES*.WQ1 is acceptable, but *91.WQ1 is not. You can use the question mark wild card, on the other hand, in any character position. Therefore, instead of the incorrect retrieval name *91.WQ1, you can type ?????91.WQ1.

Retrieving Files from Subdirectories

Quattro Pro not only keeps track of file names, but also subdirectory names. When you issue the /File Retrieve command, for example, subdirectories of the current directory are displayed with the file names.

Within a list of file
names, a name
followed by a
backslash (\)
symbol indicates
a subdirectory
name.

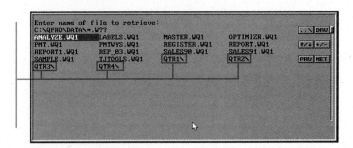

When you highlight a subdirectory name and press ↵Enter, Quattro Pro displays the list of files in that subdirectory.

Below the prompt
is the path Quattro
Pro follows to
retrieve the speci-
fied files, as shown
in this example of
the files in QTR1.

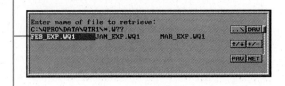

Retrieving Files from a Different Drive

When you need to access a file from a different drive, you can select the /File Retrieve command and click the DRV button from the dialog box that appears.

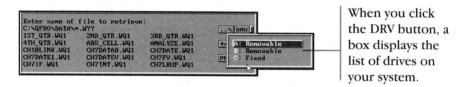

When you click the DRV button, a box displays the list of drives on your system.

This list varies according to the type of computer you have and whether you are networked. Highlight the drive from which you want to retrieve files and press ↵Enter. Alternatively, you can click the drive you want from the list.

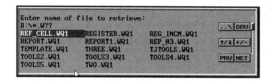

In this example, Quattro Pro displays a list of the files from drive B.

Highlight or type the name of the file you want to retrieve, and then press ↵Enter. Alternatively, you can click the name of the file you want.

When you need to access a file located in a different directory or subdirectory, press Esc or ◆Backspace after selecting /File Retrieve. When you press Esc while the default path name is displayed in the dialog box, Quattro Pro changes to EDIT mode. You can then edit the file specification as you would any label entry. When you press Esc a second time, Quattro Pro erases the current drive and directory specification. You can then enter the specification for the directory or subdirectory you want.

You can press ◆Backspace to erase the path name one directory at a time. To add to the path name, one directory at a time, select a subdirectory name from the list of files and press ↵Enter.

Some valid file directory specifications are the following:

File name	Description
C:\QPRO*.W??	Lists the spreadsheet files in the directory QPRO.
C:\QPRO\INCOME*.W??	Lists the spreadsheet files in the subdirectory INCOME.
C:\QPRO\SALES*.*	Lists all files in the subdirectory SALES.

Summary

This chapter on Quattro Pro basics covered many important concepts essential to beginning Quattro Pro users. You learned about moving the cell selector around the spreadsheet; selecting commands from menus; entering and editing labels, numbers, and formulas; using the Undo feature; and naming, saving, and retrieving Quattro Pro files.

Specifically, you learned the following key information about Quattro Pro:

■ The arrow keys move the cell selector horizontally and vertically, one cell at a time. When used with the End key, however, the arrow keys move the cell selector to the next intersection of a blank cell and a cell containing data. Using the End key with an arrow key is a quick way to move around the spreadsheet from one group of data to another group of data. You also can use the mouse to move the cell selector directly to a cell.

■ PgUp, PgDn, Tab, and ⇧Shift Tab help you move around the spreadsheet, one screen at a time (up, down, right, and left, respectively).

■ Home moves the cell selector to the upper left corner of a spreadsheet—to cell A1. When you use the GoTo (F5) key and specify a cell address, the cell selector jumps instantly to that cell in the spreadsheet.

■ To select a command from Quattro Pro's menu system, press slash (/) and then either *highlight* a menu name and press ↵Enter or *type* the boldfaced letter of the menu. You also can use the mouse by clicking the menu you want. From the pull-down menu that Quattro Pro displays, highlight the command you want to invoke and press ↵Enter, or click the command.

- You can enter two types of data into a Quattro Pro spreadsheet: labels and values. Labels are text entries, and values are numbers, formulas, or @functions.

- Label prefixes affect how text data is displayed in individual cells. The label prefixes include ' (left-justify), " (right-justify), ^ (center), and \ (repeat label). The /Style Alignment command aligns labels in a block of cells, and the /Options Formats Align Labels command changes the alignment of labels for the entire spreadsheet.

- One strength of Quattro Pro is its capability to accept and compute complex numerical data, formulas, and @functions. You use Quattro Pro's @functions—always identified by the @ symbol preceding the function's name—within formulas to provide exceptional power in your spreadsheets.

- Use the Edit (F2) key to modify any data that you already have entered (or are currently entering) into the spreadsheet. Use the direction keys to move the cursor in the input line while you are editing a cell entry.

- The Undo feature, which you activate by pressing Alt-F5, enables you to "undo" the previous command before executing the next command. You can easily reverse many potentially disastrous mistakes with this convenient feature.

- Quattro Pro's file names can be eight characters in length, followed by a period (.) and a three-character extension. File name extensions in Quattro Pro include WQ1 for spreadsheet files (WKQ for older versions of Quattro Pro) and PRN for ASCII print files.

- The /File Save command saves an existing file or a new file. If the file name already exists, Quattro Pro prompts you to Replace the existing file or Cancel the command. The Backup option ensures that the previous version of the spreadsheet will always be available. If the file is new, type the name of the file in the dialog box and press ↵Enter. To save an existing file under a new file name, use the /File Save As command.

- The /File Retrieve command recalls an existing file into memory. The file replaces the existing file in memory. The /File Open command, however, recalls an existing file into memory along with any other file currently in memory. Quattro Pro provides a list of the spreadsheet files (and subdirectories) located in the current directory. You can use the wild-card characters, * and ?, to limit the files displayed with the /File Retrieve command.

The Quattro Pro basics provided in this chapter will enable you to begin working with blocks, which are discussed in the next chapter.

3

101

4

Working with Blocks

Before you begin building and working with spreadsheets—as discussed in Chapters 5, 6, and 7—you need to understand the concept of *blocks*. This chapter teaches you the principles of using blocks to build a spreadsheet and how to use some of the fundamental Quattro Pro commands you need to build spreadsheets. Although most of the commands discussed in this chapter are from the Edit menu, you can use blocks with many Quattro Pro commands.

To make sense of the command structure, you first need to understand the concept of blocks. Although some commands affect the entire spreadsheet, others affect only certain cells. Quattro Pro uses the term *block* to describe a rectangular group of cells. Many useful actions in Quattro Pro are built around the block concept. This chapter tells you what blocks are and how to manipulate them with specific commands.

Blocks offer many advantages that can make your work less tedious and more efficient. When you use blocks, you can execute commands that affect all the cells in a group rather than one individual cell. For example, you can protect a block of cells so that no one can edit those cells.

What is a block?

Designating a block

Naming blocks

Deleting block names

Erasing blocks

Listing block names

Creating a table of block names

Attaching a note to a block name

4

Key Terms in This Chapter

Block	A rectangular group of cells you use in a spreadsheet operation. For example, the rectangular area A10..D10 is a block.
Block address	The upper left and lower right cell coordinates of a block.
Block commands	Commands you use to manipulate cells in blocks.
Block name	A name you assign to a block of cells.
Block name table	A list of all block names and their corresponding cell addresses. You produce this list with the /Edit Names Make Table command.
Block note	Text attached to a block name.

A descriptive block name will help you and others recognize the nature of the data that the block contains. When you use block names instead of cell addresses, you can quickly process blocks of cells in commands and formulas. You also can use the name with the GoTo (F5) command to move the cell selector quickly to that block in the spreadsheet.

What Is a Block?

Quattro Pro's definition of a block is *a rectangular unit of adjacent cells*. The smallest possible block is one cell.

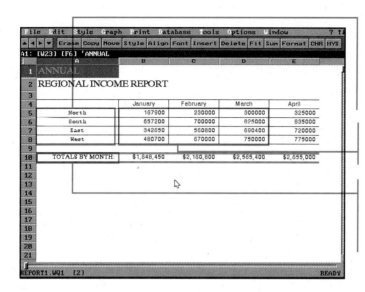

This block is one column in width. The address for the block is A5..A8.

This large block is made up of cells B5..D8.

This block is the smallest possible block: one cell. The block's address is A10.

4

Designating a Block

Many commands act on blocks. For example, the /Edit Erase Block command prompts you to specify the block you want to erase. You can respond to a prompt for a block in one of three ways:

- Type the addresses of the upper left and lower right cells in the block.
- Use the cell selector to highlight the cells in the block.
- Type the block name, or press Choices (F3) to display a list of block names and then click the block name you want.

Each method is covered in the following sections.

Typing a Block Address

Using the typing method to designate a block, type the cell addresses of the upper left and lower right corners. Be sure to separate the two addresses with one or two periods. Quattro Pro always stores a block with two periods, but you need to type only one period.

4

To specify the block B5..B8, you can type **B5..B8** or **B5.B8**. Quattro Pro stores cells B5, B6, B7, and B8 as the block.

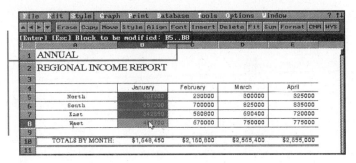

You can type cell addresses to specify a block in several situations: when the block does not have a block name, when the block is far from the current cell, and when you know the cell addresses of the block. Experienced Quattro Pro users rarely type cell addresses; they highlight a block in POINT mode or use block names instead.

Highlighting a Block

The second method of designating a block—highlighting the cells in the block in POINT mode—is used most often.

In the input line, following a prompt to enter a block, Quattro Pro displays the address of the cell selector. This single cell, shown as a one-cell block, is *anchored.* The default block with most block-related commands is an anchored one-cell block. After Quattro Pro anchors a cell, moving the cell selector highlights a block.

When a block is highlighted, the cells of that block appear in reverse video, a feature that enables you to specify blocks easily, with little chance for error. As you move the cell selector, the reverse-video rectangle expands until you finish specifying the block.

To highlight a block, you can use the normal cell selector movement keys (←, →, ↑, ↓, PgUp, PgDn, and so on), or you can use the mouse. To use the mouse, move the mouse pointer to the anchored cell, click and hold down the mouse button, and drag the mouse pointer over the cells in the block. When all the cells in the block are highlighted, release the mouse button.

Suppose, for example, that you select the /Edit Erase Block command. Quattro Pro displays the prompt Block to be modified in the input line.

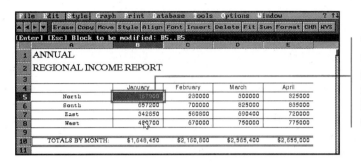

The location of the cell selector marks the beginning of the block, which is anchored.

4

You can use the End key with the direction keys to highlight large blocks quickly. You also can use the End key to move the cell selector to the boundaries of contiguous data blocks.

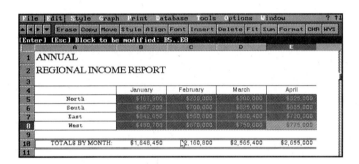

After you press [End] and then [↓] and [End] and then [→], the block B5..E8 is highlighted and the address appears in the input line.

Note: You can press [Esc] or [◄Backspace] to clear an incorrectly highlighted block. Quattro Pro collapses the block, highlights only the anchored cell, and removes the anchor—enabling you to move the cell selector to the correct location at the beginning of the block you want.

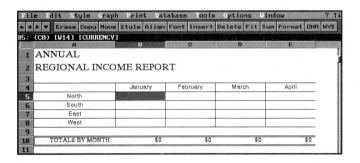

When you press [◄Enter], Quattro Pro uses the highlighted block to execute the command and then returns the cell selector to the original cell.

107

Highlighting is faster and easier than typing the block addresses. You also make fewer errors when highlighting because you can see the block as you specify it.

Typing a Block Name

Another way to specify a block is to type an existing block name at the prompt. Block names, which should be descriptive, can contain as many as 15 characters, and you can use them in formulas and commands.

Using block names is advantageous for several reasons. Block names are easier to remember than cell addresses, and using a name can be faster than highlighting a block in another part of the spreadsheet. Block names also make formulas easier to understand. For example, when you see the block name NORTH_TOT_SALES (rather than the cell address) in a formula, you have a better chance of remembering that the entry represents the total sales for the north region. The process of assigning names to blocks is described in the following section.

Naming Blocks

Block names can contain as many as 15 characters and should describe the block's contents. The advantage of naming blocks is that names are easier to understand than cell addresses, and thus they enable you to work more efficiently. For example, the block name SALES_MODEL25 is a more understandable way of describing the sales for Model #25 than its cell coordinates. (Note that the underscore is part of the block name.)

Block names can be useful tools for processing commands and generating formulas. Whenever you must designate a block that has been named, you can respond with the block name instead of entering cell addresses or highlighting cell locations. Quattro Pro's /Edit Names command enables you to tag a specific block of the spreadsheet with any name you choose. After naming the block, you can type the name instead of typing the cell addresses that indicate the block's boundaries.

The /Edit Names Create command, for example, enables you to assign the name JANSALES to the cells in the block B5..B8.

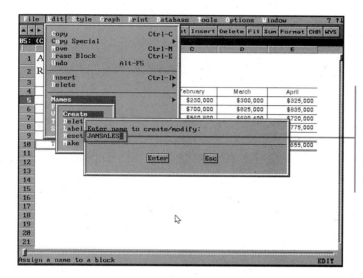

When Quattro Pro prompts you to specify a name, you would type **JANSALES**, as shown in this example.

4

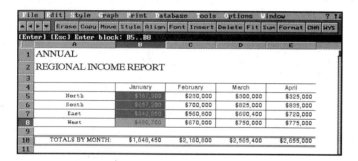

When prompted to designate the block address in the input line, you would specify **B5..B8**, as shown in this example.

The simplest way to compute the sum of this block is to use the function @SUM(JANSALES). In a similar way, you can use the function @MAX(JANSALES) to determine the maximum value in the block. In functions and formulas, you always can use block names in place of cell addresses.

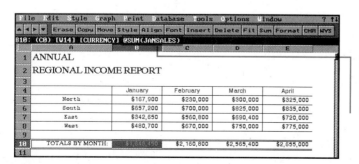

If you name a block, you can use that name in a formula.

You can use a block name in response to any command prompt that asks for a block.

You also can use a block name to jump from one part of the spreadsheet to another.

4

You can press GoTo (F5) and type **JANSALES**, for example, to move the cell selector to cell B5—the first cell (upper left corner) of the block named JANSALES.

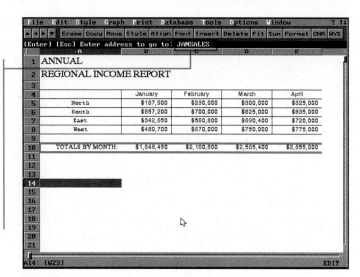

After you establish a block name, Quattro Pro automatically uses that name throughout the spreadsheet in place of the block's cell addresses. For example, your formulas change to refer to the block name rather than the block's cell addresses.

You also can designate the blocks of cells you want to print or cells you want to extract and save to another spreadsheet. If you set up special names that correspond to different areas and you want to print or extract and save those areas to another spreadsheet, you can enter a predefined block name rather than actual cell addresses. For example, if you want to print a portion of a spreadsheet, you can use the /Print Block command and then enter an existing block name, such as JAN_BUDGET or WEST_INCOME, in response to the prompt for entering a print block (see Chapter 9, "Printing Reports," for more information on printing blocks).

You name blocks in one of two ways. You can either issue the /Edit Names Create command to create a new block name, or select /Edit Names Labels to use a label already on the spreadsheet as a name for a block. When you create a name, you assign a name to one or more cells. When you use the Labels option, you select a label from the spreadsheet and make it the block name of

110

a one-cell block above, below, to the left, or to the right of the label. You can use the /Edit Names Labels command to assign more than one label at a time, but each label applies to only one adjacent cell.

Naming a Single Cell or a Group of Cells

You can use the /Edit Names Create command to give a name to a single cell or a group of cells. This command is ideal when you need to give a name to a multicell block. To use /Edit Names Create to specify a name for any block, even one cell, follow these steps:

1. Press ⌐/⌐ to access the Quattro Pro menu.
2. Press ⌐E⌐ to select Edit.

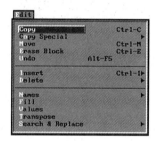

Quattro Pro displays the Edit commands.

3. Press ⌐N⌐ to select Names.

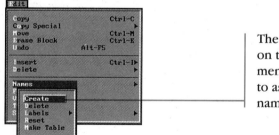

The first option on the Names menu enables you to assign a block name.

4. Press ⌐C⌐ to select Create.
5. At the Enter name to create/modify prompt, type the block name you want, and then press ⌐Enter⌐. Do not use a name that can be easily confused with a cell address.

111

For this example, type **FEBSALES** and press ↵Enter.

6. At the Enter block prompt, select the block you want to name by typing the cell addresses or highlighting the block; then press ↵Enter. To name a single cell instead of a block, type the cell address or highlight it.

4

For this example, select C5..C8 as the block you want to name, and then press ↵Enter.

Naming a Series of Single Cells

If you need to assign names to a series of one-cell entries with adjacent labels, or to a series of columns or rows with headings, use the /Edit Names Labels command. Although similar to /Edit Names Create, the /Edit Names Labels command takes block names directly from adjacent label entries. These names must be text entries (labels); you cannot use numeric entries or blank cells to name adjacent cells with the /Edit Names Labels command.

To use /Edit Names Labels to assign names to adjacent single-cell entries, follow these steps:

1. Position the cell selector on the first label you want to use as a block name. Remember that you can use this command only on adjacent cells.

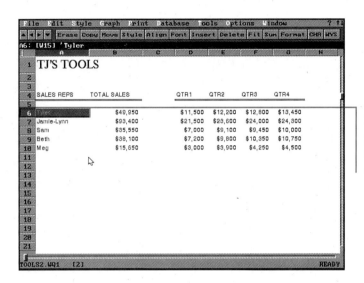

In this example, place the cell selector on cell A6.

2. Press ⃞/ to access the Quattro Pro menu.
3. Press ⃞E to select **E**dit.
4. Press ⃞N to select **N**ames.
5. Press ⃞L to select **L**abels.
6. Select the appropriate option, depending on the location of the individual cells you want to name.

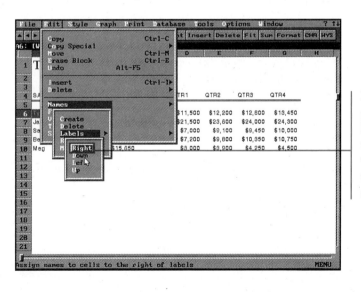

In this example, press ⃞R to select **R**ight, because the block you want to name is to the right of the cell.

7. At the prompt Enter label block, highlight the cells containing the labels you want to use as block names; then press ⏎Enter.

   In this example, highlight the block A6..A10; then press ⏎Enter. This procedure assigns the labels in cells A6, A7, A8, A9, and A10 to cells B6, B7, B8, B9, and B10, respectively—assigning five single-cell block names at once.

Changing the Cell Addresses of a Block Name

If you revise your spreadsheet, you may need to change the cell addresses of a block name. This procedure is very similar to creating a block name, because you actually re-create the block name. Follow these steps to change the cell addresses of a block name:

1. Press / to access the Quattro Pro menu.
2. Press E to select **E**dit.
3. Press N to select **N**ames.
4. Press C to select **C**reate.
5. At the Enter name to create/modify prompt, type the block name whose cell addresses you want to change.
6. Quattro Pro highlights the specified block and displays the prompt Enter block. Press ←Backspace to unanchor the highlight, type or highlight the new block address, and press ⏎Enter.

Deleting Block Names

You can delete block names individually or all at once. The /Edit Names Delete command enables you to delete a single block name, and the /Edit Names Reset command deletes all block names. The latter command is powerful; use it with caution.

To delete a single block name, follow these steps:

1. Press / to access the Quattro Pro menu.
2. Press E to select **E**dit.
3. Press N to select **N**ames.
4. Press D to select **D**elete.

5. After Quattro Pro displays a list of block names, highlight or type the block name you want to delete, and then press ⏎Enter). You also can click the block name to delete it.

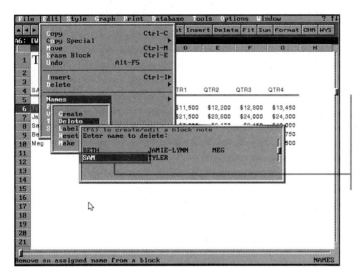

To delete the block named SAM, for example, highlight SAM in the list and press ⏎Enter).

To delete all the block names in a spreadsheet, follow these steps:

1. Press / to access the Quattro Pro menu.
2. Press E to select **E**dit.
3. Press N to select **N**ames.
4. Press R to select **R**eset.
5. Press Y to select **Y**es.

Note: Use this command with caution. Quattro Pro deletes all block names as soon as you confirm that you really want to delete them. Before issuing this command, you may want to enable the Undo (Alt)- F5)) key, which you can use to reestablish block names after you reset them.

If you delete a block name, Quattro Pro no longer uses that name and reverts to using the block's cell address. For example, @SUM(JANSALES) returns to @SUM(B5..B8). The contents of the cells within the block, however, remain intact. To erase the contents of blocks, use the /**E**dit **E**rase Block command, which is explained in the following section.

115

Erasing Blocks

With the /Edit Erase Block command, you can erase sections of the spread-sheet. You can use this command on blocks as small as a single cell or as large as the entire spreadsheet.

To erase a block, follow these steps:

1. Press ⌗ to access the Quattro Pro menu.
2. Press E to select **Edit**.
3. Press E to select **Erase Block**.
4. When Quattro Pro prompts you to specify a block, highlight the block you want to erase.

For this example, highlight the block D6..G10.

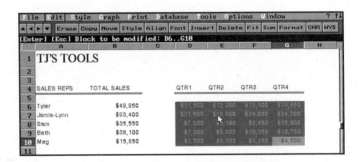

Although you can type the block address or block name of the block you want to erase, highlighting the block enables you to see the block's boundaries before Quattro Pro erases the block. Highlighting thereby helps prevent accidental erasure of important data.

5. Press ⏎Enter.

Quattro Pro immediately erases the block.

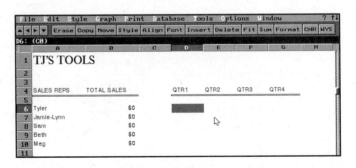

You can preselect the block of cells you want to erase by using the mouse to highlight the block before you issue the /Edit Erase Block command. If you preselect the block of cells, Quattro Pro erases the data in the block as soon as you select Erase Block. Quattro Pro does not prompt you for the block you want to modify, because you already specified the block.

After you erase a block, you cannot recover it unless the Undo key is enabled (immediately press Alt-F5 to undo the /Edit Erase Block command). If the Undo key is unavailable, you must reenter all the data to restore the block.

You also can use the Ctrl-E shortcut key combination in place of the /Edit Erase Block command.

4

Listing Block Names

Suppose that you select the /Edit Erase Block command, but cannot remember the name of the block you want to erase. You can use the Choices (F3) key to produce a list of the block names in the current spreadsheet.

To display a list of the block names in the current spreadsheet, follow these steps:

1. Make sure that the spreadsheet is in POINT mode, and then press F3 (Choices).

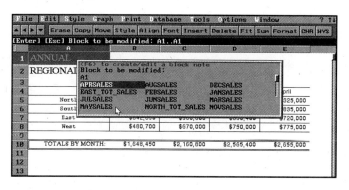

Quattro Pro displays a list of the current spreadsheet's block names.

If the block names extend below the bottom edge of the list box, use the direction keys or scroll bar to display the additional names.

2. To display a partial-screen list of block names, press F3 a second time.

117

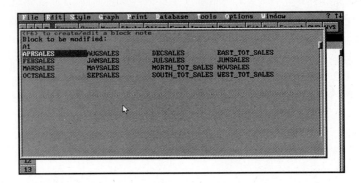

Quattro Pro displays the entire list of block names, or as much of it as can fit on-screen.

4

3. Move the cell selector to the name you want to use and press ⏎Enter. Quattro Pro returns you to the spreadsheet.

   To select the name of the block you want to use, you can press the following keys: **space bar**, ←, →, ↑, ↓, Home, and End. You also can click the name.

Note: If Quattro Pro is in Text mode and you want to print the displayed list of block names, hold down ⇧Shift and press PrtSc. If you have an enhanced keyboard, just press PrtSc. When the printer is on, ⇧Shift-PrtSc or PrtSc prints whatever appears on-screen.

To move the cell selector to a certain block, use the Choices (F3) key with the GoTo (F5) key to select the block name. When you press GoTo (F5) and then Choices (F3), Quattro Pro displays a dialog box of your spreadsheet's block names. You can press Choices (F3) again to get a partial-screen display of the block names.

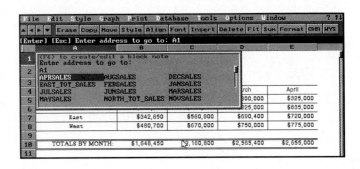

To specify the block you want to go to, click a block name from the list, or highlight the name and press ⏎Enter.

The cell selector immediately moves to the first cell of the block you specified.

Creating a Table of Block Names

If you have created several block names in your spreadsheet, you can document them in a table in the spreadsheet. Quattro Pro provides the /Edit Names Make Table command to perform this task.

To create a block name table, follow these steps:

1. Move the cell selector to the location where you want the upper left corner of the table to appear.

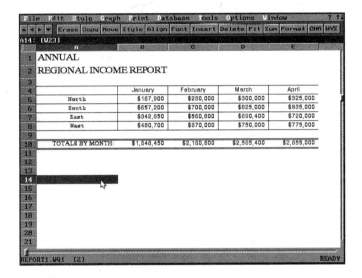

For this example, move the cell selector to cell A14, a few rows below the data in the spreadsheet.

2. Press / to access the Quattro Pro menu.
3. Press E to select **Edit**.
4. Press N to select **Names**.
5. Press M to select **Make Table**.
6. Press ↵Enter.

119

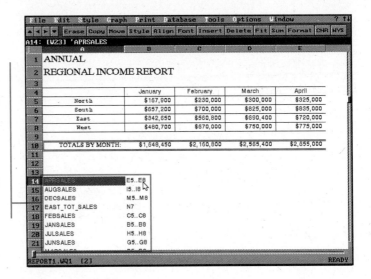

Quattro Pro produces a table with all the block names in a column and the corresponding block addresses to the immediate right of the names.

4

Note: Creating a table of block names is simple, but you must exercise care in your placement of the table. Make certain that the table does not overwrite an important part of the spreadsheet.

Attaching a Note to a Block Name

As you create more block names in a spreadsheet, one convenient Quattro Pro feature is the *note* you can attach to a block name. A block name note can describe the data in the block, state what significance the data has in the spreadsheet, and indicate whether the block is protected. You can attach a note to any block name.

To attach a note to a block name, follow these steps:

1. Press / to access the Quattro Pro menu.
2. Press E to select **E**dit.
3. Press N to select **N**ames.
4. Press C to select **C**reate.
   The list of existing block names appears.
5. Highlight the name of the block to which you want to attach the note.

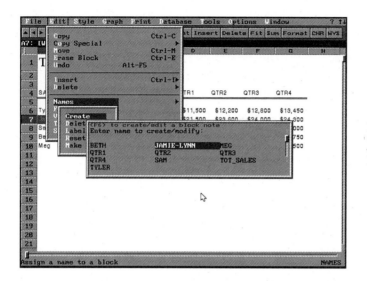

In this example, JAMIE-LYNN is highlighted.

4

6. Press F6 and enter the note you want to attach to the block name.

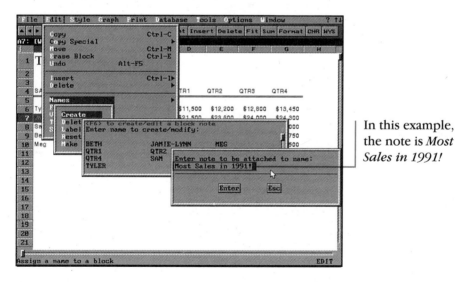

In this example, the note is *Most Sales in 1991!*

7. Press ↵Enter.

4

Now, when you highlight JAMIE-LYNN in the list of block names, Quattro Pro displays the attached note immediately below the prompt for the block name.

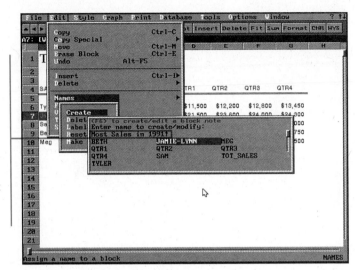

Summary

In this chapter, you learned how to use the /Edit commands to create and name blocks, delete block names, erase blocks, move quickly to a named block, and display existing block names in a list box.

Specifically, you learned the following key information about Quattro Pro:

■ A *block* in Quattro Pro is defined as a rectangular unit of adjacent cells. You specify blocks by entering the cell addresses of their upper left and lower right corners, separated by one or two periods. An example of a block is C4..G17.

■ Use the /Edit Names Create and /Edit Names Labels commands to name blocks of cells within the spreadsheet. The Create option is commonly used to name new multicell blocks. The Labels option is useful for naming a series of one-cell entries with adjacent labels, or a series of columns or rows with headings.

■ Use the /Edit Names Delete and /Edit Names Reset commands to delete one or all block names, respectively. Use the Reset option with caution because Quattro Pro deletes all your block names after you verify the deletion.

■ Use the /Edit Erase Block command (or Ctrl-E) to erase single-cell or multicell blocks. To specify a block you want to erase, type the cell addresses of the block, enter a block name, or highlight the block. Highlighting is recommended because it enables you to see the boundaries of the block you want to erase, before Quattro Pro erases it.

■ To display a list of all block names in the current spreadsheet, press Choices (F3) while in POINT mode (when Quattro Pro prompts you for a block).

■ You can use the Choices (F3) key with the GoTo (F5) key to select the name of a block to which you want to move the cell selector. If you press GoTo (F5) and then press Choices (F3), Quattro Pro displays an alphabetical list of your spreadsheet's block names in a list box.

■ Use the /Edit Names Make Table command to list within the spread-sheet all block names and their corresponding locations. You should execute this command in a remote portion of the spreadsheet to avoid overwriting your spreadsheet data.

■ You can add a note to any named block by highlighting the block name and pressing F6. You can then use the /Edit Names Create command to display the block names and any attached notes.

The following chapter, "Building a Spreadsheet," discusses the various tasks you can perform with other Quattro Pro commands—tasks such as setting column widths, creating windows, locking titles, and inserting and deleting rows and columns.

4

123

Building a Spreadsheet

After you enter data, you can use commands from Quattro Pro's pull-down menus to control the way your data is displayed and organized. In the preceding chapter, you learned how to manipulate data in specified blocks. This chapter shows you how to use commands that affect not only a block, but the entire spreadsheet.

In this chapter you learn how to change the widths of the columns, insert and delete columns and rows, recalculate formulas, protect certain areas of your spreadsheet, and perform other tasks. In the next chapter, you learn how to modify your spreadsheet with more dramatic changes.

Setting column widths

Hiding columns

Splitting the screen

Locking titles on-screen

Inserting and deleting columns and rows

Suppressing the display of zeros

Recalculating the spreadsheet

Protecting the spreadsheet

5

Key Terms in This Chapter

Windows	Two separate screens that appear, either horizontally or vertically, after you execute the /Window Options Vertical or Horizontal command. Windows enable you to view different parts of the spreadsheet at the same time.
Automatic recalculation	A default Quattro Pro setting indicating that the spreadsheet is calculated each time a cell's content changes.
Locked titles	Locking an area of the spreadsheet so that the area remains on-screen as the cell selector changes location.
Protection	The process of protecting cells against content changes.

Setting Column Widths

You can control the widths of columns in the spreadsheet to accommodate data entries that are too wide for the default column width. You also can reduce column widths to give the spreadsheet a better appearance when a column contains narrow entries. With Quattro Pro, you have three options for setting column widths: you can set widths one column at a time (with the /Style Column Width command), you can set the widths of all the columns in the spreadsheet at once (with the /Options Formats Global Width command), or you can set the widths of a number of contiguous columns at once (with the /Style Block Size Set Width command).

Suppose that you are setting up a spreadsheet of cash flow projections and want to display long labels in the first column. You can set the width of the first column of your spreadsheet individually, and then set the other columns to any smaller width you choose. The sections that follow describe the steps to execute the commands for changing column widths.

Setting the Width of a Single Column

To change the width of a single column, use the /Style Column Width command. To change the width of column A from 9 characters, the default width, to 25 characters, for example, follow these steps:

1. Position the cell selector within the column you want to change.

    For example, position the cell selector in any row of column A.

2. Press ⌐/⌐ to access the Quattro Pro menu.

3. Press ⌐S⌐ to select Style.

The Style menu appears.

4. Press ⌐C⌐ to select Column Width.

5. When the prompt Alter the width of the current column appears, either type a width between 1 and 254, or press ⌐←⌐ or ⌐→⌐ until the desired column width is displayed.

    The advantage of using ⌐←⌐ and ⌐→⌐ is that the column width expands and contracts each time you press the key. To get a good idea of the width requirements, experiment when you enter the command.

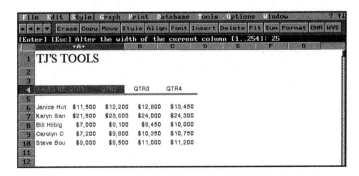

In this example, press ⌐→⌐ until the column width is 25.

6. Press ⏎Enter to complete the command.

After changing
column widths,
you can continue
entering data into
your spreadsheet.

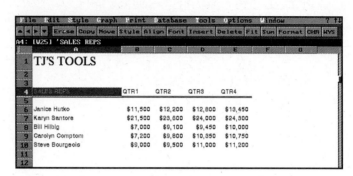

5

You also can use the Ctrl-W shortcut key combination in place of the /Style
Column Width command.

Note: The /Style Reset Width command returns the width of a single column
to the default width of nine characters or whatever width is specified with the
/Options Formats Global Width command. The Reset Width option does not
prompt you for a specific width, but returns the width of the columns to the
default column-width setting.

Setting the Widths of All Columns at Once

You can set all the column widths in the spreadsheet at one time with the
command /Options Formats Global Width. Normally, you use this command
in the early stages of creating a spreadsheet.

To change the widths of all columns in the spreadsheet at one time, follow
these steps:

1. Press / to access the Quattro Pro menu.
2. Press O to select Options.
3. Press F to select Formats.
4. Press G to select Global Width.
5. When the prompt Set the default column width to a new
   value appears, either type a width between 1 and 254, or press ← or
   → until the desired column width is displayed.

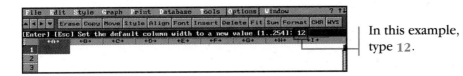

In this example, type **12**.

6. Press Enter to complete the command. Each column in the spreadsheet now has a default width of 12 characters instead of the original default width of 9.

Select Quit twice to return to READY mode.

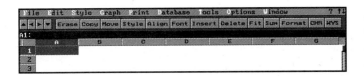

Because the columns are now wider, fewer columns are displayed on-screen.

Note: The /Options Other Global Width command does not alter the width of columns already set with either the /Style Column Width or /Style Block Size Set Width commands.

Setting the Width of Contiguous Columns

If you want to set a group of adjacent columns to the same width, use the /Style Block Size Set Width command. This command keeps you from having to set each adjacent column individually.

To change the widths of contiguous columns, follow these steps:

1. Position the cell selector in the first or last column in the block of columns you want to change. You do not have to highlight the entire column.
2. Press / to access the Quattro Pro menu.
3. Press S to select Style.
4. Press B to select Block Size.
5. Press S to select Set Width.
6. When the prompt Enter block of columns appears, highlight cells in the block of columns you want to change. Then press Enter.

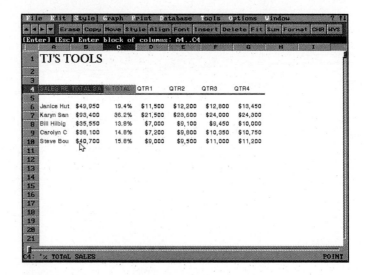

In this example, highlight the block A4..C4; then press ↵Enter.

5

7. When the prompt `Alter the width of columns` appears, either type a width between 1 and 254, or press ← or → until the desired column width is displayed. Then press ↵Enter.

In this example, type **15**; then press Enter.

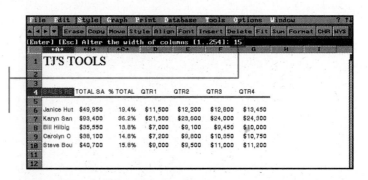

The column widths for columns A, B, and C all change to 15.

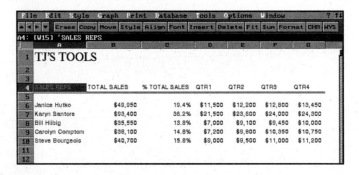

Note: The **R**eset Width command on the /**S**tyle **B**lock Size menu restores the widths of all selected columns to the default column-width setting.

Hiding Columns

With the /**S**tyle **H**ide Column command, you can suppress the display of any single column or adjacent columns in the spreadsheet. One useful function of this command is to suppress the display of unwanted columns when you print reports. When you hide intervening columns, a report can display data from two or more separated columns on a single page. Other uses of the /**S**tyle **H**ide Column command include suppressing the display of sensitive information (such as employee salaries or financial data), hiding a column of cells that contain zeros or that calculate to zeros, and fitting noncontiguous columns on-screen.

To hide one or more spreadsheet columns, follow these steps:

1. Press ⌿ to access the Quattro Pro menu.
2. Press S to select **S**tyle.
3. Press H to select **H**ide Column.
4. Press H to select **H**ide.
5. Specify the columns you want to hide by either typing the block address or highlighting the block.

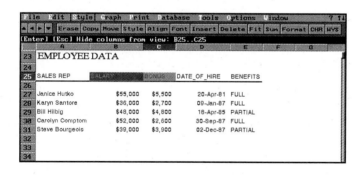

In this example, specify columns B and C.

6. Press ↵Enter to hide the specified columns from view.

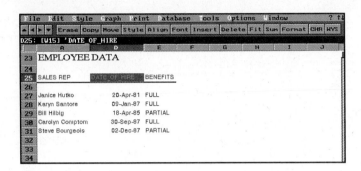

In this example,
columns B and C
are now hidden.

5

You also can use the Ctrl-H shortcut key combination in place of the /Style Hide Column command.

Although the hidden columns do not appear on-screen, numbers and formulas in hidden columns are still present, and references to cells in hidden columns continue to work properly. You can tell which columns are missing only by noting the break in column letters in the spreadsheet border at the top of the display. The hidden columns are temporarily redisplayed, however, when you use certain commands, such as /Edit Copy or /Edit Move; the hidden columns are marked with an asterisk (such as C*) during this temporary display.

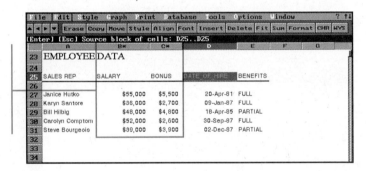

In this example,
hidden columns
are temporarily
displayed during
an /Edit Copy
operation.

To redisplay hidden columns, use the /Style Hide Column Expose command, as follows:

1. Press / to access the Quattro Pro menu.
2. Press S to select Style.
3. Press H to select Hide Column.
4. Press E to select Expose.

Quattro Pro redisplays the hidden columns and places an asterisk (*) next to the column letters.

5. In response to the prompt `Expose hidden columns`, specify the block of columns you want to redisplay.

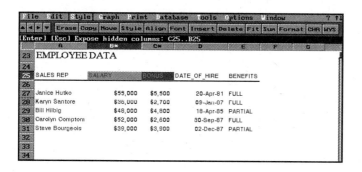

In this example, specify columns B and C.

5

6. Press ⏎Enter to redisplay the hidden columns.

Splitting the Screen

Sometimes the size of a Quattro Pro spreadsheet can be unwieldy. For example, if you want to compare data in column A with data in column N, you need to be able to "fold" the spreadsheet so that you can see both parts at the same time. To do this, you can split the Quattro Pro screen display into two windows, either horizontally or vertically. This feature helps you overcome some of the inconvenience of not being able to see the entire spreadsheet at one time. Using the /Window command to split the screen, you can make changes in one area and immediately see the effects in the other.

To split the screen into two horizontal or two vertical windows, follow these steps:

1. Position the cell selector at the location in which you want to split the screen.

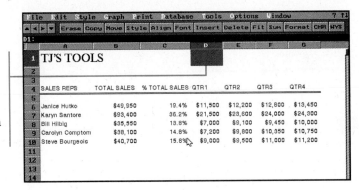

In this example, position the cell selector in any row of column D to split the screen vertically.

5

2. Press ⌐/⌐ to access the Quattro Pro menu.

3. Press ⌐W⌐ to select Window.

4. Press ⌐O⌐ to select Options.

5. Press ⌐H⌐ to select Horizontal or ⌐V⌐ to select Vertical.

In this example, press ⌐V⌐ to select Vertical.

6. Press ⌐Enter⌐ to complete the command and split the screen.

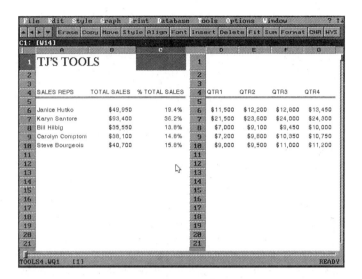

Quattro Pro splits the screen vertically into two windows.

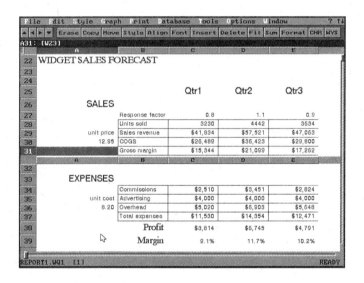

In this example, the screen is split horizontally into two windows with the /Window Options Horizontal command.

You can use the Horizontal or Vertical option of the Window Options menu to split the screen horizontally or vertically, respectively, at the point at which the cell selector is positioned when you select the command. In other words, you don't have to split the screen exactly in half. Remember that the dividing line requires you to specify either one row or one column, depending on whether you want to split the screen horizontally or vertically.

After you use the Vertical option to split the screen, the cell selector appears in the left window. After you use the Horizontal option to split the screen, the cell selector appears in the top window. To jump between the windows, use the Pane (F6) function key.

After splitting the screen, you can change the screen display so that the windows scroll independently rather than together (the default mode). To scroll the windows independently, select /Window Options Unsync. Reverse this command by selecting the /Window Options Sync command.

In Sync (synchronized) screen mode, when you scroll one window, the other window also automatically scrolls.

In Sync mode, pressing PgDn while in one window also moves the other window down the same number of rows.

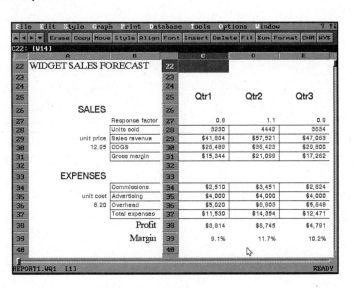

Horizontally split screens keep the same columns in view, and vertically split screens keep the same rows in view.

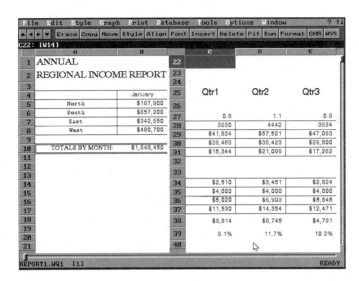

In Unsync (unsynchronized) screen mode, you control windows independently of each other in all directions.

5

To return to the single-window screen, select /Window Options Clear. If you are in Unsync mode when you use the Clear option, the single window assumes the cell selector position of the top window if the screen was split horizontally, or of the left window if it was split vertically.

Locking Titles On-Screen

If you need rows or columns, or both, along the top and left edges of the spreadsheet to remain in view as you scroll to different parts of the spreadsheet, use the /Window Options Locked Titles command. The /Locked Titles command is similar to the Horizontal and Vertical commands. With these commands, you can see one area of a spreadsheet while you work on another area. The unique function of the /Window Options Locked Titles command, however, is that it locks all the cells to the left of or above (or both to the left of and above) the cell selector's position so that those cells cannot move off-screen.

Because the default screen, without any special column widths, shows 23 rows by 10 columns in WYSIWYG mode, you have to shift the screen if your data is outside of this screen area. In fact, you may need to scroll the screen several times to enter or view all the information.

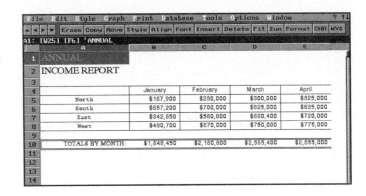

Suppose, for example, that you want to keep the headings in column A on-screen as you scroll this spread-sheet.

5

To lock spreadsheet titles on-screen, follow these steps:

1. Position the cell selector one column to the right of the column you want to lock.

   In this example, position the cell selector in column B.

2. Press ⌐/⌐ to access the Quattro Pro menu.

3. Press ⌐W⌐ to select Window.

4. Press ⌐O⌐ to select Options.

5. Press ⌐L⌐ to select Locked Titles.

6. Press ⌐H⌐, ⌐V⌐, or ⌐B⌐ to select Horizontal, Vertical, or Both, respectively. The Both option enables you to lock the rows above and columns to the left of the cell selector.

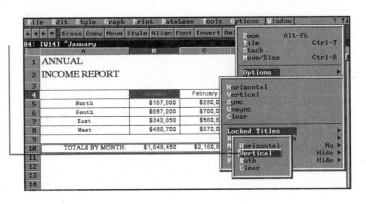

In this example, press ⌐V⌐ to select Vertical and lock all cells in the column to the left of the cell selector.

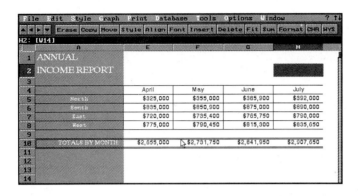

Now, no matter where you move the cell selector, column A is always displayed.

Note: After you lock columns or rows, or both, you cannot move the cell selector into the locked area while Quattro Pro is in READY mode. If you try to move the cell selector into the locked area, Quattro Pro beeps. Similarly, pressing Home moves the cell selector only to the upper left cell in the unlocked area, rather than to cell A1, as it normally does. You can avoid these restrictions, however, by using the GoTo (F5) key to move the cell selector into the locked area.

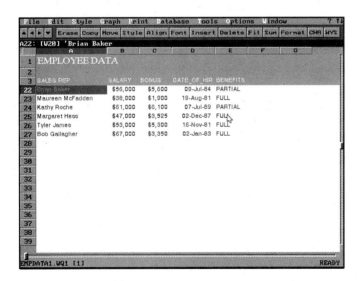

This example shows a spreadsheet in which rows 1-3 are locked with the /Window Options Locked Titles Horizontal command. Notice that rows 1-3 remain at the top of the screen, even though the cell selector is in row 22.

Sometimes you need to lock both rows and columns on-screen.

In this example,
with the cell
selector in B5,
you can issue the
/Window Options
Locked Titles
Both command to
keep the rows
above the cell
selector and the
column to the left
of the cell selec-
tor locked on-
screen.

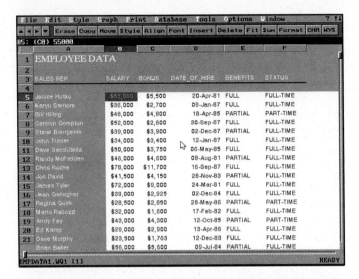

Then, when you
scroll right,
column A remains
on the left side of
the screen and,
when you scroll
down, rows 1-4
remain on top of
the screen.

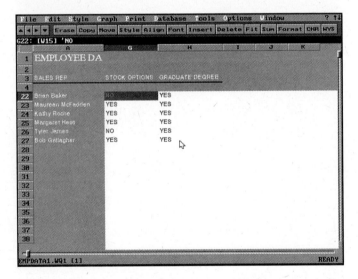

Note: To unlock spreadsheet titles, whether Vertical, Horizontal, or Both, use
the /Window Options Locked Titles Clear command. After you clear the titles,
you can freely move the cell selector throughout the spreadsheet.

Inserting Columns and Rows

Suppose that you are finished creating a spreadsheet, but you want to enhance its general appearance. You can insert blank columns and rows in
strategic places to highlight headings and other important items. Whether you
want to insert additional data or add blank rows or columns to separate
sections of your spreadsheet, you can use the /Edit Insert command to insert
columns and rows. You can insert multiple adjacent columns and rows each
time you invoke this command.

To insert a new column or row into the spreadsheet, follow these steps:

1. Position the cell selector at the location in which you want to insert
   the new column or row.

   In this example, position the cell selector in column D to add a new
   column of data.

2. Press / to access the Quattro Pro menu.

3. Press E to select Edit.

4. Press I to select Insert.

5. To insert a column, press C to select Columns. To insert a row, press
   R to select Rows.

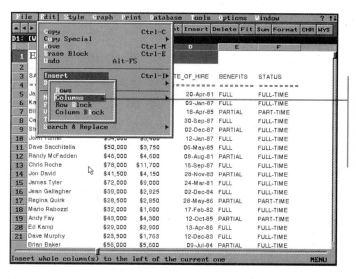

In this example,
press C to select
Columns and
insert a new
column in the
spreadsheet.

6. In response to the prompt, designate the block where you want to insert the new column or row. To insert more than one column or row, press → to highlight multiple columns or ↓ to highlight multiple rows.

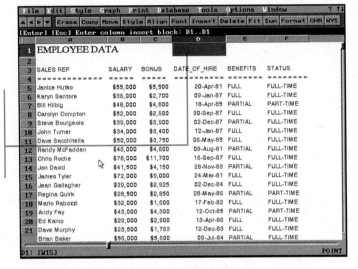

In this example, the cell selector is positioned in column D to insert a single column.

7. Press ↵Enter to complete the command. Quattro Pro moves existing spreadsheet data to the right of the cell selector when you insert columns, or below the cell selector when you insert rows.

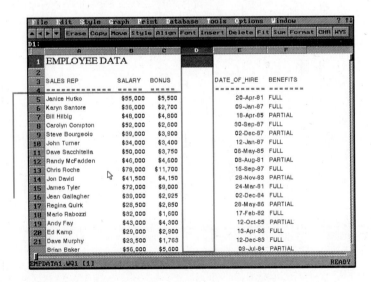

In this example, when you press ↵Enter), Quattro Pro displays a blank column in which you can enter new data.

Quattro Pro automatically shifts all values and modifies all cell formulas to accommodate the change in the spreadsheet.

Using the mouse, you can preselect the location for the new rows or columns, before issuing the /Edit Insert command. If you preselect the location for the new rows or columns and then select /Edit Insert Columns or /Edit Insert Rows, Quattro Pro immediately performs the insertion, without prompting you for a location.

Note: You also can use the Ctrl - I shortcut key combination in place of the /Edit Insert command.

Deleting Columns and Rows

You can delete single or multiple columns or rows with the /Edit Delete command. After you select this command, you then choose Columns or Rows from the Delete menu. If you choose Rows, Quattro Pro prompts you to specify the block of rows you want to delete; you need to specify only cell from each row you want to delete. Similarly, if you choose Columns, Quattro Pro prompts you to specify the block of columns you want to delete; you need to specify only one cell from each column you want to delete.

To delete existing columns or rows from the spreadsheet, follow these steps:

1. Position the cell selector in the first row or column that you want to delete.

   In this example, position the cell selector in row 5 to delete rows 5-11.

2. Press / to access the Quattro Pro menu.

3. Press E to select Edit.

4. Press D to select Delete.

5. Press C to select Columns or R to select Rows.

   In this example, press R to select Rows and delete rows from the spreadsheet.

6. In response to the prompt, designate the block of columns or rows you want to delete.

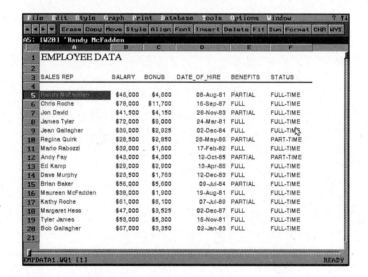

In this example, highlight rows 5 through 11 (in any column).

7. Press ↵Enter to complete the command.

In this example, when you press ↵Enter, Quattro Pro removes the original data in rows 5 through 11 and moves up the data that was below these rows.

Using the mouse, you can preselect the rows or columns you want to delete, before issuing the /Edit Delete command. If you preselect the rows or columns you want to delete and then select /Edit Delete Columns or /Edit Delete Rows, Quattro Pro immediately deletes the selected rows or columns, without prompting you to specify the block you want to delete.

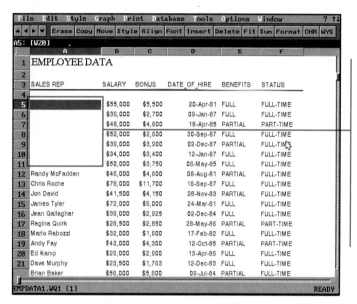

/Edit Delete is different from /Edit Block Erase. As shown in this example, /Edit Block Erase erases only the data from a cell or block of cells; it does not erase entire columns or rows of data.

5

If you plan to use the /Edit Delete command to delete a column or row containing values, keep in mind that all formulas in the spreadsheet that refer to these cells will result in ERR. Also remember that when you use the /Edit Delete command, the columns or rows you delete may be gone forever. This command deletes entire columns or rows, not just the block of cells you specify in those columns or rows.

If the Undo feature is enabled, you can undo the deletion by pressing Undo (Alt-F5) before you execute another command. Otherwise, the only remedies are to re-create the missing data or retrieve the spreadsheet file. Retrieving the spreadsheet works only if you saved a copy of your spreadsheet when it contained the deleted data.

Suppressing the Display of Zeros

The /Options Formats Hide Zeros command enables you to suppress the display of all cells in the spreadsheet that have a numeric value of zero. For example, this technique is useful if you are preparing a report for a presentation in which cells showing $0 would look odd.

You can enter formulas and values for all the items in the report, including the zero items, and then display the results with all the zeros removed. The actual formula or value is displayed in the input line when the cell selector highlights a cell that contains a zero or a formula that evaluates to zero.

5

Suppose that your spreadsheet contains dates and product sales. In some cases, the sales are $0, perhaps entered in error.

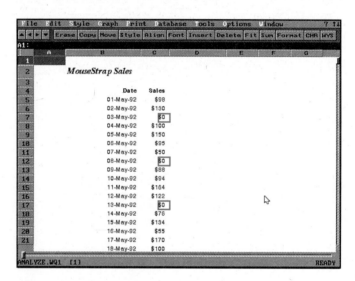

To suppress the display of zeros, follow these steps:

1. Press / to access the Quattro Pro menu.
2. Press O to select Options.
3. Press F to select Formats.
4. Press H to select Hide Zeros.

146

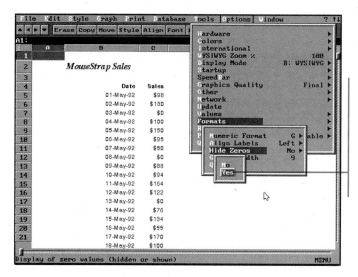

After you select
Hide Zeros,
Quattro Pro
prompts you to
specify Yes to
suppress the
display of zeros or
No display them.

5

5. Press Ⓨ to select Yes.

6. Select Quit to exit the Options Format menu. Select Quit again to
    leave the Options menu and return to READY mode.

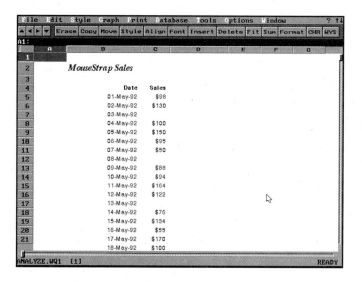

Now the zeros in
the spreadsheet
are suppressed.

If you want to make the zeros visible again, use the command /Options
Formats Hide Zeros No. When you use the /File Save command to save your
spreadsheet, Quattro Pro does not save the zero suppression feature of this

command with the spreadsheet. Unless you suppressed zeros with the /Options Format Hide Zeros command, the next time you use Quattro Pro, the spreadsheet displays zeros.

Note: This command is not selective; it affects all cells in the spreadsheet with a zero value. A cell with the value .004 is displayed as 0.00 if you use a 2-decimal place format. Because the value is not truly zero, the /Options Formats Hide Zeros command does not change it.

Recalculating the Spreadsheet

One of the primary functions of a spreadsheet program is to recalculate all the cells in a spreadsheet when a value or formula in one of the cells changes. Quattro Pro provides three basic recalculation modes: *automatic, manual,* and *background*. Using automatic recalculation, the default mode, Quattro Pro recalculates the spreadsheet whenever any cell in the spreadsheet changes. In manual recalculation, Quattro Pro recalculates only when you request it, either with the Calc (F9) key or with a macro. In background recalculation, Quattro Pro recalculates formulas between keystrokes.

Quattro Pro also provides three orders of recalculation: the *natural order* and two linear orders, either *columnwise* or *rowwise*. Natural order is the default, but you can choose any of the three orders. You also can choose the number of times the spreadsheet is recalculated. You use the /Options Recalculation command to select recalculation options.

To select recalculation settings, follow these steps:

1. Press / to access the Quattro Pro menu.
2. Press O to select Options.
3. Press R to select Recalculation.

The Recalculation menu appears, enabling you to choose from the recalculation options.

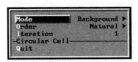

4. Select an option from the Recalculation menu.

   To change the mode of recalculation, press M to select Mode, and then select one of the following Mode options:

Option	Description
Automatic	Recalculation occurs whenever you change a cell. This option is the default setting.
Manual	Recalculation occurs only when you press Calc (F9).
Background	Recalculation occurs in the background during any pause in keyboard activity.

To change the order of recalculation, press O to select Order, and then select one of the following Order options:

Option	Description
Natural	Recalculation does not occur for any cell until the cells it depends on have been recalculated. This option is the default setting.
Columnwise	Recalculation begins at cell A1 and continues down column A, then goes to cell B1 and down column B, and so forth.
Rowwise	Recalculation begins at cell A1 and proceeds across row 1, then goes to cell A2 and across row 2, and so forth.

To change the number of recalculations, press I to select Iteration, and then specify the number of times you want recalculation to occur when you change cell contents (Automatic recalculation) or press F9 (Manual recalculation). One iteration per recalculation is the default.

As a beginning Quattro Pro user, you may not need to change the recalculation settings. To save processing time, you can switch to Manual recalculation so that Quattro Pro recalculates the spreadsheet only when you press Calc (F9).

5

149

For more specialized applications, you can use the Columnwise or Rowwise recalculation methods. Be extremely careful when you use these orders of recalculation, however; if you use them improperly, they can produce erroneous values on the spreadsheet.

For more information on automatic, manual, and iterative recalculation, and natural, columnwise, and rowwise orders of recalculation, refer to Que's *Using Quattro Pro 4*, Special Edition. You will find in-depth discussions and step-by-step examples on using each of these recalculation options.

Protecting the Spreadsheet

5

Quattro Pro has special features that protect an entire spreadsheet or areas of a spreadsheet from possible destruction. Using a series of commands, you can set up blocks of cells that cannot be changed unless you first turn off the protection. In fact, you cannot delete columns or rows that contain protected cells. These protection commands are particularly beneficial when you are setting up a spreadsheet into which people who are not familiar with Quattro Pro will enter data.

Protecting the Entire Spreadsheet

When you first create a spreadsheet, the spreadsheet protection feature is not active, enabling you to make changes and add data.

The /Options Protection Enable command turns on the spreadsheet's protection system.

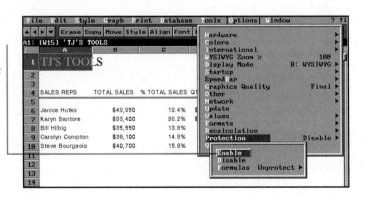

When you enable the protection, every cell in the spreadsheet is protected; you cannot add data to the spreadsheet or edit any cell's contents.

To turn on protection for the entire spreadsheet, follow these steps:

1. Press / to access the Quattro Pro menu.
2. Press O to select Options.
3. Press P to select Protection.
4. Press E to select Enable.

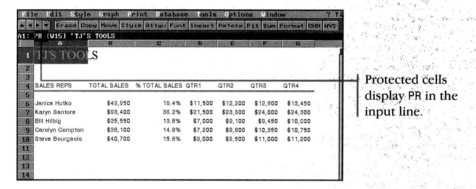

Protected cells display PR in the input line.

Protecting a Block in the Spreadsheet

Many times you may want to protect only some of the cells in a spreadsheet rather than all the cells. Quattro Pro enables you to protect blocks of cells so that you cannot change the data in the block. To protect a block, you must turn on the global spreadsheet protection, unprotect your work area, and then protect the specific block that you want to protect in the work area.

To protect a block of cells in the spreadsheet, follow these steps:

1. Select /Options Protection Enable to turn on global protection for the spreadsheet, as explained in the preceding section. (You must turn on global protection to protect cells in a worksheet.)
2. Press / to access the Quattro Pro menu.
3. Press S to select Style.
4. Press P to select Protection.

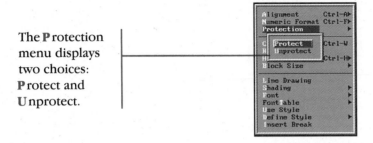

The **P**rotection menu displays two choices: **P**rotect and **U**nprotect.

5. Press U to select **U**nprotect.

6. When Quattro Pro prompts you to specify the block you want to unprotect, highlight your work area and press ↵Enter .

In this example, the work area is the block A1..G10.

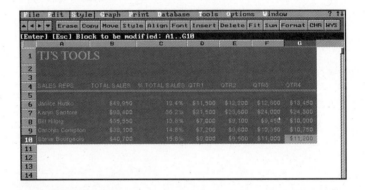

Unprotected cells display U in the input line. If you are using a color monitor, the color of the cells changes when you unprotect them.

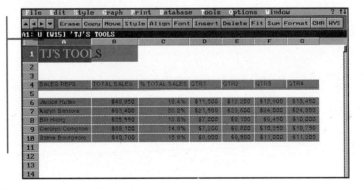

Now you can edit the cells in the block A1..G10 because these cells are no longer protected.

7. Press ⌸ to access the Quattro Pro menu.

8. Press Ⓢ to select Style.

9. Press Ⓟ to select Protection.

10. Press Ⓟ to select Protect.

11. When Quattro Pro prompts you to specify the block you want to protect, highlight a block in the work area and press ⏎Enter.

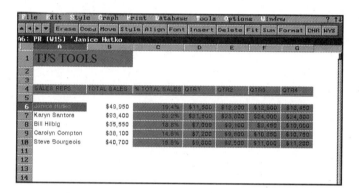

In this example, the protected block is C6..G10, the TOTAL SALES formulas for quarters 1-4.

5

Now you cannot enter or edit data in the block C6..G10.

Note: Using the mouse, you can preselect the block you want to protect or unprotect, and then issue the /Style Protection Protect or /Style Protection Unprotect command. If you preselect the block, Quattro Pro immediately protects or unprotects the block when you issue the command, without prompting you to specify a block.

Protecting Formulas in a Spreadsheet

You can spend hours building complex formulas for a spreadsheet. To prevent these formulas from being erased accidentally, Quattro Pro enables you to protect just the formula cells in a spreadsheet.

To turn on protection for only the formulas in a spreadsheet, follow these steps:

1. Press ⌸ to access the Quattro Pro menu.

2. Press Ⓞ to select Options.

153

3. Press P to select **P**rotection.

4. Press F to select **F**ormulas.

The **P**rotect option from the /**O**ptions **P**rotection **F**ormulas menu protects only the cells containing formulas in the spreadsheet.

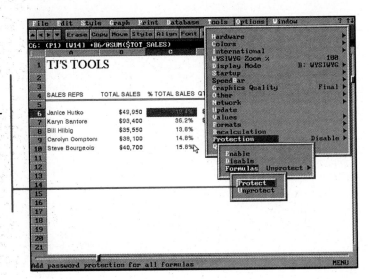

5. Press P to select **P**rotect.

Quattro Pro prompts you to enter a password, which you must provide to turn on the formula protection.

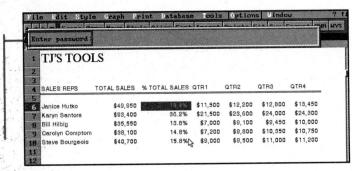

6. Type a password and press ↵Enter.

A password can be up to 15 characters and is case-sensitive. Use a password that you will remember easily.

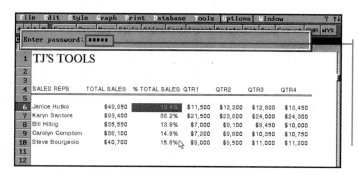

As you type the password, Quattro Pro displays a filled square for each character you type.

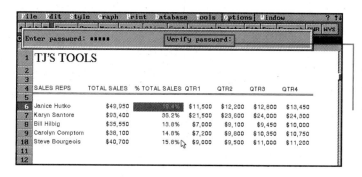

You must verify the password by reentering it.

7. Verify the password by typing it again, and then press ⏎Enter.

8. Select Quit to return to READY mode.

Quattro Pro does not indicate that you have protected the formula cells: the formula cells do not display PR when highlighted, nor does the color of the formula cells change. If you try to edit or erase a formula, however, Quattro Pro displays an error message indicating that formula protection is enabled.

To turn off formula protection, choose /Options Protection Formulas Unprotect and provide the correct password at the Enter password prompt.

Protecting important data in your worksheet is always a good idea. Accidental deletions and erasures, as well as accidentally typing over the data in a cell, are very common spreadsheet occurrences.

Summary

This chapter showed you how to set column widths (individually or globally), hide columns, split the screen into horizontal or vertical windows, and lock titles for scrolling. You also learned how to insert and delete columns and rows, suppress the display of zeros, and recalculate and protect the spreadsheet.

Specifically, you learned the following key information about Quattro Pro:

- The /Style Column Width command changes the width of a single column. To reset the column to its original default, use /Style Reset Width.

- The /Options Formats Global Width command changes the column width of all columns in the spreadsheet, except for those already changed.

- The /Style Block Size Set Width command sets the width of contiguous columns. To reset these columns to the default, select /Style Block Size Reset Width.

- The /Style Hide Column Hide command temporarily removes columns of data from the screen. Hidden columns also do not print when included in a print block. These columns can be restored with the /Style Hide Column Expose command.

- The /Window Options command splits the screen so that you can simultaneously view two different parts of the spreadsheet at the same time. You can split spreadsheets with the Horizontal or Vertical options. Use /Window Options Clear to return the spreadsheet to a single window.

- The /Window Options Locked Titles command locks titles along the top or left, or both, borders of the spreadsheet so that the titles remain in view when you scroll the spreadsheet. The /Window Options Locked Titles Clear command unlocks the titles.

- The /Edit Insert command inserts one or more columns and rows into the spreadsheet. To delete one or more columns or rows, use /Edit Delete.

- The /Options Formats Hide Zero command suppresses the display of zeros in the spreadsheet. Blank cells, instead of zeros, are displayed on-screen. The actual value (or formula) is displayed in the input line when you highlight a zero-valued cell.

5

■ The /Options Recalculation commands change the method, order, and number of iterations used in spreadsheet recalculation.

■ The /Options Protection command enables you to turn protection on or off in a spreadsheet. When protection is enabled, all the cells in the worksheet are protected and therefore cannot be edited, erased, or overwritten. You also can use the /Options Protection Formulas command to protect only the formulas in the spreadsheet. You can use the /Style Protection Protect command—in conjunction with the /Options Protection command and the /Style Protection Unprotect command—to protect specific blocks in a spreadsheet.

The next chapter shows you how to use the /Edit Copy and /Edit Move commands to modify your spreadsheet data. You also learn how to use Quattro Pro's search and replace feature.

5

157

Modifying
a Spreadsheet

As you use the basic concepts and commands described in previous chapters to create your own spreadsheets, you will need to modify your spreadsheets by moving and copying data from one location to another. Quattro Pro provides the capability to move and copy data—saving you hours of work when building and modifying your spreadsheets.

This chapter shows you how to improve your spreadsheets by effectively moving and copying data. You also learn how to search for and replace a specific string of data in a block of cells in the spreadsheet.

6

Moving the
contents of cells

Copying the
contents of cells

Searching for and
replacing cell
contents

Key Terms in This Chapter

Relative cell address	A cell reference in a formula that adjusts when you copy the formula to a new location.
Absolute cell address	A cell reference in a formula that does not adjust when you copy the formula to a new location.
Mixed cell address	A cell reference that combines both relative and absolute cell addresses.
Destination block	The block of cells to receive copied data.
Source block	The block of cells whose data is being copied.
Recalculation	The process of updating formulas in a spreadsheet.
Search string	A set of characters you use with the /Edit Search & Replace command to find specified text within a block of cells.

Moving the Contents of Cells

In the days of manual spreadsheets, the process of moving data around on the page was called *cutting and pasting* because the process involved using scissors and glue to move sections of the spreadsheet. Quattro Pro, however, enables you to cut and paste sections of the spreadsheet automatically.

With the /Edit Copy command, you can move and copy the contents of individual cells or blocks of cells from one part of the spreadsheet to another. The difference between moving and copying is that data you *move* from one cell to another disappears from the original cell; data you *copy* remains in the original cell.

Suppose that you want to move the contents of the block C3..C4 to the block A1..A2 on your spreadsheet. To move a block, follow these steps:

1. Press ⌷/⌷ to access the Quattro Pro menu.
2. Press ⌷E⌷ to select Edit.
3. Press ⌷M⌷ to select Move.

160

4. When the prompt Source block of cells appears, specify the block you want to move by highlighting the block (or typing the cell addresses), and then press ↵Enter.

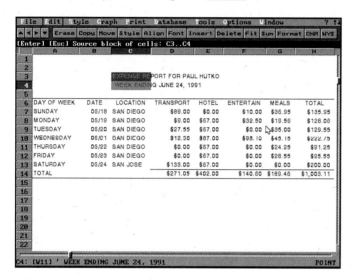

In this example, highlight C3..C4 and then press ↵Enter.

5. When the prompt Destination for cells appears, move the cell selector to (or type the cell address of) the upper left cell of the new location, and then press ↵Enter. Highlighting the entire Destination block is not necessary.

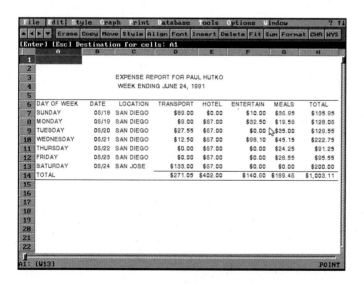

In this example, move the cell selector to cell A1, and then press ↵Enter.

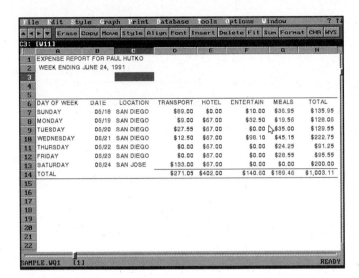

Quattro Pro moves the specified block to the new location.

The cell selector immediately returns to the cell from which you initiated the /Edit Move command.

Note: When you move a block of cells, the Source block (the block you are moving) completely overwrites the Destination block (the location to which you are moving the block), and you lose any cell contents in the Destination block. If any cells in the spreadsheet contain formulas that depend on the cell addresses in the Destination block, the cells containing these formulas display the message ERR.

Use the expanding cell selector to highlight a block. When you select /Edit Move and are prompted to enter a block, Quattro Pro automatically makes the current cell one corner of the block. If you do not want that cell to be a part of the Source block, press Esc, move the cell selector to the cell you want as the upper left corner of the Source block, and then press ⋅. Press → and ↓ to move the cell selector to the right and down, respectively. Notice that the cell selector "expands" so that the entire block is highlighted. After you highlight the Source block you want to move, press ⏎Enter. The expanding cell selector enables you to use the /Edit Move command without first positioning the cell selector at the beginning of the Source or Destination block.

Use the End key to highlight a large block. Suppose that you want to move the contents of the block A1..E15 to the block that begins at cell A20. When the block prompt A1..A1 appears, press End and then ↓. The cell selector jumps to cell A15, and the prompt reads A1..A15. The cell selector jumps down to cell A15 because that cell is the last one in that column that contains data. Now move the cell selector by pressing End and then →. The prompt now reads A1..E15. The cell selector jumps to cell E15 because that cell is the last one in that row that contains data. This process takes 18 keystrokes if you use only the arrow keys. Instead, using End reduces the number of required keystrokes to 4. The difference is even more dramatic when you work with larger blocks.

Remember that when you press an arrow key after you press End, the cell selector moves in the direction of the arrow key to the next intersection between a blank cell and a cell that contains data. If gaps (blank cells) exist within the blocks of data, however, using End is less useful because the cell selector will go to the boundary of each gap.

Note that you can use the Ctrl- M shortcut key combination in place of the /Edit Move command.

6

Copying the Contents of Cells

You will often want to copy the contents of cells to other locations in a spreadsheet. In this section, you will look at the four different ways in which you can copy data in Quattro Pro:

- Copy from one cell to another cell.
- Copy from one cell to every cell in a block.
- Copy from one block to a block of equal size.
- Copy from one block to a larger block.

The procedure for each copy operation is basically the same. To copy a block, follow these steps:

1. Press / to access the Quattro Pro menu.
2. Press E to select Edit.
3. Press C to select Copy.
4. When the prompt Source block of cells appears, specify the Source block.
5. When the prompt Destination for cells appears, specify the Destination block.

The only elements that change are the dimensions and locations of the Source and Destination blocks. Remember that you can either type the coordinates of the Source and Destination blocks, or highlight the blocks in POINT mode.

When you copy a cell, Quattro Pro automatically copies the format of the cell with it. This automatic format-copying feature saves you from having to set the format for an entire block of cells before or after copying it. The format of a cell includes shading, font size, line drawings (such as outline), and numeric format (such as currency).

The four methods of copying data are described in the text that follows.

Method 1: Copying from one cell to another cell

1. Press ☐ to access the Quattro Pro menu.
2. Press ☐ to select **E**dit.
3. Press ☐ to select **C**opy.
4. When the prompt `Source block of cells` appears, move the cell selector to the cell whose contents you want to copy, and then press ☐Enter.

In this example, select A1 as the Source block and press ☐Enter.

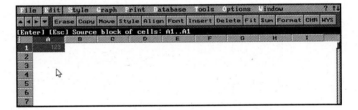

5. When the prompt `Destination for cells` appears, move the cell selector to the cell where you want to copy the data, and then press ☐Enter.

In this example, move the cell selector to cell A2 and press ☐Enter.

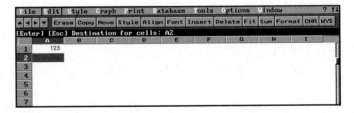

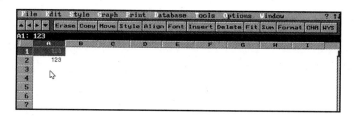

Quattro Pro copies the contents of cell A1 to cell A2, as shown in this example.

Method 2: Copying from one cell to a block of cells

1. Press ⌐/⌐ to access the Quattro Pro menu.

2. Press ⌐E⌐ to select **E**dit.

3. Press ⌐C⌐ to select **C**opy.

4. When the prompt Source block of cells appears, move the cell selector to the cell whose contents you want to copy, and then press ⌐Enter⌐.

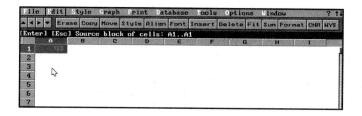

In this example, select A1 as the Source block and press ⌐Enter⌐.

5. When the prompt Destination for cells appears, highlight the block of cells in which you want to copy the data, and then press ⌐Enter⌐.

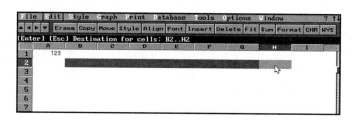

In this example, highlight B2..H2 as the Destination block and press ⌐Enter⌐.

Quattro Pro copies the contents of cell A1 to each cell in the block B2..H2, as shown in this example.

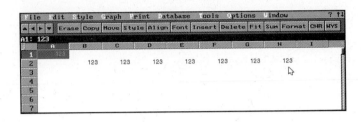

Method 3: Copying from one block to a block of equal size

1. Press / to access the Quattro Pro menu.

2. Press E to select Edit.

3. Press C to select Copy.

4. When the prompt Source block of cells appears, highlight the block of cells whose contents you want to copy, and then press Enter.

In this example, highlight the block A1..H1, and then press Enter.

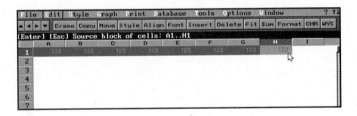

5. When the prompt Destination for cells appears, move the cell selector to the first cell of the block in which you want to copy the data, and then press Enter. Highlighting the entire Destination block is not necessary.

In this example, specify the Destination block by moving the cell selector to cell A2, and then press Enter.

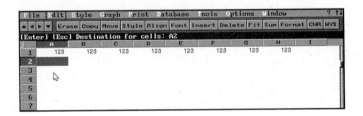

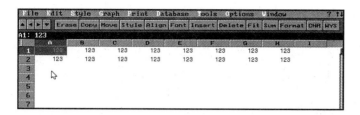

Quattro Pro copies the block A1..H1 to A2..H2, as shown in this example.

Method 4: Copying from one block to a larger block

1. Press ⁄ to access the Quattro Pro menu.
2. Press E to select **E**dit.
3. Press C to select **C**opy.
4. When the prompt `Source block of cells` appears, highlight the block of cells whose contents you want to copy, and then press ↵Enter.

In this example, highlight the block A1..F1, and then press ↵Enter.

5. When the prompt `Destination for cells` appears, highlight only the first cells in the rows or columns to which you want to copy the data, and then press ↵Enter.

167

For example, to copy the data from row 1 (cells A1..F1) to rows 2 through 22 (cells A2..F22), specify the Destination block by highlighting the first cells in rows 2 through 22 (cells A2..A22), and then press Enter.

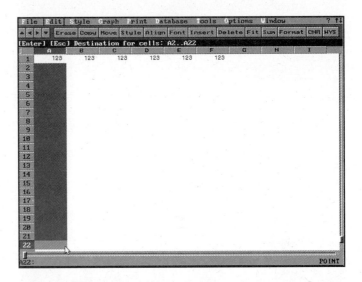

Quattro Pro copies the block A1..F1 to the larger block A2..F22.

6

This method of copying is simply an extension of the third method. The results of this copy operation could have been reached by repeating the copy command 21 times and specifying 21 different single-row Destination blocks. The first Destination block would be A2, the second would be A3, the third A4, and so on. The results are the same for either method, but you can save a great deal of time by copying to the A2..A22 block, as shown.

The best way to learn how to use different Source and Destination blocks is to experiment. After a while, the rules of copying become second nature to you. Note that you can use the Ctrl-C shortcut key combination in place of the /Edit Copy command.

Copying Only the Contents of a Cell

Rather than copy both the contents and the format of a cell or block, you can choose to copy only its contents, which can be very useful when you want only the data without the specific format of the Source block.

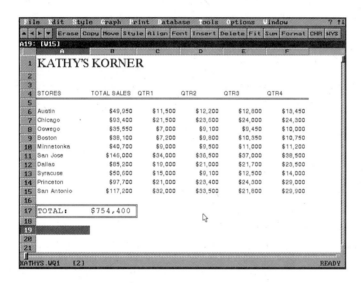

In this spreadsheet, cells A17 and B17 have special formats. A double line surrounds the cells, and the cells contain a different font size than the default for the spreadsheet. Also, B17 has a currency numeric format.

6

To copy only the contents of a cell or block, follow these steps:

1. Press / to access the Quattro Pro menu.
2. Press E to select Edit.
3. Press O to select Copy Special.

After you select
/Edit Copy
Special, you then
select to copy
only the cell's
contents or only
the cell's format.

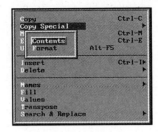

4. Press C to select Contents.

5. When the prompt Source block of cells appears, highlight the block of cells whose contents you want to copy, and then press ↵Enter

6

In this example,
highlight the
block A17..B17,
and then press
↵Enter

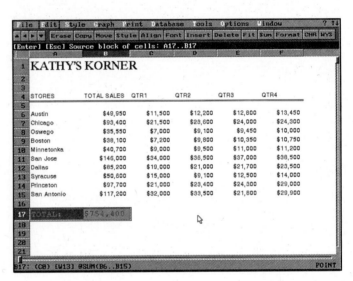

6. When the prompt Destination for cells appears, highlight only the first cell or cells in the rows or columns to which you want to copy the data, and then press ↵Enter

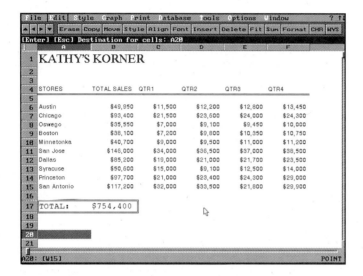

Highlight cell A20 as the Destination cell and press ↵Enter.

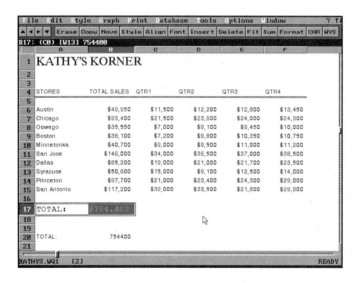

Quattro Pro copies only the data from cells A17..B17 to A20..B20. It does not copy the format of cells A17..B17 to the new location.

Copying Only the Format of a Cell

You can choose to copy only the format of a cell or block, rather than copy its contents. This feature can be very useful when you want to apply a special format to another area of the spreadsheet.

To copy only the format of a cell or block, follow these steps:

1. Press ⎵/⎵ to access the Quattro Pro menu.

2. Press ⎵E⎵ to select **E**dit.

3. Press ⎵O⎵ to select C**o**py Special.

4. Press ⎵F⎵ to select **F**ormat.

5. When the prompt Source block of cells appears, highlight the block of cells whose format you want to copy, and then press ⎵↵Enter⎵.

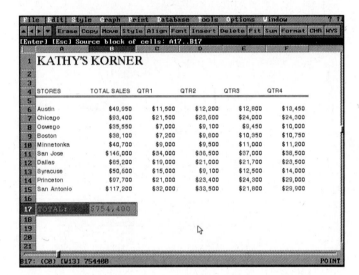

In this example, highlight the block A17..B17, and then press ⎵↵Enter⎵.

6. When the prompt Destination for cells appears, highlight only the first cell or cells in the rows or columns to which you want to copy the format, and then press ⎵↵Enter⎵.

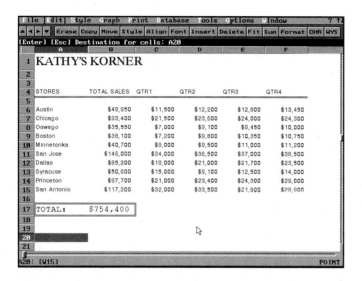

Highlight cell A20 as the Destination cell and press ⏎Enter.

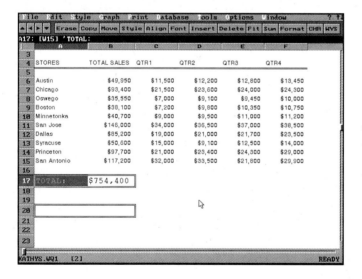

Quattro Pro copies only the format from cells A17..B17 to A20..B20. The data in cells A17..B17 is not copied to the new location.

6

173

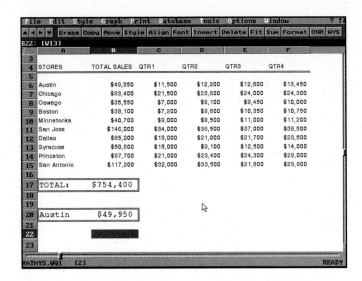

If you enter the label *Austin* in cell A20 and the number *49950* in cell B20, you can see that Quattro Pro applied the format from A17..B17 to the new location.

Addressing Cells

Although the connection may not be readily obvious, the way you address cells is tied closely to copy operations. When copying, you can choose between two different methods of addressing cells: *relative addressing* and *absolute addressing*. These two methods of referencing cells are important for building formulas. The type of addressing you use when you reference cells in formulas can affect the results produced by these formulas when you copy them to different locations in the spreadsheet. The following sections discuss relative and absolute addressing, as well as the combination of both methods—known as *mixed addressing*.

Referencing Cells with Relative Addressing

Relative addressing, Quattro Pro's default for referencing cells, means that when you copy a formula, the addresses of the cells in the formula are adjusted automatically to fit the new location. Suppose that you have summed the contents of one column and need to sum the contents of several adjacent columns, but you don't want to enter the @SUM function over and over again.

To copy a formula with a relative address, follow these steps:

1. Press / to access the Quattro Pro menu.
2. Press E to select Edit.
3. Press C to select Copy.

174

4. When the prompt `Source block of cells` appears, move the cell selector to the cell containing the formula you want to copy, and then press ⏎Enter.

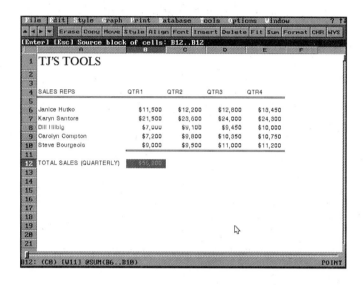

In this example, move the cell selector to cell B12, and then press ⏎Enter.

6

5. When the prompt `Destination for cells` appears, highlight the block of cells in which you want to copy the formula, and then press ⏎Enter.

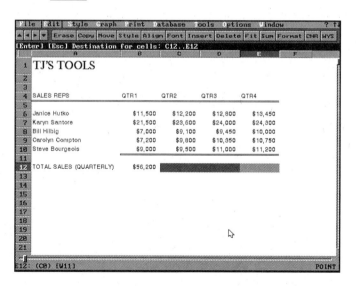

In this example, highlight C12..E12 as the Destination block and press ⏎Enter.

Quattro Pro copies the @SUM function to all the cells in the specified Destination block, C12..E12.

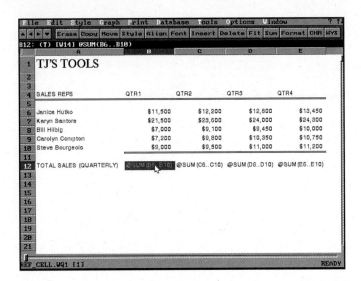

In the preceding illustration, the block of formulas is displayed in text format to show that each copied formula has adjusted to its new location.

Referencing Cells with Absolute Addressing

Absolute addressing means that when you copy a formula, the addresses of the cells in the formula do not change. In some cases, a formula has an important address that should not change when you copy the formula. To keep an address absolute, type $ before the cell's column letter and before the cell's row number. For example, E12 is an absolute address.

Now that you have summed the contents of several columns of sales, suppose that you want to calculate the percentage of sales. In the example, the best way to do this is to copy a formula that contains an absolute address. When you create the formula in cell B14, type $ before the E and A$ before the 12 in the second part of the formula.

To copy a formula with an absolute address, follow these steps:

1. Press / to access the Quattro Pro menu.
2. Press E to select Edit.
3. Press C to select Copy.
4. When the prompt Source block of cells appears, move the cell selector to the cell containing the formula with the absolute address you want to copy, and then press ⏎Enter.

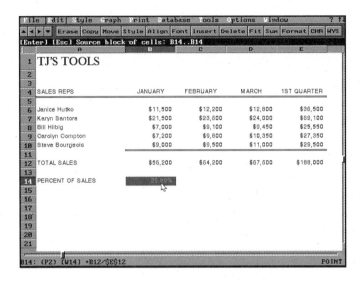

In this example, move the cell selector to cell B14 and press ⏎Enter. Note that cell B14 contains an absolute address in the formula +B12/E12, as shown in the status line.

6

5. When the prompt `Destination for cells` appears, highlight the block of cells in which you want to copy the formula with the absolute address, and then press ⏎Enter.

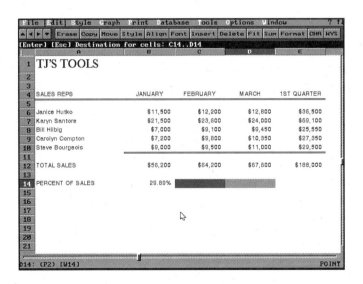

In this example, specify the Destination block by highlighting C14..D14 and pressing ⏎Enter.

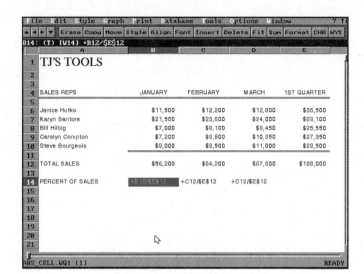

Quattro Pro
copies the
formula in B14
to the block
C14..D14.

In the preceding illustration, the block of formulas in row 14 is displayed in
text format to show that each copied formula has adjusted to its new location.
Note that in all three formulas, the first address of each formula varies, but the
second address remains absolute as *E12*.

Referencing Absolute Cell Addresses Using a Block Name

You also can use a block name to create the same formula, making sure that
the cell reference to cell E12 does not change. If you have created the block
name TOTAL for cell E12, for example, you can reference *TOTAL* rather than
E12 in the formula. To keep an address absolute with a block name, type $
before the block name; for example, $TOTAL is an absolute address. To
Quattro Pro, $TOTAL is exactly the same as E12 in this example.

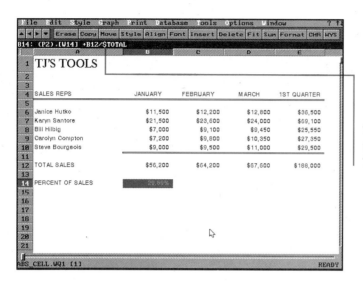

This formula uses
the block name
TOTAL.

To copy a formula with a block name absolute address, follow these steps:

1. Press ⃞/ to access the Quattro Pro menu.

2. Press ⃞E to select **E**dit.

3. Press ⃞C to select **C**opy.

4. When the prompt `Source block of cells` appears, move the cell
   selector to the cell containing the formula with the absolute address
   you want to copy, and then press ⃞⏎Enter.

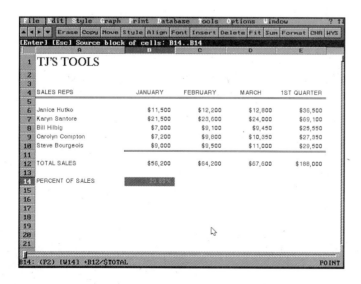

In this example,
move the cell
selector to cell
B14 and press
⏎Enter. Note that
cell B14 contains
an absolute
address in the
formula
+B12/$TOTAL.

6

5. When the prompt Destination for cells appears, highlight the
block of cells in which you want to copy the formula with the absolute
address, and then press ⏎Enter.

In this example,
specify the
Destination block
by highlighting
C14..D14 and
press ⏎Enter.

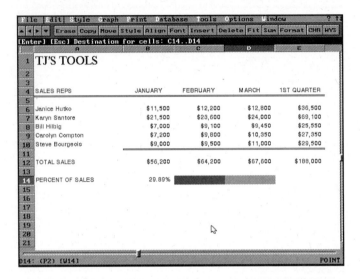

The block of
formulas in row
14 is displayed in
text format to
show that each
copied formula
has adjusted to its
new location.

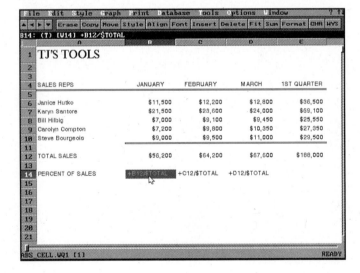

Note that although the first address of each formula varies, the second address
remains absolute as *$TOTAL* in all three formulas.

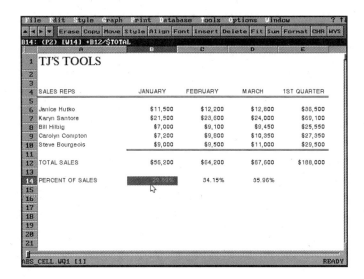

The block of formulas in row 14 is displayed in percent format and shows the percentages calculated by the formulas.

6

Mixing Relative and Absolute Addressing

The preceding two sections discuss absolute addresses, which do not change at all when you copy the address. You also can create a mixed address, which sometimes changes, depending on the direction of the copy operation. *Mixed addressing* refers to a combination of relative and absolute addressing. Because a cell address has two components—a column and a row—it is possible to fix (make absolute) either portion, but leave the other part unfixed (relative).

Keeping a running total in a spreadsheet requires a mixed address. When you copy the formula, you want the row number to change but you do not want the column letter to change. The formula in the following example contains mixed addresses and keeps a running total for the McFadden Associates account at Austin Federal Bank.

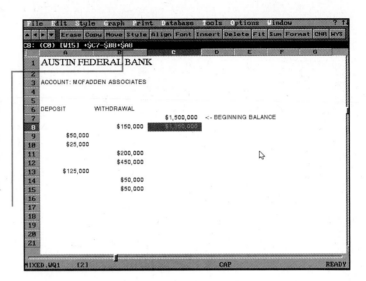

The formula in cell C8 has mixed references. The formula takes the previous balance, subtracts withdrawals, and then adds deposits.

You do not want the column letter references to change as you copy the formula; therefore, you precede the column letters with dollar signs to indicate that they are absolute. You do want the row number reference to change as you copy the formula; therefore, you do not precede the row numbers with dollar signs, indicating that they are relative.

To copy a formula with mixed cell addresses, follow these steps:

1. Press ⌷/⌷ to access the Quattro Pro menu.
2. Press ⌷E⌷ to select **E**dit.
3. Press ⌷C⌷ to select **C**opy.
4. When the prompt Source block of cells appears, move the cell selector to the cell containing the formula with the absolute address you want to copy, and then press ⌷↵Enter⌷.

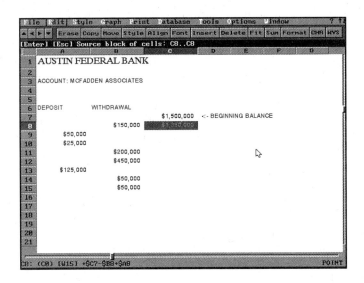

In this example, move the cell selector to cell C8 and press ⏎Enter.

5. When the prompt Destination for cells appears, highlight the block of cells in which you want to copy the formula with the absolute address, and then press ⏎Enter.

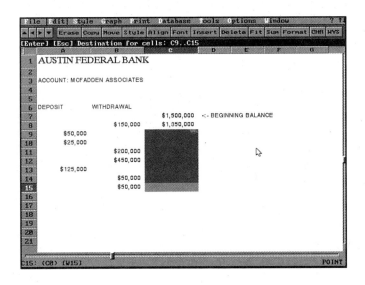

In this example, specify the Destination block by highlighting C9..C15, and then press ⏎Enter.

183

The row number reference changes when you copy the formula, but the column letter reference remains unchanged.

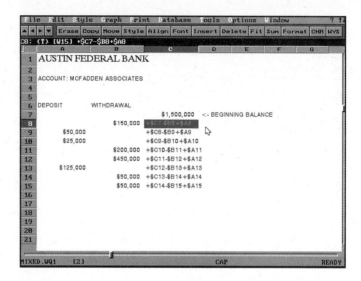

In the preceding illustration, the block of formulas in column C is displayed in text format to show that the row numbers in the copied formula have adjusted to their new location.

The block of formulas in column C is displayed in currency format to show how the running total is calculated.

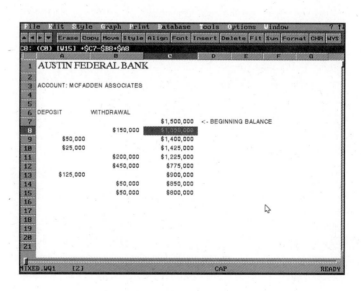

184

Using the Abs (F4) Key To Change a Cell Address

In a formula, you can enter dollar signs for absolute or mixed addresses in two ways. You can type the dollar signs as you create the formula, or you can modify the formula later by using the Abs (F4) key to have Quattro Pro enter the dollar signs for you. Use the Abs (F4) key in POINT mode or EDIT mode to make a cell address absolute, mixed, or relative. The Abs (F4) key is a four-way toggle: you repeatedly press F4 until you get the kind of cell reference you want.

To change a cell address with the Abs (F4) key, follow these steps:

1. Highlight the formula you want to change, and then press F2 (Edit).

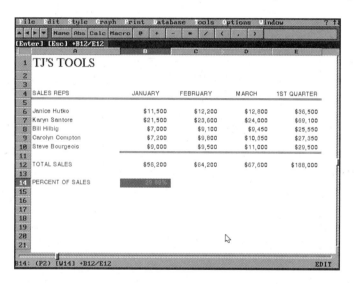

In this example, highlight cell B14 and press F2 (Edit).

2. With the cursor located on any character of the cell address in the input line, press F4 (Abs) once to change the address to absolute.

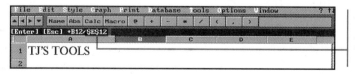

In this example, press F4 (Abs) to change E12 to E12.

3. Press F4 a second time to change the address to mixed—making the column relative and the row absolute.

6

185

In this example, E12 changes to E$12.

4. Press F4 a third time to transpose the mixed address—making the column absolute and the row relative.

In this example, E$12 changes to $E12.

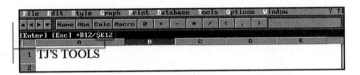

5. Press F4 a fourth time to change the address from mixed back to relative (the default).

In this example, $E12 changes to E12.

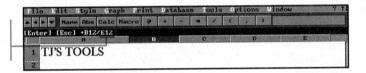

Transposing Rows and Columns

For copy operations that are difficult to perform with Quattro Pro's normal copy commands, Quattro Pro has two specialized copy commands: /Edit Transpose and /Edit Values. The /Edit Transpose command copies columns into rows and rows into columns. The /Edit Values command, which is explained in the next section, copies the values (but not the formulas) from one block to another. The /Edit Transpose command copies each row of the Source block into the corresponding column of the Destination block, or each column of the Source block into the corresponding row of the Destination block. The result is a transposed copy of the Source block.

Suppose that you want to transpose the data in two rows to columnar format. To transpose the data, follow these steps:

1. Press / to access the Quattro Pro menu.

2. Press E to select Edit.

3. Press T to select Transpose.

4. When the prompt `Source block of cells` appears, highlight the block of cells you want to transpose, and then press ↵Enter.

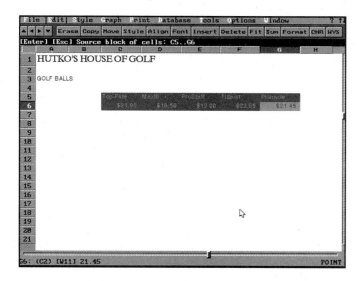

In this example, highlight the block C5..G6 and press ↵Enter.

5. When the prompt `Destination for cells` appears, highlight the cell into which you want to begin copying the data and then press ↵Enter.

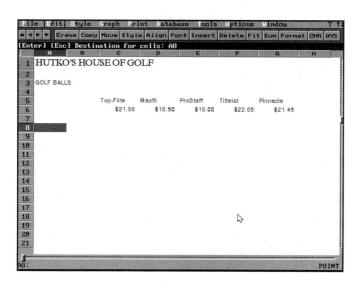

In this example, highlight cell A8 and press ↵Enter.

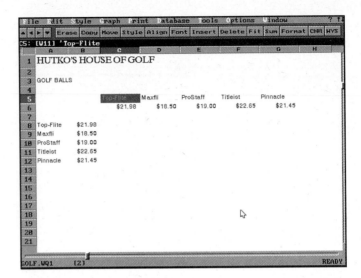

The data appears in its original location as well as transposed in its new location.

You can use the /Edit Transpose command to copy data from row to column format (as in this example) or from column to row format.

When copying formulas, the /Edit Transpose command behaves just like the /Edit Copy command. When you transpose a block, Quattro Pro adjusts the cell references in the transposed block, just as it adjusts references in an /Edit Copy command. This adjustment of cell references can lead to serious trouble when you use the /Edit Transpose command to transpose a block containing formulas. The transposed formulas will be incorrect; the values, however, will remain in the same order. Because the cell references are not transposed, the relative and mixed cell references in the transposed block will refer to incorrect locations after the transposition.

You can avoid the problem of incorrect cell references in transposed blocks by converting the formulas in the Source block to values before transposing. Using the /Edit Values command, discussed in the following section, is a convenient way to convert a block of formulas to values.

Converting Formulas to Values

The /Edit Values command enables you to copy only the values of the cells in one block to another block. This command is useful whenever you want to preserve the current formula values of a block of cells when you update your spreadsheet. An important function of the /Edit Values command is its capability to convert formulas to values. You don't have to worry, therefore, about formulas that depend on cell references (when using /Edit Transpose, for example).

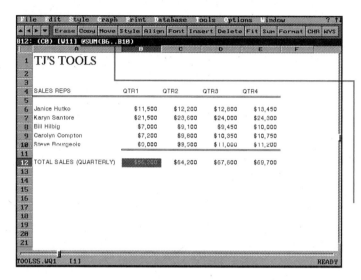

In this spread-sheet, each cell in the block B12..E12 contains a formula. The input line displays the formula stored in cell B12.

6

To convert formulas to values when copying, follow these steps:

1. Press / to access the Quattro Pro menu.
2. Press E to select Edit.
3. Press V to select Values.
4. When the prompt Source block of cells appears, highlight the block of formulas you want to copy, and then press ↵Enter.

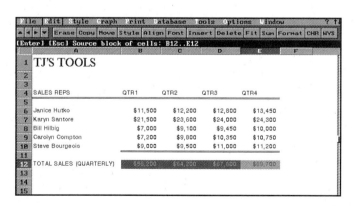

In this example, highlight the block B12..E12 and press ↵Enter.

189

5. When the prompt Destination for cells appears, move the cell selector to the first cell in the block in which you want to copy the values, and then press ⏎Enter.

In this example, move the cell selector to cell B14 and press ⏎Enter.

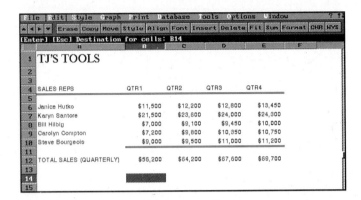

6

Notice that the formula from cell B12 has become a value in cell B14.

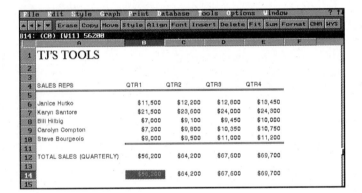

Tips for Copying

Remember the following tips whenever you intend to copy data within the spreadsheet:

- Sometimes the Source and Destination blocks will overlap when you copy. The general rule is to avoid overlapping the end points of the Source and Destination blocks to prevent problems with the copy operation. If you do overlap them, you may get mixed results. You can, however, overlap blocks without error when the Source and Destination blocks have the same upper left boundary (such as when you use the /Edit Values command to copy formulas onto themselves).

190

- Note that when the Undo feature is disabled, the /Edit Copy command is final. If you copy over the contents of a cell, you cannot retrieve the contents. Make sure that you have properly designated your blocks before you complete the command. You can retrieve the spreadsheet again if it has already been saved, but all changes made since the last save will be lost.

Searching for and Replacing Cell Contents

Looking for a word or string of characters in a large spreadsheet can be time-consuming and tedious. Quattro Pro offers a feature that enables you to search for text easily. If necessary, you can replace a specified string of characters with other text everywhere the string occurs. Frequent users of word processing software are familiar with this capability. It can be particularly useful for correcting all occurrences of a particular misspelling.

Whether you want to find the first occurrence of a string or you want to replace it with another string, you start with the same command: /Edit Search & Replace. By default, Quattro Pro performs the search row by row in the defined search block. If you do not define a block, Quattro Pro automatically searches the entire spreadsheet. The following section shows you how to search for a given string, and the subsequent section shows you how to search for a string and replace it with another string.

Searching for a String

To search a specified block for a particular string in labels and formulas, follow these steps:

1. Press ⏢/ to access the Quattro Pro menu.
2. Press ⏢E to select Edit.
3. Press ⏢S to select Search & Replace.
4. Press ⏢B to select Block.
5. Highlight the block in which you want to search, and then press ⏢↵Enter.

6

191

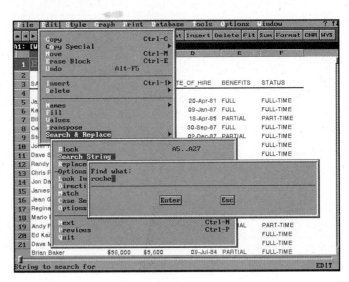

In this example, highlight the block A5..A27 and press *Enter*.

6. Press S to select Search String.

7. At the Find what prompt, specify the string you want to search for; then press *Enter*. Note that the search string is not case-sensitive; you can enter the string in upper- or lowercase characters.

In this example, to search for all occurrences of *Roche* in the highlighted block, type **roche**, and then press *Enter*.

8. Press N to select Next. Quattro Pro highlights the first appearance of the string.

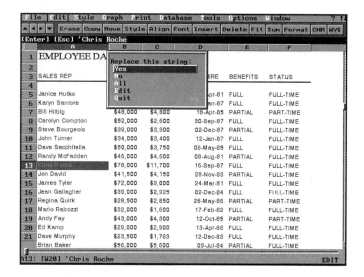

In this example, Quattro Pro highlights the first occurrence of *Roche* in the search block.

6

9. To search for the next appearance of the string, press [N] to select **N**o. Quattro Pro highlights the second occurrence of the string, if it is present.

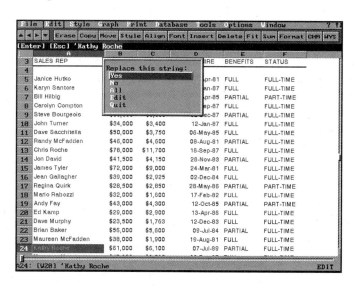

In this example, the next appearance of *Roche* in the search block is highlighted.

10. At each of the successive prompts, press [N] to select **N**o until Quattro Pro finds the last occurrence of your string in the block.

Note: To end the search before all occurrences of the string have been found, press Q to select Quit.

When Quattro Pro cannot locate another string, the cell selector returns to the anchor cell in the search block.

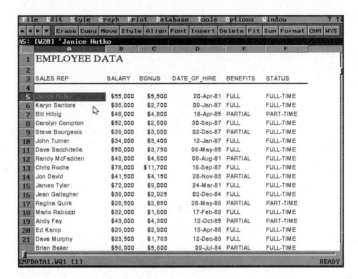

Replacing One String with Another String

To replace a string in the spreadsheet with another specified string, you follow a procedure similar to that which finds a string within a block. You must, however, supply the string of characters with which you want to replace the existing string.

To search a block for a particular string and replace that string with another string, follow these steps:

1. Press / to access the Quattro Pro menu.
2. Press E to select Edit.
3. Press S to select Search & Replace.
4. Press B to select Block.
5. Highlight the block in which you want to search, and then press ↵Enter. If you do not highlight a block, Quattro Pro searches the entire spreadsheet.

194

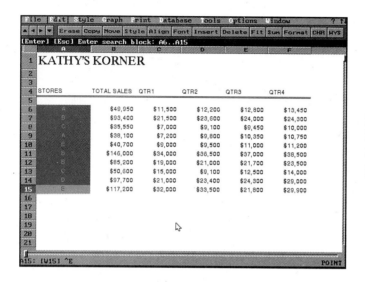

In this example, highlight the block A6..A15 and press ↵Enter.

6. Press $\boxed{S}$ to select **S**earch String.

7. Specify the string you want to search for, and then press ↵Enter. Note that the search string is not case-sensitive.

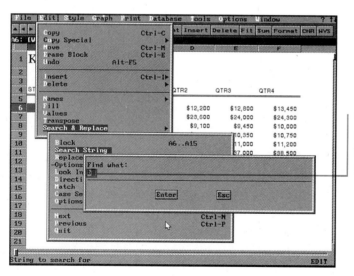

To search for *B* in the highlighted block, type **b** and press ↵Enter.

8. Press $\boxed{R}$ to select **R**eplace String.

9. Specify the string you want to use to replace occurrences of the search string you specified in step 7, and then press ↵Enter. Note that this

195

string *is* case-sensitive; Quattro Pro uses your exact pattern of upper- and lowercase letters to replace the search string.

In this example, to replace the occurrences of *B* with *West 5th Street*, type West 5th Street and press ↵Enter.

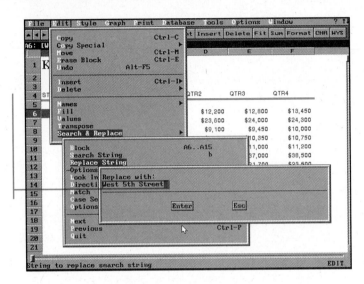

10. Press N to select Next. Quattro Pro highlights the first occurrence of the search string and provides a menu with five options. Select one of the five options:

Option	Description
Yes	Replaces the string.
No	Continues the search without replacing the string.
All	Replaces *every* matching string with the new string, without further prompting.
Edit	Changes the string.
Quit	Ends the search and returns Quattro Pro to READY mode.

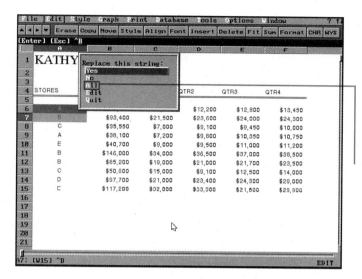

For this example, press A to select All.

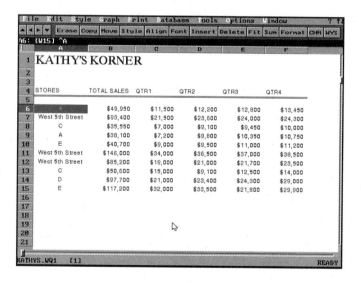

Note that all occurrences of the string *B* are replaced with the string *West 5th Street*.

When Quattro Pro cannot locate another appearance of the string after you select **All**, **Yes**, or **No**, the program returns to READY mode.

Tips for Using the Search-and-Replace Feature

Remember the following tips when using Quattro Pro's search-and-replace feature:

- Confining your search to a given block accelerates the search and reduces your chance of accidentally replacing strings you want to leave undisturbed.

- The search string can consist of more than a single word. In fact, the string can be as long as 254 characters and can contain many words.

- The string you are searching for is not case-sensitive. Quattro Pro will find any string that matches the characters you type, regardless of whether you type the string in uppercase characters, lowercase characters, or a combination of both.

- Unlike the search string, the replacement string is case-sensitive. The substitution consists of precisely what you type, in keeping with your use of uppercase and lowercase characters.

- The /Edit Search & Replace command does not search hidden columns; however, you can use the command to search individual cells formatted with the /Style Numeric Format command.

- Be careful when you use the /Edit Search & Replace command to replace values in formulas. Unintentional changes to formulas cause inaccurate results that are difficult to identify and correct.

Summary

In this chapter, you learned that when building a spreadsheet, you can use the /Edit Move command to relocate cells and cell blocks, and the /Edit Copy command to duplicate the contents of cells and cell blocks throughout the spreadsheet. By specifying relative, absolute, or mixed addressing, you can control cell references for formulas you use in your spreadsheets. You also learned that Quattro Pro provides a search-and-replace feature that enables you to find or replace specified strings of data in your spreadsheets.

Specifically, you learned the following key information about Quattro Pro:

- The /Edit Move command enables you to move the contents of one or more cells to any location in the spreadsheet. The data you move appears only in the new location.

- The /Edit Copy command enables you to copy information to other parts of the spreadsheet in four different ways. After being copied, the data appears in both locations.

- The /Edit Copy Special command enables you to copy only the data or only the format of a cell or a block.

6

■ In combination with the arrow keys, you can use the End key with the /Edit Move and /Edit Copy commands to move or copy large blocks of data.

■ Two types of cell addresses that are helpful when you copy formulas are relative and absolute cell addresses. Combinations of relative and absolute cell addresses are called mixed cell addresses. You use dollar signs to indicate absolute and mixed cell addresses.

■ When creating or modifying relative, absolute, and mixed cell addresses, you can use the Abs (F4) key to toggle between the different types of cell references.

■ The /Edit Transpose command copies data from columns into rows, and rows into columns.

■ The /Edit Values command copies a block of formulas to their equivalent values in another (or the same) block in the spreadsheet.

■ The /Edit Search & Replace command finds a specified string of data in a block. You also can replace this string with a new string.

In the next chapter, you learn how to format a spreadsheet. Quattro Pro 4 is equipped with strong formatting capabilities. You can outline, shade, bold, and underline a cell or block. You also can change the typeface and size of the text. Quattro Pro's formatting features enable you to create spectacular spreadsheets.

6

Formatting a Spreadsheet

The last two chapters taught you the commands to construct your spreadsheet and the commands to modify your spreadsheet, respectively. This chapter teaches you how to change the appearance of your spreadsheet. Most of the commands discussed in this chapter are from the Style menu. You can control how numbers are displayed, whether data cells should be outlined or shaded, and how large the text should appear in a label cell. One of the powerful features of Quattro Pro is its presentation-quality spreadsheets, which you learn to create in this chapter. And remember, because Quattro Pro is a WYSIWYG product, if you are in WYSIWYG display mode, whatever your spreadsheet looks like on-screen is what the spreadsheet will look like when you print it.

Formatting cell contents

Changing the font in a block

Setting a border and shading for a block

Defining and using styles

Key Terms in This Chapter

Formatting   The process of changing the way data is displayed in the spreadsheet. You accomplish formatting with the /Style Numeric Format and /Options Formats commands.

Font   The characteristics of a block, such as the typeface, style, color, and size.

Formatting Cell Contents

Quattro Pro expects you to enter data a certain way. If you try to enter 1,234, for example, the program beeps, switches to EDIT mode, and waits for you to remove the comma. You get the same result if you try to enter 10:08 AM—in this case, the colon and *AM* are the offenders.

Quattro Pro 4 would have limited usefulness if you could not change the way data is displayed on-screen. You can, however, control not only the display of data with commas, time, and currency, but also with a variety of other formats. You determine formats with one of the options of the /Style Numeric Format or /Options Formats Numeric Formats commands.

The formats available in Quattro Pro 4 primarily affect the way numeric values appear in a spreadsheet. Notice that Text format causes a formula to appear in a cell as a formula rather than a value, and Hidden format hides the display of a cell's contents.

Cell formats specified with /Style Numeric Format are automatically displayed within parentheses in the input line.

The format for cell D6, as depicted by (C0) in the input line, is Currency with zero decimal places.

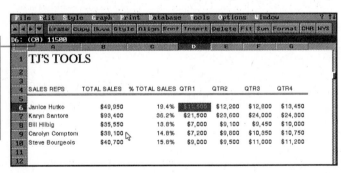

202

The spreadsheet's default cell format, however, does not appear in the input line.

Table 7.1 shows numbers formatted with different format options. Note that the examples of the data displayed for each format choice are shown with zero decimal places; however, you can specify up to 15 decimal places.

Table 7.1
Quattro Pro Format Options

| | | Examples | |
Format	Description	Data entered	Data displayed
Fixed	Controls the number of decimal places displayed.	15.56	16
Scientific	Displays large or small numbers, using scientific (exponential) notation.	–21	–2E+01
Currency	Displays currency symbols and commas.	234567.75	$234,568
, (Comma)	Inserts commas to mark thousands and multiples of thousands.	1234567	1,234,567
General	Displays values with up to 10 decimal places or uses scientific notation. This option is the default format in a new spreadsheet.	26.003	26.003
+ /–	Creates horizontal bar graphs or time-duration graphs; useful for computers that cannot display graphs.	5 –3	+++++ - - -
Percent	Displays a decimal number as a whole number with a % symbol.	0.25	25%

continues

7

Table 7.1 *(Continued)*

Format	Description	Examples Data entered	Data displayed
Date	Displays serial-date numbers. /Style Numeric Format Date Time sets time formats.	@DATE(89,8,1) @NOW	01-Aug-89 07:48 AM
Text	Displays formulas as text, not the computed values that Quattro Pro normally displays.	14 145	+B5+B6 @SUM(C4..C8)
Hidden	Hides contents from the display and does not print them; hidden contents are still evaluated.	289	
Reset	Returns the format to the current spreadsheet format.		

Setting Block and Spreadsheet Formats

Although you will frequently use the /Style Numeric Format command to format individual blocks in your spreadsheet, you also can change the default format for the entire spreadsheet. The /Options Formats Numeric Format command controls the format of all cells in the spreadsheet, and the /Style Numeric Format command controls specific blocks.

Generally, you use the /Options Formats Numeric Format command when you are just starting to enter data in a spreadsheet. Be sure to choose a format that you will use for the majority of cells; for example, a financial spreadsheet has many currency values, so a default format of Currency is a smart choice for this type of spreadsheet. After you set all the cells to that format, you can use the /Style Numeric Format command to override the overall spreadsheet format setting for specific cell blocks.

The /Style Numeric Format command takes precedence over the /Options Formats Numeric Format command. As a result, whenever you change the spreadsheet format, Quattro Pro automatically changes all the affected numbers and formulas, unless you previously formatted them with the /Style Numeric Format command.

204

Although you generally use the /Style Numeric Format command on cells that contain data, you may choose to select a format for cells that are now blank but will eventually contain data. Any information you enter in these cells later will be displayed according to the format you chose with /Style Numeric Format.

To change the format of a cell or block of cells, follow these steps:

1. Press ⟨/⟩ to access the Quattro Pro menu.
2. Press ⟨S⟩ to select Style.
3. Press ⟨N⟩ to select Numeric Format.
4. Select the type of format you want to set by pressing the first character (or symbol) of the option.

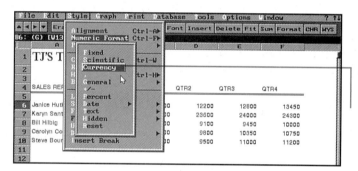

In this example, press ⟨C⟩ to select Currency.

7

If you are prompted to enter the number of decimal places, type a number and press ⟨↵Enter⟩, or press ⟨↵Enter⟩ to accept the default number.

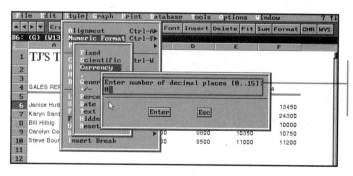

In this example, type 0 for zero decimal places, and press ⟨↵Enter⟩.

5. Highlight the block you want to format.

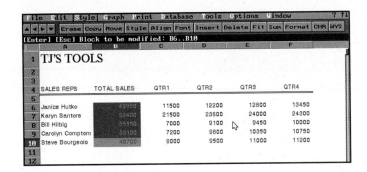

In this example, highlight the block B6..B10.

6. Press `⏎Enter` to complete the command.

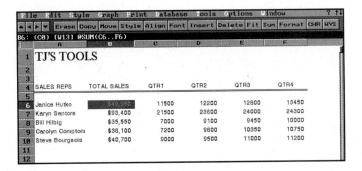

The cell selector is located on the first cell of the formatted block; the input line indicates the designated format.

Note: Using a mouse, you can preselect the block of cells you want to format. If you highlight the block before issuing the /S tyle N umeric Format command, Quattro Pro formats the block as soon as you select the format (and specify the number of decimal places, if necessary). Because you preselected a block, Quattro Pro does not prompt you to specify the cells you want to format.

Note: You can use the `Ctrl`-`F` shortcut key combination in place of the /S tyle N umeric Format command.

General Format

G eneral format is the default format for all new spreadsheets. When numbers are displayed in G eneral format, commas that separate thousands and multiples of thousands are not displayed. Trailing zeros to the right of the decimal point also are suppressed. If numbers are too large or too small to be displayed normally, Quattro Pro uses scientific notation.

Fixed Format

Quattro Pro's Fixed format is similar to General format in that it does not display commas or dollar signs. The difference is that Fixed format enables you to choose the number of decimal places (up to 15) you want to display.

Scientific Format

The Scientific format causes Quattro Pro to display numbers in exponential form (scientific notation). Unlike General format, Scientific format enables you to control the number of decimal places; you thereby determine the amount of precision displayed. You can specify up to 15 decimal places.

Currency Format

The Currency format displays a dollar sign ($) before the numbers in cells and inserts commas to separate thousands and multiples of thousands. Negative values appear in parentheses ( ). Although the dollar sign is the default symbol, you can use other symbols as currency indicators. The Currency format also gives you the option of controlling the number of decimal places. You can specify up to 15 decimal places.

Comma (,) Format

The , (Comma) format is similar to Currency format, except that no dollar signs appear with the numbers. Commas separate hundreds from thousands, hundreds of thousands from millions, and so on. Parentheses ( ) identify negative numbers. After you select the , (Comma) format, you can specify the number of decimal places you want. You can specify up to 15 decimal places.

Only in Currency and , (Comma) formats are negative values displayed within parentheses. In other formats, negative values are preceded by a minus sign.

+/– Format

The +/– format creates a horizontal bar graph of plus or minus signs within the cell, depending on the value of the number you enter in the cell. Asterisks appear if the size of the bar graph exceeds the column width. If you enter zero in a cell, a period (.) appears on the graph and left-justified in the cell.

You can use this format to mark a value in a long column of numbers. As you scan the column, the + and – signs stand out and are easy to locate.

7

Percent Format

The Percent format displays percentages. After you select the Percent format, you can specify the number of decimal places you want (no more than 15 decimal places). The values displayed in the spreadsheet are the values you enter, multiplied by 100 and followed by a percent sign. When you use the Percent format, remember to enter numbers with the correct decimal point. To display 12%, for example, you must enter .12 or 12%, not 12. If you enter % at the end of your entry, Quattro Pro automatically divides that number by 100. For example, if you enter 12%, Quattro Pro divides 12 by 100 (or 12/100) and stores .12 in that cell.

Date and Time Formats

Quattro Pro internally represents any given date as an integer equal to the number of days from December 31, 1899, to the given date. For example, January 1, 1900, is represented by the number 2; December 31, 2099 (the last date in Quattro Pro's calendar), is represented by 73,050. To enter a date into the spreadsheet, use one of the following date functions: @DATE, @DATEVALUE, @NOW, or @TODAY. You also can enter a date by pressing Ctrl-D and then typing the date, such as 12/22/68.

Quattro Pro calculates a period of hours as a fraction expressed in decimals. The calculations are based on a 24-hour clock (military time). Use one of the time functions (@TIME, @TIMEVALUE, or @NOW) to enter a time into the spreadsheet. You can specify nine date and time formats with the /Style Numeric Format Date and /Options Formats Date commands.

Text Format

Text format displays formulas in cells just as they appear in the input line, not as the computed values that Quattro Pro normally displays. Although Quattro Pro displays the formulas and numbers as text, it evaluates them correctly. Numbers you enter with this format appear as they do in General format.

The two most important applications of this format are setting up table blocks for /Tools What-If commands and formula debugging. Because you can display all the formulas on-screen with the Text format, finding and correcting problems is a relatively easy task. You may, however, have to widen the column width to see your complete formulas when you use this technique.

Hidden Format

The /Style Numeric Format Hidden command suppresses the cell contents for any given block. To hide all the cells in a column or block of columns, use the /Style Hide Column command instead, as discussed in the next chapter.

Although a cell with Hidden format appears as a blank cell on-screen, its contents are displayed in the input line when you highlight that cell, and the contents are still available for calculations or formulas. All formulas and values are calculated and readjusted when you modify the spreadsheet. If you print your spreadsheet, the contents of hidden cells do not appear on the printed copy.

Reset Format

The /Style Numeric Format Reset command resets the format of the indicated block to the spreadsheet default setting. When you reset the format of a block, the format indicator for any cell within the block disappears from the input line. The Reset option does not appear on the /Options Formats command menu.

Controlling the International Formats

Quattro Pro enables you to control the punctuation and currency sign displayed by the , (Comma) and Currency formats, and to control the way the date and time are displayed when you use the special international Date and Time formats. To control these settings globally for the spreadsheet, use the /Options International command.

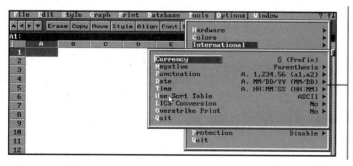

The /Options International command enables you to choose the format Quattro Pro uses to display the date, time, currency symbols, and punctuation.

Changing the Font in a Block

Many times you will want to showcase a particular portion of your spreadsheet. Using the /Style Font command, you can change the size, style, color, or typeface of the data in a block. These changes enable you to present your spreadsheet creatively for greater effect.

To change the font of a cell or block of cells, follow these steps:

1. Press / to access the Quattro Pro menu.
2. Press S to select Style.
3. Press F to select Font.
4. Highlight the block for which you want to set the font, and then press Enter.

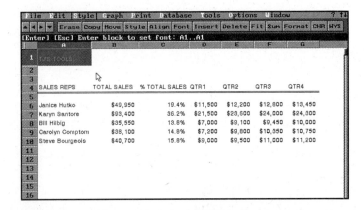

In this example, highlight cell A1 as the block, and press Enter.

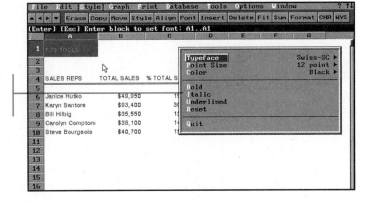

After you press Enter, the Font menu appears.

5. Press ⊤ to select **T**ypeface and then, after the list of typefaces appears, either click the typeface name you want or highlight it and press ↵Enter.

The **T**ypeface option enables you to specify the type of lettering you want to apply to the characters in the block.

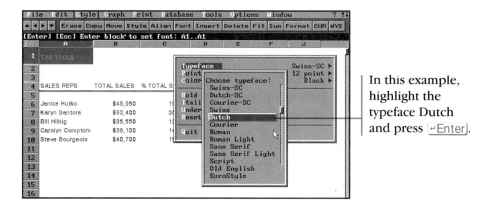

In this example, highlight the typeface Dutch and press ↵Enter.

6. Press P to select **P**oint Size and then, after the list of point sizes appears, either click the point size you want, or highlight it and press ↵Enter.

The **P**oint Size option enables you to specify how large the characters appear.

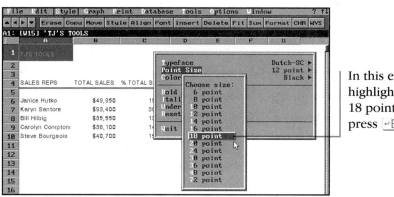

In this example, highlight the size 18 point and press ↵Enter.

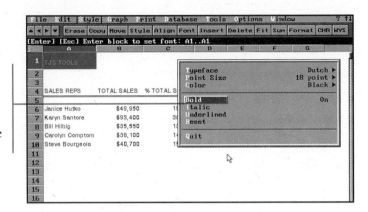

Press B to turn on the **Bold** option, which enables you to specify a boldface character.

7. Press Q to select **Q**uit and apply the font to the specified block.

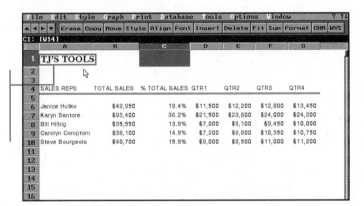

The characters in cell A1 now appear in a boldface 18-point Dutch font.

Changing the Font Color in a Block

The steps to change the font color in a block are very similar to the preceding steps. In this example, however, you are going to preselect the block and then execute the commands. Note that by default, the font color is black.

To change the font color in a block, follow these steps:

1. Select the block in which you want to change the font color.

212

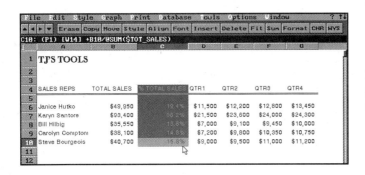

In this example, select the block C4..C10.

2. Press ⟨/⟩ to access the Quattro Pro menu.

3. Press ⟨S⟩ to select **S**tyle.

4. Press ⟨F⟩ to select **F**ont.

   Note that because you preselected the block, Quattro Pro does not display the prompt Enter block to set font.

5. Press ⟨C⟩ to select **C**olor.

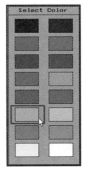

The color palette appears on-screen.

6. Press ⟨↓⟩ to select the color you want, and then press ⟨↵Enter⟩; alternatively, click the box displaying the color you want.

7. Press ⟨Q⟩ to select **Q**uit and apply the font color to the specified block.

7

213

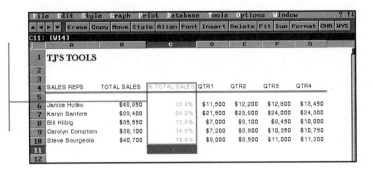

Quattro Pro
applies the
specified color
(light green in
this example)
to the block.

Note: The big advantage to preselecting a block before you set the font is that
after Quattro Pro applies the font, the block remains highlighted. You can
therefore quickly affect the block again with another command or go back to
the /Style Font menu to make another adjustment.

Using Prearranged Fonts

The Style menu also contains the FontTable command. The FontTable dialog
box lists eight prearranged fonts you can quickly apply by clicking a font
option, pressing a font option's number, or highlighting a font option and
pressing ⏎Enter.

Select the /Style
FontTable com-
mand to display
the FontTable
dialog box.

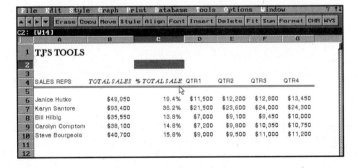

In this example,
Font 8 from the
FontTable dialog
box is applied to
cells B4 and C4.

You can change the fonts in the FontTable by selecting Edit Fonts from the FontTable dialog box. For more information on editing fonts in the FontTable, see Que's *Using Quattro Pro 4*, Special Edition.

In WYSIWYG display mode, each font change you make to a cell or block appears instantly on-screen. Font changes you make in Text display mode, however, are not displayed. In Text mode, the correct font will appear on the printed spreadsheet. Text mode is not useful if you plan to experiment with font attributes.

Setting a Border and Shading for a Block

The Quattro Pro spreadsheet can appear with or without grid lines. By default, Quattro Pro's grid lines are off; however, you can turn them on with the /Window Options Grid Lines Display command. Note that the grid lines do not appear when you print your spreadsheet.

7

This example shows a spreadsheet with grid lines.

When the grid is turned off in your spreadsheet, the /Style Line Drawing command is especially useful. You can create borders for a block to set it off from the rest of the data. Shading a block is an excellent way to mark off a block, separating it from the other data in the spreadsheet. The appearance of a shaded area immediately draws attention to that area.

Setting a Border for a Block

You can set borders on all sides of a block, on only one side of a block, or inside a block.

To set a border for a block of cells, follow these steps:

1. Select the block around which you want to draw a border.

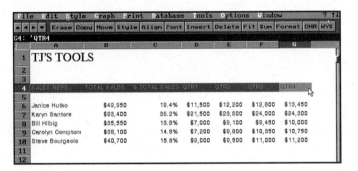

In this example, block A4..G4 is selected.

2. Press ⃞/ to access the Quattro Pro menu.

3. Press ⃞S to select **S**tyle.

4. Press ⃞L to select **L**ine Drawing.

   Note that because you preselected a block, Quattro Pro does not prompt you to enter a block address.

5. Select a line placement option for the border. (Line placement options are explained in detail in table 7.2.)

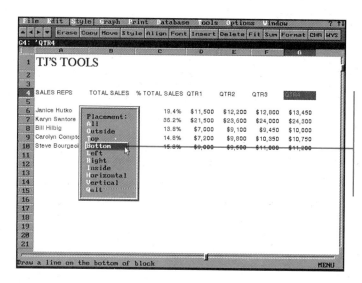

In this example, select **Bottom** from the Placement list to place the border along the bottom of the block.

6. Select a line type for the border.

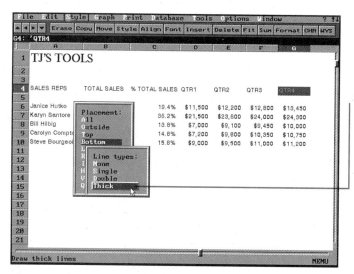

In this example, select **Thick** from the Line types list to draw a thick border.

7. Press Q to select **Quit**.

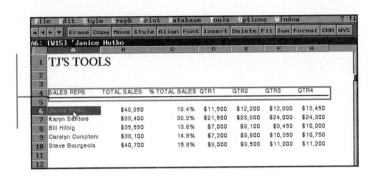

A thick line appears across the bottom border of the block A4..G4.

Table 7.2 describes the line placement options.

Table 7.2
Line Placement Options

Option	Description
All	Draws a box around the block and draws vertical and horizontal lines between all the cells in that block.
Outside	Draws a box around the perimeter of the block.
Top	Draws a horizontal line on top of the first row of the block.
Bottom	Draws a horizontal line under the last row of the block.
Left	In the leftmost column, draws a vertical line along the left edge of the cells in the block.
Right	In the rightmost column, draws a vertical line along the right edge of the cells in the block.
Inside	Draws vertical and horizontal lines between all the cells in the block.
Horizontal	Draws lines between each row in the block.
Vertical	Draws lines between each column in the block.
Quit	Returns to the spreadsheet.

Setting Shading for a Block

Shading is a very effective way to make a block stand out in your spreadsheet. You can shade in either grey or black.

To set shading for a block, follow these steps:

1. Select the block you want to shade.

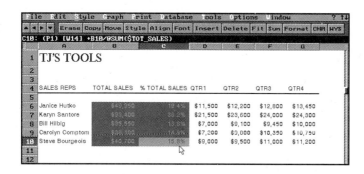

In this example, the block B6..C10 is selected.

2. Press ⟨/⟩ to access the Quattro Pro menu.
3. Press ⟨S⟩ to select **S**tyle.
4. Press ⟨S⟩ to select **S**hading.
5. Select **G**rey or **B**lack as the shade.

7

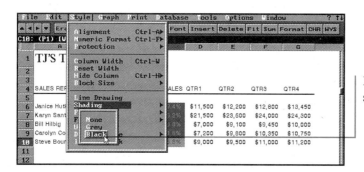

In this example, select **B**lack.

Note that because you preselected the block, Quattro Pro does not prompt you to specify a block address.

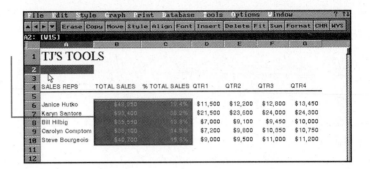

Quattro Pro applies a black shade to the block B6..C10.

Defining and Using Styles

You can define your own styles and then apply them as you would any other style. This flexibility gives you quick access to styles you have created and use frequently.

To define a style, follow these steps:

1. Press ☐/☐ to access the Quattro Pro menu.

2. Press ☐S☐ to select **S**tyle.

3. Press ☐D☐ to select **D**efine Style.

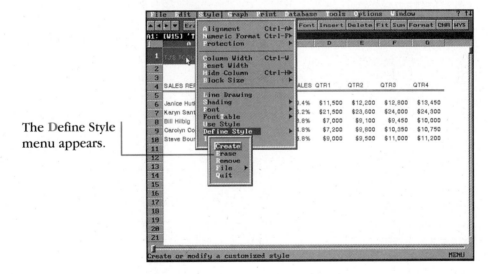

The **D**efine Style menu appears.

4. Press ☐C☐ to select **C**reate.

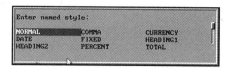

Quattro Pro displays an alphabetical list of all predefined styles.

5. Type the name of the style you want to create, and press ⏎Enter.

In this example, type **Title** and press ⏎Enter.

6. Select the Font, Line Drawing, Shading, Alignment, Data Entry, and Numeric Format settings you want to use as the definition of the style called *Title*.

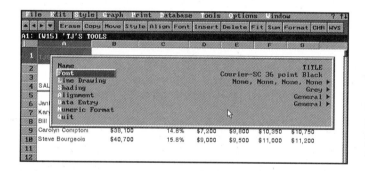

In this example, define the font as Courier-SC 36-point Black and the shading as Grey, as ex-plained in previous sections of the chapter.

7. Press ⬛Q to select Quit. Quattro Pro establishes *Title* as a style.

To apply the style, follow these steps:

1. Select the block to which you want to apply the style.
2. Press ⬛/ to access the Quattro Pro menu.
3. Press ⬛S to select Style.
4. Press ⬛U to select Use Style.

221

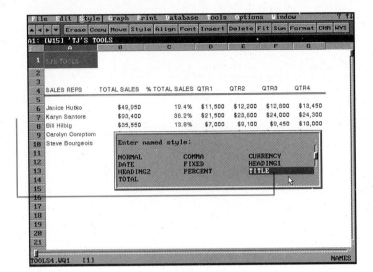

Title is displayed
in the list of
styles.

5. Highlight Title and press ⏎Enter, or click Title.

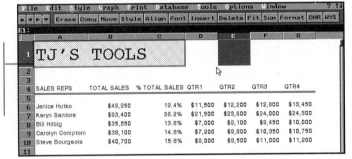

In this example,
Quattro Pro
applies the style
Title to the title of
this spreadsheet.

The power of custom styles can help you create spectacular spreadsheets
quickly.

Summary

In this chapter, you learned how to use the /Style Numeric Format command
to format a cell or a block of cells so that you can determine how values and
formula results appear on-screen. You learned how to apply a font, shading, a
border, and color to a block. You also learned how to create and use custom
styles.

Specifically, you learned the following key information about Quattro Pro 4:

■ The /Style Numeric Format commands change the way data is displayed within the spreadsheet. Some available formatting options within Quattro Pro 4 include Currency, Fixed, Percent, Text, Hidden, and , (Comma).

■ Use the /Style Font command to change the typeface, point size, color, and attribute of the data block. The /Style FontTable command displays a table of preset fonts you can quickly apply to the data in a block.

■ The /Style Line Drawing command draws borders for a block. You can position the border on all sides of the block or on just one (for example, the bottom) side of the block.

■ Use the /Style Shading command to shade a block to make it stand out in the spreadsheet. Two styles of shade are available: Grey and Black.

■ You can use the /Style Define Style command to customize styles. You can create whatever style suits your needs so that it is available each time you start Quattro Pro 4. The /Style Use Style command lists the defined styles, from which you can select a style to apply it to a block.

7

The next chapter explores Quattro Pro's built-in @functions, which you use in formulas to perform complex calculations. You learn about the most widely used Quattro Pro @functions, including mathematical, financial, and string @functions.

Using @Functions

8

In addition to the spreadsheet formulas you can create, you can take advantage of a variety of ready-made formulas provided by Quattro Pro. These built-in formulas—called *functions*—enable you to take advantage of Quattro Pro's analytical capability and are helpful when used with business, engineering, scientific, and statistical applications. You can use many of these powerful functions in even the simplest of spreadsheets. You can use functions by themselves, in your own formulas, or in macros and advanced macro command programs to calculate results and solve problems.

Quattro Pro provides 113 functions in the following categories:

* Mathematical
* Date and time
* Financial
* Statistical
* Database statistical
* Logical
* String
* Miscellaneous

Entering a
Quattro Pro
@function

Mathematical
functions

Date and time
functions

Financial
functions

Statistical
functions

Database
statistical
functions

Logical functions

String functions

Miscellaneous
functions

This chapter first describes the basic steps for using Quattro Pro functions and then covers each of these categories in more detail. Although all Quattro Pro functions are listed and briefly described within tables, only the most commonly used Quattro Pro functions are discussed in detail in separate sections of this chapter. Refer to Que's *Using Quattro Pro 4*, Special Edition, for comprehensive coverage of each of Quattro Pro's functions.

Key Terms in This Chapter

@Functions   Quattro Pro's built-in formulas that perform many different types of calculations.

Arguments   Input that most functions need to perform their calculations. Arguments in brackets (<>) are optional.

Syntax   The format of a specific @function.

Entering a Quattro Pro @Function

8

Before you continue with this chapter, you should study the section "Using @Functions in Formulas" in Chapter 3 for an introduction to Quattro Pro's functions. In that section, you learn about the eight categories of functions that this chapter covers, as well as about the steps you use to enter specific functions.

This chapter does not include numbered steps for entering each function, because you use the same procedure to enter all functions. To enter a Quattro Pro function into a spreadsheet, follow this general four-step process:

1. Press @ to tell Quattro Pro that you want to enter a function.
2. Type a function name, or press Alt - F3 to select from a list box the function you need.
3. Type within parentheses any input, or arguments, that the function needs.
4. Press Enter.

An example of a function is @AVG. If you type the function *@AVG(1,2,3)*, Quattro Pro returns the calculated result 2, which is the average of the three arguments—the numbers 1, 2, and 3.

Some functions do not require arguments. For example, the mathematical function @PI returns the value of pi and the mathematical function @RAND produces a random number between zero and one.

Using Mathematical Functions

Quattro Pro's nine mathematical functions and ten trigonometric functions are useful in engineering and scientific applications. These functions are also convenient tools you can use to perform a variety of standard arithmetic operations, such as rounding values or calculating square roots.

Table 8.1 lists the mathematical and trigonometric functions, their arguments, and the operations they perform. The sections that follow cover the @INT and @ROUND mathematical functions in detail.

Table 8.1
Mathematical Functions

Function	Description
@ABS(*number* or *cell_reference*)	Computes the absolute value of the argument.
@ACOS(*angle*)	Calculates the arccosine, given an angle in radians.
@ASIN(*angle*)	Calculates the arcsine, given an angle in radians.
@ATAN(*angle*)	Calculates the arctangent, given an angle in radians.
@ATAN2(*number1, number2*)	Calculates the four-quadrant arctangent.
@COS(*angle*)	Calculates the cosine, given an angle in radians.
@DEGREES(*number*)	Converts a specified number of radians to degrees.
@EXP(*number* or *cell_reference*)	Computes the number *e* raised to the power of the argument.
@INT(*number* or *cell_reference*)	Returns the integer portion of a number.
@LN(*number* or *cell_reference*)	Calculates the natural logarithm of a number.
@LOG(*number* or *cell_reference*)	Calculates the common, or base 10, logarithm of number.

continues

8

Table 8.1 *(Continued)*

Function	Description
@MOD(*number, divisor*)	Computes the remainder of a division operation.
@PI	Returns the value of pi.
@RADIANS(*x*)	Returns the number of radians in *x* degrees.
@RAND	Generates a random number between 0 and 1.
@ROUND(*number* or *cell_reference,precision*)	Rounds a number to a specified precision.
@SIN(*angle*)	Calculates the sine, given an angle in radians.
@SQRT(*number* or *cell_reference*)	Computes the positive square root of a number.
@TAN(*angle*)	Calculates the tangent, given an angle in radians.

Computing Integers with @INT

The @INT function converts a decimal number into an *integer*, or whole number. @INT creates an integer by truncating, or removing, the decimal portion of a number (without rounding). @INT uses the following format, or syntax:

@INT(*number* or *cell_reference*)

@INT has one argument, which can be either a numeric value or a cell reference to a numeric value. The result of applying @INT to the values 3.1, 4.5, and 5.9 yields integer values of 3, 4, and 5, respectively.

@INT is useful for computations in which the decimal portion of a number is irrelevant or insignificant. Suppose, for example, that you have $1,000 to invest in XYZ company and that shares of XYZ sell for $17 each. You divide 1,000 by 17 to compute the total number of shares you can purchase. Because you cannot purchase a fractional share, you can use @INT to truncate the decimal portion.

8

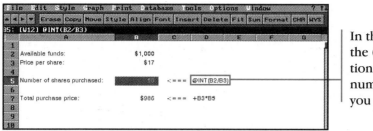

In this example, the @INT function calculates the number of shares you can purchase.

Rounding Numbers with @ROUND

The @ROUND function rounds values to the precision you specify. The function uses two arguments: the value you want to round and the precision you want to use when rounding that value. @ROUND uses the following syntax:

@ROUND(*number* or *cell_reference,precision*)

The first argument can be a numeric value or a cell reference to a numeric value. The *precision* argument determines the number of decimal places and can be a numeric value between −15 and +15. You use positive precision values to specify positions to the right of the decimal place and negative values to specify positions to the left of the decimal place. A precision value of 0 rounds decimal values to the nearest integer.

8

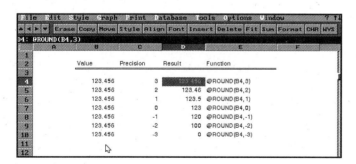

In this example, notice the variety of results that the @ROUND function returns in column D, all based on the value 123.456.

Note: The @ROUND function and the /Style Numeric Format command perform differently. @ROUND actually changes the contents of a cell; /Style Numeric Format alters only how the cell's contents are displayed.

Using Date and Time Functions

The twelve date and time functions enable you to convert dates, such as November 26, 1989, and times, such as 6:00 p.m., to serial numbers. You can then use the serial numbers to perform date and time arithmetic. These functions are valuable tools when dates and times affect calculations and logic in your spreadsheets.

The date and time functions available in Quattro Pro are summarized in table 8.2. The sections that follow review examples of the @DATE, @DATEVALUE, and @NOW functions.

Table 8.2
Date and Time Functions

Function	Description
@DATE(*year,month,day*)	Calculates the serial number of the specified date.
@DATEVALUE(*date_string*)	Converts a date expressed as a string into a serial number.
@DAY(*date_number*)	Extracts the day number from a serial number.
@HOUR(*time_number*)	Extracts the hour number from a serial number.
@MINUTE(*time_number*)	Extracts the minute number from a serial number.
@MONTH(*date_number*)	Extracts the month number from a serial number.
@NOW	Calculates the serial date and time from the current system date and time.
@SECOND(*time_number*)	Extracts the seconds from a serial number.
@TIME(*hour,minutes,seconds*)	Calculates the serial number of the specified time.
@TIMEVALUE(*time_string*)	Converts a time expressed as a string into a serial number.

Function	Description
@TODAY	Returns the numeric value of the current system date.
@YEAR(*date_number*)	Extracts the year number from a serial number.

Converting Date Values to Serial Numbers with @DATE

The first step in using dates in arithmetic operations is to convert the dates to serial numbers, which you can then use in arithmetic operations and sorting. Probably the most frequently used date function is @DATE. This function converts any date into a serial number you can use in calculations and display as a date in Quattro Pro. @DATE uses the following syntax:

@DATE(*year,month,day*)

Use numbers to identify a year, month, or day. For example, enter the date *November 26, 1989* into the @DATE function as @DATE(89,11,26). The serial number that results is 32838.

Quattro Pro's internal calendar begins with the serial number *1*, which represents December 31, 1899. A single day is represented by an increment of 1; therefore, Quattro Pro represents January 1, 1900, as 2.

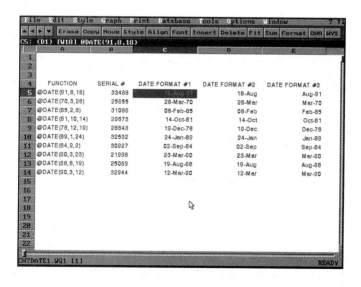

To display a serial number as a text date, format the cell with the /Style Numeric Format Date command. You have three date format styles (not including the international choices), as illustrated in columns C, D, and E of this example.

8

The @DATE function in column E of this example calculates the number of days a bill is overdue as of May 1, 1991.

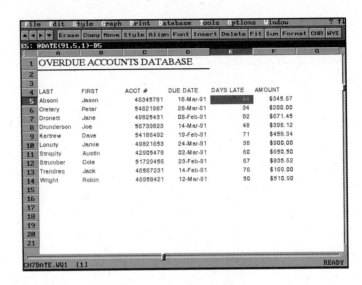

Note: The numbers you enter to represent the year, month, and day must constitute a valid date; otherwise, Quattro Pro returns the message ERR. For example, Quattro Pro is programmed so that you can specify February 29 only during leap years, and you never can specify February 30 or 31.

Converting Date Strings to Serial Numbers with @DATEVALUE

@DATEVALUE computes the serial number for a date text string typed into a referenced cell. The text string must use one of the date formats recognized by Quattro Pro. @DATEVALUE requires the following syntax:

@DATEVALUE(*date_string*)

If Quattro Pro cannot recognize the format used for the argument, the function results in the message ERR. After you correctly enter a function, use the /Style Numeric Format Date command to display the serial date number as a text date.

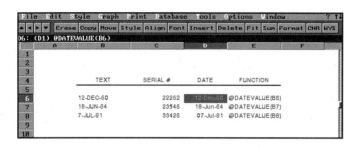

The @DATEVALUE function converts date strings entered as text into serial date numbers, which you can then format as Quattro Pro dates.

Finding the Current Date and Time with @NOW

The @NOW function displays as a serial number both the current system date and the current system time. The numbers to the left of the decimal point specify the date, and the numbers to the right of the decimal point indicate the time. This function, which requires no arguments, provides a convenient tool for adding dates to spreadsheets and reports.

After you enter a @NOW function, use the /Style Numeric Format Date command to display the serial date number as a text date or time.

8

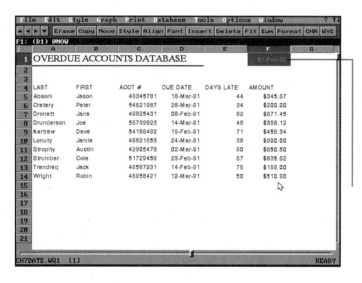

The @NOW function, format- ted as a date, inserts the current date in a spreadsheet.

Using Financial Functions

Quattro Pro's 18 financial functions enable you to perform a variety of business-related calculations. These calculations include discounting cash flows, computing loan amortization, calculating depreciation, and analyzing the return on investments. This set of functions helps you perform investment analysis and accounting, or budgeting for depreciable assets.

Table 8.3 summarizes the financial functions available in Quattro Pro. Normally, you will want to use Quattro Pro's financial functions in your spreadsheets; however, if you are developing applications for Lotus 1-2-3 users, you should use the 1-2-3-compatible financial functions. Quattro Pro's financial functions are more precise than 1-2-3's financial functions, but are not compatible with 1-2-3's WK1 file format.

The sections that follow table 8.3 describe the @PAYMT, @PVAL, and @FVAL functions in greater detail.

Table 8.3
Financial Functions

Function	Description
Quattro Pro Financial Functions	
@DDB(*cost,salvage,life,period*)	Calculates depreciation using the double-declining balance method.
@FVAL(*rate,number_periods, payment,<present_value>, <type>*)	Calculates the future value of an ordinary annuity.
@IPAYMT(*rate,payment_period, number_periods,present_value, <future_value>,<type>*)	Calculates the value of the interest portion of a loan payment.
@IRATE(*number_periods, payment,present_value, <future_value>,<type>*)	Calculates the interest rate earned on an investment.
@IRR(*estimate,block*)	Calculates the internal rate of return on an investment.
@NPER(*rate,payment, present_value,<future_value>, <type>*)	Calculates the number of periods it will take a present value amount to grow to a future value amount at a periodic interest rate.

Function	Description
@NPV(*rate,block,<type>*)	Calculates the present value of a series of future cash flows at equal time intervals when the payments are discounted by the periodic interest rate.
@PAYMT(*rate,number_periods, present_value,<future_value>, <type>*)	Calculates a loan payment amount.
@PPAYMT(*rate, period, number_periods,present_value, <future_value>,<type>*)	Calculates the principal portion of a loan payment.
@PVAL(*rate,number_periods, payment,<future_value>, <type>*)	Calculates the present value of a series of future cash flows of equal payments discounted by the periodic interest rate.
@SLN(*cost,salvage,life*)	Calculates straight-line depreciation for one period.
@SYD(*cost,salvage,life,period*)	Calculates sum-of-the-years' digits depreciation for a specified period.

Lotus 1-2-3-Compatible Financial Functions

@CTERM(*interest,future_value, present_value*)	Calculates the number of periods required for a present value amount, to grow to a future value amount, given a periodic interest rate.
@FV(*payment,interest,term*)	Calculates the future value of a series of equal payments compounded at the periodic interest rate.
@PMT(*principal,interest,term*)	Calculates the loan payment amount.
@PV(*payment,interest,term*)	Calculates the present value of a series of future cash flows of equal payments discounted by the periodic interest rate.

8

continues

235

Table 8.3 (*Continued*)

Function	Description
@RATE(*future_value, present_value,term*)	Calculates the periodic rate required to increase the present-value amount to the future-value amount in a specified length of time.
@TERM(*payment, interest,future_value*)	Calculates the number of payment periods necessary to accumulate the future value, when payments are compounded at the periodic interest rate.

Calculating Loan Payment Amounts with @PAYMT

You use the @PAYMT function to calculate the periodic payments necessary to pay the principal on a loan with a given interest rate and time period. Therefore, to use @PAYMT, you need to know the periodic interest rate, the number of periods, and the total loan amount (present value), as shown in the following syntax:

@PAYMT(*rate,number_periods,present_value,<future_value>,<type>*)

The interest rate and the number of periods must be expressed as the same units of time. For example, if you make monthly payments, you should use the annual interest rate divided by 12, and the number of months should be the number of months you will be making payments.

You can use the @PAYMT function to calculate the monthly car payment on a $12,000 car loan. The loan is repaid over 48 months, and the loan rate is 1 percent—12 percent divided by 12 periods per year.

In this example, the @PAYMT function calculates loan payments.

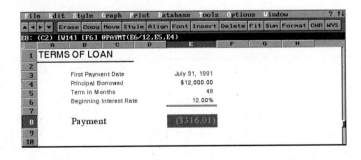

Calculating Present and Future Values
with @PVAL and @FVAL

@PVAL calculates the present value of a series of future cash flows of equal payments discounted by the periodic interest rate. The interest rate and the number of periods must be expressed as the same units of time. The @PVAL function uses the following syntax:

@PVAL(*rate,number_periods,payment,<future_value>,<type>*)

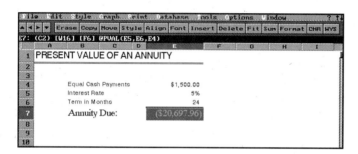

One example of using @PVAL is to determine the present value of a series of annuity payments.

The @FVAL function calculates the future value of the current amount, based on a specified interest rate and the number of years. Again, the interest rate and the number of periods must be expressed as the same units of time. @FVAL uses the following syntax:

@FVAL(*rate,number_periods,payment,<present_value>,<type>*)

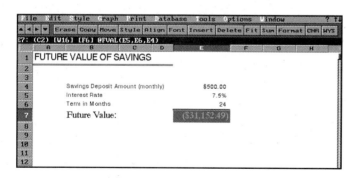

You can use @FVAL to calculate the future value of a savings account that receives equal automatic deposits on a monthly basis.

8

Using Statistical Functions

A set of ten statistical functions enables you to perform all the standard statistical calculations on data in your spreadsheet. You can find minimum and maximum values, calculate averages, and compute standard deviations and variances.

Table 8.4 lists Quattro Pro's statistical functions, their arguments, and the statistical operations they perform. The sections that follow cover the @AVG, @COUNT, @MAX, and @MIN statistical functions. The @SUM function, probably the most commonly used Quattro Pro function, is illustrated in the @functions sections of Chapter 3.

Table 8.4
Statistical Functions

Function	Description
@AVG(*list*)	Calculates the arithmetic mean of a list of values.
@COUNT(*list*)	Counts the number of cells that contain entries.
@MAX(*list*)	Returns the maximum value in a list of values.
@MIN(*list*)	Returns the minimum value in a list of values.
@STD(*list*)	Calculates the population standard deviation of a list of values.
@STDS(*list*)	Calculates the sample standard deviation of a list of values.
@SUM(*list*)	Sums a list of values.
@SUMPRODUCT (*block1,block2*)	Calculates the sum and product of *block1* and *block2*.
@VAR(*list*)	Calculates the population variance of a list of values.
@VARS(*list*)	Calculates the sample population variance of a list of values.

Note: When you specify a block of cells, Quattro Pro ignores empty cells within the specified block. When you specify cells, keep in mind that Quattro Pro treats cells containing labels as zeros.

8

Computing the Arithmetic Mean with @AVG

To calculate the average of a set of values manually, you add all the values and then divide the sum by the number of values. The @AVG function calculates the average of a series of numbers. Use the following syntax for this function:

@AVG(*list*)

The *list* argument can contain any combination of values, cell addresses, single and multiple blocks, and block names.

You can use the @AVG function to calculate the mean price per share of a company's stock. The function's argument includes the list of stock prices you want to average.

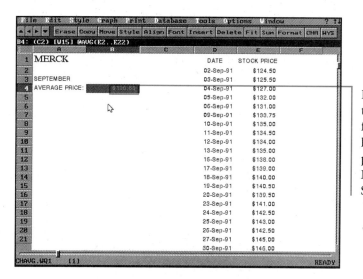

In this example, the @AVG function calculates the average price per share of Merck stock in September 1991.

8

Counting Cell Entries with @COUNT

The @COUNT function totals the number of cells that contain entries of any kind:

@COUNT(*list*)

The *list* argument can contain any combination of values, cell addresses, single and multiple blocks, and block names. For example, you can use @COUNT to show the number of share prices included in the @AVG calculation of the preceding example.

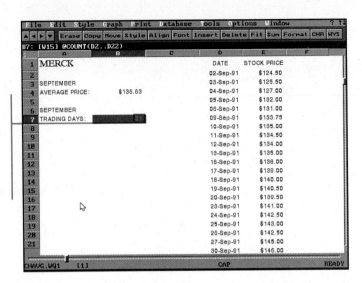

Here, the @COUNT function calculates the number of share prices used in the @AVG calculation.

Note: The @COUNT function counts any cells containing data. Therefore, if a cell contains a label, that cell is counted by @COUNT. This function is unlike other statistical functions, where, because a label equates to a numerical value of 0, the label cell is ignored.

Finding Maximum and Minimum Values with @MAX and @MIN

The @MAX function finds the largest value included in the *list* argument; the @MIN function finds the smallest value included in the *list* argument. These functions respectively use the following syntax:

@MAX(*list*)

@MIN(*list*)

Using the stock prices example, the @MAX and @MIN functions can help you find the highest and the lowest prices. These two functions are especially useful if your list consists of several dozen or several hundred items.

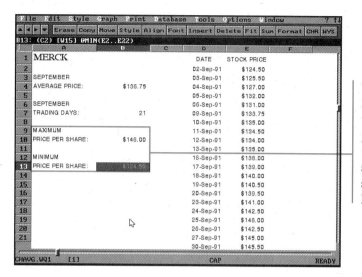

The @MAX function shows the highest price per share. The @MIN function shows the lowest stock price in the list.

Using Database Statistical Functions

Quattro Pro's nine database statistical functions are similar to the statistical functions but have been modified for use with database fields. Like other functions, the database statistical functions perform in one simple statement calculations that may otherwise require several statements. This efficiency and ease of application make these functions excellent tools for manipulating Quattro Pro databases. The database statistical functions are described in table 8.5.

The general syntax of each of these functions is as follows:

@DSUM(*block,column,criteria*)

The *block* and *criteria* arguments are the same as those used by the /Database Query command, discussed in Chapter 12. The *block* specifies the database or the part of a database you want to search, and the *criteria* specifies which records you want to select. The *column* indicates which field to select from the database records; the column value must be either zero or a positive integer. A value of zero indicates the first column in the database, a value of one indicates the second column, and so on.

8

Table 8.5
Database Statistical Functions

Function	Description
@DAVG(*block,column,criteria*)	Calculates the arithmetic mean of specific items in a list.
@DCOUNT(*block,column,criteria*)	Counts the number of specific entries in a list.
@DMAX(*block,column,criteria*)	Returns the maximum value among specific items in a list.
@DMIN(*block,column,criteria*)	Returns the minimum value among specific items in a list.
@DSTD(*block,column,criteria*)	Calculates the standard deviation of items in a list.
@DSTDS(*block,column,criteria*)	Calculates the sample standard deviation of items in a list.
@DSUM(*block,column,criteria*)	Sums the values of items in a list.
@DVAR(*block,column,criteria*)	Computes the variance of items in a list.
@DVARS(*block,column,criteria*)	Calculates the sample variance of items in a list.

Suppose that you want to compute database statistics of the average interest rates offered by money market funds for a given week. Quattro Pro's database statistical functions enable you to find the count, sum, mean (average), variance, standard deviation, maximum, and minimum rates of return.

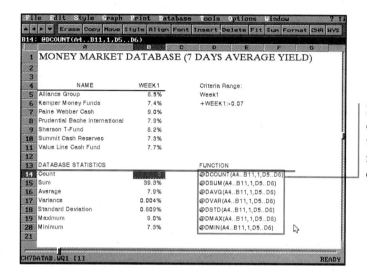

Database statistical functions are used here with a money market database.

As displayed in the input line of this example, the block is A4..B11, the column value of 1 indicates column B, and the criteria is D5..D6. Also, the database functions are located in column B (the functions are shown in text format in column D).

8

Using Logical Functions

Each of Quattro Pro's eight logical functions enables you to test whether a condition is true or false. Many of these functions operate in a similar manner—by returning a 1 if the test is true or a 0 if the test is false. These logical tests are important for creating decision-making functions; the results of these functions depend on conditions elsewhere in the spreadsheet.

The eight logical functions that Quattro Pro provides are summarized in table 8.6. In the text that follows, the @IF and @ISERR logical functions are described in more detail.

**Table 8.6
Logical Functions**

Function	Description
@FALSE	Returns the logical value 0, for false.
@FILEEXISTS(*filename*)	Returns the logical value 1 when *filename* exists.
@IF(*condition, true_expression, false_expression*)	Tests a condition and returns one result if the condition is true and another result if the condition is false.
@ISERR(*cell_reference*)	Tests whether the argument results in ERR.
@ISNA(*cell_reference*)	Tests whether the argument results in NA.
@ISNUMBER(*cell_reference*)	Tests whether the argument is a number.
@ISSTRING(*cell_reference*)	Tests whether the argument is a string.
@TRUE	Returns the logical value 1, for true.

8

Creating Conditional Tests with @IF

The @IF function represents a powerful tool—one you can use both to manipulate text within your spreadsheets and to affect calculations. You can use an @IF statement, for example, to test the condition "Is the inventory on-hand below 1,000 units?" and then return one value or label if the answer to the question is true, or another value or label if the answer is false. The @IF function uses the following syntax:

@IF(*condition,true_expression,false_expression*)

The @IF function can use six operators when testing conditions. The following list shows the operators and their corresponding definitions:

Operator	Definition
>	Greater than
<	Less than
=	Equal to
>=	Greater than or equal to

Operator	Definition
< =	Less than or equal to
< >	Not equal to

In addition, you can perform more complex conditional tests by using @IF functions with logical operators that enable you to test multiple conditions in one @IF function. These complex operators and their descriptions are summarized in the following list:

Operator	Description
#AND#	Tests two conditions, both of which must be true for the entire test to be true.
#NOT#	Tests one condition, which must be false for the entire test to be true.
#OR#	Tests two conditions; if either condition is true, the entire test is true.

8

You can use the @IF function to check whether a specified cell's content is between two numbers, whether a cell contains a specified text string, and whether a Quattro Pro date falls before or after the current date. The results of these tests depend on whether the condition evaluates as true or false.

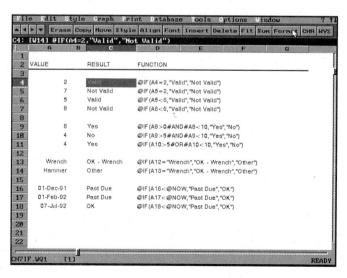

Examples of the @IF function test for specified values or labels.

245

Checking for Errors with @TRUE and @FALSE

You use the @ISERR function to check whether a cell contains ERR. You can use this logical function with the @IF logical function to present a warning if an important cell contains ERR, as shown in the following example:

@IF(@ISERR(C42),"CELL C42 has an ERROR","OK")

This statement says, "If the value in cell C42 is equal to ERR, display 'CELL C42 has an ERROR'; otherwise, display 'OK.'"

One way to ensure the integrity of your spreadsheet is to set up a table containing formulas like the preceding example to evaluate the important cells in your spreadsheet. If one of the cells in the table is not OK, you know that an important data cell has a problem.

Using String Functions

Another set of Quattro Pro functions includes the 21 string functions, which manipulate text. You can use string functions to repeat text characters (a handy trick for creating spreadsheet and row boundaries and visual borders), to convert letters in a string to uppercase or lowercase, to change strings into numbers, and to change numbers into strings. String functions also are important when you prepare Quattro Pro data to be used in other programs, such as word processing programs.

Table 8.7 summarizes the string functions available in Quattro Pro. The sections that follow discuss the @LOWER, @UPPER, @PROPER, and @REPEAT string functions in more detail.

Table 8.7
String Functions

Function	Description
@CHAR(*code*)	Displays the ASCII character of code.
@CLEAN(*string*)	Removes nonprintable characters from the specified string.
@CODE(*string*)	Returns the ASCII code that corresponds to the first character of the specified string.

Function	Description
@EXACT(*string1,string2*)	Returns 1 (true) if arguments are exact matches; otherwise, returns 0 (false).
@FIND(*search_string, string,start_number*)	Locates the start position of one string within another string.
@HEXTONUM(*string*)	Converts the hexidecimal number in the string to its equivalent decimal value.
@LEFT(*string,number*)	Extracts the leftmost specified number of characters from the string.
@LENGTH(*string*)	Returns the number of characters in the string.
@LOWER(*string*)	Converts all characters in the string to lowercase.
@MID(*string, start_number,number*)	Extracts a specified number of characters from the middle of another string, beginning at the specified starting position.
@N(*block*)	Returns as a value the contents of the cell in the upper left corner of a block.
@NUMTOHEX(*string*)	Converts the decimal number in the string to its equivalent hexidecimal value.
@PROPER(*string*)	Converts the first character in each word of the string to uppercase, and the remaining characters in each word to lowercase.
@REPEAT(*string,number*)	Duplicates the string the specified number of times in a cell.
@REPLACE(*original_string, start_number,number, new_string*)	Replaces a number of characters in the original string with new string characters, starting at the character identified by the start number.
@RIGHT(*string,number*)	Extracts the rightmost specified number of characters from the string.

continues

8

Table 8.7 *(Continued)*

Function	Description
@S(*block*)	Returns as a label the contents of the cell in the upper left corner of a block.
@STRING(*number, decimal_places*)	Converts a value to a string with the specified number of decimal places.
@TRIM(*string*)	Removes blank spaces from the string.
@UPPER(*string*)	Converts all characters in the string to uppercase.
@VALUE(*string*)	Converts the string to a value.

Strings are labels or portions of labels. Strings used within functions consist of characters enclosed in quotation marks, such as "Total." Some functions produce strings, but other functions produce numeric results. If a function's result is not of the data type you need, use the @STRING and @VALUE functions to convert a numeric value to a string, or a string to a numeric value.

Converting the Case of Strings with @LOWER, @UPPER, and @PROPER

Quattro Pro offers three different functions for converting the case of a string value. The @LOWER and @UPPER functions convert all characters in the referenced string to lowercase or uppercase, respectively. The @PROPER function converts characters in the string to proper capitalization—with the first letter in uppercase and all remaining letters in lowercase. The general syntax of these functions is as follows:

@LOWER(*string*)

@UPPER(*string*)

@PROPER(*string*)

These three functions work with strings or references to strings. If a cell contains a number or is empty, Quattro Pro returns ERR for these functions.

8

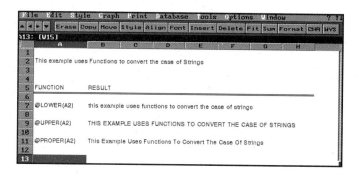

These functions convert the case of alphanumeric strings. The text versions of the formulas appear in column A, and the formulas and their results are in column B.

You can use @LOWER, @UPPER, or @PROPER to modify the contents of a database so that all entries in a field appear with the same capitalization. This technique produces reports with a consistent appearance.

Repeating Strings with @REPEAT

The @REPEAT function repeats a string a specified number of times, much as the backslash (\) repeats strings to fill a single cell. But @REPEAT has some distinct advantages over the backslash. With @REPEAT, you can repeat the string the precise number of times you want. If the result is wider than the cell width, the result is displayed in empty adjacent cells to the right. @REPEAT uses the following syntax:

@REPEAT(*string,number*)

The *number* argument indicates the number of times you want to repeat a string in a cell. For example, to repeat the string ** four times, you can enter the following function:

@REPEAT("**",4)

The resulting string will appear as ********.

Using Miscellaneous Functions

Quattro Pro provides a set of 16 special functions you can use to perform a variety of tasks. For example, two miscellaneous functions return up to ten different characteristics of a cell. Other special functions count the number of rows or columns in a block, enable you to trap spreadsheet errors, and use specified keys in the functions' arguments to look up values in tables or lists.

Table 8.8 lists Quattro Pro's miscellaneous functions. The sections that follow discuss the @ERR, @NA, @HLOOKUP, and @VLOOKUP functions.

Table 8.8
Special Functions

Function	Description
@@(*location*)	Returns the contents of the cell referenced in the specified location.
@CELL(*attribute,block*)	Returns an attribute of the cell in the upper left corner of the block.
@@CELLINDEX(*attribute, block,column,row*)	Returns an attribute of a cell in the block specified by the offset column and row.
@CELLPOINTER(*attribute*)	Returns an attribute of the current cell.
@CHOOSE(*number,list*)	Locates in a list the entry specified by the offset number.
@COLS(*block*)	Counts the number of columns in a block.
@CURVALUE(*general_action, specification*)	Describes the most recent menu command execution.
@ERR	Displays ERR in the cell.
@HLOOKUP(*x,block,row*)	Locates the number in a table and returns a value from that row of the block.
@INDEX(*block,column,row*)	Returns the contents of a cell specified by the intersection of a row and column within a block.
@ISAFF(*addin.function*)	Tests whether an add-in function is in a loaded add-in; displays 0 if negative and 1 if positive.
@ISAPP(*addin*)	Tests whether an add-in is loaded; displays 0 if negative and 1 if positive.
@MEMAVAIL	Displays the number of available bytes of conventional memory currently available to Quattro Pro.

8

Function	Description
@MEMEMSAVAIL	Displays the number of available bytes of expanded (EMS) memory currently available to Quattro Pro.
@NA	Displays NA in the cell.
@ROWS(*block*)	Counts the number of rows in a block.
@VERSION	Displays the Quattro Pro version number.
@VLOOKUP(*x, block, column*)	Locates the number in a lookup table and returns a value from that column of the block.

Trapping Errors with @ERR and @NA

When you create Quattro Pro applications, you may want to use @ERR or @NA to distinguish certain cell entries. Suppose, for example, that you are creating a checkbook-balancing spreadsheet in which checks with dollar amounts less than or equal to zero are unacceptable. One way to indicate that these checks are unacceptable is to use @ERR to signal that fact. You can use the following version of the @IF function:

@IF(B9<=0,@ERR,B9)

This statement says, "If the amount in cell B9 is less than or equal to zero, display ERR in that cell; otherwise, display the amount."

You can use the @NA function with a database containing inventory items to display NA in empty cells (or cells containing zeros) in a Number of Items column. You also can use the @IF function in this example, as follows:

@IF(C4=0,@NA,C4)

This statement says, "If the value in cell C4 is equal to zero, display NA in that cell; otherwise, display the value."

Finding Table Entries with @HLOOKUP and @VLOOKUP

The @HLOOKUP and @VLOOKUP functions retrieve a string or value from a table, based on a specified key used to find the information. The operation

8

and format of the two functions are essentially the same except that @HLOOKUP searches horizontal tables and @VLOOKUP searches vertical tables. These functions use the following syntax:

@HLOOKUP(*x,block,row*)

@VLOOKUP(*x,block,column*)

The *x* argument is the string or value that indicates the column (@HLOOKUP) or row (@VLOOKUP) you want to search. The key strings or values belong in the first column or row; numeric keys must be in ascending order for the functions to work properly. The *block* argument is the area that makes up the entire lookup table. The *column* argument specifies the row (@HLOOKUP) or column (@VLOOKUP) from which the data is to be retrieved. The *column* argument is always a number, ranging from 0 to the highest number of columns or rows in the table.

The @HLOOKUP and @VLOOKUP functions are useful for finding any type of value you would have to look up manually in a table, such as a tax amount, shipping zones, or interest charges.

In this example, @VLOOKUP and @HLOOKUP functions retrieve values from the table.

Summary

This chapter described the functions that Quattro Pro provides to make formula and spreadsheet construction easier and, usually, more error-free. After you become accustomed to using these functions, you can use them regularly in your spreadsheets. You can use the tables in this chapter as a reference for the types of functions available, their syntax, and the types of arguments they require.

Specifically, you learned the following key information about Quattro Pro:

■ Quattro Pro includes 113 built-in functions you can use with 8 different types of applications. These functions perform a variety of powerful calculations that save you a great deal of time when building spreadsheets.

■ Quattro Pro functions are entered by typing the @ sign, followed by the function name and any required arguments within parentheses. Press ⏎Enter to complete the process.

■ The mathematical functions perform standard arithmetic operations, such as computing an integer with @INT and rounding numbers with @ROUND.

■ The date and time functions convert dates and times to serial numbers, which you can then format as dates and use in sorting and arithmetic calculations. Examples include @DATE and @DATEVALUE, which convert date values and date strings to serial numbers; and the @NOW function, which you can use to date-stamp a spreadsheet or report.

■ The financial functions calculate cash flows, loans, annuities, and asset depreciation. The @PAYMT function calculates loan payments, and the @PVAL and @FVAL functions calculate present and future values, respectively.

■ The statistical functions perform standard statistical calculations on lists. For example, @AVG calculates the average of values in a list, @COUNT counts the total number of entries in a list, and @MAX and @MIN find the maximum and minimum values in a list, respectively.

■ The database statistical functions are similar to the statistical functions but perform calculations and queries on databases.

■ The logical functions test whether a condition is true or false. The @IF function returns a different value or label, depending on the outcome of a specified condition. You can use the @ISERR function in conditional tests to ensure a cell content's integrity.

■ You can use the string functions, which include the ASCII functions, to manipulate text. For example, the @LOWER, @UPPER, and @PROPER functions convert the case of a specified label. The @REPEAT function repeats a string a specified number of times.

8

253

■ Quattro Pro's miscellaneous functions perform a variety of spread-sheet tasks. The @ERR and @NA functions trap errors or distinguish certain cell entries. The @HLOOKUP and @VLOOKUP functions return values from a specified row and column of a table.

In the next chapter, "Printing Reports," you learn how to print reports created in Quattro Pro. The various options available for enhancing reports are also discussed.

8

Printing
Reports

Selecting a print
option

Printing draft-
quality reports

Excluding
segments within
a print block

Controlling paper
movement

Enhancing reports
with print options

Previewing a
printed report

Printing a listing
of cell contents

Resetting the
print options

Preparing output
for other
programs

Quattro Pro is a powerful tool for developing
information presented in a column-and-row format. You
can enter and edit your spreadsheet and database files
on-screen and then store the input on-disk. To make
good use of your data, however, you often need it in
printed form—such as a target production schedule, a
summary report to your supervisor, or a detailed reorder
list to central stores.

Using Quattro Pro's /Print command, you can access
different options to meet your printing needs. You can
elect to print from Quattro Pro directly to the printer by
using the /Print Destination Printer command; alternatively, you can use the /Print Destination File command
to print the file to a disk, thus creating a print file. Later,
you can produce a printout of the print file from within
Quattro Pro or from DOS, or you can incorporate the
file into a word processing file.

To make this chapter effective for learning the basics
of printing, and not just a complex series of options,
several things are assumed: (1) that you have not
modified Quattro Pro's preset printing defaults; (2) that
you need to produce reports on 8 1/2-by-11-inch paper;

and (3) that you want to use basic report-enhancement techniques such as hiding columns and rows, adding headers and footers, and repeating column and row headings. To modify Quattro Pro's default settings, consult Que's *Using Quattro Pro 4*, Special Edition.

Key Terms in This Chapter

Print defaults	Preset, standard specifications for a Quattro Pro print job.
Headings	One or more rows and/or columns of data and/or labels repeated on a multiple-page report.
Header	Information displayed on one line at the top of each printed page. A header may include a date and a page number.
Footer	Information displayed on one line at the bottom of each printed page. A footer may include a date and a page number.

9

Selecting a Print Option

Every print command in Quattro Pro starts from the Print option of the main menu.

This illustration shows the Print menu.

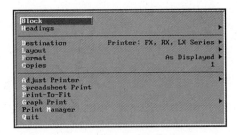

To print directly to a printer, select Destination Printer. To create a *print file* on-disk, select Destination File; later you can incorporate the print file into a word processing file printed from the word processor.

If you choose File, respond to the prompt for a print file name by typing a name up to eight characters long. A file extension is not necessary because Quattro Pro automatically assigns the extension PRN (print file).

You can incorporate a PRN file back into a Quattro Pro spreadsheet by using the /Tools Import command. The file, however, will not be the same as your original spreadsheet file; none of the formats of a spreadsheet are saved in a PRN file. Also, the data saved in a PRN file is saved row by row, not cell by cell; therefore, when you import a PRN file, all the data for a row is in the leftmost cell of the row. Quattro Pro therefore creates one long label in each row, instead of a series of short labels with each label in its own cell.

In any /Print command sequence, you start with /Print and then branch to either Destination Printer or Destination File. Table 9.1 gives you an overview of the various options on the Print pull-down menu. Not only do you select a print destination, but you also must select Block and specify a block to print, select Spreadsheet Print, and then select Quit to return to the spreadsheet. All other selections are optional.

Table 9.1
Print Menu Options

Option	Description
Block	Indicates the section of the spreadsheet you want to print or save to disk as a print file.
Headings	Indicates the rows and/or columns you want to display on each printed page.
Destination	Indicates the location of printing.
Layout	Establishes settings to enhance the appearance of the printout.
Format	Indicates how spreadsheet contents will be printed.
Copies	Indicates the number of copies you want to print.
Adjust Printer	Controls paper movement and position before or after printing.
Spreadsheet Print	Starts printing a spreadsheet block to the printer or a disk file.
Print to Fit	Automatically prints the print block on one page.
Graph Print	Starts printing a graph to the printer.
Print Manager	Enables you to view, suspend from printing, or stop printing any files being printed.
Quit	Exits the Print menu and returns Quattro Pro to READY mode.

9

Printing Draft-Quality Reports

Printing doesn't have to be an arduous process. With Quattro Pro, you can print quick reports by issuing a few simple commands. In this section, you learn a variety of printing techniques. Specifically, you learn to print a full screen of data, to print a draft-quality report of one page or less, and to print a multipage report with headings.

Printing a Full Screen of Data

Before you print any portion of a Quattro Pro spreadsheet, decide whether the output must be suitable for distribution or whether all you need is a copy of the screen's contents. If a copy of what you see on-screen is sufficient, make sure that Quattro Pro is in Text display mode (select /Options Display Mode A: 80x25). Then send the data to the printer by pressing ⇧Shift⊦ PrtSc or, on an enhanced keyboard, by pressing PrtSc.

9

Suppose that you want a quick printout of the portion of the spreadsheet you see on-screen.

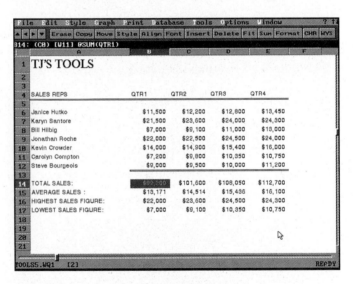

Press ⇧Shift⊦ PrtSc (PrtSc on an enhanced keyboard) to begin printing.

```
     File  Edit  Style  Graph  Print  Database  Tools  Options  Window      ?
  A1: [W28] 'TJ'S TOOLS                                                      Öáàá
  1                 A            B        C        D        E     End        ±
  1    TJ'S TOOLS                                                            ÿ
  2                                                                          ÿ
  3                                                                          ÿ
  4    SALES REPS              QTR1     QTR2     QTR3     QTR4               ÿáàá
     ======================================================================ÿERS
  5                                                                          ÿáàá
  6    Janice Hutko          $11,500  $12,200  $12,800  $13,450  ÿCPY
  7    Karyn Santore         $21,500  $23,600  $24,000  $24,300  ÿáàá
  8    Bill Hilbig            $7,000   $9,100  $11,000  $13,000  ÿMOV
  9    Jonathan Roche        $22,000  $22,500  $24,500  $24,000  ÿáàá
 10    Kevin Crowder         $14,000  $14,900  $15,400  $16,000  ÿSTY
 11    Carolyn Compton        $7,200   $9,800  $10,350  $10,750  ÿáàá
 12    Steve Bourgeois        $9,000   $9,500  $10,000  $11,200  ÿALN
 13                   ========================================ÿáàá
                                                                             ÿFNT
 14    TOTAL SALES:          $92,200 $101,600 $108,050 $112,700  ÿáàá
 15    AVERAGE SALES :       $13,171  $14,514  $15,436  $16,100  ÿINS
 16    HIGHEST SALES FIGURE: $22,000  $23,600  $24,500  $24,300  ÿáàá
 17    LOWEST SALES FIGURE:   $7,000   $9,100  $10,350  $10,750  ÿBAR
 18                                                                          ááá
  ±ÿÿÿÿÿÿÿÿÿÿÿÿÿÿÿÿÿÿÿÿÿÿÿÿÿÿÿÿÿÿÿÿÿÿÿÿÿÿÿÿÿÿÿÿÿÿÿÿÿÿÿÿÿÿÿÿÿÿÿÿÿÿÿÿÿÿÿÿÿÿÿÿÿÿÿÿÿÿÿÿÿÿÿÿÖ
  TJTOOLS.WQ1  [2]                                                      READY
```

The resulting printout captures everything on-screen, including the menu and the mode indicator.

A "snapshot" printout, such as this example, is usually adequate for document-ing a spreadsheet or as a printout for yourself.

Printing a One-Page Report

If you don't change any of the default print settings and you haven't entered other print settings during the current spreadsheet session, printing one or fewer pages involves only a few steps:

1. Choose to print to the printer or file.

2. Highlight the block you want to print.

3. Choose the command to begin printing.

Two other steps may be necessary if another person uses your copy of Quattro Pro and either changes the default settings or enters new settings in the Print menu. First, you can check the default settings by selecting /Print. A quick review of the Print pull-down menu will show you whether the printer and page layout settings are the ones you need. Second, you can reset any settings that may have been entered by another user by selecting /Print Layout Reset, which is explained further in this chapter.

If you are certain that all default settings are correct, you can print a draft-quality report of one or fewer pages by completing the following steps:

9

1. Make sure that your printer is on-line and that your paper is positioned properly.
2. Press ⌷/⌷ to access the Quattro Pro menu.
3. Press ⌷P⌷ to select **P**rint.
4. Press ⌷D⌷ to select **D**estination.
5. Press ⌷P⌷ to select **P**rinter.
6. Press ⌷B⌷ to select **B**lock to specify the spreadsheet block you want to print.
7. Indicate the portion of the spreadsheet you want to print by highlighting that area; then press ⌷↵Enter⌷.

   To designate a block, you can press ⌷←⌷, ⌷→⌷, ⌷↑⌷, ⌷↓⌷, ⌷PgUp⌷, or ⌷PgDn⌷. You also can press ⌷End⌷ and then ⌷←⌷, ⌷→⌷, ⌷↑⌷, or ⌷↓⌷. To use the mouse, move the mouse pointer to the top left cell of the block you want to print, click and drag to the bottom right cell of the block, release the mouse button when the desired block is highlighted, and then press ⌷↵Enter⌷.

   To designate a block that includes the *entire* active area of the spreadsheet, position the cell selector at the top left corner of the active area and press ⌷.⌷ to anchor the block. Then press ⌷End⌷-⌷Home⌷ to move the cell selector to the bottom right corner of the active area. Finally, press ⌷↵Enter⌷.

In this example, highlight the block A1..E14 and press ⌷↵Enter⌋.

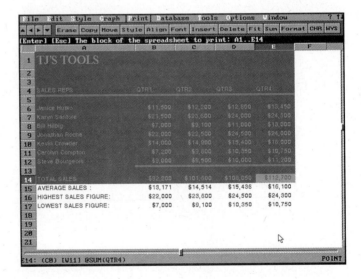

8. After you highlight the exact block you want to print, press ⌷A⌷ to select **A**djust Printer.

9. Press 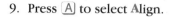 to select **A**lign.

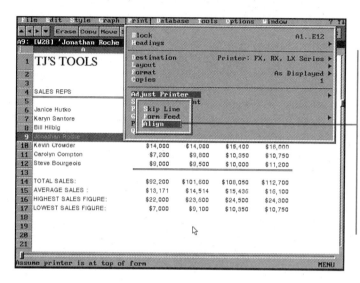

The **A**lign option ensures that printing will begin at the top of each successive page after the first. Before printing, always make sure that your printer paper is correctly positioned.

10. To begin printing, press Ⓢ to select **S**preadsheet Print.

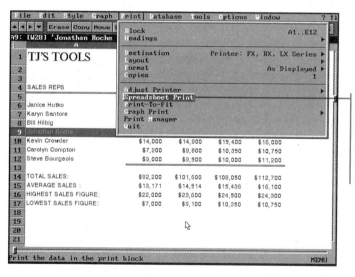

The **S**preadsheet Print option on the **P**rint menu sends your spreadsheet data to the printer.

11. After printing is completed, press Ⓐ to select **A**djust Printer, and then press Ⓕ to select **F**orm Feed to advance to the top of the next page.

12. Press Ⓠ to select **Q**uit.

```
TJ'S TOOLS

SALES REPS               QTR1      QTR2      QTR3      QTR4
-----------------------------------------------------------------
Janice Hutko           $11,500   $12,200   $12,800   $13,450
Karyn Santore          $21,500   $23,600   $24,000   $24,300
Bill Hilbig             $7,000    $9,100   $11,000   $13,000
Jonathan Roche         $22,000   $22,500   $24,500   $24,000
Kevin Crowder          $14,000   $14,900   $15,400   $16,000
Carolyn Compton         $7,200    $9,800   $10,350   $10,750
Steve Bourgeois         $9,000    $9,500   $10,000   $11,200
```

This example shows a draft-quality report less than one page long, printed with the default settings.

If you accidentally press ⏎Enter after you select the Spreadsheet Print option, the file will print a second time. You can press Ctrl-Break to stop printing.

You can use the /Print Headings command to repeat certain labels on each page. This command is discussed in the following section.

Printing Two or More Pages with Headings

When printing two or more pages, you can repeat certain columns or rows on each printed page. In Quattro Pro, the repeated columns and rows are called *headings*.

To repeat column or row headings on each printed page, follow these steps:

1. Press / to access the Quattro Pro menu.

2. Press P to select Print.

3. Press H to select Headings.

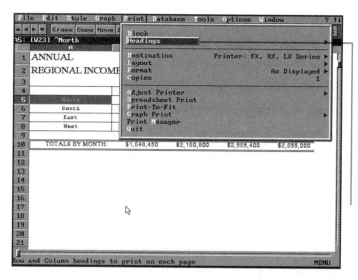

The Headings command enables you to select row or column headings to repeat on each page of the printout.

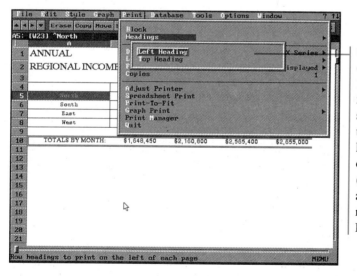

Quattro Pro displays the Headings menu, from which you specify whether the labels are located down one or more columns (Left Heading) or across one or more rows (Top Heading).

9

4. Press ⎣L⎦ to select Left Heading or ⎣T⎦ to select Top Heading.

To print a report of two or more pages and repeat labels displayed down a column, select Left Heading. To print a report of two or more pages and repeat labels displayed across a row, select Top Heading.

In this example, press L to select **L**eft Heading.

After you choose **L**eft Heading, Quattro Pro displays the prompt Row headings to print on the left of each page.

5. Indicate the rows or columns you want to print on each page by highlighting a cell in those rows or columns; then press ⏎Enter.

In this example, highlight A5 (to specify the labels in column A as headings) and press ⏎Enter.

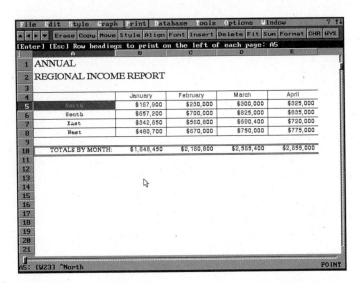

6. To choose the block you want to print, press B to select **B**lock.

7. Highlight the desired print block, *excluding* those columns or rows you entered using the **H**eadings command from the **P**rint menu; then press ⏎Enter.

Note: When you specify a print block, you should *not* include the headings you want repeated on each page. Quattro Pro automatically prints the headings on every page of the printout. If you *do* include the headings in the print block, Quattro Pro will print them twice on each page.

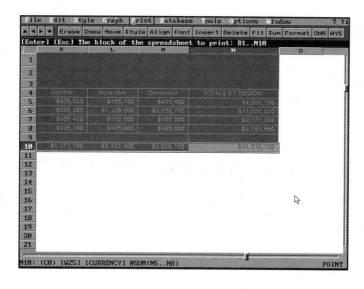

In this example, highlight B1..N10 as the print block and press ⏎Enter. Note that this block does not include column A, which you specified as the headings.

8. Press [A] to select **A**djust Printer.

9. Press [A] to select **A**lign to synchronize the printer's line counter with Quattro Pro.

10. Press [S] to select **S**preadsheet Print.

11. After printing is completed, press [A] to select **A**djust Printer, and then press [F] to select **F**orm Feed to advance to the top of the next page.

12. Press [Q] to select **Q**uit.

ANNUAL
REGIONAL INC OME REPORT

	January	February	March	April
North	$167,900	$230,000	$300,000	$325,000
South	$657,200	$700,000	$825,000	$835,000
East	$342,650	$560,800	$690,400	$720,000
West	$480,700	$670,000	$750,000	$775,000
TOTALS BY MONTH:	$1,648,450	$2,160,800	$2,565,400	$2,655,000

This printout shows the first page of a three-page report that has column headings repeated on each page.

ANNUAL
REGIONAL INC

	May	June	July	August
North	$355,000	$385,900	$392,000	$410,500
South	$850,900	$875,000	$890,000	$945,700
East	$735,400	$765,750	$790,000	$855,900
West	$790,450	$815,300	$835,650	$855,300

TOTALS BY MONTH:	$2,731,750	$2,841,950	$2,907,650	$3,067,400

This printout shows the second page of the report with headings.

ANNUAL
REGIONAL INC

	September	October	November	December
North	$418,750	$435,600	$450,700	$495,400
South	$970,250	$995,000	$1,125,800	$1,550,750
East	$875,000	$905,400	$950,900	$985,000
West	$885,450	$935,700	$965,000	$995,000

TOTALS BY MONTH:	$3,149,450	$3,271,700	$3,492,400	$4,026,150

This printout shows the third page of the report with headings.

Excluding Segments within a Print Block

Because the /Print commands require that you specify the block you want to print, you can print only rectangular blocks from the spreadsheet. Nevertheless, you can suppress the display of cell contents within the block. You can hide entire rows or columns, or you can remove from view a segment that spans only part of a row or column. Whether you want to hide a column (or block) of sensitive financial information or want to compress the spreadsheet so that the most important data fits on a one-page report, you can use Quattro Pro to prevent certain data from printing.

Excluding Columns

As you learned in Chapter 5, you can use Quattro Pro's /Style Hide Column command to hide columns you don't want to display on-screen. This command therefore enables you to exclude columns of data from printing.

To print a spreadsheet block and exclude one or more columns within that block, follow these steps:

1. Press / to access the Quattro Pro menu.
2. Press S to select Style.
3. Press H to select Hide Column.
4. Press H to select Hide.
5. When the prompt Hide columns from view appears, highlight a cell in the column or columns you want to hide; then press ↵Enter.

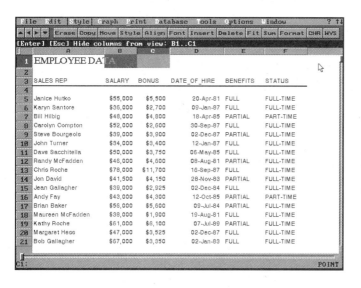

In this example, specify columns B and C as the columns you want to hide, and press ↵Enter.

6. Press / to access the Quattro Pro menu.
7. Press P to select Print.

8. Press ⃞D to select **D**estination.

9. Press ⃞P to select **P**rinter.

10. To assign the block to print, press ⃞B to select **B**lock.

11. Highlight the block you want to print; then press ⃞↵Enter.

In this example, highlight A1..G21 as the print block and press ⃞↵Enter.

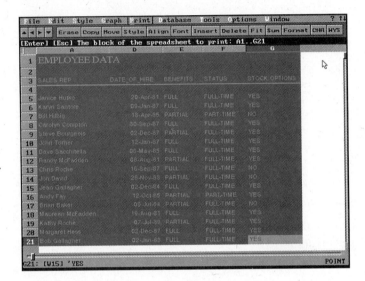

12. Press ⃞A to select **A**djust Printer.

13. Press ⃞A to select **A**lign.

14. Press ⃞S to select **S**preadsheet Print.

15. After printing is completed, press ⃞A to select **A**djust Printer, and then press ⃞F to select **F**orm Feed to advance to the top of the next page.

16. Press ⃞Q to select **Q**uit.

EMPLOYEE DATA

SALES REP	DATE_OF_HIRE	BENEFITS	STATUS	STOCK OPTION
Janice Hutko	20-Apr-81	FULL	FULL-TIME	YES
Karyn Santore	09-Jan-87	FULL	FULL-TIME	YES
Bill Hilbig	18-Apr-85	PARTIAL	PART-TIME	NO
Carolyn Compton	30-Sep-87	FULL	FULL-TIME	YES
Steve Bourgeois	02-Dec-87	PARTIAL	FULL-TIME	YES
John Turner	12-Jan-87	FULL	FULL-TIME	YES
Dave Sacchitella	06-May-85	FULL	FULL-TIME	YES
Randy McFadden	08-Aug-81	PARTIAL	FULL-TIME	YES
Chris Roche	16-Sep-87	FULL	FULL-TIME	NO
Jon David	28-Nov-83	PARTIAL	FULL-TIME	NO
Jean Gallagher	02-Dec-84	FULL	FULL-TIME	YES
Andy Fay	12-Oct-85	PARTIAL	PART-TIME	YES
Brian Baker	09-Jul-84	PARTIAL	FULL-TIME	NO
Maureen McFadden	19-Aug-81	FULL	FULL-TIME	YES
Kathy Roche	07-Jul-89	PARTIAL	FULL-TIME	YES
Margaret Hess	02-Dec-87	FULL	FULL-TIME	YES
Bob Gallagher	02-Jan-83	FULL	FULL-TIME	YES

The printed report excludes the salary and bonus information contained in the hidden columns, B and C.

Note: To restore hidden columns, select /Style Hide Column Expose. When the hidden columns (marked with an asterisk) reappear on-screen, you can specify which column or columns you want to display.

Excluding Rows

To prevent specific rows of the spreadsheet from printing, you must mark these rows with a special symbol for nonprinting. You enter the symbol for nonprinting by typing two vertical bars (¦¦) in the first column of the print block in each row you want to exclude.

Only one of the vertical bars appears on-screen, and neither vertical bar appears on the printout. If the row you want to exclude contains data in the first column of the print block, you must insert a new column in which you can place the vertical bars. The column with the vertical bars must be the first column of the print block. To avoid alignment problems when inserting a new column for the vertical bars, you can use /Style Hide Column to suppress printing of that column after you specify the print block.

To print a spreadsheet block and suppress one or more rows within that block, follow these steps:

1. In the first column of the print block, highlight the first cell in the row you want to suppress from the printout.

269

Note: If the first cell in the row you want to mark for omission already contains data, use the **/Edit Insert Columns** command to insert a new blank column into your spreadsheet at column A.

In this example, highlight A6, which is the leftmost cell in the first row you want to suppress from the printout.

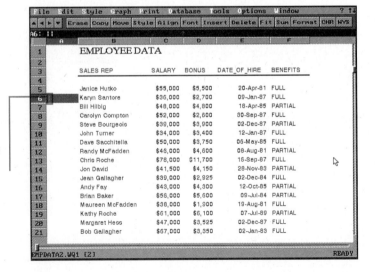

2. Type ¦¦, the symbol for nonprinting, and press ↵Enter.

The symbol for nonprinting appears as a single bar in the spreadsheet.

9

3. Repeat steps 1 and 2 until all rows you want to suppress from the printout are marked.

4. Press ⌐/⌐ to access the Quattro Pro menu.

5. Press ⌐P⌐ to select **P**rint.

6. Press ⌐D⌐ to select **D**estination.

7. Press ⌐P⌐ to select **P**rinter.

8. Press ⌐B⌐ to select **B**lock.

9. Highlight the block you want to print and press ⌐◄Enter⌐.

   Note: You *must* include the column containing the vertical bars as the *first* column in the print block.

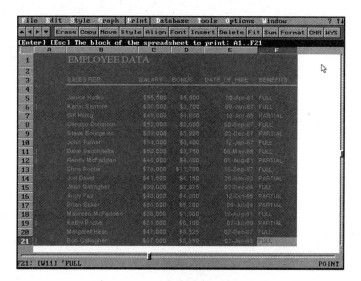

In this example, highlight A1..F21 as the print block and press ◄Enter.

9

10. If you have inserted a new column for the vertical bars, hide that column to avoid alignment problems in your printout. To do this, select **Q**uit from the **P**rint menu, highlight the new column, select /**S**tyle **H**ide Column **H**ide, and press ◄Enter. Then select /**P**rint to access the **P**rint menu again, and continue with the next step.

    In this example, you must hide column A before printing, to avoid alignment problems. Quattro Pro will still suppress the marked rows, even though the symbols for nonprinting are not visible on-screen.

11. Press ⌐A⌐ to select **A**djust Printer.

12. Press ⌐A⌐ to select **A**lign.

13. Press S to select Spreadsheet Print.

14. After printing is completed, press A to select **Adjust Printer**, and then press F to select **Form Feed** to advance to the top of the next page.

15. Press Q to select **Quit**.

```
EMPLOYEE DATA

SALES REP              SALARY     BONUS     DATE_OF_HIRE    BENEFITS
-------------------------------------------------------------------------

Janice Hutko           $55,000    $5,500     20-Apr-81  FULL
Bill Hilbig            $48,000    $4,800     18-Apr-85  PARTIAL
Carolyn Compton        $52,000    $2,600     30-Sep-87  FULL
Steve Bourgeois        $39,000    $3,900     02-Dec-87  PARTIAL
John Turner            $34,000    $3,400     12-Jan-87  FULL
Chris Roche            $78,000   $11,700     16-Sep-87  FULL
Jon David              $41,500    $4,150     28-Nov-83  PARTIAL
Jean Gallagher         $39,000    $2,925     02-Dec-84  FULL
Andy Fay               $43,000    $4,300     12-Oct-85  PARTIAL
Brian Baker            $56,000    $5,600     09-Jul-84  PARTIAL
Maureen McFadden       $38,000    $1,900     19-Aug-81  FULL
Margaret Hess          $47,000    $3,525     02-Dec-87  FULL
```

Rows marked with two vertical bars in the first column of the print block do not appear in the printed output.

9

To restore the spreadsheet after you finish printing, remove the vertical bars from the leftmost cells of the marked rows. If you inserted a column for the vertical bars, redisplay the column, if necessary, with /Style Hide Column Expose, and then delete the column with /Edit Delete Column.

Excluding Blocks

If you want to hide only part of a row or column, or an area that partially spans one or more rows and columns, use the /Style Numeric Format Hidden command to hide the block.

To exclude a spreadsheet block from a printout, follow these steps:

1. Press / to access the Quattro Pro menu.

2. Press S to select **Style**.

272

3. Press N to select **N**umeric Format.

4. Press H to select **H**idden.

5. Highlight the block you want to hide, and press ↵Enter.

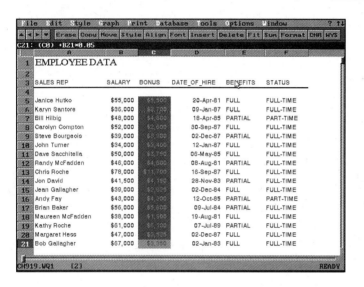

In this example, highlight C5..C21 as the block you want to hide, and press ↵Enter.

6. Press / to access the Quattro Pro menu.

7. Press P to select **P**rint.

8. Press D to select **D**estination.

9. Press P to select **P**rinter.

10. Press B to select **B**lock.

11. Highlight the block you want to print, and press ↵Enter.

    Note: Be sure to include the hidden block within the print block.

12. Press A to select **A**djust Printer.

13. Press A to select **A**lign.

14. Press S to select **S**preadsheet Print.

15. After printing is completed, press A to select **A**djust Printer, and then press F to select **F**orm Feed to advance to the top of the next page.

16. Press Q to select **Q**uit.

9

273

EMPLOYEE DATA

SALES REP	SALARY	BONUS	DATE OF HIRE	BENEFITS	STATUS
Janice Hutko	$55,000		20-Apr-81	FULL	FULL-TIME
Karyn Santore	$36,000		09-Jan-87	FULL	FULL-TIME
Bill Hilbig	$48,000		18-Apr-85	PARTIAL	PART-TIME
Carolyn Compton	$52,000		30-Sep-87	FULL	FULL-TIME
Steve Bourgeois	$39,000		02-Dec-87	PARTIAL	FULL-TIME
John Turner	$34,000		12-Jan-87	FULL	FULL-TIME
Dave Sacchitella	$50,000		06-May-85	FULL	FULL-TIME
Randy McFadden	$46,000		08-Aug-81	PARTIAL	FULL-TIME
Chris Roche	$78,000		16-Sep-87	FULL	FULL-TIME
Jon David	$41,500		28-Nov-83	PARTIAL	FULL-TIME
Jean Gallagher	$39,000		02-Dec-84	FULL	FULL-TIME
Andy Fay	$43,000		12-Oct-85	PARTIAL	PART-TIME
Brian Baker	$56,000		09-Jul-84	FULL	FULL-TIME
Maureen McFadden	$38,000		19-Aug-81	FULL	FULL-TIME
Kathy Roche	$61,000		07-Jul-89	PARTIAL	FULL-TIME
Margaret Hess	$47,000		02-Dec-87	FULL	FULL-TIME
Bob Gallagher	$67,000		02-Jan-83	FULL	FULL-TIME

The block hidden with /Style Numeric Format Hidden is suppressed from the printout.

After you finish printing, restore the hidden block to the global format with the /Style Numeric Format Reset command.

If you find yourself repeating print operations (hiding the same columns, suppressing and then restoring the same documentation, and so forth), remember that you can save time and minimize frustration by developing and using print macros. Chapter 13 explains the basics about macros; for more detailed information, see Que's *Using Quattro Pro 4*, Special Edition.

Controlling Paper Movement

With Quattro Pro, if you print a one-page report containing fewer lines than the default page length, the printer does not automatically advance the paper to the top of the next page. Instead, the next print operation begins wherever the preceding operation ended. Similarly, if you print a multipage report, Quattro Pro automatically inserts page breaks in the document between pages, but the paper does not advance to the top of the next page after Quattro Pro prints the last page.

You can control movement of the paper in your printer from within Quattro Pro. You can specify the "top" of a page in any paper position, advance the paper by line or by page, and insert page breaks exactly where you want them.

Using the Skip Line, Form Feed, and Align Options

If you are using continuous-feed paper, position the paper so that your printer's print head is even with the perforations at the top of the paper, and then turn on your printer. If your printer is already on, turn it off and then on again. Do not advance the paper manually after the printer is on. Because Quattro Pro coordinates a line counter with the current page-length setting, any lines you advance manually are not counted, and page breaks will occur in strange places.

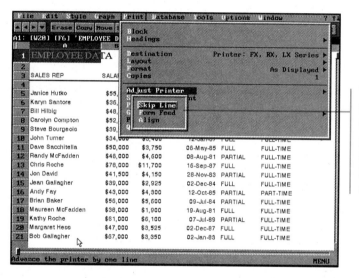

You can control the movement of the paper in your printer with the Skip Line, Form Feed, and Align options.

9

The Skip Line option from the /Print Adjust Printer menu advances the paper one line at a time, and the Form Feed option advances the paper one page at a time. You use the Align option to set the beginning of a page.

If you want to advance the paper one line at a time (to separate several small printed blocks that fit on one page, for example), issue the /Print Adjust Printer Skip Line command. This command causes the printer to skip a line.

To advance the paper one line at a time, follow these steps:

1. Press / to access the Quattro Pro menu.

2. Press P to select Print.

3. Press A to select Adjust Printer.

4. Press S to select Skip Line.

To advance to a new page after printing less than a full page, select /Print Adjust Printer Form Feed. Whenever you issue this command, the printer advances to a new page. (Note that the following section shows how to embed in the print block a page-break symbol that instructs Quattro Pro to advance automatically.)

To advance to a new page after printing less than a full page, follow these steps:

1. Press ⌑ to access the Quattro Pro menu.
2. Press ⊡ to select **P**rint.
3. Press ⊡ to select **A**djust Printer.
4. Press ⊡ to select **F**orm Feed.

Use the /Print Adjust Printer **A**lign command when the paper perforation and print head are aligned to establish (or reestablish) correct page breaks. Whenever you begin a print job at the top of a page, always select **A**lign before printing.

To align the printer and set the beginning of a page, follow these steps:

1. Press ⌑ to access the Quattro Pro menu.
2. Press ⊡ to select **P**rint.
3. Press ⊡ to select **A**djust Printer.
4. Press ⊡ to select **A**lign.

Setting Page Breaks within the Spreadsheet

You use the /Style Insert Break command to insert page breaks into a spreadsheet. You should execute this command with the cell selector at the first column of the block you want to print, in the row that should begin the new page. The command automatically inserts a new blank row containing a page-break symbol (¦::) in the cell where the cell selector is located.

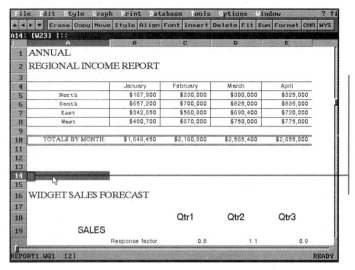

Quattro Pro displays the page-break character (::) in the cell in which you originally positioned the cell selector.

The vertical bar (¦) that precedes the page-break character (visible only in the input line) tells Quattro Pro not to print the row. The /Style Insert Break command is similar to the /Edit Insert Row command that inserts one or more rows at the row specified by the cell selector.

To enter the page-break symbol into a spreadsheet, follow these steps:

1. Position the cell selector in the first column of the block you want to print, at the row location where you want a new page to begin.
2. Press ⌐/⌐ to access the Quattro Pro menu.
3. Press ⌐S⌐ to select Style.
4. Press ⌐I⌐ to select Insert Break.

When you print the block containing the page-break symbol, Quattro Pro automatically starts a new page at that point. Then, on the new page, Quattro Pro prints the data that follows the page-break symbol.

Note: Exercise caution when entering page breaks into the spreadsheet, either manually or with the /Style Insert Break command, because you can accidentally delete the wrong row after you finish printing. You can avoid such

9

accidents by typing the page-break symbol into the first column in the print block of a row that is already blank in your spreadsheet. First check to be sure that the row is blank by pressing [End] [←] and then [End] [→] to scan across the row.

The page break is effective only when positioned at the left edge of the block you are printing. If you add contents to cells in the page-break row, the contents of those cells are not printed.

Enhancing Reports with Print Options

If you are preparing a report for distribution to others, you can add some simple enhancements. For example, you can add headers and footers, or you can change the page layout by adjusting the margins and page length.

Adding Headers and Footers

Quattro Pro reserves three lines on each page of a document for a header and an additional three lines for a footer. If specified, headers and footers appear at the top and bottom, respectively, of each page on your printout.

The Header and Footer options, accessed from the /Print Layout menu, enable you to specify up to 254 characters of text within one line of your printed output. You can position the header and footer at the left, right, or center of the page. The number of characters in the header and footer lines, however, is limited by the size of both the paper and the printed characters. When you are printing on 8 1/2-by-11-inch paper with 1/2-inch margins and 10-characters-per-inch type, for example, you can print only 75 characters in the header or footer.

The header text, which is printed on the first line after any blank top margin lines, is followed by two blank header lines (for spacing). The footer text line is printed above any blank bottom margin lines and below two blank footer lines (for spacing).

Quattro Pro provides special characters for controlling page numbers, the current date, and the positioning of text within a header or footer. The following list gives you an overview of the characters you use to place page numbers and dates in headers, and to set the alignment of the header.

Character	Function
#	Automatically prints consecutive page numbers, starting with 1.
@	Automatically prints the current date.
¦	Automatically separates text. Absence of a ¦ symbol left-justifies all text. The first ¦ symbol centers the text that follows. The second ¦ symbol right-justifies remaining text.

To add a header or footer, follow these steps:

1. Press / to access the Quattro Pro menu.

2. Press P to select Print.

3. Press B to select Block, highlight the desired print block, and press Enter.

   For this example, highlight the block A1..F21 and press Enter.

4. Press L to select Layout.

5. Press H to select Header or F to select Footer.

In this example, press H to select Header to add a header to the report.

6. At the Header text or Footer text prompt, enter the desired header or footer characters and press ↵Enter.

For example, type @¦NATIONAL MICRO¦# as the header text, and press ↵Enter.

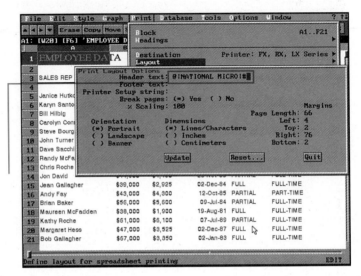

@¦NATIONAL MICRO¦#

The @ sign tells Quattro Pro to include the date in your header (or footer). Make sure that your computer is set to the correct date.

The ¦ symbol tells Quattro Pro how to align the different items within the header (or footer) line.

The # symbol tells Quattro Pro to print the page number.

7. To return to the main **P**rint menu, press Q to select **Q**uit.

8. Press A to select **A**djust Printer.

9. Press A to select **A**lign.

10. Press S to select **S**preadsheet Print.

11. After printing is completed, press A to select **A**djust Printer, and then press F to select **F**orm Feed to advance to the top of the next page.

12. Press Q to select **Q**uit.

280

21-Apr-92			NATIONAL MICRO			1

EMPLOYEE DATA

SALES REP	SALARY	BONUS	DATE OF HIRE	BENEFITS	STATUS
Janice Hutko	$55,000	$5,500	20-Apr-81	FULL	FULL-TIME
Karyn Santore	$36,000	$2,700	09-Jan-87	FULL	FULL-TIME
Bill Hilbig	$48,000	$4,800	18-Apr-85	PARTIAL	PART-TIME
Carolyn Compton	$52,000	$2,600	30-Sep-87	FULL	FULL-TIME
Steve Bourgeois	$39,000	$3,900	02-Dec-87	PARTIAL	FULL-TIME
John Turner	$34,000	$3,400	12-Jan-87	FULL	FULL-TIME
Dave Sacchitella	$50,000	$3,750	06-May-85	FULL	FULL-TIME
Randy McFadden	$46,000	$4,600	08-Aug-81	PARTIAL	FULL-TIME
Chris Roche	$78,000	$11,700	16-Sep-87	FULL	FULL-TIME
Jon David	$41,500	$4,150	28-Nov-83	PARTIAL	FULL-TIME
Jean Gallagher	$39,000	$2,925	02-Dec-84	FULL	FULL-TIME
Andy Fay	$43,000	$4,300	12-Oct-85	PARTIAL	PART-TIME
Brian Baker	$56,000	$5,600	09-Jul-84	PARTIAL	FULL-TIME
Maureen McFadden	$38,000	$1,900	19-Aug-81	FULL	FULL-TIME
Kathy Roche	$61,000	$6,100	07-Jul-89	PARTIAL	FULL-TIME
Margaret Hess	$47,000	$3,525	02-Dec-87	FULL	FULL-TIME
Bob Gallagher	$67,000	$3,350	02-Jan-83	FULL	FULL-TIME

The header appears at the top of the printed report.

Whenever the print block exceeds one page, the header is reproduced on each succeeding page, and the page number increases by one. If you have used the special page-number character (#) and want to print your report a second time before you leave the Print menu, reset the page counter and set the top of the form by selecting Adjust Printer Align before you select Spreadsheet Print.

If you have specified a header line, but the centered or right-justified text doesn't print, make sure that the right-margin setting (discussed in the next section) is appropriate for the current type size and paper width. To change the header, repeat the sequence to establish the text, press Esc to remove the display of the existing header from the dialog box, and press ↵Enter. (You can delete a header or footer without removing other specified options.)

To print a footer on the last page of a report (or on a single-page report), you must use the Form Feed command at the end of the printing session. If you select the Quit command from the Print menu without issuing the Form Feed command, this final footer will not print. You can, however, reissue the /Print Adjust Printer command and select Form Feed; in this case, the footer still prints.

9

Changing the Page Layout

Before you change the page layout defaults, be aware of the current settings. Quattro Pro initially assumes 8 1/2-by-11-inch paper and a printer output of six lines per inch; the default length of a page is 66 lines. Quattro Pro reserves two lines at the top and bottom of each page for the top and bottom margins. Also, Quattro Pro automatically reserves three lines at the top for headers and three lines at the bottom for footers (one line for the header or footer, and two lines for spacing before or after the main text).

Note: If you have a laser printer and are using the lines/characters dimension, you should change the page length to 60 lines instead of 66.

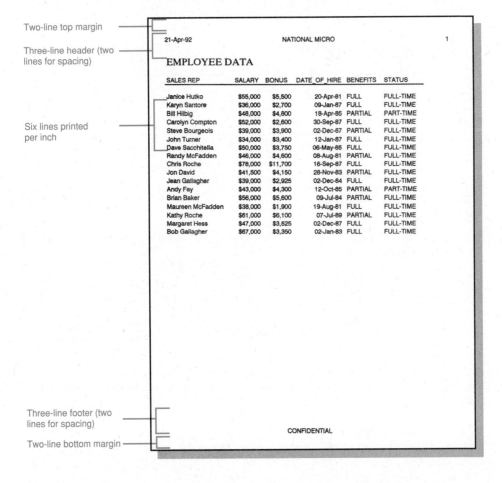

Two-line top margin

Three-line header (two lines for spacing)

Six lines printed per inch

Three-line footer (two lines for spacing)

Two-line bottom margin

SALES REP	SALARY	BONUS	DATE OF HIRE	BENEFITS	STATUS
Janice Hutko	$55,000	$5,500	20-Apr-81	FULL	FULL-TIME
Karyn Santore	$36,000	$2,700	09-Jan-87	FULL	FULL-TIME
Bill Hilbig	$48,000	$4,800	18-Apr-85	PARTIAL	PART-TIME
Carolyn Compton	$52,000	$2,600	30-Sep-87	FULL	FULL-TIME
Steve Bourgeois	$39,000	$3,900	02-Dec-87	PARTIAL	FULL-TIME
John Turner	$34,000	$3,400	12-Jan-87	FULL	FULL-TIME
Dave Sacchitella	$50,000	$3,750	06-May-85	FULL	FULL-TIME
Randy McFadden	$46,000	$4,600	08-Aug-81	PARTIAL	FULL-TIME
Chris Roche	$78,000	$11,700	16-Sep-87	FULL	FULL-TIME
Jon David	$41,500	$4,150	28-Nov-83	PARTIAL	FULL-TIME
Jean Gallagher	$39,000	$2,925	02-Dec-84	FULL	FULL-TIME
Andy Fay	$43,000	$4,300	12-Oct-85	PARTIAL	PART-TIME
Brian Baker	$56,000	$5,600	09-Jul-84	PARTIAL	FULL-TIME
Maureen McFadden	$38,000	$1,900	19-Aug-81	FULL	FULL-TIME
Kathy Roche	$61,000	$6,100	07-Jul-89	PARTIAL	FULL-TIME
Margaret Hess	$47,000	$3,525	02-Dec-87	FULL	FULL-TIME
Bob Gallagher	$67,000	$3,350	02-Jan-83	FULL	FULL-TIME

21-Apr-92   NATIONAL MICRO   1

EMPLOYEE DATA

CONFIDENTIAL

9

To change the page layout of the current spreadsheet, follow these steps:

1. Press ⃞/ to access the Quattro Pro menu.
2. Press ⃞P to select **P**rint.
3. Press ⃞L to select **L**ayout.

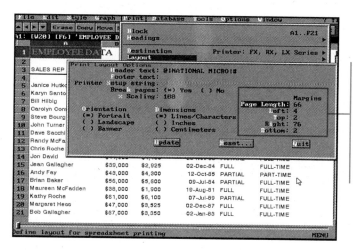

The Margins area of the Print Layout Options dialog box enables you to modify the size of the margins in the printed report.

4. Select **P**age Length, **L**eft, **T**op, **R**ight, or **B**ottom (press ⃞P, ⃞L, ⃞T, ⃞⃞, or ⃞B, respectively).

5. In response to the dialog box instructions to enter the margin or change the page length, type a value within the dialog box and press ⃞Enter.

To change the length of a page, select **P**age Length and enter a value from 0 through 100 (lines). When you select **L**eft, you are prompted to enter a new left margin setting from the values 0 through 254 (characters). To change the right margin, select **R**ight and enter a value from 0 through 511 (characters) in the dialog box. For the top and bottom margins, select **T**op or **B**ottom and enter a margin specification from 0 through 32 (lines).

Be sure that you set left and right margins that are consistent with the width of your paper and the established pitch (characters per inch) of your printer. The right margin must be greater than the left margin. Also, make sure that the settings for the top and bottom margins are consistent with the paper's length and the established number of lines per inch.

9

Previewing a Printed Report

After you have enhanced your report with headings or layout changes, you can view the report on-screen before sending it to your printer. To access the Screen Previewer, first specify a print block and then follow these steps:

1. Press / to access the Quattro Pro menu.
2. Press P to select **P**rint.
3. Press D to select **D**estination.
4. Press S to select **S**creen Preview.
5. Press S to select **S**preadsheet Print.

Quattro Pro displays your spreadsheet as it will be printed.

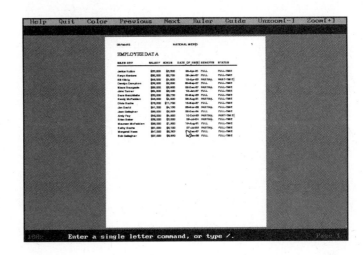

6. Press Esc to exit the Screen Previewer.

Table 9.2 describes the Screen Previewer commands, and table 9.3 describes the movement keys you can use in the Screen Previewer.

Table 9.2
Screen Previewer Commands

Command	Description
Help	Invokes a context-sensitive window.
Quit	Exits to the spreadsheet.

Command	Description
Color	Toggles between a monochrome and color screen.
Previous	Displays the preceding page.
Next	Displays the next page.
Ruler	Overlays a one-inch grid on-screen.
Guide	Displays in the upper right corner of the screen a miniature spreadsheet containing a box. Press ←, →, ↑, or ↓ to move the box around the miniature spreadsheet, or use the mouse to click and drag the box. Press ↵Enter to relocate the screen to the portion of the spreadsheet indicated by the box. (This command works only when in a zoomed view.)
Unzoom[−]	Reduces the screen display one zoomed level. You can press U or − to activate this command.
Zoom[+]	Enlarges the display by 100%, 200%, and 400%. You can press Z or + to activate this command.

Table 9.3
Screen Previewer Movement Keys

Key	Description
Esc	Exits the Screen Previewer.
← → ↑ ↓	Scrolls the zoomed display in the direction of the arrow.
PgUp	Moves to the preceding page.
PgDn	Moves to the next page.
Home	Displays the top of a zoomed page.
End	Displays the bottom of a zoomed page.
Del	Removes the page guide when a page is zoomed.

9

Printing a Listing of Cell Contents

You can spend hours developing and debugging a spreadsheet application and spend additional time entering and verifying data. You should safeguard your work by making backup copies of your important files. You also can print a listing of the cell contents of important spreadsheets. Be aware, however, that this print job can eat up lots of time (and paper) if you have a large spreadsheet.

You can produce printed documentation of cell contents by selecting /Print Format and then selecting either As Displayed or Cell-Formulas. The two options are related. Selecting Cell-Formulas produces a listing with one cell per line that shows the cell format, the width of the cell (if different from the default), the cell-protection status, and the contents of cells (including any formulas) in the print block. With As Displayed, the data prints as it appears—showing the cell format, cell width, and protection status—but the contents of the cells are printed as they appear on-screen rather than as formulas.

To print a cell-by-cell listing of the contents of a particular block, follow these steps:

1. Press / to access the Quattro Pro menu.
2. Press P to select Print.
3. Press F to select Format.
4. Press C to select Cell-Formulas to print a listing of formulas in cells; or press A to select As Displayed to print the block as it appears on-screen.

In this example, press C to select Cell-Formulas.

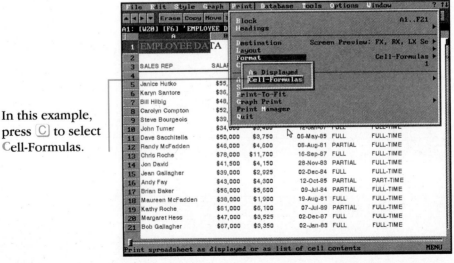

5. Press B to select Block, highlight the block of cells you want to print, and press ↵Enter.

   In this example, highlight A1..F21 as the print block and press ↵Enter.

6. Press A to select Adjust Printer.

7. Press A to select Align.

8. Press S to select Spreadsheet Print.

9. After printing is completed, press A to select Adjust Printer, and then press F to select Form Feed.

10. Press Q to select Quit.

Each entry in the resulting printout is listed in the following format.

```
A1: [W20] [F6] 'EMPLOYEE DATA
A3: [W20] 'SALES REP
B3: 'SALARY
C3: 'BONUS
D3: [W15] 'DATE_OF_HIRE
E3: [W11] 'BENEFITS
F3: [W12] 'STATUS
A5: [W20] 'Janice Hutko
B5: (C0) 55000
C5: (C0) +B5*0.1
D5: (D1) [W15] @DATE(81,4,20)
E5: [W11] 'FULL
F5: [W12] 'FULL-TIME
A6: [W20] 'Karyn Santore
B6: (C0) 36000
C6: (C0) +B6*0.075
D6: (D1) [W15] @DATE(87,1,9)
E6: [W11] 'FULL
F6: [W12] 'FULL-TIME
A7: [W20] 'Bill Hilbig
B7: (C0) 48000
C7: (C0) +B7*0.1
D7: (D1) [W15] @DATE(85,4,18)
E7: [W11] 'PARTIAL
F7: [W12] 'PART-TIME
A8: [W20] 'Carolyn Compton
B8: (C0) 52000
C8: (C0) +B8*0.05
D8: (D1) [W15] @DATE(87,9,30)
E8: [W11] 'FULL
F8: [W12] 'FULL-TIME
A9: [W20] 'Steve Bourgeois
B9: (C0) 39000
C9: (C0) +B9*0.1
D9: (D1) [W15] @DATE(87,12,2)
E9: [W11] 'PARTIAL
F9: [W12] 'FULL-TIME
A10: [W20] 'John Turner
B10: (C0) 34000
C10: (C0) +B10*0.1
D10: (D1) [W15] @DATE(87,1,12)
E10: [W11] 'FULL
F10: [W12] 'FULL-TIME
```

Moving horizontally across each row of the print block, Quattro Pro prints the contents of each cell.

9

287

Note: If a cell has been unprotected with the /Style Protection Unprotect command, an uppercase U appears after the cell format. Cells protected with /Style Protection do not display U or any other character in this location.

Resetting the Print Options

When you select Print options, the settings you specify are automatically saved with the spreadsheet when you select /File Save. Saving the settings with the spreadsheet for a future print job, rather than resetting them after each printing, is good practice. You then can quickly make minor changes to the existing settings.

At times, however, resetting all or some of the print settings may be beneficial; you can accomplish this task with the /Print Layout Reset command. For example, you may want to print a report from the same spreadsheet you printed from earlier, but specify a different print block. You can use /Print Layout Reset Print Block to eliminate only the block setting, thereby enabling you to select the new block quickly. All other print settings remain intact. The /Print Layout Reset All command can be helpful when a report isn't printing properly and you want to reenter the print settings.

To reset some or all print settings, follow these steps:

1. Press ⌐/⌐ to access the Quattro Pro menu.
2. Press ⌐P⌐ to select Print.
3. Press ⌐L⌐ to select Layout.
4. Press ⌐R⌐ to select Reset.

Quattro Pro displays the options for resetting the print settings.

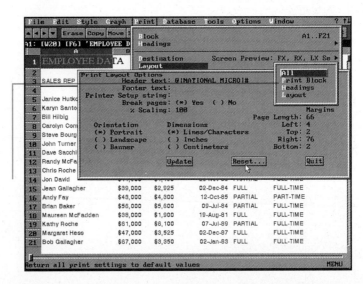

5. Press [A], [P], [H], or [L] to select All, Print Block, Headings, or Layout, respectively. Each option is described in table 9.4.

Table 9.4
Print Reset Options

Option	Description
All	Resets every Print setting, including the print block.
Print Block	Removes only the previous print-block specification.
Headings	Cancels columns and rows specified as headings.
Layout	Returns Margins, Page Length, and Setup string settings to the default settings.

6. Press [Q] to select Quit.

Preparing Output for Other Programs

Many word processing, database, and other software programs import ASCII text files. You can maximize your chances of successfully exporting Quattro Pro files to other programs if you select several Print command sequences that eliminate unwanted specifications for page layout and page breaks. This section shows you how to use this command to create a PRN file you can import into another program.

To prepare output for other programs, follow these steps:

1. Press [/] to access the Quattro Pro menu.
2. Press [P] to select Print.
3. Press [D] to select Destination.
4. Press [F] to select File to direct output to a PRN file rather than to your printer.
5. Type a file name of up to eight characters and press [⏎Enter].

   To change the current drive and directory, press [Esc] before you enter the file name, type the new path name, and then type a file name.

9

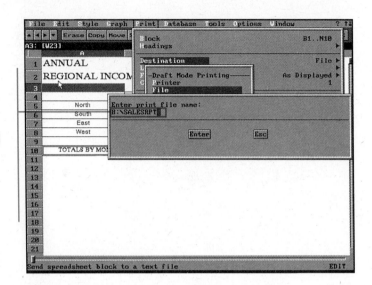

In this example, press Esc twice, type **B:\SALESRPT**, and press ↵Enter to direct the output to a PRN file named SALESRPT on drive B.

6. Press B to select **B**lock, specify the block you want to send to the PRN file, and press ↵Enter.

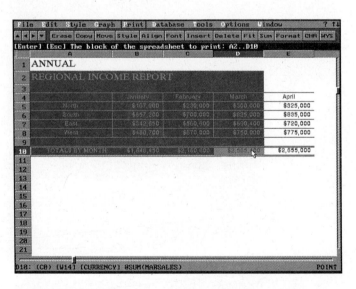

In this example, select **B**lock, highlight A2..D10 as the print block, and then press ↵Enter.

7. Press L to select **L**ayout.

290

8. Press ⌊L⌋ to select **L**eft, type **0**, and press ⏎Enter; press ⌊T⌋ to select **T**op, type **0**, and press ⏎Enter; press ⌊⌋ to select **R**ight, type **511**, and press ⏎Enter; and press ⌊B⌋ to select **B**ottom, type **0**, and press ⏎Enter.

9. Press ⌊Q⌋⌊Q⌋ to select **Q**uit twice to return to the **P**rint menu.

10. To create the PRN file on-disk, press ⌊S⌋ to select **S**preadsheet Print.

    Note: The **A**lign and **F**orm Feed commands are not necessary when creating a PRN file because you are not using printer paper.

11. To return to READY mode, press ⌊Q⌋ to select **Q**uit.

12. Follow the instructions in your word processing, database, or other software program to import the ASCII file.

```
MEMO TO:      T. Ryan
FROM:         T.J. Roche
DATE:         April 21, 1992
SUBJECT:      REGIONAL SALES REPORT

As you requested in our meeting on April 13, I have reviewed the
first quarter's sales for each of our four regional offices.  The
South office, as indicated in the following table, remains our
strongest sales force in the country.

REGIONAL INCOME REPORT

                  January      February      March

North            $167,900     $230,000     $300,000
South            $657,200     $700,000     $825,000
East             $342,650     $560,800     $690,400
West             $480,700     $670,000     $750,000

TOTALS BY MONTH: $1,648,450   $2,160,800   $2,565,400


B:\SLSRPT.MMO                     Doc 1 Pg 1 Ln 2.5" Pos 1"
```

In this example, the PRN file just created has been imported into WordPerfect, a popular word processing program.

9

Note: If you use a PostScript printer and want to create an ASCII file, you need to specify a non-PostScript printer driver. To specify a non-PostScript printer driver, select /**O**ptions **H**ardware **P**rinters **1**st (or **2**nd) Printer. Then select **T**ype of Printer and specify a non-PostScript printer, such as an IBM graphics printer. If you then print to a file while using a PostScript driver, you will produce an ASCII file of PostScript instruction codes.

Summary

This chapter showed you how to print reports by selecting the **P**rint command from Quattro Pro's main menu. You can use the /**P**rint **D**estination **P**rinter command to print a report to a printer, or the /**P**rint **D**estination **F**ile command to create a PRN file on-disk that you or someone else can print later.

You learned how to print a document of one page or less, to add headings to a multipage report, and to hide spreadsheet segments within the print block. You also learned how to control paper movement with the **S**kip Line, **F**orm Feed, and **A**lign options and how to create page breaks within a spreadsheet.

The chapter also indicated ways to enhance printouts. You can add headers and footers that can include the date and a page number. You also can change the layout of a page by adjusting the margins and the page length.

Specifically, you learned the following key information about Quattro Pro:

- The /**P**rinter **D**estination **P**rinter command enables you to print reports on a printer, and the /**P**rinter **D**estination **F**ile command enables you to "print" a block to a file you can import within other software programs.

- To print the current information as it is shown on-screen, press ⬆Shift-PrtSc (or PrtSc if you have an enhanced keyboard) when your screen is in Text mode.

- The /**P**rint **H**eadings command enables you to print specified rows and/or columns on each page of a printed report.

- When you are printing reports, you can hide specific rows, columns, or blocks. Columns are hidden by selecting /**S**tyle **H**ide Column after specifying a print block; rows are hidden by the /**S**tyle **I**nsert Break command or by entering the symbol for nonprinting—two vertical bars (¦¦)—in the first cell of the row; blocks are hidden with the command /**S**tyle **N**umeric Format **H**idden.

- The /**P**rint **A**djust Printer **S**kip Line command advances the paper one line in the printer, and the /**P**rint **A**djust Printer **F**orm Feed command advances the paper to the top of the next page.

- The /**P**rint **A**djust Printer **A**lign command ensures that printing will begin at the top of all succeeding pages after the first. Before printing, always make sure that your printer paper is correctly positioned.

- The /**P**rint **D**estination **S**creen Preview command enables you to view your report on-screen before you send it to your printer.

9

■ The /Print Format Cell-Formulas command prints a cell-by-cell listing of a specified block. The listing includes the cell's location, format, width, protection status, and contents (including formulas). The /Print Format As Displayed command prints cell contents as they appear on-screen.

■ The /Print Layout Reset command resets some or all of a spreadsheet's print settings. /Print Layout Reset Print Block clears only the specified print block, and /Print Layout Reset All clears all settings, including the print block, headings, margins, and other settings.

The next chapter discusses some useful file-management techniques. You learn how to erase a file in memory, protect files with passwords, save and retrieve parts of files, and link cells between spreadsheets. You also learn how to change the drive and directory and import files from other programs into Quattro Pro.

9

10

Managing Files

In Chapter 3, you learned some of the basic file management tasks. You learned to name, save, and retrieve files. In this chapter, you learn some of the other valuable procedures for managing files. For example, you learn how to remove a file from memory. Also, you learn how to protect files with passwords so that unauthorized users cannot access them. Each password you assign can be easily changed or deleted, but only by those who know the current password.

This chapter also explains how to save and retrieve parts of files. You learn how to extract a section of data from a spreadsheet and save that section as a file, and you learn how to combine sections of several files into one master file. The latter capability is useful for consolidating data from similar spreadsheets. Individual cells can contain formulas that reference information in another spreadsheet on-disk. These linked cells are automatically updated when you retrieve a file containing the links.

You also learn to list different types of files on-screen, change the default drive and directory (either permanently or temporarily for only the current Quattro Pro session), delete spreadsheet and other Quattro Pro files, and import files from outside programs into Quattro Pro.

Erasing a file from memory

Protecting files with passwords

Saving and retrieving partial files

Linking cells between files

Specifying a drive and directory

Deleting files

Importing files into Quattro Pro

Key Terms in This Chapter

Password	A string of up to 15 characters you can use to limit access to spreadsheet files.
File linking	A Quattro Pro feature that enables you to use formulas in the current spreadsheet to refer to values in other spreadsheets.
ASCII file	A text (or print) file created in another program; you can import an ASCII file into a Quattro Pro spreadsheet with the /Tools Import command.
Template	An empty master file that is useful when combining files. A template normally contains the same labels as the spreadsheets you are combining, but the area containing the specific data values remains blank.

Erasing a File from Memory

The /File Erase command clears the current spreadsheet from the screen and memory and replaces it with a blank spreadsheet. The effect is the same as if you were to quit Quattro Pro and restart it from the operating system. You can use this command to create a new spreadsheet—with no data and the default spreadsheet settings. This command does not erase the spreadsheet file stored on-disk.

Be sure that you understand the difference between the /File Erase command and the /Edit Erase Block command. The /File Erase command removes the entire spreadsheet and replaces it with a new spreadsheet. The /Edit Erase Block command removes a block from the current spreadsheet. After you issue the /File Erase command, the spreadsheet is exactly as it was when you loaded Quattro Pro—all the default settings are instituted because you are working with a new spreadsheet. If you want to preserve the settings and simply remove the data from the spreadsheet, use the /Edit Erase Block command to erase every cell in the spreadsheet. The /Edit Erase Block command does not alter any of the global settings, such as column widths, cell formats, and print settings.

To erase a spreadsheet from the screen and the computer's memory, follow these steps:

10

1. Press ⧄ to access the Quattro Pro menu.
2. Press ⟨F⟩ to select **F**ile.

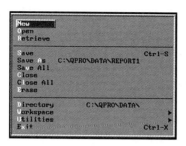

Quattro Pro displays the menu of **F**ile commands.

3. Press ⟨E⟩ to select **E**rase.

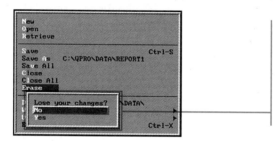

Because this command is potentially destructive, Quattro Pro prompts you for verification.

4. To erase the spreadsheet, press ⟨Y⟩ to select **Y**es.

   Or

   If you change your mind or need to save your file before erasing the spreadsheet, press ⟨↵Enter⟩ to select the default option **N**o.

Note: After you erase a spreadsheet with /**F**ile **E**rase, you cannot recover it unless the Undo feature is active and you press ⟨Alt⟩-⟨F5⟩ before you issue the next command. You should always save a spreadsheet that you want to keep, before you clear the spreadsheet with this command.

Protecting Files with Passwords

You can protect your files by using Quattro Pro's password protection system. When saving files, you can specify passwords that prevent unauthorized users from accessing the protected files. Only those who know the password for a

10

protected file can retrieve that file. This feature is particularly useful for confidential information such as sales and payroll data.

Creating a Password

You can create a /File Save command so that your file can be retrieved only by entering the exact password.

To assign a password to a spreadsheet, follow these steps when saving a file:

1. Press ⌿ to access the Quattro Pro menu.
2. Press F to select File.
3. For a previously saved file, press A to select Save As.

   For a new file, press S to select Save.
4. In the dialog box that appears, type a file name, press **space bar**, type **P**, and press ⏎Enter.

In this example, the name of the file being assigned a password is INCOME91.

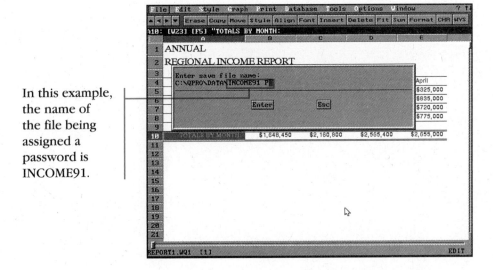

5. When the dialog box appears, type a password (no more than 15 characters) and press ⏎Enter.

10

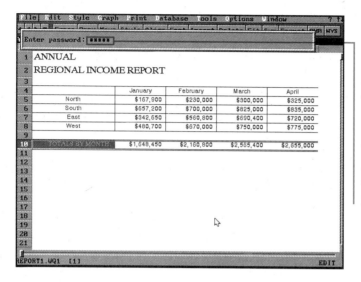

The password never appears on-screen; it is "hidden" by small boxes that appear as you type each character of the password.

6. When prompted to verify the password, type the password a second time and press ⏎Enter.

If the first and second passwords do not match exactly (including case), Quattro Pro does not accept the password.

10

If the passwords match, Quattro Pro saves the file with the new password. In the future, only those who know the password can retrieve the file.

Note: Quattro Pro accepts any character in a password, including spaces. A password can contain as many as 15 characters. You need to be careful, however, because Quattro Pro accepts the password only in the exact upper-case or lowercase letters you entered. For example, if you entered **pdfund** as your password, Quattro Pro does not retrieve the file if you type **PDFUND**, **PDfund**, or any other combination of uppercase and lowercase letters. Be sure to remember your password. If you forget your password, it is impossible to open the file. As a precaution, you may want to copy the file before you password protect it, and keep it in a secure place such as a safe.

Retrieving a Password-Protected File

Use the /File Retrieve command and type the file's password to open a protected file.

To retrieve a file protected with a password, follow these steps:

1. Press [/] to access the Quattro Pro menu.
2. Press [F] to select File.
3. Press [R] to select Retrieve.
4. Select the file you want to retrieve by highlighting or typing the file name, and then press [↵Enter].
5. When the prompt Enter password appears, type your password exactly as you did when you created it; then press [↵Enter].

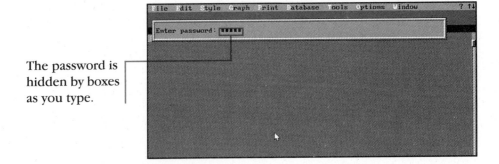

The password is hidden by boxes as you type.

If you enter the password correctly, the spreadsheet appears. If you enter the wrong password, however, Quattro Pro displays the error message Invalid Password, and the mode indicator flashes ERROR. Press [Esc] or [↵Enter] to return to a blank spreadsheet.

Deleting a Password

Quattro Pro enables you to delete passwords. First, you must retrieve the file containing the password you want to delete. Then, when you are ready to save the file, you select the /File Save As command and erase the [Password protected] message.

To delete password protection from a file, follow these steps:

1. Press [/] to access the Quattro Pro menu.

10

2. Press [F] to select **F**ile.

3. Press [A] to select Save **A**s.

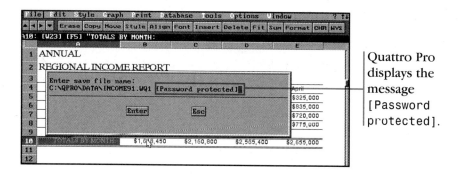

Quattro Pro displays the message [Password protected].

4. Press [◆Backspace] once to erase [Password protected].

5. Press [↵Enter] to save the file without the password.

Changing a Password

To change a password, you must delete the existing password during a /**F**ile **S**ave operation and then enter a new one. The first part of the procedure is the same as you use to delete a password, and the last part is the same as you use to create a new password.

To change a password, follow these steps:

1. Press [/] to access the Quattro Pro menu.

2. Press [F] to select **F**ile.

3. Press [A] to select Save **A**s.

4. Press [◆Backspace] once to erase [Password protected].

5. In the dialog box that appears, type a file name, press **space bar**, type **P**, and press [↵Enter].

6. When the dialog box appears, type the password and press [↵Enter].

7. When prompted to verify the password, retype the password and press [↵Enter].

After you complete these steps, Quattro Pro saves the file with the new password.

10

Saving and Retrieving Partial Files

Sometimes you may want to store only part of a spreadsheet, such as a block of cells, in a separate file on-disk. For example, suppose that you want to extract payments from an expense report or revenues from an income statement. Quattro Pro's /Tools Xtract command enables you to make such extractions. One of the best uses for an extraction is to break up spreadsheet files that are too large to fit on a single disk.

Conversely, you may have several spreadsheets with similar information. Suppose that you own a store in which each department is its own profit center. At the end of the month, you may want to retrieve a partial file from each department's spreadsheet and combine the files to get the overall picture of the store's profit and loss. You can use the /Tools Combine command to perform this operation.

Extracting Data

With the /Tools Xtract command, you can save part of the spreadsheet file—either the formulas in a block of cells or the current values of the formulas in that block, depending on the option you select. Both options (Formulas and Values) create a separate spreadsheet file you can reload into Quattro Pro with the /File Retrieve command.

The /Tools Xtract command requires you to specify the portion, or block, of the spreadsheet you want to save. The block can be as small as a cell or as large as the entire spreadsheet.

To copy part of your spreadsheet to a separate file, follow these steps:

1. Press / to access the Quattro Pro menu.
2. Press T to select Tools.
3. Press X to select Xtract.
4. To extract data and preserve any formulas in the extract block, press F to select Formulas.

   Or

   To extract data and convert formulas to values, press V to select Values.

10

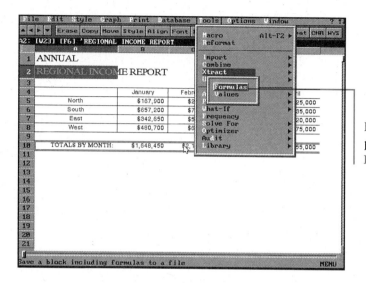

In this example, press F to select Formulas.

5. When the dialog box appears, type a file name for the file in which you want to save the extracted data, and press ⏎Enter.

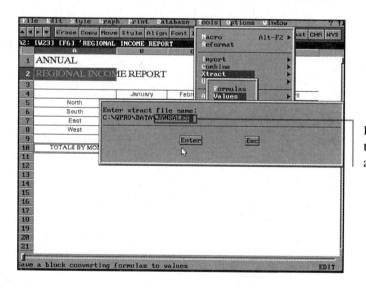

In this example, type **JANSALES** and press ⏎Enter.

6. As prompted in the input line, specify the block you want to extract; then press ⏎Enter.

In this example, highlight the block A2..B10 and press ⏎Enter.

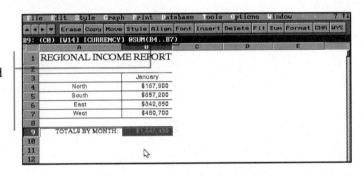

The formula in cell B9 (displayed in the input line) is retained in the new file.

10

In this example, the same block has been extracted; however, the formulas are converted to values with the /Tools Xtract Values command, as shown in cell B9.

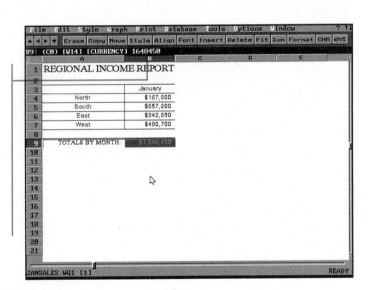

If you choose to select /Tools Xtract Values to save only the current values, remember that the resulting spreadsheet file will contain numbers but no formulas. The /Tools Xtract Formulas command preserves any formulas in the extract block. If your spreadsheet is too large to fit on one disk, the Formulas option is useful because you can split the file across two disks and still preserve the formulas you need. Make sure, however, that all formulas in the block you are extracting refer only to cells in that same block; otherwise the created file has formulas that refer to blank cells. Use /Tools Xtract Values to avoid this problem.

When you select the /Tools Xtract Values command, you "lock" the current values into a spreadsheet. Think of this process as taking a snapshot of the current spreadsheet. You can then reload the new, values-only file into the spreadsheet to perform operations that do not require formulas (such as printing and graphing). Before using /Tools Xtract Values, however, be sure to press Calc (F9) if the CALC indicator appears at the bottom of the screen. This step ensures that the correct formula values are extracted.

Combining Files

Another file management task you may need to perform is copying blocks of cells from other spreadsheets and placing them in strategic spots in the current spreadsheet. For example, if you work in the sales department of a large firm, you may want to combine quarterly sales information by region into one consolidated spreadsheet.

A simple technique for accomplishing this kind of consolidation is to start with and keep a copy of a master file, or *template*. A template can contain the same labels as the spreadsheets you are combining, but the area containing the specific data values remains blank. You should prepare a template before you attempt to combine data. When you start with a blank template, you can copy the first quarterly sales spreadsheet to the template, leaving the original copy of that spreadsheet untouched. Copying a block of cells also can be helpful when you want to combine divisional data into a single consolidated spreadsheet.

Use the /Tools Combine command to combine data from similar files. The Copy option of this command copies the incoming spreadsheet or block into the current spreadsheet. The Add option adds the values from the incoming spreadsheet or block to the values in the current spreadsheet. The Subtract option decreases the values in the current spreadsheet by the values in the incoming spreadsheet or block.

10

To combine data from similar files, follow these steps:

1. Select /File Retrieve to retrieve the blank template file into which you want to combine files.

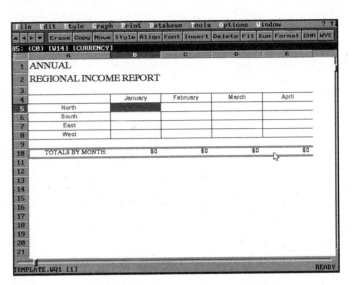

Because this blank template file contains no monthly data, the formulas in row 10 evaluate to zero.

2. Position the cell selector on the first cell of the block in which you want to combine data.

3. Press ⟨/⟩ to access the Quattro Pro menu.

4. Press ⟨T⟩ to select **Tools**.

5. Press ⟨C⟩ to select **Combine**.

6. Press ⟨C⟩ to select **Copy** to copy a spreadsheet or block from another file on top of the existing spreadsheet, starting at the location of the cell selector.

   Or

   Press ⟨A⟩ to select **Add** to add the incoming values in a spreadsheet or block to the values in the existing spreadsheet or block, starting at the location of the cell selector.

   Or

   Press ⟨S⟩ to select **Subtract** to decrease the existing values in a spreadsheet or block by the values in an incoming spreadsheet or block, starting at the location of the cell selector.

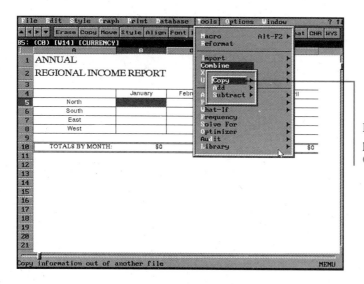

In this example, press C to select Copy.

7. To copy an entire file, press F to select File.

   Or

   To copy a specific block from a file, press B to select Block.

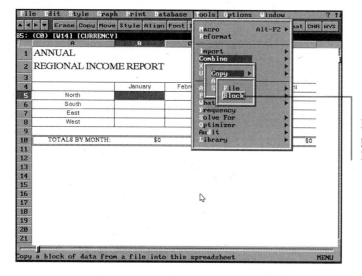

In this example, press B to select Block.

8. If you selected File in step 7, skip to step 9.

   If you selected Block in step 7, type the block name or location of the incoming block and press ⏎Enter.

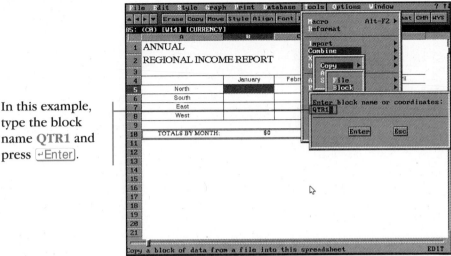

In this example, type the block name **QTR1** and press ⏎Enter.

9. When the dialog box appears, enter the name of the file containing the data you want to combine, and press ⏎Enter.

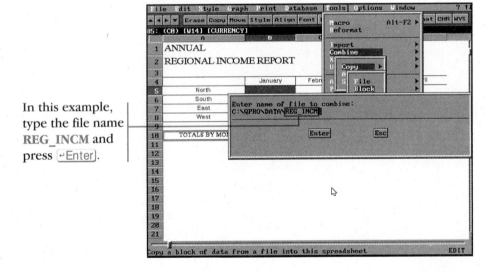

In this example, type the file name **REG_INCM** and press ⏎Enter.

10

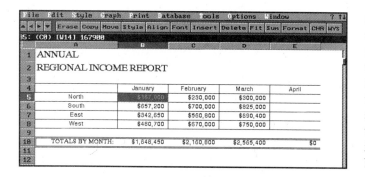

Quattro Pro copies the first-quarter data to the block B5..D8 in the blank template and automatically updates the formulas in the block B10..D10.

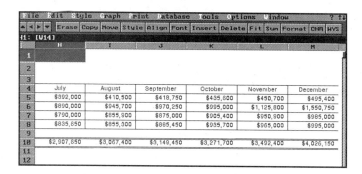

After you have combined data for all quarters, the result is a filled-in version of the template. The formulas in row 10 display values.

The /Tools Combine Copy command pulls in an entire spreadsheet or named block and causes the new contents to write over the corresponding cells in the current spreadsheet. Make sure that you correctly position the cell selector before you execute the /Tools Combine command.

10

In this example, the Add option has added the values in the center spreadsheet to the values in the corresponding cells of the top (current) spreadsheet, resulting in the combined values shown in the bottom spreadsheet.

10

With the Add option, you can pull in the values from an entire spreadsheet or a named block and add those values to corresponding cells in the current spreadsheet. The Add option affects only the blank cells in the spreadsheet, or cells that contain numeric values. In the current spreadsheet, cells that contain formulas or labels do not change. In the spreadsheet being combined, cells that contain labels or string formulas are not added.

In this example, the Subtract option has subtracted the values in the center spreadsheet from the values in the corresponding cells of the top (current) spreadsheet, resulting in the combined values shown in the bottom spreadsheet.

With the Subtract option, you can pull in the values from an entire spreadsheet or a named block and subtract those values from the corresponding cells in the current spreadsheet. When an existing cell is blank, the incoming value is subtracted from zero. Like Add, Subtract affects only the blank cells in the spreadsheet or cells that contain numeric values. In the current spreadsheet, cells containing formulas or labels are unaffected. In the spreadsheet being combined, cells that contain labels or string formulas are not subtracted.

Linking Cells between Files

Quattro Pro enables you to use formulas to link a cell in one spreadsheet to a cell in another. The cell that receives the information is called the *primary* cell, and the one that sends the information is the *supporting* cell. After you establish this link for a given cell in a spreadsheet and save the spreadsheet with /File Save or /File Save As, Quattro Pro automatically updates the linked formulas whenever you retrieve the file.

Unlike the /Tools Combine command, which you must use every time you want to copy information from file to file, the cell link feature is automatic and requires no active use of commands.

The following section discusses how to create links from a spreadsheet in memory to a spreadsheet on-disk. You also can use this technique to create links among several spreadsheets in memory. To learn more about linking multiple spreadsheets in memory, see Que's *Using Quattro Pro 4*, Special Edition.

Establishing a Link

Linking is performed within the target cell, using a special kind of formula. The formula begins with a plus sign (+), followed by the left-bracket symbol ([), the name of the sending file (including the directory name if the file is not in the current directory), the right-bracket symbol (]), and finally, the address or block name of the source cell.

The entry +[NORTH]NORTH_JAN in cell B5 of the current spreadsheet, for example, means that B5 is to contain the data found in cell C7 of the file NORTH.WQ1 in the current directory. When this cell entry is complete, data copying occurs at once. For the link to become permanent and automatic (occurring with every subsequent /File Retrieve operation), use the /File Save command on the current spreadsheet.

10

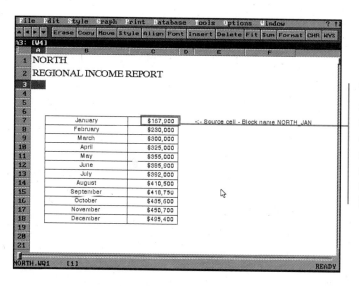

The regional income report for the North region contains a source cell—C7. The source cell has the block name NORTH_JAN.

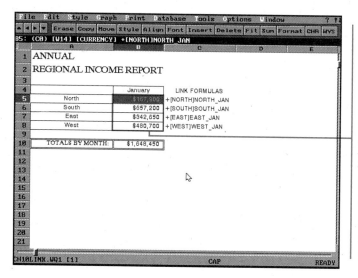

Cells B5..B8 of the target file (the annual regional income report) contain link formulas that link these cells to the supporting cells in the files NORTH, SOUTH, EAST, and WEST. The link formulas are shown in text format in column C.

10

In this example, cell B5 is linked to cell C7 (a block called NORTH_JAN) of a file named NORTH.WQ1. Cell B6 is linked to block SOUTH_JAN of a file named SOUTH.WQ1. Cell B7 is linked to block WEST_JAN of a file named WEST.WQ1. Cell B8 is linked to block EAST_JAN of a file named EAST.WQ1. When you enter the link formulas, you do not have to type the file extension WQ1 after the file name. Quattro Pro assumes that you are linking to another Quattro Pro spreadsheet.

313

Whenever you retrieve the target file, Quattro Pro automatically updates cells B5 through B8 with information from the supporting files. When you alter a cell that serves as a supporting cell, Quattro Pro does not immediately copy its contents to the primary cell or cells to which it is linked. In fact, you may change a supporting cell and save its file many times, yet the primary cell may not reflect any of these interim values. The contents of the primary cell are updated only upon retrieval of the file containing the primary cell.

When you retrieve or open the primary file, Quattro Pro displays a dialog box with three choices regarding the linked information.

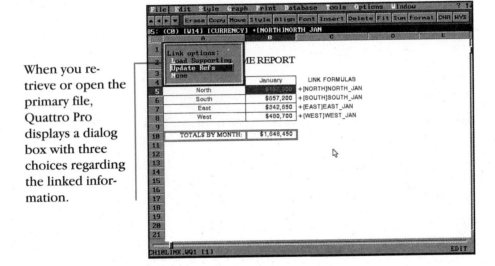

The Load Supporting option opens all files that are source files for the primary file, which is handy if you need to adjust figures in the source files. The Update Refs option updates the primary file links. This option ensures that the linked information is updated for any changes to the source files. You should choose the None option if you do not want Quattro Pro to update the linking references in the primary file. This option causes Quattro Pro to display NA (Not Available) in each cell that contains a link in the primary file.

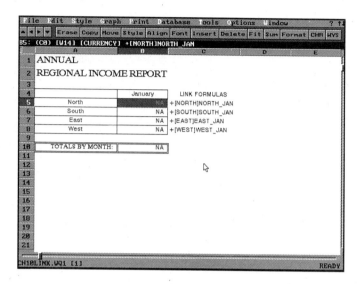

This primary file was retrieved with the None option chosen for linked references.

You can change a link from NA status to the source cell contents while working with the primary file; you use the /Tools Update Links Refresh command, discussed in the next section.

Refreshing Links

If you are using Quattro Pro in a network or multiuser environment, others may be altering files that contain supporting cells for the spreadsheet you are using. In this case, you may want periodic updating of your primary cells. Use the /Tools Update Links Refresh command to update some or all of the primary cells in the current spreadsheet to reflect the current contents of the supporting cells.

To refresh the cells linked to the current spreadsheet, follow these steps:

1. Press / to access the Quattro Pro menu.
2. Press T to select Tools.
3. Press U to select Update Links.
4. Press R to select Refresh.

10

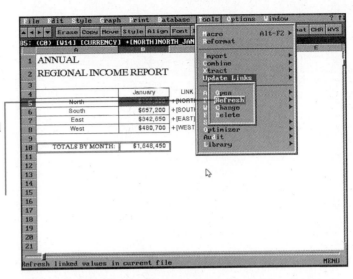

The **U**pdate Links
Refresh command
updates the
values of cells
linked to other
spreadsheets.

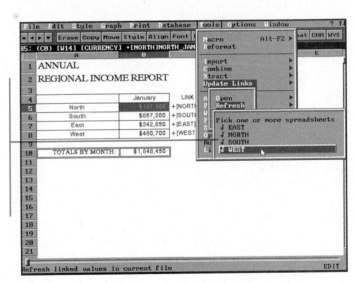

Quattro Pro lists
each source file
for the primary
file. In this
example, each file
is checked so that
all the links in the
primary file are
updated.

You can use the mouse to check each file quickly; click each file name to
check it.

10

316

Specifying a Drive and Directory

You use the /Options Startup Directory command or the /File Directory command to change the drive and directory. After installing Quattro Pro, the default directory is the directory containing the Quattro Pro program files.

/Options Startup Directory changes the default drive and directory to one that contains your data files. /File Directory, on the other hand, changes the drive and directory temporarily for only the current spreadsheet session.

To change the default directory, follow these steps:

1. Press / to access the Quattro Pro menu.
2. Press O to select Options.
3. Press S to select Startup.
4. Press D to select Directory. The current default directory appears.

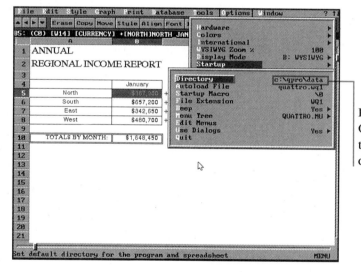

In this example, C:\QPRO\DATA is the default directory.

5. Press +Backspace to clear the current default directory, type the new default directory name, and press ↵Enter. Remember to type the drive letter before the directory name.

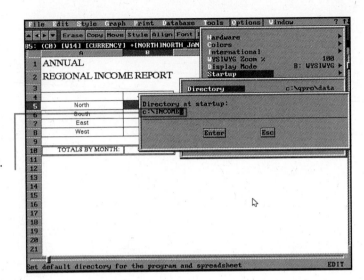

In this example,
type **C:\INCOME**
and press ⏎Enter.

6. Press Q to select **Q**uit.

7. Press U to select **U**pdate.

   This command updates a program file that enables Quattro Pro to use the new default directory in future sessions.

8. Press Q to select **Q**uit to return to READY mode.

With a hard disk, you can use the default directory setting to your advantage. As in the preceding example, you can set the default directory to C:\INCOME. When you want to retrieve a file, Quattro Pro displays all the subdirectories and files stored in the C:\INCOME directory. After you choose the proper directory, Quattro Pro again displays the subdirectories and files stored in that directory so that you can make a choice. Setting the default directory this way saves time if you use spreadsheets in different subdirectories.

If you are working with files in a different directory than the one you normally use, you can change the directory temporarily with the /File Directory command. This command overrides the default directory for only the current session.

To change the current directory, follow these steps:

1. Press / to access the Quattro Pro menu.

2. Press F to select **F**ile.

10

318

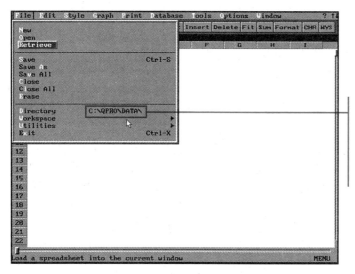

The **File** menu in this example shows C:\QPRO\DATA as the current directory.

3. Press D to select **Directory**. Quattro Pro displays the name of the current directory.

4. Type the new directory name and press Enter (the current directory name automatically clears when you start typing). Remember to type the drive letter before the directory name.

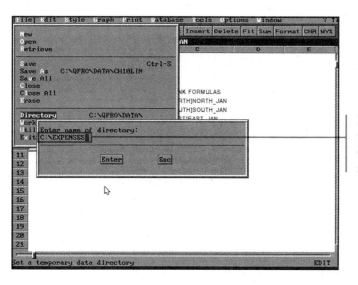

In this example, type **C:\EXPENSES** and press Enter.

10

Quattro Pro changes the directory for only the current session. The next time you access Quattro Pro, the default directory again becomes the current directory.

Deleting Files

When you save files to a diskette, you may sometimes find that the diskette is full. To alert you, Quattro Pro displays the message Disk full at the bottom of the screen, and the mode indicator flashes ERROR. You can then either swap diskettes or delete one or more of the files occupying space on the diskette.

To delete files from within Quattro Pro, access DOS with the /File Utilities DOS Shell command and erase the files at the DOS level with the DOS commands ERASE or DEL.

To delete a file from within Quattro Pro, follow these steps:

1. Press / to access the Quattro Pro menu.
2. Press F to select File.
3. Press U to select Utilities.
4. Press D to select DOS Shell.

After you select DOS Shell, Quattro Pro prompts you to press ↵Enter to suspend Quattro Pro temporarily and go to DOS.

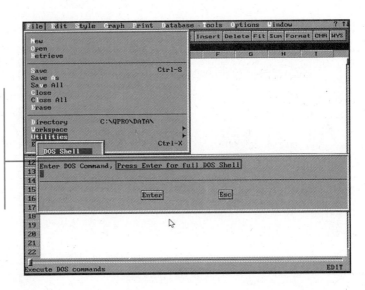

10

320

5. Press ⏎Enter to go to DOS.

6. Type **DIR** at the DOS prompt and press ⏎Enter.

```
Type Exit to return to Quattro

COMPAQ DOS Version 4.01
              (C)Copyright Compaq Computer Corp 1982-1989
              (C)Copyright Microsoft Corp 1981-1988

C:\QPRO\DATA>dir t*.*

 Volume in drive C is INVENT
 Volume Serial Number is 2428-07ED
 Directory of  C:\QPRO\DATA

TJTOOLS   WQ1      3478 02-03-92   10:00a
TOOLS3    WQ1      3469 02-04-92    3:18p
TOOLS4    WQ1      4189 02-04-92    4:35p
TOOLS2    WQ1      3664 02-04-92   12:09p
TOOLS5    WQ1      4370 02-08-92    2:58p
TEST1     WQ1      8855 02-09-92   10:56a
TEMPLATE  WQ1      9189 02-08-92    9:49p
TWO       WQ1      9597 02-08-92   10:19p
THREE     WQ1      9562 02-08-92   10:20p
        9 File(s)     7307264 bytes free

C:\QPRO\DATA>
```

In this example, type **dir t*.*** and press ⏎Enter to list all files that begin with the letter *T*.

7. Type **DEL** or **ERASE**, press **space bar** once, type the name and file extension of the file you want to delete, and press ⏎Enter.

```
Type Exit to return to Quattro

COMPAQ DOS Version 4.01
              (C)Copyright Compaq Computer Corp 1982-1989
              (C)Copyright Microsoft Corp 1981-1988

C:\QPRO\DATA>dir t*.*

 Volume in drive C is INVENT
 Volume Serial Number is 2428-07ED
 Directory of  C:\QPRO\DATA

TJTOOLS   WQ1      3478 02-03-92   10:00a
TOOLS3    WQ1      3469 02-04-92    3:18p
TOOLS4    WQ1      4189 02-04-92    4:35p
TOOLS2    WQ1      3664 02-04-92   12:09p
TOOLS5    WQ1      4370 02-08-92    2:58p
TEST1     WQ1      8855 02-09-92   10:56a
TEMPLATE  WQ1      9189 02-08-92    9:49p
TWO       WQ1      9597 02-08-92   10:19p
THREE     WQ1      9562 02-08-92   10:20p
        9 File(s)     7307264 bytes free

C:\QPRO\DATA>
C:\QPRO\DATA>del test1.wq1
```

In this example, delete the file TEST1.WQ1.

10

321

8. To return to Quattro Pro, type **exit** and press ⏎Enter.

As you saw in the example, before you delete files in DOS, you can use the wild-card characters described in Chapter 3 to display a list of files that begin or end with specific characters. These characters are the same familiar wild-card characters used for DOS and other commands throughout Quattro Pro. The following list shows some examples of using wild-card characters:

Wild card	Description
*	Matches the remaining characters of a file name. For example, C*.WQ1 matches CHICAGO.WQ1, CASHFLOW.WQ1, and CENTERS.WQ1. You also can use the wild card to match all files, whether they are Quattro Pro files or not. For example, B*.* matches BUDGET91.WQ1, BOSS.DOC, and BOSTON.WK1.
?	Matches all characters in a single position in a file name. For example, SALES8? matches SALES88 and SALES89, but not SALES90 or SALES.

Be careful when you delete files. After you delete a file, you cannot recover it by conventional means. Always double-check before you delete a file.

You also can use Quattro Pro's File Manager to delete files, accessed with the /File Utilities File Manager command. To learn more about the File Manager, see Que's *Using Quattro Pro 4*, Special Edition.

10

Importing Files into Quattro Pro

Powerful features of Quattro Pro are its capability to transfer data between Quattro Pro and other programs and to import ASCII text files. To perform a transfer, you use the /Tools Import and /Print Destination File commands (the latter command is fully discussed in Chapter 9, "Printing Reports").

Importing ASCII Text Files

The /Tools Import command enables you to "import," or copy, standard *ASCII files* to specific locations in the current spreadsheet. ASCII, an acronym for

American Standard Code for Information Interchange, is a file format that many programs can understand and has therefore become a standard means of data communication in the computer industry. PRN (print) files, for example, are standard ASCII text files created to print after the current Quattro Pro session. Other standard ASCII files include those produced in various word processing and BASIC programs. Many programs, such as database and word processing programs, have the capability to produce ASCII files, as does Quattro Pro.

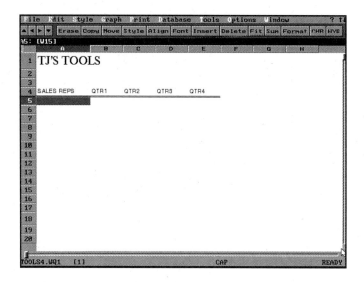

Suppose that you want to import data from an ASCII file into this blank Quattro Pro database.

10

To import an ASCII text file into Quattro Pro, follow these steps:

1. Press ⟦/⟧ to access the Quattro Pro menu.
2. Press ⟦T⟧ to select **T**ools.
3. Press ⟦I⟧ to select **I**mport.
4. Press ⟦A⟧ to select **A**SCII Text File.

   Generally, you should use the **A**SCII Text File option to import an ASCII file created with your word processing program.

   Use the **O**nly Commas option when you import delimited files—that is, ASCII files that contain commas as separator characters to distinguish items of data.

   You should use the **C**omma & " " Delimited File option when you import ASCII files delimited by commas and quotation marks.

5. To display files in a different drive or directory, or with a different extension, type the appropriate drive and directory. Then use wild-card characters (* or ?) and press ⏎Enter to display the desired files.

As shown here, typing *.**PRN** causes Quattro Pro to display a list of all subdirectories and PRN files in the current directory (C:\QPRO\DATA, in this example).

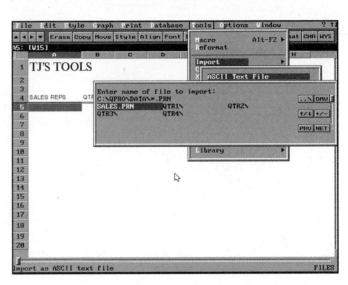

6. Highlight the name of the text file you want to import, and press ⏎Enter. For example, highlight the file name SALES.PRN and press ⏎Enter.

10

The ASCII text file is imported into Quattro Pro.

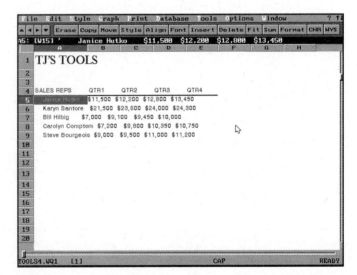

Notice that the imported data does not correctly line up in columns. You must use the /Data Parse command to line up the data in columns (see Chapter 12, "Managing Data," for information on this command). If you select /Tools Import Only Commas or /Tools Import Comma & " " Delimited File, Quattro Pro separates the labels and numbers in the imported file with commas, colons, semicolons, or spaces. Remember that if you use either of these options to import a file, Quattro Pro does not import any column headings that aren't enclosed in commas or commas and quotation marks, respectively. Headings enclosed in quotation marks are imported as labels.

Importing and Exporting Files from Other Programs

Quattro Pro can import files from and export files to the programs listed in table 10.1.

Table 10.1
Files Quattro Pro Can Import and Export

Program	File Extension
Spreadsheets	
Allways	ALL
Impress	FMT
Impress (1-2-3 3.0 WYSIWYG	FM3
Lotus 1-2-3, Educational Release	WKE
Lotus 1-2-3, Release 1A	WKS
Lotus 1-2-3, Release 3.0	WK3
Lotus 1-2-3, Releases 2.01, 2.2, 2.3	WK1
MultiPlan	SLK
Quattro	WKQ
Surpass	WKP
Symphony 1.2	WRK
Symphony 2.0, 2.2	WR1
VisiCalc	DIF

continues

325

Table 10.1 *(Continued)*

Program	File Extension
Databases	
dBASE II	DB2
dBASE III, III PLUS, IV	DBF
Paradox	DB
Reflex 1.0	RXD
Reflex 2.0	R2D
Graphics	
Harvard Graphics	CHT

To export a Quattro Pro WQ1 file to one of the preceding formats, select the /File Save As command. Type the name of the file and the appropriate extension, and press ⏎Enter. Quattro Pro automatically performs the translation for you and saves the file in the format you selected.

Note: You need to perform an additional step to retrieve a file saved in dBASE II format with Quattro Pro. At the DOS prompt, type RENAME *filename*.DB2 *filename*.DBF, where *filename* is the name of your dBASE II file, and press ⏎Enter. This step is necessary because dBASE II and dBASE III use the same file-name extension (DBF) but have different file formats.

To import a file from one of the programs listed in table 10.1 into Quattro Pro, select the /File Retrieve command. Type the name of the file and its extension, and press ⏎Enter. Quattro Pro automatically performs the translation and loads the file into memory.

Summary

Knowing how to manage files is essential to use Quattro Pro efficiently. Aside from the basic tasks of naming, saving, and retrieving files, which you learned in Chapter 3, you sometimes need to perform other file management tasks. This chapter showed you how to erase a file from memory and protect files with passwords. You also learned how to save partial files when you want to extract or combine portions of a spreadsheet. You can delete files with ease if you know how to specify drives, subdirectories, and file names accurately. You

10

can even import and export files from other leading spreadsheet and database programs.

Specifically, you learned the following key information about Quattro Pro:

■ The /File Erase command removes a file from memory.

■ You can add passwords to your files with the /File Save and /File Save As commands so that only those who know the exact password can retrieve your files.

■ The /Tools Xtract command enables you to save part of a spreadsheet file. You can save either the formulas existing in a block of cells or the current values of the formulas in that block.

■ The /Tools Combine command combines data from different files. You can *copy* the spreadsheet or block you want to combine on top of the current spreadsheet, *add* the values from the combined spreadsheet or block to the values in the current spreadsheet, or *decrease* the values in the current spreadsheet by the values in the combined spreadsheet or block.

■ The /Tools Update Links Refresh command updates all primary cells in the current spreadsheet to reflect the current contents of the supporting cells. This command is particularly helpful for users on a network.

■ The /Options Startup Directory command and the /File Directory command change the current drive and directory. The latter command affects only the current session of Quattro Pro.

■ You can delete files by accessing DOS with the /File Utilities DOS Shell command and erasing the files at the DOS level with the ERASE or DEL commands.

■ The /Tools Import command enables you to transfer data between Quattro Pro and other programs. This command is commonly used to copy standard ASCII files to specific locations in the current spreadsheet.

■ You can use files created in other popular spreadsheet and database programs: select the /File Retrieve command and type the file's name and extension.

The next chapter shows you how to create graphs within Quattro Pro. You learn about the graph creation process, how to select graph types and data blocks, how to enhance the appearance of a graph, and how to print a graph.

10

Creating and Printing Graphs

Even if Quattro Pro were to provide only spreadsheet capabilities, the program would remain extremely powerful. More information can be quickly assembled and tabulated electronically than can possibly be developed manually. But despite the importance of keeping detailed spreadsheets that show real or projected data, that information can be worthless if you cannot readily understand it.

To help decision-makers who are pressed for time or unable to draw conclusions from countless rows of numeric data, and those who may benefit from seeing key figures displayed graphically, Quattro Pro offers graphics capabilities. The program has 11 types of basic business graphs and 4 three-dimensional graph types, as well as many options for enhancing a graph's appearance. Although Quattro Pro is equal to many stand-alone graphics packages, the strength of its graphics capability lies in its integration with the spreadsheet. Using Quattro Pro, you can quickly design and alter graphs as your spreadsheet data changes. This capability means that graphs can be changed almost as fast as Quattro Pro recalculates the data. You also can place a "live" graph into a spreadsheet, further excelling the presentation of data.

Creating a graph: an overview

Selecting a graph type

Enhancing the appearance of a graph

Zooming and panning a graph

Saving graph settings

Placing a graph in a spreadsheet

Printing graphs

11

Key Terms in This Chapter

Graph type	The manner in which data is represented graphically.
X-axis	The horizontal bottom edge of a graph.
Y-axis	The vertical left edge of a graph.
Origin	The intersection of the x-axis and y-axis.
Legend	The description of the shading, color, or symbols assigned to data blocks in line or bar graphs. The legend appears across the bottom or to the right of the graph.
Tick marks	The small marks on the axes of a graph that indicate the increments between the minimum and maximum graph values.

You create graphs with Quattro Pro's /Graph commands. Although the program has a number of options, you need to specify only a graph type and a single data block to create a basic graph. After providing the required information, you select the View option from the Graph menu. This command plots the graph to the screen, temporarily replacing the spreadsheet until you press a key.

With Quattro Pro, you can quickly perform true graphics "what-if" analyses by using the Graph (F10) key to replot a graph after making changes to the spreadsheet. This replotting immediately shows the effects of changes on the current graph.

This chapter explains how to perform the simple four-step procedure for creating a basic graph, how to create 11 basic types of graphs from the data on your spreadsheet, and how to enhance your graphs so that they are presentation quality. You also learn to name and save your graphs in a spreadsheet file you can retrieve and modify at any time, and to place a graph directly into the spreadsheet. Finally, this chapter explains how to print graphs.

Creating a Graph: An Overview

Before creating your first graph, you must determine whether or not the spreadsheet on-screen contains data you want to graph. You also should

330

understand which type of graph is best suited for presenting specific numeric data in picture form.

You can use Quattro Pro's graphics feature to create and view a graph, store its specifications for later use, and print it. Creating and storing a graph requires only that you have the Quattro Pro software installed on your computer, that you correctly select options from the Graph menu, and that you save these options with the associated spreadsheet file.

Hardware Requirements

You must make sure that your hardware supports viewing and printing graphs, and that your Quattro Pro software is correctly installed for graphics.

To view a graph on-screen, you need a graphics monitor or a monitor with a graphics-display adapter. Without this monitor, you can construct and save a Quattro Pro graph, but you must print the graph to view it.

To print a graph, you need a graphics printer that Quattro Pro supports and a separate set of printing procedures, as explained later in this chapter.

The Graph Creation Process

To create a Quattro Pro graph, you begin by retrieving the spreadsheet containing the data you want to graph and then selecting the Graph command from the main menu.

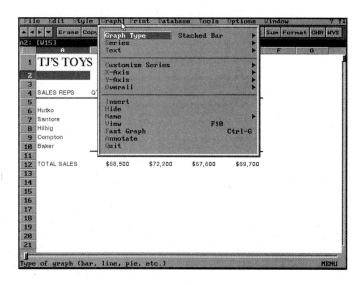

The Graph pull-down menu appears.

Each option on the Graph menu is described in table 11.1.

Table 11.1
Graph Menu Options

Option	Description
Graph Type	Provides options for creating 11 two-dimensional types of graphs: line, bar, XY, stacked bar, pie, area, rotated bar, column, high-low, text, and bubble; and 4 three-dimensional graphs.
Series	Specifies the block you want to use as x-axis labels or values, or labels of pie slices.
Text	Adds titles and legends to a graph.
Customize Series	Customizes the display of an individual data series in your graph.
X-Axis	Adjusts the display and scaling of the x-axis.
Y-Axis	Adjusts the display and scaling of the y-axis.
Overall	Adds lines, patterns, and colors to a graph.
Insert	Inserts a copy of a graph into a spreadsheet.
Hide	Removes a copy of a graph from a spreadsheet.
Name	Assigns a name to one or more graphs and stores the graph settings so that you can re-display the graph(s) whenever you retrieve the spreadsheet file.
View	Displays a graph on the computer monitor.
Fast Graph	Creates a basic graph from a block of cells.
Annotate	Adds text, lines, arrows, and other shapes to a graph.
Quit	Quits the Graph menu and returns the spreadsheet to READY mode.

You use some of these commands every time you create a graph. Other commands (particularly some commands available through Customize Series and Overall) are used less frequently; you use these commands when you

11

need to enhance or customize your graph or when you want to save your graph in a form that can be printed. If you do not need to enhance, customize, or print the graph, creating a graph that displays nothing more than data points is easy.

Only four steps are required to produce a simple graph:

1. Select a graph type (if different from the default type, which is a stacked-bar graph) by selecting the /Graph Graph Type command and specifying the type of graph you want; then press ↵Enter.

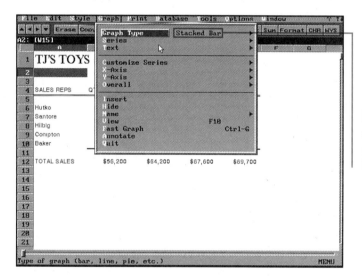

For this example, accept the default graph type, Stacked Bar.

2. Press S to select Series, and then indicate the spreadsheet data blocks you want to graph by selecting one or more of the 1st-6th Series options.

11

To graph Hutko's quarterly sales, for example, select 1st Series, highlight the block B6..E6, and press ⏎Enter.

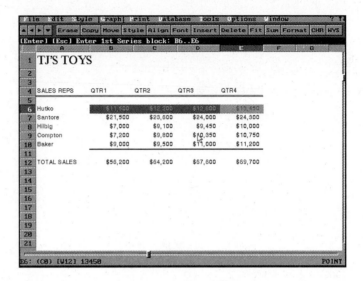

Select series 2nd, 3rd, 4th, and 5th and set up the correct block for each salesperson. Follow the same procedure you followed for setting up series 1st.

In this example, each series is set up for the graph.

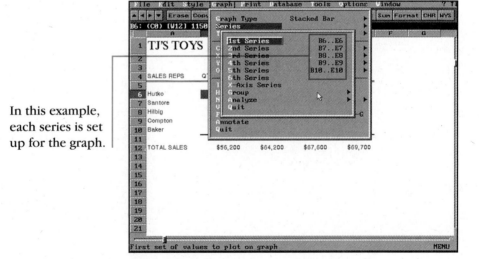

3. Use the X-Axis Series option from the Series menu to indicate the data block for labeling each tick mark along the x-axis.

334

11

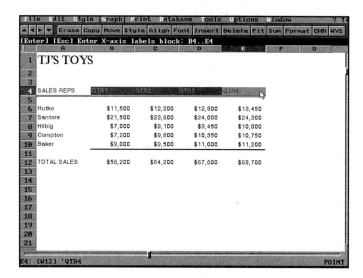

For this example, select **X**-Axis Series, highlight the labels QTR1 through QTR4 in row 4, and press ⏎Enter. Select **Q**uit to leave the **S**eries menu.

You also can use the /**G**raph **S**eries **G**roup command to set all data blocks at once from a contiguous block of cells. By using /**G**raph **S**eries **G**roup, you can combine steps 2 and 3 into a one-step operation. This command is described later in this chapter.

4. Display the graph on-screen by selecting the **V**iew command from the **G**raph menu or by pressing F10 (Graph) when in READY mode. Press ⏎Enter to return to the spreadsheet.

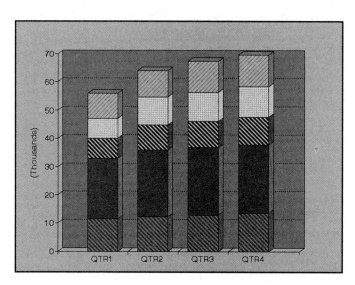

The resulting graph illustrates the default features of a stacked-bar graph.

335

Creating a Basic Graph with Fast Graph

The /Graph Fast Graph command enables you to create a basic graph quickly. By default, Quattro Pro creates a stacked-bar graph when you invoke this command; however, you can change this default graph type. The /Graph Fast Graph command is an alternative to the four-step graph creation process discussed in the preceding section. The data you want to graph, however, must be contiguous; that is, no blank rows or columns can be in the data block.

To create a basic graph with the Fast Graph command, follow these steps:

1. Use the mouse to preselect the block you want to graph, or press ⇧Shift-F7 (Select) and use the arrow keys to highlight the block.

In this example, highlight the block B4..E9.

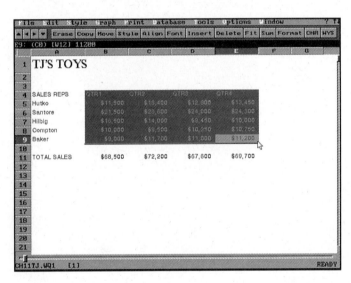

2. Press / to access the Quattro Pro menu.

3. Press G to select **G**raph.

4. Press F to select **F**ast Graph.

11

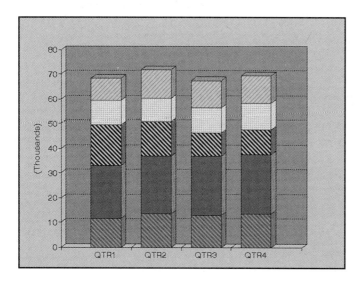

Using the data from the preselected block, Quattro Pro displays a basic graph.

You also can use the Ctrl - G shortcut key combination as an alternative to using the /**G**raph **F**ast Graph command to create a basic graph.

The following line graph illustrates some elements of the Quattro Pro graph.

11

Because Quattro Pro sets a scale based on minimum and maximum values, the program automatically displays a numeric indicator, such as *Thousands*, along the y-axis.

The y-axis measures the amounts of the data being graphed along the vertical axis.

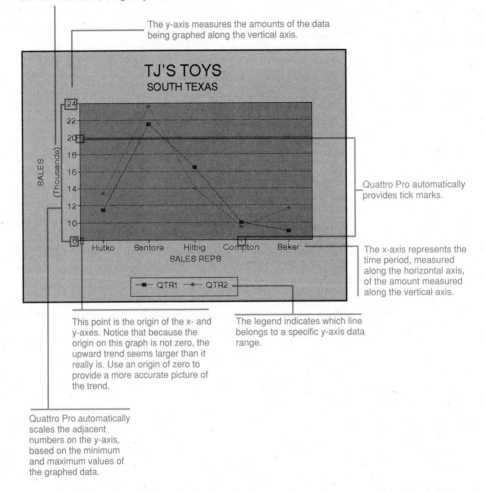

Quattro Pro automatically provides tick marks.

The x-axis represents the time period, measured along the horizontal axis, of the amount measured along the vertical axis.

This point is the origin of the x- and y-axes. Notice that because the origin on this graph is not zero, the upward trend seems larger than it really is. Use an origin of zero to provide a more accurate picture of the trend.

The legend indicates which line belongs to a specific y-axis data range.

Quattro Pro automatically scales the adjacent numbers on the y-axis, based on the minimum and maximum values of the graphed data.

After you create a basic graph using the four-step process or the Fast Graph method, you can choose from among numerous options to change the graph type and add titles, labels, grid lines, and legends. The above line graph, for example, is enhanced in a number of ways to display the data in presentation-quality form. Later in this chapter, you learn more about the many ways in which you can enhance a graph. First, though, you learn the process for creating a basic graph. Specifically, you learn how to select the graph type you need and how to indicate the spreadsheet data you want in the graph.

Selecting a Graph Type

Quattro Pro's graphic capabilities increase the program's power by giving you a way to represent your data visually. Do you want to see whether a trend exists in the latest sales increase of a particular product? A Quattro Pro graph can show you the answer quickly, whereas deciphering that type of information from columns of numbers would be difficult. Quattro Pro offers 11 basic two-dimensional graph types: line, bar, XY, stacked bar, rotated bar, pie, area, high-low, column, text, and bubble; and it offers 4 three-dimensional graph types: area, bar, ribbon, and step.

A line graph is best used for showing numeric data across time.

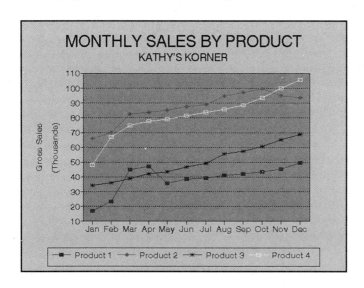

For example, you can track the sales trend of several products with a line graph.

A bar graph, often comparing two or more data items, shows the trend of numeric data across time.

11

For example, you can track the progress of two or more products with a bar graph.

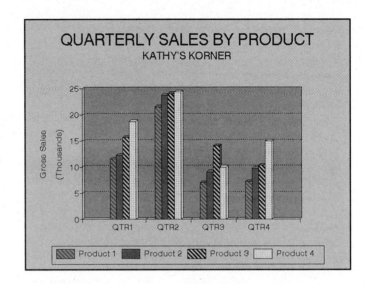

An XY graph compares one numeric data series to another across time to determine whether one set of values (the dependent variable) depends on the other (the independent variable).

Use an XY graph, for example, to plot total sales and advertising percentages to assess whether sales data depends on the share of advertising.

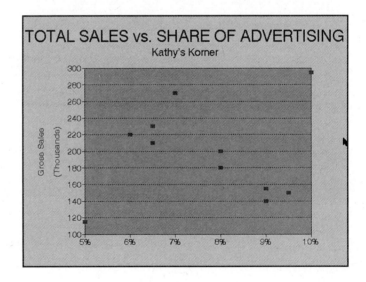

A stacked-bar graph shows two or more data series that total 100 percent of a specific numeric category. (Do not use this type of graph if your data contains negative numbers.)

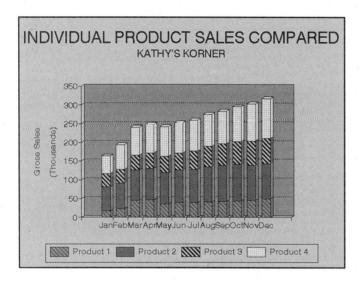

Use a stacked-bar graph, for example, to graph data series for four products (displayed one above the other) to depict the proportion each represents of total product sales throughout the year.

Use a pie graph to graph only one data series in which the components total 100 percent of a specific numeric category. (Do not use this type of graph if your data contains negative numbers.)

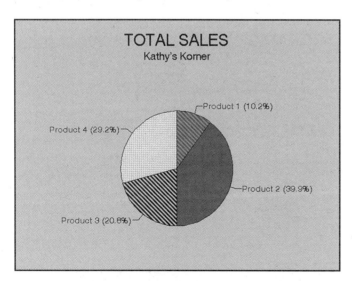

Use a pie graph, for example, to graph the percentage of total sales by month.

11

An area graph is a combination of the line and bar graphs.

Use an area graph to display changes in magnitude (like a bar graph) at points in time, and to display trends over time (like a line graph).

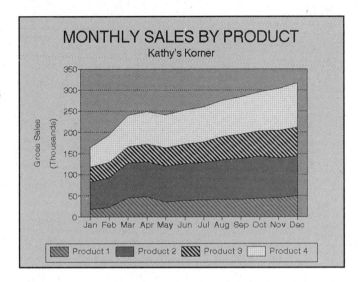

A rotated bar graph, like the bar graph, displays trends over time.

Use a rotated bar graph rather than a bar graph to display the trend of numeric data across time in a horizontal fashion.

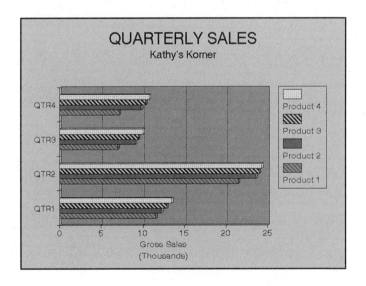

11

A column graph, like a pie graph, shows the individual components of a total.

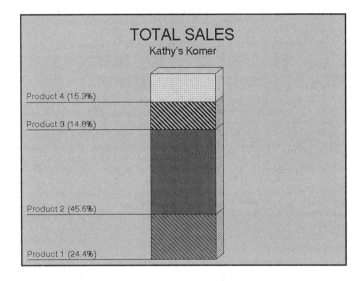

Use a column graph rather than a pie graph when you want to display portions of a total in a vertical fashion.

A high-low graph displays the opening and closing prices of investments.

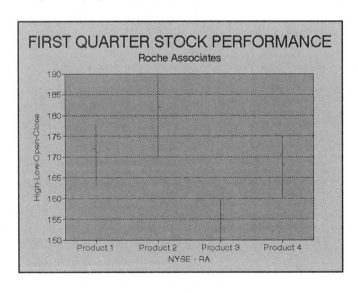

Use a high-low graph to display high, low, open, and closing prices of stocks, commodities, and other items with minimum and maximum values over time.

11

A text graph is a graph that has no x- or y-axis, and no data series. As its name implies, a text graph contains only text.

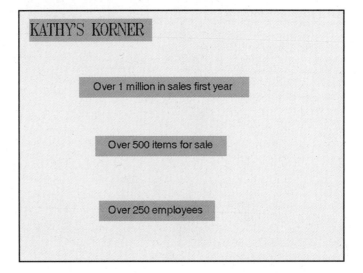

Use text graphs to create organizational charts or bulleted lists for presentations.

A bubble graph is useful because the relative size of the bubbles shows their relationship to each other, not only their positions on the XY grid.

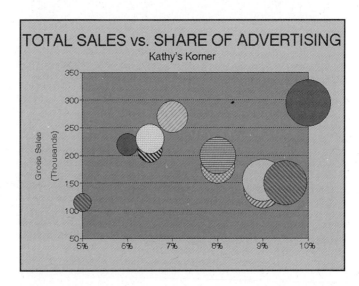

A bubble graph, like an XY graph, shows the relationship between two sets of data.

344

Quattro Pro's three-dimensional graphs add depth to the area, line, and bar graphs. In 3-D graphs, the data series appear in front of each other rather than on top of or beside each other. Quattro Pro places the first data series in the back of the graph, the second data series in front of that one, and so on. Therefore, to see all the data series, you should arrange the spreadsheet with the larger numbers before the smaller numbers. Four types of 3-D graphs are available: ribbon, bar, step, and area.

The 3-D ribbon graph is similar to the two-dimensional line graph. Like the regular line graph, the 3-D ribbon graph is useful for showing time progression.

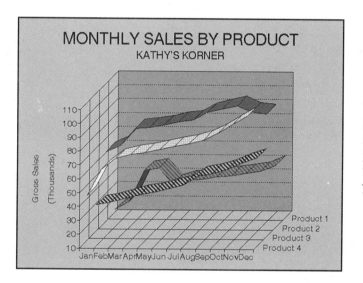

This 3-D ribbon graph shows the sales growth for products 1-4 over the course of a year.

The 3-D area graph is a 3-D ribbon graph with the area under the ribbons filled in. Like the 3-D ribbon graph, the 3-D area graph helps you track trends by displaying a progression of values over a period of time.

11

This 3-D area graph shows the growth trends for products 1-4 over the course of one year.

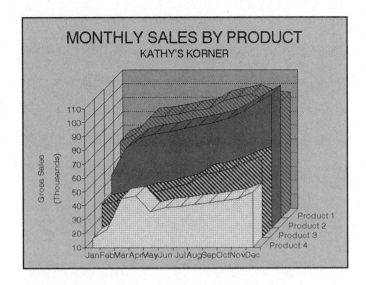

The 3-D bar graph is similar to the two-dimensional bar graph. Like the regular bar graph, the 3-D bar graph is useful for comparing the values of different items at set periods in time.

This 3-D bar graph compares four different products' sales figures for each quarter.

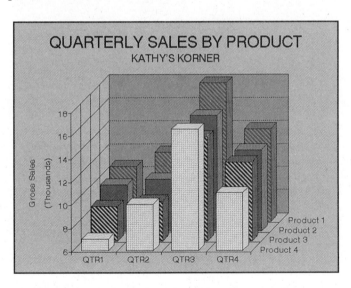

The 3-D step graph resembles the 3-D bar graph, except that the bars for the 3-D step graph are connected, forming a series of steps. The 3-D step graph is an excellent way to compare the margin of growth between products during a period in time.

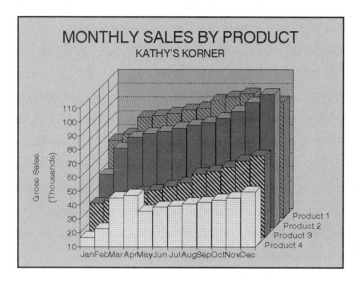

This 3-D step graph shows the product margin of change over the course of one year.

Selecting one of the 11 available graph types is easy. When you select **G**raph Type from the **G**raph menu, Quattro Pro displays the following options: **L**ine, **B**ar, **XY**, **S**tacked Bar, **P**ie, **A**rea, **B**ar, **C**olumn, **H**igh-Low, **T**ext, **B**ubble, and **3**-D Graphs. By selecting one of these options, you set that graph type and automatically return to the **G**raph menu.

To understand which type of graph best displays specific numeric data, you must know something about plotting points on a graph. Take a few minutes now to review two basic terms: *x-axis* and *y-axis*.

All graphs (except pie and text graphs) have two axes: the x-axis is the horizontal bottom edge, and the y-axis is the vertical left edge. Quattro Pro automatically provides tick marks for both axes. The program also scales the adjacent numbers on the y-axis, based on the minimum and maximum figures included in the plotted data block(s).

Every point plotted on a graph has a unique location (x,y): *x* represents the time period or the amount measured along the horizontal axis; *y* measures the corresponding amount along the vertical axis. The intersection of the x-axis and the y-axis is called *the origin*. To avoid the misinterpretation of graph results and to make graphs easier to compare, use a zero origin in your graphs. Later in this chapter, you learn how to manually change the high or low limits of the scale initially set by Quattro Pro.

Of the 11 Quattro Pro graph types, all but the pie and text graphs display both x- and y-axes. All other graphs display numbers (centered on the tick marks) along only the y-axis. The XY graph displays numbers on both axes.

Specifying a Data Series Block

Because more than one type of graph can accomplish the desired presentation, you need to consider which data blocks you want to graph and what relationships among data you want to show. To create a graph, you must specify the block(s) of cells from the current spreadsheet that you want to use as data series.

To enter a data series from the Series menu, select from the following options: 1st Series, 2nd Series, 3rd Series, 4th Series, 5th Series, 6th Series, X-Axis Series, or Group.

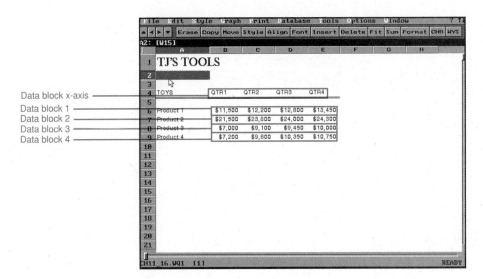

You have the option of separately defining each data block on the spreadsheet or simultaneously defining all the data blocks you want to plot. To define one data block at a time, use the X-Axis Series option and 1st-6th Series options from the Graph Series menu. If all the blocks you want to plot are contiguous (next to each other without any intervening rows or columns), you can use the Group option to define all the blocks at once.

Defining One Data Block at a Time

If the blocks you want to plot are located in various parts of the spreadsheet—that is, the blocks are not all contiguous—you must define one block at a time. You can do so by selecting from among the options **X**-Axis Series and **1**st-6th Series.

To specify the data blocks containing x-axis and y-axis data, follow these steps:

1. Press ⟨ / ⟩ to access the Quattro Pro menu.
2. Press ⟨G⟩ to select **G**raph.
3. Press ⟨G⟩ to select **G**raph Type.

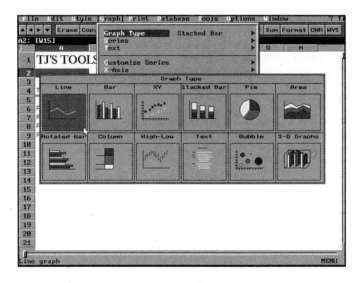

Quattro Pro displays the various graph types.

4. Select the Line graph by pressing ⟨ᴇEnter⟩ or clicking the Line graph display box.
5. Press ⟨S⟩ to select **S**eries from the **G**raph menu.

11

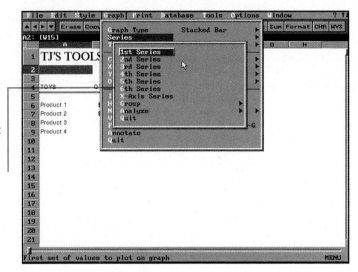

The **S**eries menu enables you to set up as many as six series.

6. From the following options, select the blocks for x- or y-axis data, or labels:

Option	Description
X-Axis Series	Specifies the x-axis label block. X-axis labels are labels such as JAN, FEB, MAR, and so on. This option creates labels for pie graphs and graphs with an x-axis.
1st Series	Specifies the first y-axis data block. This data block is the only one used by a pie graph.
2nd through **6**th Series	Specifies the second through sixth y-axis data blocks.

When you select one of the **X**-Axis or **1**st-**6**th Series options, Quattro Pro prompts you for the cell or block of cells containing the data you want to graph. You cannot enter data directly into the dialog box.

7. Highlight the data block you want to graph, and press ⏎Enter].

11

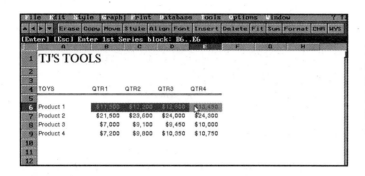

In this example, select **1**st Series, highlight the block B6..E6, and then press ↵Enter.

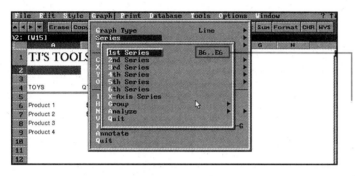

The **1**st Series is specified.

8. Repeat steps 6 and 7 to enter the other series.

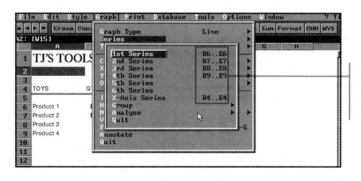

In this example, series **1**st-**4**th and the **X**-Axis are specified.

9. To view the graph, press Q to select **Q**uit; then press V to select **V**iew.

11

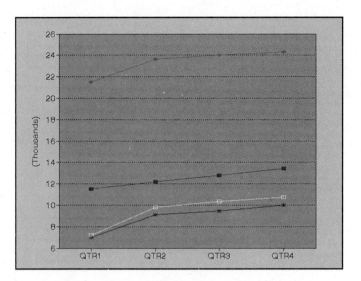

Although this line
graph shows four
data series, you
can enter as many
as six data series
by separately
specifying the **1st-
6**th Series from
the **S**eries menu.

You can specify blocks in any order; the block you select will always correspond with the number you assign in the selection process. Use the **X**-Axis
Series option to plot the time or amount measured along the x-axis. The data
points in each data series are marked by a unique symbol that you select.

With bar graphs or stacked-bar graphs, you also can enter as many as six data
series.

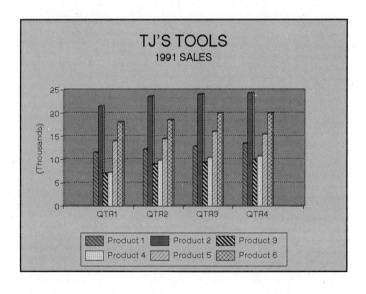

In a bar graph,
multiple data
blocks appear on
the graph from
left to right in
order of the six
series.

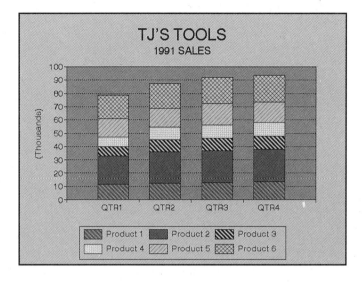

In a stacked-bar graph, multiple data blocks appear on the graph from bottom to top in order of the six series.

In bar and stacked-bar graphs, the X-Axis Series option enables you to indicate the time or amount measured along the x-axis. Every data series displayed in monochrome (one color) has unique shading. Data series displayed in color are assigned one of 16 colors. Quattro Pro enables you to select the shading or color you prefer.

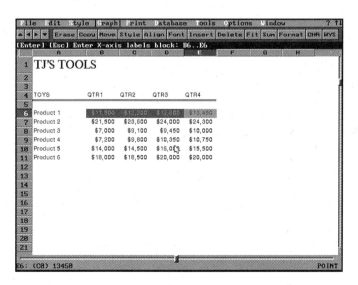

In a bubble or XY graph, to enter the data series being plotted as the independent variable, select X-Axis Series from the Series menu and highlight the correct data.

11

Plot at least one dependent variable (usually the **1**st Series). The unique markers that mark the data points depend on the dependent variables you select.

With pie graphs, choose **X**-Axis Series to identify each piece of the pie. Then enter only one data series by selecting **1**st Series from the **S**eries menu.

This example shows a pie graph with some of the different types of shading and one exploded slice.

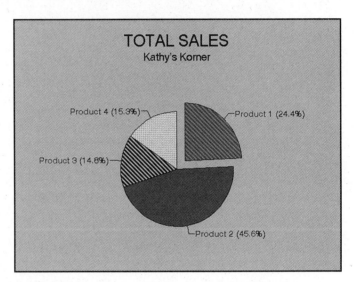

Defining All Data Blocks at Once

If the **X**-Axis and **1**st-**6**th Series blocks are in one contiguous block, you can use the /**G**raph **S**eries **G**roup command to define all the blocks at once. The command /**G**raph **S**eries **G**roup provides a quick way to define the **X**-Axis and **1**st-**6**th Series blocks without having to specify them individually. For this option to work properly, the cells for the **X**-Axis block must be immediately to the left of or immediately above the cells of the **1**st Series block. The cells for the **2**nd through **6**th Series blocks, if present, must be adjacent to the **1**st Series block. After you define the location of the block, the command prompts you for a "columnwise" or "rowwise" orientation.

To select all the data blocks for a graph, **X**-Axis Series and **1**st-**6**th Series, when data in adjacent rows and columns is in consecutive order, follow these steps:

1. Press ⌀ to access the Quattro Pro menu.
2. Press Ⓖ to select **G**raph.
3. Press Ⓖ to select **G**raph Type; then select the type of graph from the selections provided.

354

4. Press S to select **S**eries.

5. Press G to select **G**roup.

6. Press C to select **C**olumns if the data blocks are in columns, or press R to select **R**ows if the data blocks are in rows.

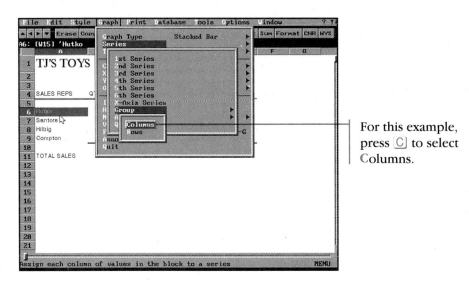

For this example, press C to select **C**olumns.

7. Specify the block that contains the **X**-Axis and one or more **1**st Series through **6**th Series data blocks, and then press ⏎Enter. The rows or columns must be adjacent and in the order X, 1, 2, 3, and so on.

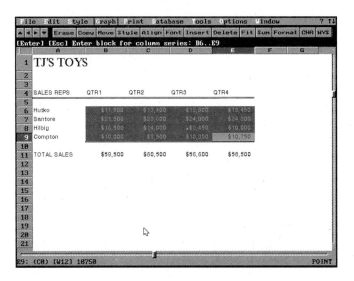

For this example, specify the group block as B6..E9 and press ⏎Enter.

11

8. To view the graph, press $\boxed{Q}$ to select **Q**uit; then press $\boxed{V}$ to select **V**iew.

This graph shows the result of selecting columnwise orientation with the /**G**raph **S**eries **G**roup command.

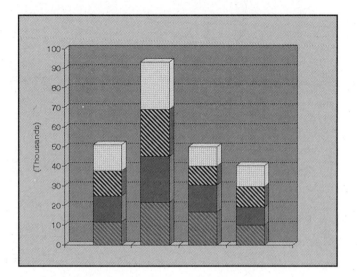

Enhancing the Appearance of a Graph

After you create a basic graph using the simple four-step procedure or the **F**ast Graph command described earlier in this chapter, you can improve the appearance of your graphs and produce final-quality output suitable for business presentations. By selecting choices from the **G**raph menu, you can enhance a graph by adding descriptive labels and numbers, adding arrows or shapes, and by changing the default graph display items.

To add descriptive information to a graph, you can use the **C**ustomize Series and **T**ext menus. The **I**nterior Labels option places labels within the graph. You can enter as many as four titles: two at the top and one to describe each axis. Legends describing the shadings, colors, or markers assigned to data blocks in line or bar graphs appear across the bottom or to the right of those graphs.

To add arrows or text notes to a graph, you can use the **A**nnotate menu options. When you select **A**nnotate, the screen changes and a graphics work area containing your graph appears. This work area enables you to customize your graph with graphic objects such as rectangles, bullets, arrows and ovals, and to enter text notes anywhere on the graph.

11

You also can enhance a graph by changing any of the default graph display items. For example, you can use the /Graph Customize Series Markers & Lines command to change the connecting lines or symbols in a line or XY graph. You also can use the /Graph Overall Grid option to display horizontal or vertical grid lines. You can adjust the axes scales with the X-Axis or Y-Axis Scale options, and you can adjust the spacing of the labels displayed on the x-axis with the /Graph X-Axis or Y-Axis No. of Ticks command.

The following sections of this chapter describe and illustrate how you can create basic graphs using only a few commands. You also learn how to use additional commands from the Customize Series, Text, and Annotate menus to create presentation-quality graphs.

As you add enhancements to your graphs, check the results frequently. Return to the main Graph menu and select View to check the most recent version of the graph. Press any key to exit the graph display and restore the Graph menu to the screen.

To view the current graph, press the Graph (F10) key, which instantly re-draws the graph with any updated spreadsheet data. You can use the Graph (F10) key to toggle between the spreadsheet and the graph.

Using the Text Option

If you select /Graph Text, the following options are displayed in the menu box: 1st Line, 2nd Line, X-Title, Y-Title, Secondary, Legends, Font, and Quit.

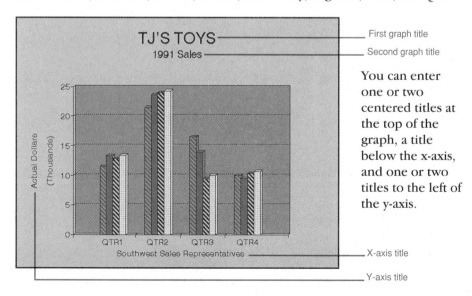

First graph title

Second graph title

You can enter one or two centered titles at the top of the graph, a title below the x-axis, and one or two titles to the left of the y-axis.

X-axis title

Y-axis title

357

11

You can enter titles by typing a new description, by specifying a block name, or by referencing the cell location of a label or a number already in the spreadsheet.

To add titles to a graph (after you have chosen the graph type and entered data blocks), complete the following steps:

1. Press ⌷ to access the Quattro Pro menu.
2. Press Ⓖ to select Graph.
3. Press Ⓣ to select Text.
4. From the Text menu, choose from six options: 1st Line, 2nd Line, X-Title, Y-Title, Secondary Y-Axis, or Legends.

To display a title on the top line of a graph, press ① to select 1st Line, type a title (TJ'S TOYS, in this example), and press ⏎Enter.

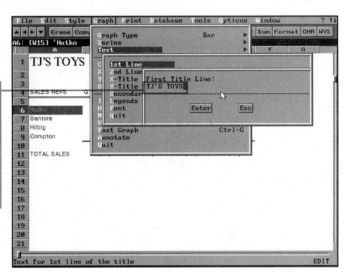

11

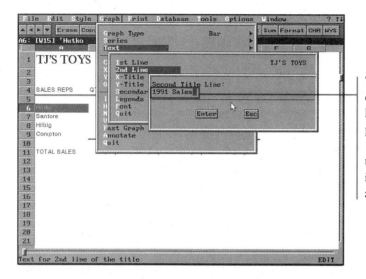

To display a title on the second line of a graph, press [2] to select 2nd Line, type a title (1991 Sales, in this example), and press [↵Enter].

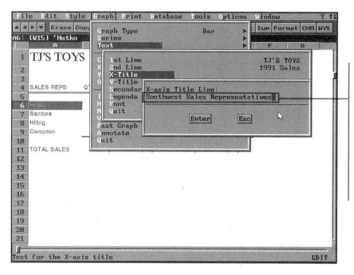

To display a title below the x-axis, press [X] to select X-Title, type a title (Southwest Sales Representatives, in this example), and press [↵Enter].

11

To display a title
to the left of the
y-axis, press [Y] to
select **Y**-Title, type
a title (Actual
Dollars, in this
example), and
press [↵Enter].

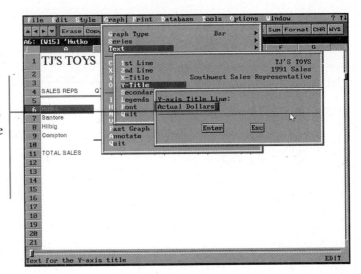

Note: The X-Axis and Y-Axis titles do not apply when you construct a pie graph.

5. To view the graph with titles displayed, press [Q] to select **Q**uit; then press [V] to select **V**iew.

To edit a title, use the same command sequence you used to create the title: /**G**raph **T**ext. The existing text, cell reference, or block name appears in the dialog box, ready for editing. To modify the title, use the keys [←], [→], [◆Backspace], and [Esc]. If you want to eliminate a title entirely, press [Esc] and then press [↵Enter].

Entering Labels within a Graph

After you graph a data series, you can enter values or labels to explain each point plotted on a bar, line, or XY graph. For example, you can label points on a line graph illustrating sales figures with the specific values for each point.

To add labels to be displayed within a graph, follow these steps:

1. Press [/] to access the Quattro Pro menu.
2. Press [G] to select **G**raph.
3. Press [C] to select **C**ustomize Series.

11

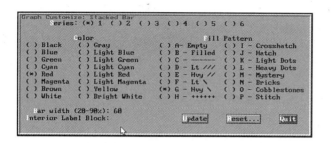

The Customize dialog box appears.

4. Specify the Series (1-6) to which the interior labels apply.

5. Press ⌶ to select Interior Label Block.

   In a line graph that includes only one data block, choose Series 1 to assign labels to the block.

6. Enter the block containing the text or values you want to use as labels for the graph, and press ⏎Enter.

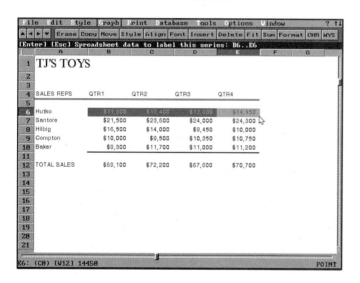

To label data points in a sales graph, highlight the block containing the sales figures (B6..E6, in this example) and press ⏎Enter.

Note: Instead of typing the labels (as you typed the titles), you must specify each interior label block by highlighting an existing block in the spreadsheet, providing cell coordinates, or specifying a previously determined block name.

7. Indicate the location of the data labels by selecting from the menu options: Center, Left, Above, Right, and Below.

11

Using these options, you may need to experiment with two or more data label positions to determine which position is best for your graph.

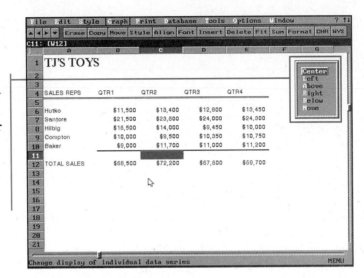

8. To view the graph with interior labels displayed, press Q Q to select **Q**uit twice; then press V to select **V**iew.

This graph shows the result of choosing the **B**elow option for the location of interior labels.

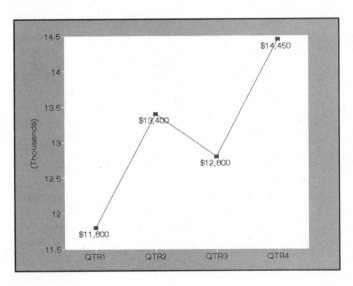

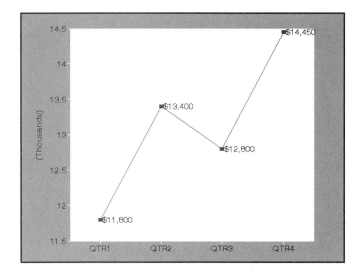

11

This graph shows the result of choosing the **R**ight option for the location of interior labels.

If you graph more than one data series, attach the interior labels to the data series with the largest figures; then select **A**bove to position the interior labels above the data points plotted. To enter text or numbers as the plotted points, use the **C**enter option with line graphs that display **N**either Line Styles nor Markers.

To edit either the block or position of the interior label, use the same command sequence you used to create the interior label. Edit the current block or specify a different position.

To eliminate interior labels that were specified, you must issue the command you used to specify the interior labels, and then select **N**one from the menu box for the interior label location.

Using the Legends Option

Whenever a graph contains more than one set of data, you need to be able to distinguish between those sets. In addition to enhancing your data with **C**olors and **F**ill Patterns, you can provide explanatory text for data represented by markers or fill patterns. Use the **/G**raph **L**egend command to display legends below the x-axis. To add a legend to your graph, follow these steps:

1. Press ⃞/ to access the Quattro Pro menu.
2. Press ⃞G to select **G**raph.

11

3. Press ⊤ to select **T**ext.

4. Press ⊔ to select **L**egends.

5. Select **1**st Series to specify the legend for the first data block.

6. When the dialog box appears, type \, type the cell address containing the label, and press ⏎Enter; alternatively, just type the label and press ⏎Enter.

For this example, type \a6 and press ⏎Enter.

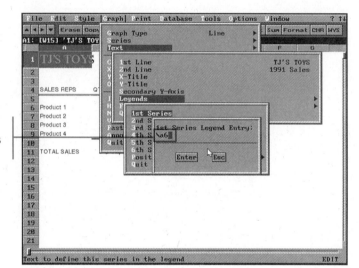

7. Select the next Series option and repeat step 6 for each data block contained in your graph.

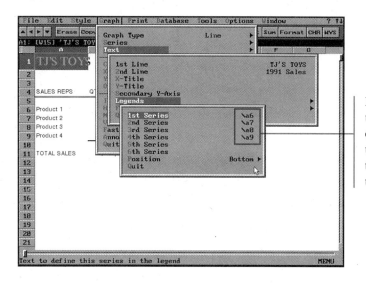

In this example, the legend for each series is set up to look for the text in a cell in the spreadsheet.

8. To view the graph with a legend displayed, press Q to select Quit; then press V to select View.

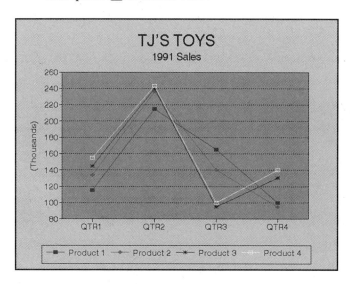

In this example, the legend clearly identifies which line in the line graph corresponds to which product.

You can use the /Graph Text Legends Position command to select the location of the legends. You can locate legends below the x-axis or to the right of the graph with the Bottom and Right options, respectively, of the /Graph Text Legends Position command.

11

The legends for the different data blocks in bar and stacked-bar graphs are marked with unique shadings.

If you want to edit a legend, use the same command sequence you used to create it. The existing text, cell reference, or block name appears in the dialog box, ready for you to edit it. To eliminate a legend, select the /Graph Text Legends Position None command. You cannot use the Legends option for pie graphs, which can have only one data series.

Setting a Background Grid

By default, when Quattro Pro displays a line, bar, stacked-bar, or XY graph, data blocks are displayed without a *background grid*; however, you may sometimes want to impose a grid on a graph so that the data-point amounts are easier to read. To display and print line, bar, stacked-bar, or XY graphs with a grid, use the /Graph Overall Grid command.

To add a grid to your line, bar, stacked-bar, or XY graph, follow these steps:

1. Press / to access the Quattro Pro menu.
2. Press G to select Graph.
3. Press O to select Overall.

The Overall dialog box appears.

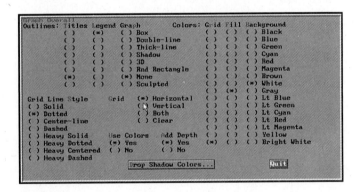

4. Press G to select Grid.
5. From the Grid options, select the type of grid you want to display: Horizontal, Vertical, or Both. (The default setting is Clear, which displays no background grid.)

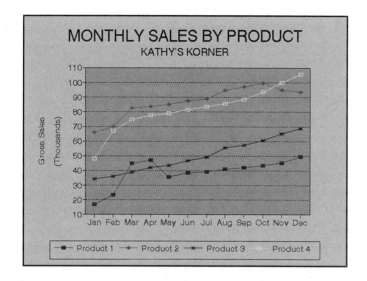

Select **H**orizontal to display a graph with a horizontal grid. Grid lines are spaced according to the tick marks on the y-axis.

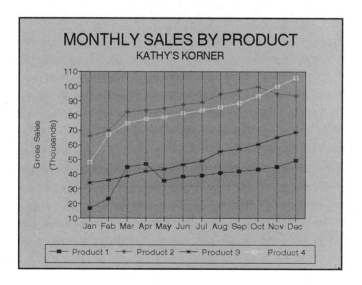

Select **V**ertical to display a graph with a vertical grid. Grid lines are spaced according to the tick marks on the x-axis.

11

Select **B**oth to display a graph with both horizontal and vertical grid lines.

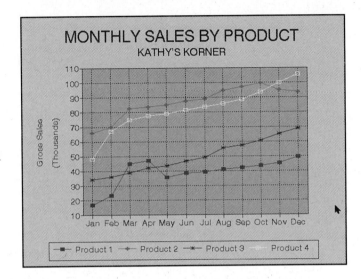

6. To view the graph with grid lines displayed, press ⒬ to select **Q**uit; then press ⒱ to select **V**iew.

Experiment with different grids, repeating the command sequence and specifying other options. Whenever you want to eliminate a grid display, select /**G**raph **O**verall **G**rid **C**lear.

Note: You cannot add grids to pie graphs.

Annotating Graphs

After you create a graph, you can add arrows, text boxes, and shapes to further enhance your graph. You can showcase specific data on the graph by annotating the graph to point out a specific piece of data. This feature is very helpful when preparing a presentation that includes graphs.

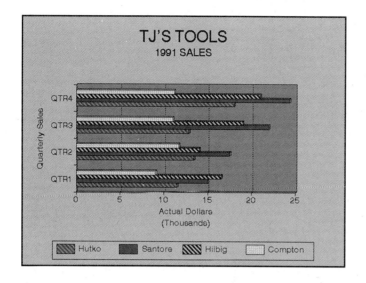

Suppose that you want to add text and an arrow to this rotated bar graph.

To annotate a graph, follow these steps:

1. Press ⌷/⌷ to access the Quattro Pro menu.
2. Press ⌷G⌷ to select **G**raph.
3. Press ⌷A⌷ to select **A**nnotate.

Toolbox

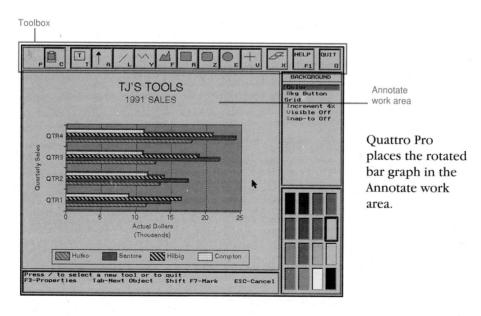

Annotate work area

Quattro Pro places the rotated bar graph in the Annotate work area.

11

Above the Annotate work area is the *Toolbox*. The Toolbox enables you to accomplish tasks such as drawing a rectangle.

4. Select the Text tool—the third icon from the left—by clicking the Text icon in the Toolbox, and then click wherever you want to add text. You also can press / T and click wherever you want to add the text; or use the arrow keys and ⇧Shift-arrow keys to position the cursor, and then press ⏎Enter.

Text tool

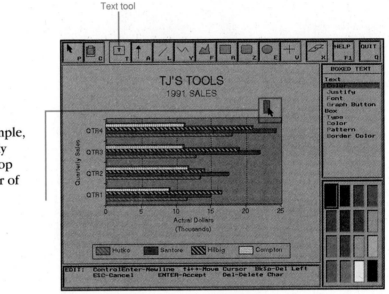

In this example, click directly above the top right border of the graph.

5. Type the text you want to display in the selected area.

Arrow tool

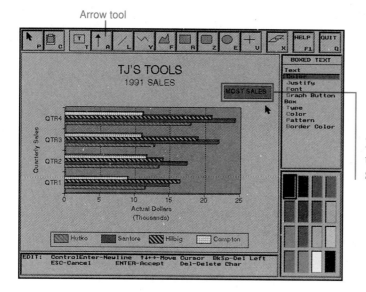

In this example, type **MOST SALES**.

6. Select the Arrow tool—the fourth icon from the left—by clicking the Arrow icon in the Toolbox. Click and hold the mouse pointer at the point where you want to position the tail of the arrow, and then drag the mouse pointer toward the point where you want to position the tip of the arrow. Release the mouse button when the arrow is the correct length.

   Alternatively, you can press ⎵/A and then click and drag the mouse pointer to position the arrow. You also can use the arrow keys to position the cursor where you want the tail of the arrow, press ⎵, use the arrow keys to position the cursor where you want the tip of the arrow, and then press ⏎Enter.

11

Quit tool

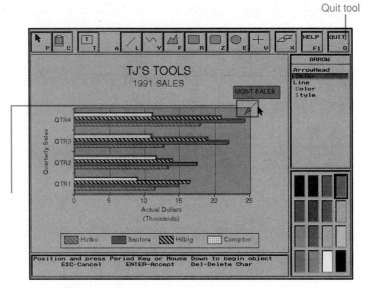

Quattro Pro adds an arrow that, in this example, points to the bar representing the most sales.

7. Select the Quit tool (click the last icon on the right) to return to the spreadsheet.

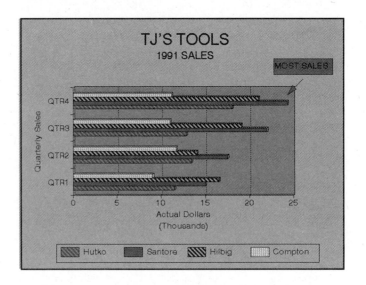

This example shows the annotated graph.

Zooming and Panning a Graph

Quattro Pro enables you to *zoom* in on a specific portion of a graph. Rather than displaying the complete graph, the program displays only a small section of it. After you zoom in on a portion of a graph, you can then *pan* across the graph to see the other portions of it. Panning is simply adjusting the zoomed view of the graph to look at a different section of it.

To zoom in on a specific area of a graph and then pan the graph, you can use the Zoom and Pan palette. While you are viewing a graph, you can display the Zoom and Pan palette by clicking the left and right mouse buttons at the same time. You can access this feature only with a mouse.

To zoom and pan a graph, follow these steps:

1. Press ⁄ to access the Quattro Pro menu.
2. Press G to select **G**raph.
3. Press V to select **V**iew.
4. Press the left and right mouse buttons at the same time.

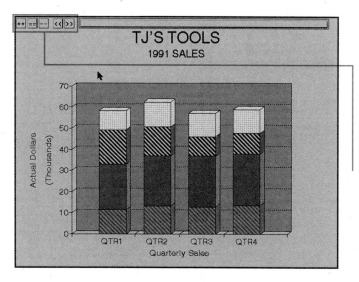

The Zoom and Pan palette appears at the top of the screen.

The double-plus sign (+ +) button zooms the view of the graph in one level.

The double-minus sign (– –) button zooms the view of the graph out one level.

The double-equal sign (= =) button redisplays the original graph.

11

5. Click the double-plus sign (++) button to zoom the graph in one level.

This graph is zoomed in so that only two quarters, QTR2 and QTR3, are displayed.

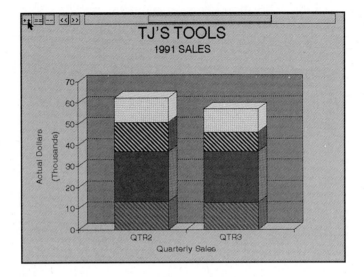

The left (<<) or right (>>) pan buttons pan the display to the right or left, respectively.

6. Click the right pan button to pan the view of the graph to the right.

This graph is panned right so that QTR3 and QTR4 are displayed.

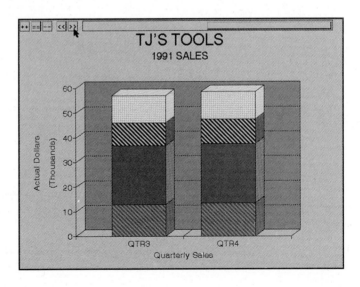

7. Click the double-equal sign (==) button to redisplay the original graph.

Zooming and panning can be very useful for busy graphs that display many data points.

Saving Graph Settings

To view on-screen a graph that you created in an earlier graphing session, you must have given the graph a name when you originally constructed the graph and saved the spreadsheet, unless the same spreadsheet is still active. To name a graph, you issue the /Graph Name Create command. Use the /Graph Name options to save the graph and the underlying spreadsheet or to retrieve or delete a named graph that you saved.

Only one graph at a time can be the current graph. If you want to save a graph that you just completed (for subsequent recall to the screen) and build a new graph, you must first issue the /Graph Name Create command. The only way to store a graph for later screen display is to issue this command, which instructs Quattro Pro to remember the specifications used to define the current graph. If you do not name a graph and subsequently either reset the graph or change the specifications, you cannot restore the original graph without rebuilding it.

To store the settings for a graph you created, or to retrieve a graph you saved, follow these steps:

1. Press ⌷/⌷ to access the Quattro Pro menu.
2. Press ⌷G⌷ to select Graph.
3. Press ⌷N⌷ to select Name.
4. Select from the following options to specify the graph-naming activity you want to perform:

Option	Description
Display	Displays a graph whose settings were saved with /Graph Name Create. This option enables you to recall any named graph from within the active spreadsheet.
Create	Creates a name for the currently defined graph so that you can later access and modify the graph.

11

375

11

Option	Description
Autosave Edits	Saves changes automatically to the current named graph when you switch to another graph.
Erase	Erases an individual graph name and the settings associated with that graph.
Reset	Erases all graph names.
Slide	Creates an on-screen "slide show" by displaying named graphs, each for a specified number of seconds.
Graph Copy	Copies a named graph from one spreadsheet to another.

Quattro Pro displays a dialog box so that you can enter a graph name, and displays a listing of the graph names (if any) in the current directory.

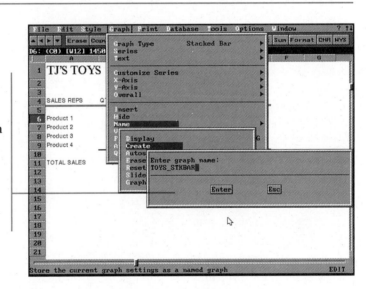

5. If you selected Create in step 4, type a new name (up to 15 characters in length), and then press ⏎Enter.

Or

If you selected a different option in step 4, click a graph name, or press → or ← to highlight the graph name; then press ⏎Enter.

Note: If you want to store graph names with their spreadsheet, remember to save the spreadsheet file by using /File Save or Save As after creating the names.

Placing a Graph in a Spreadsheet

11

You can insert a graph into a spreadsheet and simultaneously view the graph and the data from which the graph was created. Combining them also enables you to make a single printout of the graph and the data. You must be in WYSIWYG mode to be able to view an inserted graph in a spreadsheet. You can insert a graph in Text mode, but it appears as a solid rectangle.

To insert a graph into a spreadsheet, follow these steps:

1. Press ⌿ to access the Quattro Pro menu.
2. Press G to select Graph.
3. Press I to select Insert.
4. Select the graph name or macro that you want to insert.

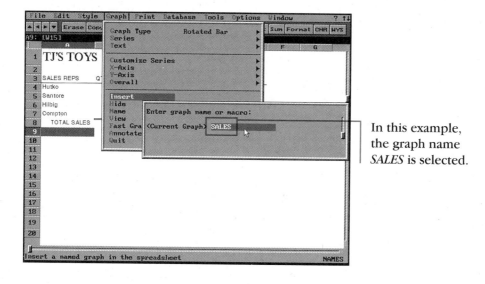

In this example, the graph name *SALES* is selected.

5. Highlight the area on the spreadsheet into which you want to insert the graph.

11

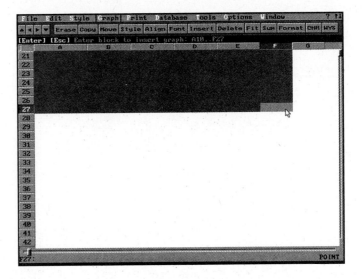

In this example,
the block
A10..F27 is
highlighted.

6. Press ⏎Enter.

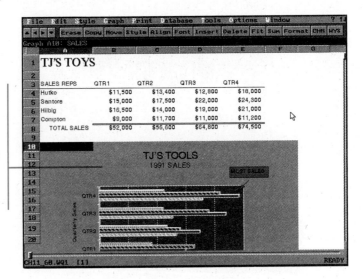

Quattro Pro
inserts the graph
into the spread-
sheet and auto-
matically sizes the
graph for the
block highlighted
in step 5.

Printing Graphs

Printing graphs in Quattro Pro is similar to printing spreadsheets. Your printer should be turned on and the print head should be aligned with the paper perforations. To print a graph, you use the /Print Graph Print command. To print a graph in Quattro Pro, follow these steps:

1. Press / to access the Quattro Pro menu.
2. Press P to select Print.
3. Press G to select Graph Print.
4. Press N to select Name.

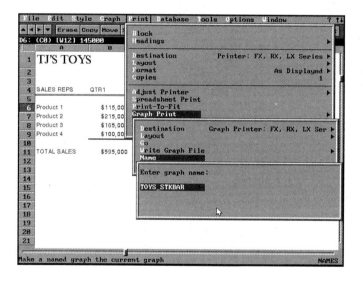

Quattro Pro prompts you to specify a graph name.

5. Select a graph name and press ⏎Enter.
6. Press Q to select Quit.
7. Press G to select Go.

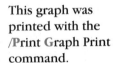

11

This graph was printed with the /Print Graph Print command.

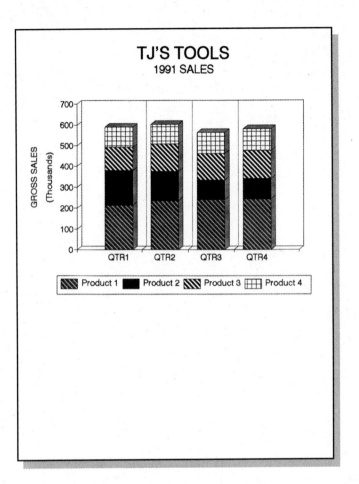

If you have more than one graph named with your spreadsheet, issue the /Print Graph Print Name command to select the graph you want to print. If you need to change the margins, size, orientation, or aspect ratio of the printed graph, use the /Print Graph Print Layout command. This command is similar to the /Print Layout command discussed in Chapter 9.

Summary

In this chapter, you learned how to create and save graphs. You learned the four basic steps for creating a basic graph and how to select any one of Quattro Pro's 11 types of two-dimensional graphs—line, XY, bar, stacked bar, pie, area, rotated bar, high-low, column, text, and bubble; and 4 types of three-dimensional graphs—ribbon, area, step, and bar.

You also learned how to improve the appearance of graphs by adding titles, interior labels, legends, grids, and formatting. The chapter showed you how to add text and arrows to a graph. After you created the graph, you learned how to insert the graph into a spreadsheet and how to print the graph.

Specifically, you learned the following key information about Quattro Pro:

■ The **G**raph option on the Quattro Pro main menu enables you to create graphs associated with data in the Quattro Pro spreadsheet.

■ The /**G**raph **G**raph Type command enables you to select from the following graph types: **L**ine, **B**ar, **XY**, **S**tacked Bar, **P**ie, **A**rea, **R**otated Bar, **C**olumn, **H**igh-Low, **T**ext, and **3**-D graphs. The graph type most appropriate for you depends on your data and your graphing needs.

■ Using the /**G**raph **S**eries **X**-Axis Series and **1**st through **6**th Series commands, you can choose the data blocks you want to display in your graph. The /**G**raph **S**eries **G**roup command enables you to select all data blocks at once, as long as they form a contiguous block of cells in the spreadsheet.

■ The /**G**raph **C**ustomize Series, **T**ext, **O**verall, and **X**-Axis and **Y**-Axis commands enable you to select from many different options that you can use to enhance the appearance of your graph. You can use these commands to add interior labels, titles, a legend, and a grid, and to change the scale of the axes.

■ The /**G**raph **A**nnotate command enables you to add text, arrows, and shapes to your graph.

■ The /**G**raph **N**ame command enables you to use existing graph specifications, create a new graph name, delete a graph name, and reset all graph names.

■ To modify a graph in a later session of Quattro Pro, you must use the /**G**raph **N**ame **C**reate command and then save the file with /**F**ile **S**ave or Save **A**s. Otherwise, your graph specifications are lost.

11

■ You can insert a graph into a spreadsheet with the /Graph Insert command, which enables you to view both the graph and the data you used to create the graph simultaneously.

■ The /Print Graph Print command enables you to print a graph created from data in the spreadsheet.

The next chapter shows you how to begin using the database features of Quattro Pro to manage your data. You will learn how to build and modify a database, and how to sort and search for database records.

Managing Data

In addition to the electronic spreadsheet and business graphics, Quattro Pro provides a third element: data management. Quattro Pro's database feature is fast, easy to access, and relatively simple to use.

The database's speed results from a reduction in the time required to transfer data to and from disks. By doing all the work inside the spreadsheet, Quattro Pro saves the time required for input and output to disk, the way many database programs function.

The Quattro Pro database is easily accessed because Borland International has made the entire database visible from the spreadsheet. You can view the contents of the whole database by using spreadsheet windows and direction keys to scroll through the database.

The relative ease with which you can use Quattro Pro is a result of integrating data management with the program's spreadsheet and graphics functions. The procedures for adding, modifying, and deleting items in a database are the same as those you have already seen for manipulating cells or groups of cells within a spreadsheet, and creating graphs from blocks in a database is as easy as creating them in a spreadsheet.

What is a database?

Using Quattro Pro as a database

Understanding the Database menu

Planning and building a database

Modifying a database

Sorting database records

Searching for records

> **12**

Key Terms in This Chapter

Database	A collection of data organized so that you can list, sort, or search its contents.
Field	One information item, such as an address or a name.
Record	A collection of associated fields. In Quattro Pro, a record is a row of cells within a database.
Key field	A column (field) to which you attach precedence when sorting the database.
Data block	The spreadsheet block on which database operations are performed.
Output block	The block to which data is copied when extracted from the database.
Criteria table	The block of the database in which you enter criteria on which a search is conducted.

What Is a Database?

A *database* is a collection of data organized so that you can list, sort, or search its contents. The list of data may contain any kind of information, from addresses to tax-deductible expenditures. A card file is one form of a database, as is an address book and a file cabinet full of employee records.

In Quattro Pro, the word *database* means a block of cells that spans at least one column and more than one row. This definition, however, does not distinguish between a database and any other block of cells on a spreadsheet. Because a database is actually a list, its manner of organization sets it apart from ordinary cells. Just as a list must be organized to be useful, a database must also be arranged in a manner that makes the information easy to access.

12

The smallest unit in a database is a *field*, or single data item. For example, if you were to develop an information database of customer accounts that are overdue, you might include the following fields of information:

Customer Last Name

Customer First Name

Street

City

State

ZIP Code

Account Number

Payment Due Date

Date Paid

Amount Due

A database *record* is a collection of associated fields. For example, the accumulation of all data about one customer forms one record. In Quattro Pro, a record is a row of cells within a database, and a field is one type of information, such as City.

You must set up a database so that you can access the information it contains. Retrieval of information usually involves relying on key fields. A database *key field* is any field (column) on which you base a list, sort, or search operation. For example, you can use the ZIP code field as a key field to sort the data in the overdue accounts database, and then assign contact representatives to specific geographic areas.

12

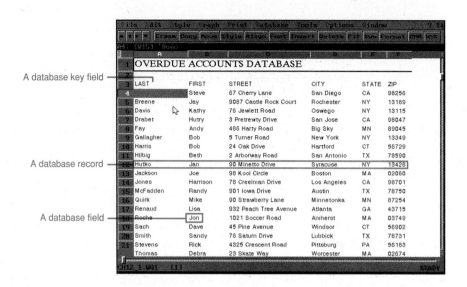

A database key field

A database record

A database field

Using Quattro Pro as a Database

After you build a database in Quattro Pro (which is no different from building any other spreadsheet table), you can perform a variety of functions on it. Some of the tasks you perform on a Quattro Pro database can be accomplished with standard Quattro Pro commands. For example, you can use simple spreadsheet commands such as /Edit Insert to add records and fields. Editing data in the database is the same as editing spreadsheet cells: highlight the cell, press Edit (F2), and make the correction.

You also can sort data. You can sort on up to five key fields, in ascending or descending order.

Some database operations specifically require database commands, such as /Database Query Locate and /Database Query Unique. Database commands can help you make inquiries, such as locating all database records of customers from Texas or all records of clients with the last name Koenig. Database commands also can remove duplications from the database. You perform these operations with the /Database Query commands.

You have several options for defining selection criteria with Quattro Pro. The criteria table can contain up to 32 cells across the spreadsheet, with each cell containing multiple criteria. You can use numbers, text, and complex formulas as criteria.

12

Quattro Pro also has a special set of statistical @functions that operate only on information stored in the database. Like the /Database Query commands, the statistical @functions use criteria to determine the records on which they will operate. The database @functions include @DCOUNT, @DSUM, @DAVG, @DVAR, @DSTD, @DMAX, and @DMIN. See Chapter 8, "Using @Functions," for information on database @functions.

If your computer has 640K of internal memory, you can store only about 1,000 400-byte (character) records or 8,000 50-byte records in a single database. Disk operating system commands and the Quattro Pro program instructions occupy the remaining memory. For large databases, you need to extend the internal memory capacity beyond 640K. If you use floppy diskettes for external storage of database files, you are limited to files that total approximately 360,000 characters (or 1.2 million characters on a high-density diskette). On a hard disk, a database of 8,000 500-byte records occupies 4 million characters, or approximately 4M of disk space. Fortunately, however, if you have Paradox 3.5 or higher, you can switch to Paradox while in Quattro Pro; you use the /Database Paradox Access command.

Understanding the Database Menu

You will use the Database menu for many of Quattro Pro's data management tasks. All other options from the Quattro Pro main menu work as well on databases as they do on spreadsheets. When you select Database from the Quattro Pro main menu, the following options are displayed: Sort, Query, Restrict Input, Data Entry, and Paradox Access. Each of these options is described in table 12.1.

Table 12.1
Database Menu Options

Option	Description
Sort	Organizes the database in ascending or descending order, based on one or two specified key fields.
Query	Offers different options for performing search operations and manipulating the found data items.
Restrict Input	Restricts data entry to a block you specify.

continues

387

12

	Table 12.1 *(Continued)*
Option	*Description*
Data Entry	Enables you to specify the type of data you want to enter into the database.
Paradox Access	Enables you to access the Paradox database program from Quattro Pro.

In the Database menu, the Sort, Query (search), and Data Entry options are considered true data management operations. Sort enables you to specify the order in which you want the records of the database organized: by number, by name, or by date, for example. With Query, you can perform a wide range of search operations, enabling you to display a specific record quickly, without having to scan a multitude of records. Data Entry enables you to determine the type of data you want to enter into your database.

Planning and Building a Database

Before you begin to create a database in Quattro Pro, you should determine the categories (fields) of information you want to include. You can best determine these fields by planning what kind of output you expect to produce from your data. Next, decide which area of the spreadsheet to use, and then create a database by specifying field names across a row and entering data in cells beneath these names, as you would for any other Quattro Pro application. Entering database contents is simple; the most critical step in creating a database is choosing your fields accurately.

Determining Required Output

Quattro Pro's data-search techniques rely on finding data by field names. Before you begin typing the kinds of data items you think you may need, write down the output you expect from the database. You also need to consider any source documents already in use that can provide input to the file.

Before you set up the items in your database, be sure to consider how you might look for data in each field. For example, consider how you will look for a particular information item. Will you search by date? By last name? Knowing how you will use your database before you design it will save you a great amount of time that you can lose if you later have to redesign the database.

Overdue Accounts Database		
Item	*Column Width*	*Type of Entry*
1. Customer Last Name	15	Label
2. Customer First Name	10	Label
3. Street Address	25	Label
4. City	15	Label
5. State	7	Label
6. ZIP Code	6	Label
7. Area Code	6	Number
8. Telephone Number	11	Label
9. Account Number	10	Number
10. Payment Due Date	11	Date
11. Date Paid	11	Date
12. Amount Due	12	Number

Structuring a database on paper before you create it in Quattro Pro is always a good idea.

After you decide on the fields, you need to choose the level of detail needed for each item of information, select the appropriate column width (you can modify this width later), and determine whether you will enter the data as a number, label, or date.

Here are some tips for planning various types of fields (columns) in your database:

- For ease in sorting, either put last and first names in separate columns, or put both names in the same cell with the last and first names separated by a comma.

- Some ZIP codes begin with zero, which does not appear in the cell if you enter it as a value. Enter ZIP codes as labels by preceding them with a label prefix.

- Set up a separate area code field apart from your telephone number field if you want to search, sort, or extract records by area code.

- Enter a telephone number as a label. This number must be a label because of the hyphen that separates the first three and last four digits of a telephone number. A hyphen indicates subtraction in a number you enter as a value.

Be sure to plan your database carefully before you establish field names, set column widths and block formats, or enter data. Although you can make changes after you set up your database, careful planning helps you reduce the time required to make such changes.

Positioning the Database

You can create a database as a new database file or as part of an existing spreadsheet. If you decide to build a database as part of an existing spreadsheet, choose a spreadsheet area where inserting or deleting lines won't affect the spreadsheet or another database.

12

If you place a database directly to the right of a spreadsheet, inserting and deleting rows may affect the spreadsheet.

If you place a database directly below a spreadsheet, inserting and deleting columns may affect the spreadsheet.

An ideal location for a database is an area in which inserting and deleting rows and columns won't affect other applications above, below, to the right, or to the left of the database.

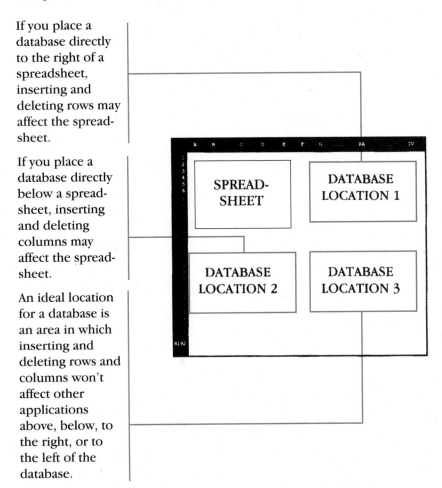

Entering Data

After you plan your database and decide which area of the spreadsheet to use, you can start entering data. Build a database by specifying field names as labels across a row, making sure that each field name is unique and in a separate column.

You can use one or more rows for field names, but Quattro Pro processes only the bottom row; therefore, using only one row for field names is highly recommended. After you enter the field names, enter data in cells as you would for any other Quattro Pro application. Use the /Style Column Width command to change the column width to fit the information you will enter.

To build a Quattro Pro database, follow these general steps:

1. Choose an area of your spreadsheet for your database.

   For your first database, you should start with a blank spreadsheet. If you would rather use an existing spreadsheet, select an area that is out of the way of the data you have entered.

2. Enter the field names across a single row.

   The field names must be labels, even if they are numeric labels. Although you can use more than one row for the field names, Quattro Pro processes only the entries that appear in the bottom row. For example, if you have the field name DATE DUE assigned to a column, with DATE in row 5 and DUE in row 6, Quattro Pro will reference only DUE as a key field in sort or query operations. Remember that all field names should be unique; any repetition of names can be confusing.

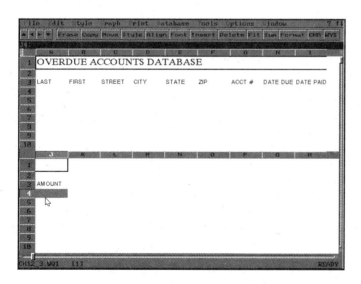

This example shows all field names in an overdue accounts database, displayed in two windows.

3. Set the column widths and cell display formats. Use Quattro Pro's /Style Column Width and /Style Numeric Format commands to control the width of the columns and the way Quattro Pro displays the data.

12

In this example, the column widths are adjusted to accommodate the width of the fields.

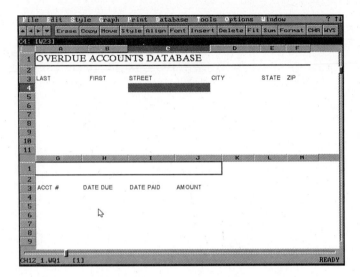

Note: Whenever a right-justified column of numeric data is adjacent to a left-justified column of label information, the data looks crowded. You can insert blank columns and adjust the column width of the blank column to change the spacing between fields.

4. Add records to the database.

To enter the first record, move the cell selector to the row *directly below* the field-names row, and then enter the data across the row in each applicable column (field).

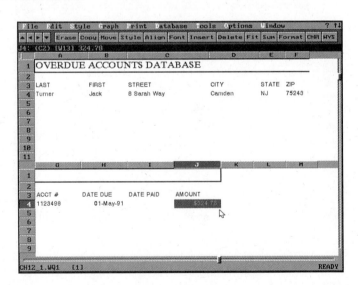

Restricting Data Entry Movement to a Particular Block

You can use the /Database Restrict Input command to limit the movement of the cell selector to only unprotected cells. In this manner, you can specify the block that will contain your data and prevent overwriting other cells with data. You must use the /Database Restrict Input command to set up special data input areas.

For example, suppose that you create a simple spreadsheet in which you want to restrict cell-selector movement to cells A4..J20, which is your data input area. By restricting cell-selector movement to just the data input area, no one entering data can enter information outside the input area. First you use the /Style Protection Unprotect command to identify this block as unprotected cells; then you use the /Database Restrict Input command to restrict movement of the cell selector to only those unprotected cells.

To restrict input to unprotected cells in a spreadsheet, follow these steps:

1. Press ⟨/⟩ to access the Quattro Pro menu.

2. Press ⟨D⟩ to select Database.

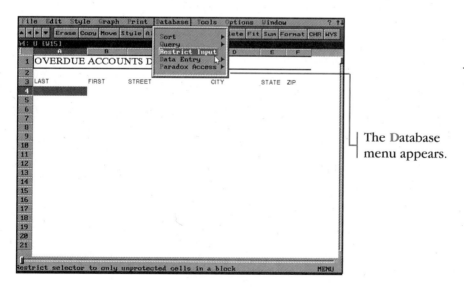

The Database menu appears.

3. Press ⟨R⟩ to select Restrict Input.

4. Highlight the block of cells that includes the unprotected cells in the data input area; then press ⟨↵Enter⟩.

12

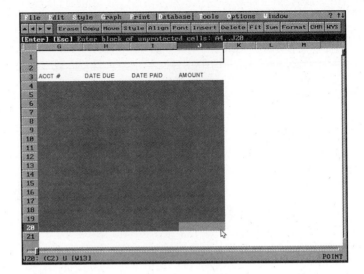

In this example, specify the block A4..J20 and press ⏎Enter.

Note: You can include protected cells in the /Database Restrict Input block, but the cell selector will move only to the unprotected cells in the block.

After you specify a block and press ⏎Enter, the first cell of the /Database Restrict Input block moves to the upper left corner of the screen, and the cell selector jumps immediately to the first cell available for input (the first unprotected cell) in the block.

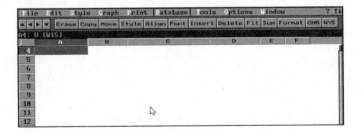

In this example, the cell selector jumps to cell A4.

You now can begin to enter or edit data in the unprotected cells, which are all the cells in this block. After completing an entry, use the arrow keys to move the cell selector to the next unprotected cell.

The /Database Restrict Input command remains in effect until you press ⏎Enter or Esc. The cell selector then returns to the upper left corner of the /Database Restrict Input block, and the spreadsheet returns to the same position it was in before you issued the /Database Restrict Input command.

12

Modifying a Database

After you collect the data for your database and decide which field names, field types, column widths, and formats to use, creating a database is easy. Thanks to Quattro Pro, maintaining the accuracy of the database contents also is simple. The commands you use to modify a database, which are the same commands you use to modify spreadsheets, are summarized in table 12.2.

Table 12.2
Commands for Modifying a Database

Command	Action
/Edit Insert Rows	Adds a record
/Edit Insert Columns	Adds a field
/Edit Delete Rows	Deletes a record
/Edit Delete Columns	Deletes a field
Edit (F2)	Edits a field

The process of modifying fields in a database is the same as that of modifying the contents of cells in any other application. As you know, you change the cell contents either by retyping the cell entry or by using the Edit (F2) key and editing the entry. You learn more about editing in the section "Editing Records During a Search," further in this chapter.

Other Quattro Pro commands, such as those for copying, moving, and formatting cells, are the same for both database and other spreadsheet applications. For more information about these commands, see Chapters 4 through 7 of this book.

Inserting and Deleting Records

To add and delete records in a database, use the Quattro Pro commands for inserting and deleting rows. Because records correspond to rows, you use the /Edit Insert Rows command to insert one or more records. You then fill in the various fields in each row with the appropriate data. To delete one or more rows, you use the /Edit Delete Rows command.

To insert one or more rows (records) in the database, follow these steps:

1. Press ⌐/⌐ to access the Quattro Pro menu.
2. Press ⌐E⌐ to select **Edit**.
3. Press ⌐I⌐ to select **Insert**.
4. Press ⌐R⌐ to select **Rows**.
5. Highlight (or type the cell address of) the location in which you want to insert the row (record); then press ⌐Enter⌐.

   You can insert several rows at once by highlighting multiple rows in this step. Quattro Pro moves down all current rows and inserts the new row or rows at the highlighted location.

When you press ⌐Enter⌐, a blank row (or rows) appears at the highlighted location, ready for you to enter a new record.

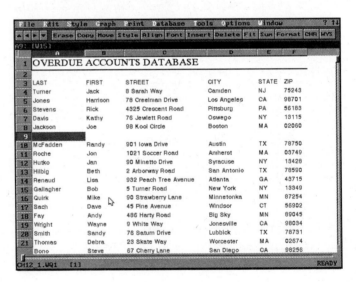

Using the mouse, you can preselect the row or rows you want to insert, and then use the ⌐Ctrl⌐-⌐I⌐ shortcut key combination to insert the row or rows.

You also can move to the bottom of the database and begin to add records in that row. The problem with this method is that each time you add new records to the database, you have to reset the data block used for sort and search operations so that it includes the new records. If you insert a row or rows and add new records, the data block automatically expands to include the new records.

To delete one or more rows (records) from the database, follow these steps:

1. Press ⃞/ to access the Quattro Pro menu.

2. Press ⃞E to select **E**dit.

3. Press ⃞D to select **D**elete.

4. Press ⃞R to select **R**ows.

5. Highlight (or type the cell addresses of) the rows (records) you want to delete; then press ⃞Enter. Note that you do not have to highlight each column in the row; you need to highlight only one cell in each row you want to delete.

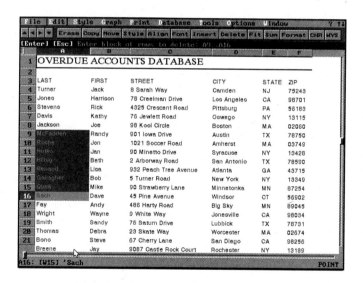

In this example, to delete rows 9 through 16, highlight a cell in those rows and press ⃞Enter.

When you press
⏎Enter, Quattro
Pro deletes the
records in the
highlighted block.

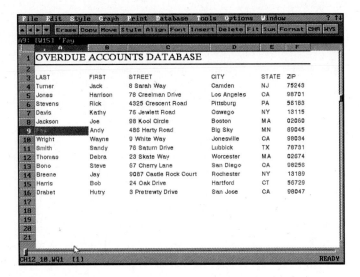

Because you do not have an opportunity to verify the block before you issue
the /Edit Delete Rows command, be extremely careful when you specify the
records you want to delete. If you want to remove only inactive records,
consider using the /Database Query Extract command to store the inactive
records in a separate location (or file) before you permanently delete the
records (this command is explained in "Searching for Records," further in this
chapter).

Inserting and Deleting Fields

To add and delete fields from a database, use the Quattro Pro /Edit commands
for inserting and deleting columns. To add one or more fields, use the /Edit
Insert Columns command; to delete one or more fields, use the /Edit Delete
Columns command.

To insert one or more new fields (columns) into the database, follow these
steps:

1. Press / to access the Quattro Pro menu.
2. Press E to select Edit.
3. Press I to select Insert.

4. Press C to select Columns.

5. Highlight (or type the cell address of) the location in which you want to insert the column or columns; then press ⏎Enter.

   You need to highlight only one cell in the column or columns you specify—anywhere in the column. Quattro Pro moves all current columns to the right of the inserted column or columns.

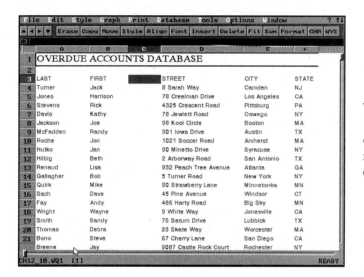

When you press ⏎Enter, a blank column appears— ready for you to enter new data.

Because maintaining data takes up valuable memory, you may decide to remove seldom-used data fields from the database.

To delete one or more fields (columns) from the database, follow these steps:

1. Press / to access the Quattro Pro menu.

2. Press E to select Edit.

3. Press D to select Delete.

4. Press C to select Columns.

5. Highlight the columns (fields) you want to delete; then press ⏎Enter.

12

In this example,
to delete column
C, highlight a cell
in that column
and press ⏎Enter.

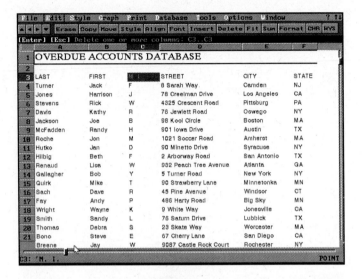

When you press
⏎Enter, Quattro
Pro deletes the
specified field
or fields.

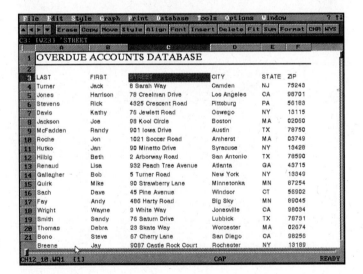

Sorting Database Records

Storing data in a database would be meaningless if you were unable to alpha-
betize the data or sort it numerically. Sorting is an important function of any

database. Quattro Pro's data management capability enables you to change the order of records by sorting them according to the contents of the fields. To sort data, you use the options available when you select /Database Sort: Block, 1st Key, 2nd Key, 3rd Key, 4th Key, 5th Key, Go, Reset, Sort Rules, and Quit. Each of these options is described in table 12.3.

Table 12.3
Database Sort Menu Options

Option	Description
Block	Enables you to specify the data block you want to sort.
1st through 5th Keys	Enable you to specify the first through fifth items you want to sort.
Go	Starts the sorting.
Reset	Resets the sort options.
Sort Rules	Specifies the rules you want Quattro Pro to use when sorting database records.
Quit	Exits the Database Sort menu.

Before you issue a /Database Sort command, you should save the database to disk. That way, if the sort procedure does not produce the results you expected, you can restore the file to its original order by retrieving it.

To sort a database, use this general procedure (specific procedures are discussed in following sections):

1. Select the /Database Sort command.

2. Select Block and designate the data block you want to sort.

    Note: Do not include the field-names row in the data block you want to sort. (If you are unfamiliar with designating or naming blocks, see Chapter 4, "Working with Blocks.")

    The data block does not necessarily have to include all rows in the database, but must include all fields (columns) to maintain the proper contents of each record. If some of the database records already have the organization you want, or if you don't want to sort all the records, you can sort a portion of these records.

3. Specify the key field(s) for the sort, and specify ascending or descending order for each key field.

   Key fields are the columns to which you attach the highest precedence when sorting the database. The column (or field) with the highest precedence is the 1st Key, and the field with the next highest precedence is the 2nd Key, and so on. You must set a 1st Key; setting the 2nd through 5th Keys is optional.

4. Press G to select Go and perform the sort.

A One-Key Row Sort

One of the simplest examples of a database sorted according to a 1st Key is a telephone book's white pages. All the records in the white pages are sorted in ascending alphabetical order, using the last name as the 1st Key.

Suppose, for example, that you want to sort records alphabetically according to last names. To perform a one-key sort operation, follow these steps:

1. Press / to access the Quattro Pro menu.

2. Press D to select Database.

3. Press S to select Sort.

The Database Sort menu appears. By default, Quattro Pro sorts by rows.

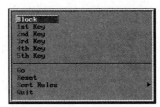

4. Press B to select Block.

5. Highlight (or enter the cell addresses or the block name of) the data block you want to sort; then press ↵Enter.

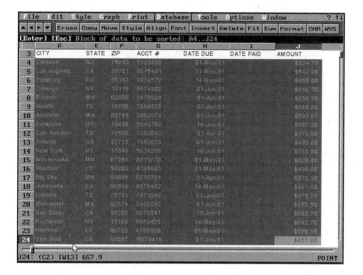

12

In this example, highlight the block for the entire database, A4..J24 (excluding the field names in row 3), and press ↵Enter.

6. From the Sort menu, press ① to select 1st Key.

7. Highlight (or type the cell address of) any cell in the column containing the 1st Key field on which you want to sort; then press ↵Enter.

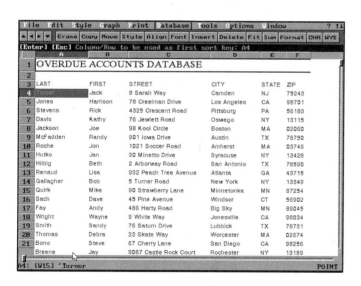

In this example, highlight any cell in column A to sort the database by the LAST (last name) field, and then press ↵Enter.

8. When prompted, type A to sort your database in ascending order of the selected 1st Key, or type D to sort in descending order; then press ↵Enter.

12

In this example, type **A** and press ⏎Enter to sort the database so that the last names are alphabetized from A to Z.

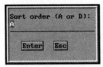

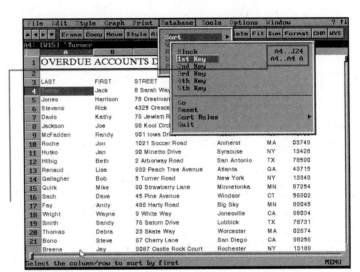

Quattro Pro will use these settings to sort the overdue accounts database by last name in ascending order.

9. Press Ⓖ to select **G**o to perform the sort.

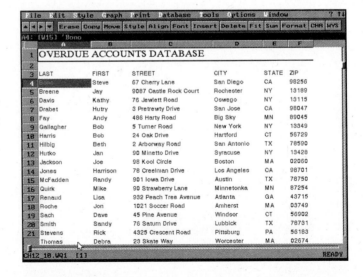

The database now displays the result of the one-key sort on the LAST field.

A Two-Key Row Sort

A two-key database sort uses both a first and second key. In the yellow pages of a telephone book, for example, records are sorted first according to business type (the **1**st Key) and then by business name (the **2**nd Key). Another example of a two-key sort—first by one key and then by another key within the first sort order—is an addresses database, sorted first by state and then by city within the state.

Suppose, for example, that you want to perform a two-key sort on the overdue accounts database. First you want to sort the records according to due date; then, when more than one record has the same due date, you want to sort those records according to the amount owed.

To perform a two-key sort operation, follow these steps:

1. Press ⃞/ to access the Quattro Pro menu.
2. Press ⃞D to select **D**atabase.
3. Press ⃞S to select **S**ort.
4. Press ⃞B to select **B**lock.
5. Highlight (or enter the cell addresses or block name of) the data block you want to sort; then press ⃞↵Enter.

   For this example, highlight the block A4..J24 and press ⃞↵Enter.
6. From the **S**ort menu, select **1**st Key to indicate the first field on which you want to sort the data.
7. Type or highlight any cell in the column containing the **1**st Key field on which you want to sort; then press ⃞↵Enter. Alternatively, you can click the cell and press ⃞↵Enter.
8. Indicate the sort order by typing **A** for ascending or **D** for descending; then press ⃞↵Enter.

12

12

In this example, to first sort the database by the DATE DUE field, highlight any cell in column H and press ⏎Enter. Then type **A** and press ⏎Enter to sort the database so that the due dates are arranged from earliest to most recent.

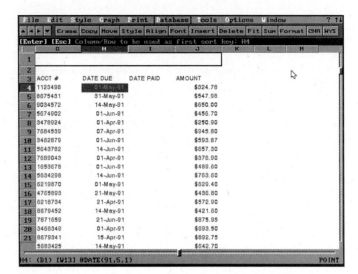

9. Select **2**nd Key to sort the data a second time for all records that have the same data in the **1**st Key field.

10. Type or highlight any cell in the column containing the **2**nd Key field on which you want to sort; then press ⏎Enter. Alternatively, you can click the cell and press ⏎Enter.

To sort according to AMOUNT after sorting by DUE DATE, highlight any cell in column J and press ⏎Enter.

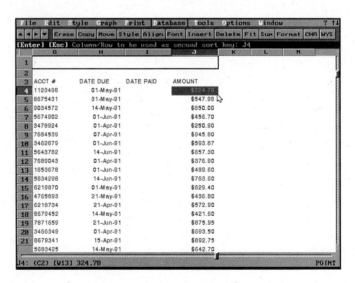

11. Indicate the sort order by typing **A** for ascending or **D** for descending; then press ⏎Enter.

For this example, type **D** and press ⏎Enter.

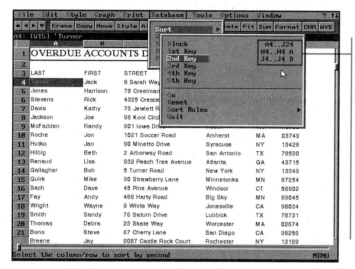

12

Quattro Pro will use these settings to sort the overdue accounts database first by due date in ascending order and then by amount in descending order for all records with the same due date.

12. Press G to select **G**o and start the sort.

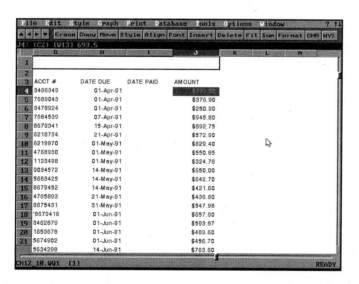

The database now displays the result of the two-key sort on the DATE DUE and AMOUNT fields. Accounts due on the same day are sorted according to their amount due.

A One-Key Column Sort

12

Quattro Pro has the capability to sort by columns if your database requires that method of sorting. Suppose, for example, that you want to sort records alphabetically according to the LAST field in a database set up with the field names in a column rather than a row.

Here is an example of a database with the field names in a column rather than a row.

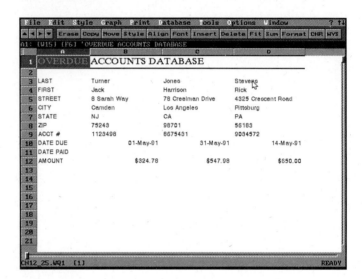

To perform a one-key sort operation, follow these steps:

1. Press [/] to access the Quattro Pro menu.
2. Press [D] to select **D**atabase.
3. Press [S] to select **S**ort.
4. Press [B] to select **B**lock.
5. Highlight (or enter the cell addresses or block name of) the data block you want to sort; then press [⏎Enter].

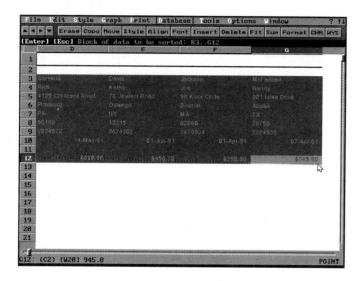

In this example, highlight the block B3..G12 (the entire database, excluding the field names in column A) and press ⏎Enter.

6. From the Sort menu, press ⬜1 to select 1st Key.

7. Type or highlight any cell in the row containing the 1st Key field on which you want to sort; then press ⏎Enter.

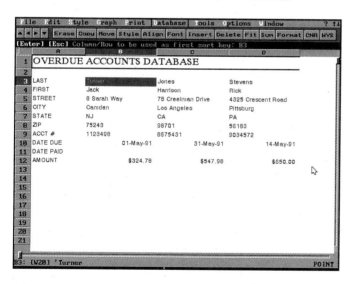

In this example, to sort the database by the LAST (last name) field, highlight any cell in row 3 and press ⏎Enter.

8. When prompted, type A to sort your database in ascending order of the selected 1st Key, or type D to sort in descending order; then press ⏎Enter.

12

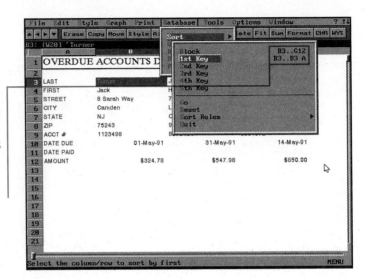

Quattro Pro will use these settings to sort the overdue accounts database by last name in ascending order.

9. Press S to select **S**ort Rules.

10. Press S to select **S**ort Rows/Columns.

11. Press C to select **C**olumns, and then press ⏎Enter.

The **C**olumns command changes the sort method from rows to columns.

12. Press Q to select **Q**uit and return to the **S**ort menu.

13. When the **S**ort menu returns, press G to select **G**o and start the sort.

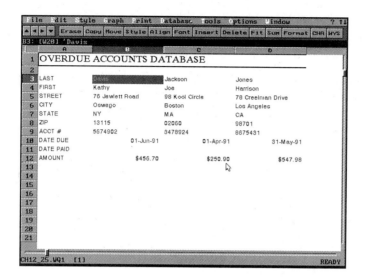

12

The database now displays the result of the one-key column sort on the LAST field.

Tips for Sorting Database Records

The following tips will help you sort database records more successfully.

Tip 1: Don't include blank rows in your data block before you sort the database.

If you accidentally include one or more blank rows in your data block, the blank rows will appear at the top of your data block. Therefore, when specifying the data you want to sort, remember to include only rows that contain data.

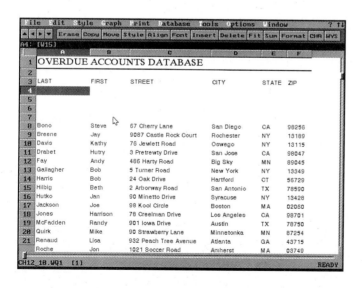

Because blanks have precedence over all other characters in an ascending sort, blank rows included in the sort data block appear at the top of the sorted database.

Tip 2: Use the /Edit Insert Columns and /Edit Fill commands to create a "counter" field so that you can easily re-sort the database to its original order if necessary.

After you sort the original contents of the database on any field, you cannot restore the records to their original order. If you add a "counter" column to the database before any sort, however, and include this column in the sort block, you can restore the original order by re-sorting on the counter field. The counter field assigns a number to each record so that you can restore the records to their original order.

To create a counter field, follow these steps:

1. Insert a blank column by pressing ⌐/⌐ ⌐E⌐ ⌐I⌐ ⌐C⌐ to select /Edit Insert Columns. You can reduce the column width of this new column with the /Style Column Width command.
2. Press ⌐/⌐ ⌐E⌐ ⌐F⌐ to select /Edit Fill.
3. Within the blank column, highlight the rows of your database in which you want to enter counter numbers; then press ⌐Enter⌐.

In this example, highlight the block A4..A21 and press ⌐Enter⌐.

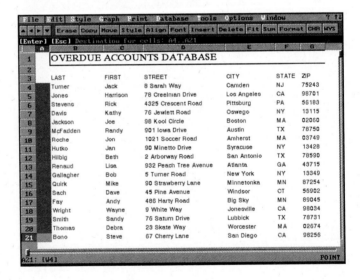

12

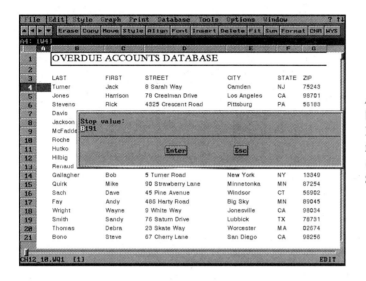

After you press ⏎Enter), Quattro Pro prompts you for the Start, Step (increment), and Stop values.

4. Type **1** and press ⏎Enter for Start; press ⏎Enter to accept the default Step value of 1; and then press ⏎Enter to accept the default Stop value of 8191.

Note: Although the default Stop value of 8191 is larger than it needs to be, Quattro Pro uses only the numbers necessary to fill the specified block.

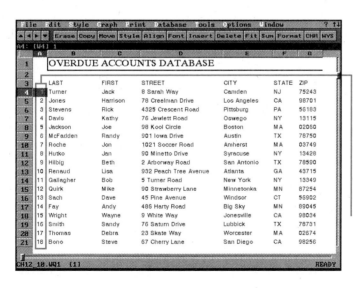

Quattro Pro fills the block with consecutive numbers, beginning with 1 and ending with the number of the last record in the specified block.

12

When you sort the database, include the counter column—column A in this example—in your data block. To re-sort the database to its original order, use the counter field as your 1st Key field and sort in ascending order.

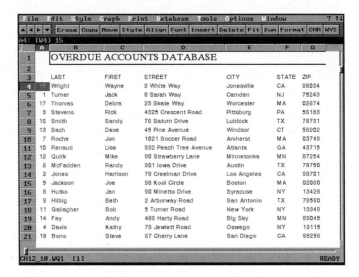

Tip 3: Add new records anywhere in the database and then re-sort them.

When adding new records, insert as many rows as you need by using the mouse to highlight the rows and then pressing Ctrl-I (the shortcut key combination for the /Edit Insert command). Select Rows, press ⏎Enter, and enter the new records. Do not worry about the order in which you enter them. After you enter all the new records into the database, sort the database by the field (key) that best suits your needs.

Searching for Records

You have learned how to use the /Database Sort command to reorganize information from the database by sorting records according to key fields. In this section of the chapter, you learn how to use /Database Query to search for records and then edit, extract, or delete the records you find.

Looking for records that meet one condition is the simplest form of searching a Quattro Pro database. In an inventory database, for example, you can determine when to reorder items by using a search operation to find any records with an on-hand quantity of fewer than four units. After you find the information you want, you can extract or copy the found records from the database to another section of the spreadsheet, separate from the database. For example, you can extract all records with a future purchase order date and print the newly extracted area as a record of pending purchases.

With Quattro Pro's search operations, you also have the option to search for only the first occurrence of a specified field value to develop a unique list of field entries. For example, you can search and extract a list of all the states represented in your database.

Minimum Search Requirements

The /Database Query command enables you to search for and extract data that meets specific criteria. After you choose /Database Query, a menu of the ten options is displayed for performing search and extract operations: Block, Criteria Table, Output Block, Assign Names, Locate, Extract, Unique, Delete, Reset, and Quit. These options are described in table 12.4.

Table 12.4
Database Query Menu Options

Option	Description
Block	Enables you to specify the location of the search area.
Criteria Table	Enables you to specify the conditions on which the search is based.
Output Block	Enables you to specify the block in which you want to locate the records extracted from the database.
Assign Names	Assigns block names to the cells in the second row of the database, using the first-row labels.
Locate	Finds records based on specified criteria.
Extract	Copies from the database the records that match the specified criteria, and places them in the output block.
Unique	Eliminates duplicates when copying records that match the specified criteria to the output block.
Delete	Removes from the data block records that match the specified criteria.
Reset	Resets the data block, criteria table, and output block.
Quit	Returns Quattro Pro to READY mode.

12

The first three options specify blocks applicable to the search operation. In all Query operations, you must specify the Block and Criteria Table—which set the location of the search area and the search conditions, respectively. You use the Output Block option to establish an output block only when you select a /Database Query command that copies records or parts of records to an area outside the database.

The next four options of the Database Query menu perform a variety of search functions. Locate moves down through a database and positions the cell selector on records that match given criteria. You can enter or change data in the records as you move the cell selector through them. Extract creates, in a specified area of the spreadsheet, copies of all or some of the fields in certain records that match given criteria. Unique is similar to Extract, but ignores duplicates that it copies as entries to the output block. Delete erases from a database all the records that match the given criteria and shifts the remaining records to fill in the remaining gaps.

The last two options of the Database Query menu, Reset and Quit, signal the end of the current search operation. Reset removes all previous search-related blocks so that you can specify a different search location, condition, and output block (if applicable). Quit restores Quattro Pro to READY mode.

Searching for Specific Records

To search for one or more specific records that meet certain criteria, you need to use three commands from the Database Query menu: Block, Criteria Table, and Locate. Suppose, for example, that you want to search a database containing a list of customers with overdue accounts to find a specific customer. The following sections describe the procedure.

Defining the Data Block

The *data block* for the /Database Query command is the block of records you want to search. The specified area does not have to include the entire database. Whether you search all or only part of a database, you *must* include the field-names row in the data block. (In contrast, remember that you do *not* include the field names in a sort operation.) If field names occupy space on more than one row, include only the bottom row in the data block. As defined by Quattro Pro, the first record is the row directly under the field names; therefore, do not use a blank row or a dashed line to separate the field names from the database records.

Select /Database Query Block, and then specify the data block by either highlighting the block or typing the cell addresses. You also can specify an assigned block name. You do not have to specify the data block again in later query operations, unless you change the search area.

The data block for the database containing the list of overdue accounts includes the entire database and the field names. To define the data block containing the records you want to search, follow these steps:

1. Press ⏴/⏵ to access the Quattro Pro menu.

2. Press ⏴D⏵ to select Database.

3. Press ⏴Q⏵ to select Query.

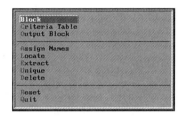

The Database Query menu appears.

4. Press ⏴B⏵ to select Block.

5. Specify the data block by highlighting the block or typing the block cell addresses or an assigned block name; then press ⏴Enter⏵.

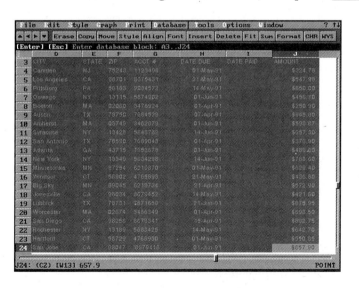

In this example, highlight the block A3..J24 and press ⏴Enter⏵.

12

6. To return to READY mode, press ⟨Q⟩ to select **Q**uit.

After you define the data block, the next step in a data query operation is to define the criteria table. This procedure is described in the following section.

Defining the Criteria Table

To search for data that meets certain conditions, or criteria, you must set up a special block called a *criteria table*, which specifies the criteria on which Quattro Pro will conduct the search. After you find an empty area of the spreadsheet for your criteria table, use the /**D**atabase **Q**uery **C**riteria Table command to specify the criteria.

You can use numbers, labels, or formulas as criteria. A criteria table can be up to 32 columns wide and two or more rows long. The first row must contain the field names of the search criteria, such as STATE. The rows below the unique field names contain the actual criteria, such as TX for Texas. The field names of the data block and the criteria table must match exactly.

Suppose that in an overdue accounts database, you want to identify all records for customers with the last name *Smith*. To define the criteria table containing the search conditions, follow these steps:

1. Locate an area of the spreadsheet where you can enter the criteria on which you want Quattro Pro to search the database.

In the top left cell of the area you choose (cell N3 in this example) type the label **CRITERIA TABLE** and press ⟨↵Enter⟩ to mark the area.

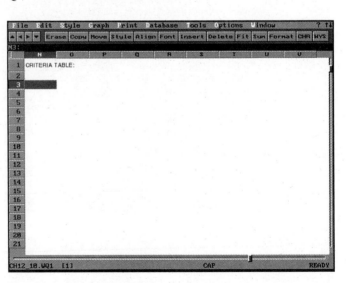

2. Copy the exact field names of your database to the section of the spreadsheet in which you want to locate the criteria table.

   Note: You do not have to include each field name in the criteria table; however, you should copy all field names, because later you may choose to enter criteria based on different field names.

   In this example, use the /Edit Copy command to copy all field names from the block A3..J3 to cell N3.

3. Type the search criteria just below the field name and press ⏎Enter.

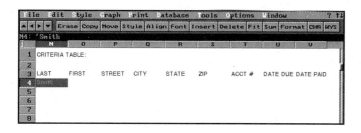

In the cell below the field name LAST, type **Smith** and press ⏎Enter.

4. Press / D Q C to select /Database Query Criteria Table.

5. Highlight (or enter the cell addresses of) the block of cells containing the field names and specific criteria; then press ⏎Enter.

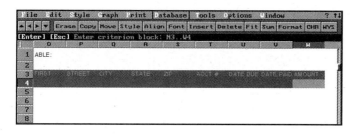

In this example, highlight the block N3..W4 and press ⏎Enter.

419

12

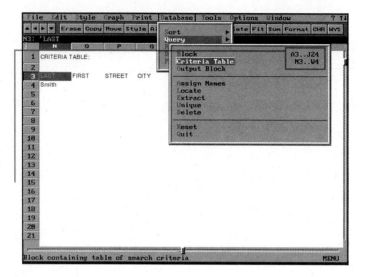

This example shows the Database Query menu with the Block and Criteria Table set.

6. To return to READY mode, press Q to select Quit.

After you define the criteria table, the next step involves searching for, but not copying, the specified records, as explained in the following section.

Finding Records That Meet the Criteria

After you enter the data block and criteria table, you have completed the minimum requirements for executing a Locate or Delete command.

To search for records that meet the criteria you have specified, follow these steps:

1. Press / to access the Quattro Pro menu.
2. Press D to select Database.
3. Press Q to select Query.
4. Press L to select Locate.

Quattro Pro places a highlight bar on the first record (in the data block) that meets the conditions specified in the criteria table. Notice that the mode indicator changes to FIND during the search.

12

In this example, the highlight bar rests on the first record that includes *Smith* in the LAST field, in row 8 of the spreadsheet.

5. Press ⊥ to move the highlight bar to the next record that meets the specified criteria. You can continue pressing ⊥ until Quattro Pro has highlighted the last record that meets the search conditions.

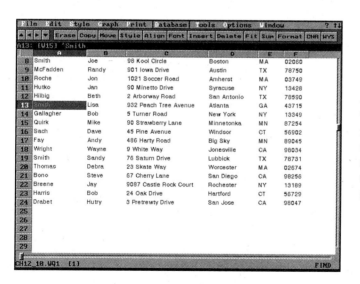

In this example, the highlight bar moves to row 13, the next occurrence of *Smith* in the LAST field of the database.

6. When you want to end the search, press Esc or ↵Enter to return to the Database Query menu.

12

7. To return to READY mode, press Q to select Quit.

Pressing Esc or ↵Enter and then selecting Quit moves the cell selector back to the cell location from which you initiated the /Database Query Locate command. You can press F7 (Query) to exit FIND mode and leave the cell selector in its current FIND mode location.

Press ↑ and ↓ to position the highlight bar on the next and previous records, respectively, that meet the search condition specified in the criteria table. You can press Home and End to position the highlight bar respectively on the first and last records in the database, even if those records do not meet the search criteria.

In FIND mode, you can press ↑ and ↓ to move the cursor to different fields in the current highlighted record. Then enter new values or use the Edit (F2) key to update the current values in the field. The next section discusses editing while in FIND mode.

Editing Records During a Search

To change a record while conducting a search, you can temporarily switch from FIND to EDIT mode, edit the record, and then return to FIND mode to search for other records. Suppose, for example, that you want to update a record in the overdue accounts database. Follow these steps to edit a record during a search:

1. To begin the search operation, press / D Q L to select /Database Query Locate.

2. In FIND mode, press ↑ or ↓ until the cursor is in the cell where you want to edit data.

3. Press F2 (Edit) to change from FIND to EDIT mode. The cell contents (if any) appear in the input line.

4. Type new data or press F2 (Edit) to edit existing data; then press ↵Enter.

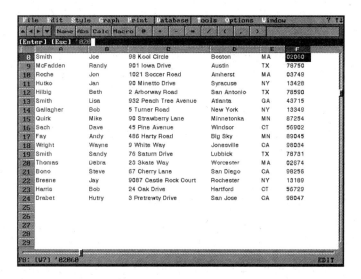

12

In this example,
edit Joe Smith's
ZIP code and
press ↵Enter.
Note that the
mode indicator is
EDIT.

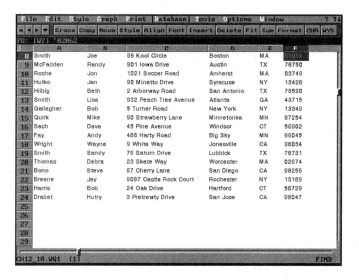

After you edit the
record, Quattro
Pro returns to
FIND mode and
displays the new
or edited data.
You can continue
searching for
records that meet
the criteria and
edit as necessary.

Listing All Specified Records

The Locate command has limited use, especially in a large database, because
the command must scroll through the entire file if you want to view each
record that meets the specified criteria. As an alternative to using the Locate
command, you can use the Extract command to copy to a blank area of the

423

12

spreadsheet only those records that meet specified conditions. Before you issue the command, you must define the blank area of the spreadsheet as an output block. You can view a list of all the extracted records, print the block of the newly extracted records, or even use the /Tools Xtract command to copy only the extracted record block to a new file on-disk.

Defining the Output Block

Choose a blank area in the spreadsheet as the output block to receive records copied in an extract operation. Designate the block to the right of or below the database. In the first row of the output block, type the names of only those fields whose contents you want to extract. You do not have to type these names in the same order as they appear in the database.

The field names in both the criteria and output blocks must exactly match the corresponding field names in the database. If you enter a database field name incorrectly in the output block—for example, if you enter FIRSTNAME instead of FIRST, or FORST instead of FIRST—an extract operation based on that field name will not work. To avoid mismatch errors, use the /Edit Copy command to copy the database field names to the criteria table and output block.

You can create an open-ended output block by entering only the field-names row as the block. The output block, in this case, can be any size, according to how many records meet the criteria. Alternatively, you can set the exact size of the extract area so that you do not accidentally overwrite any data located below the area.

To define the output block where you want to copy records meeting the specified criteria, follow these steps:

1. Locate an area of the spreadsheet where you want Quattro Pro to copy the records meeting the criteria. Type the label OUTPUT BLOCK and press ⏎Enter to mark the area.

2. Copy the exact field names of your database to the section of the spreadsheet where you want the output block located.

   Note: You do not have to extract entire records or maintain the order of field names in the output block. If you do not need to see information for every field in the output block, copy only the desired field names.

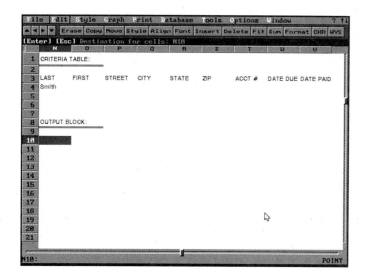

12

In this example, use the /Edit Copy command to copy all field names from the block A3..J3 to cell N10.

3. Press ⌐/⌐ D ⌐ Q ⌐ O to select /Database Query Output.

4. When the prompt Enter block to copy to with Extract or Unique appears, highlight the block where you want to copy the records, and press ⏎Enter. You can indicate either an unlimited block or a block limited to a specific block of cells.

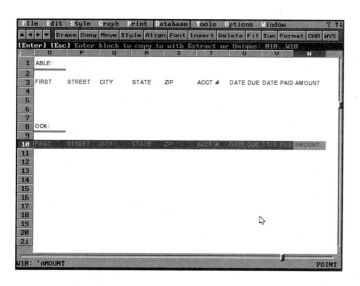

To enter an unlimited output block, highlight only the cells containing field names. In this example, highlight the block N10..W10 and press ⏎Enter.

12

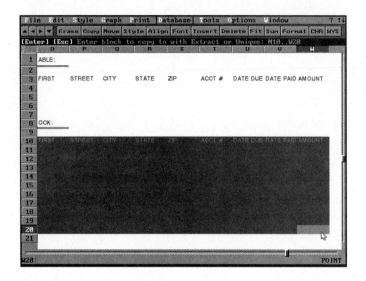

To enter a limited output block, specify additional rows below the field-names row, such as the block N10..W20, and press ⏎Enter.

5. To return to READY mode, press Q to select Quit.

To create an open-ended extract area that does not limit the number of incoming records, specify as the output block only the row containing the output field names. Keep in mind that an extract operation first removes all existing data from the output block. If you use only the field-names row to specify the output area, all data below that row (down to row 8192) will be destroyed to make room for the unknown number of incoming extracted records. Therefore, ensure that no data is located below the row of field names if you choose an open-ended output block.

To limit the size of the output block, enter the upper left to lower right cell coordinates of the entire output block. The first row in the specified block must contain the field names; the remaining rows must accommodate the maximum number of records you expect to receive from the extract operation. Use this method when you want to retain additional data that is below the extract area. If you do not allow sufficient room in the fixed-length output area, the extract operation will abort, and the message Too many records will be displayed on-screen. Nevertheless, the output area will be filled with as many records as will fit.

Each time you execute a search command that uses the output block, such as /Database Query Extract, Quattro Pro overwrites all data in the output block; therefore, you do not need to clear the data from the output block each time you use the /Database Query Extract or /Database Query Unique commands.

Executing the Extract Command

The /Database Query Extract command enables you to copy specific records from the database to the output range; you can then quickly and easily analyze those records. Before you can execute the /Database Query Extract command, however, you must type the search conditions in the criteria table of the spreadsheet, copy the output field names to the output block in the spreadsheet, and use the /Database Query commands to specify the data block, criteria table, and output block.

To extract (or copy) to the output block records that meet the specified criteria, follow these steps:

1. Press ⌷ to access the Quattro Pro menu.
2. Press Ⓓ to select Database.
3. Press Ⓠ to select Query.
4. Press Ⓔ to select Extract.

    Quattro Pro copies all records that meet the specified criteria in the criteria table to the output area, in the order of their occurrence in the block.

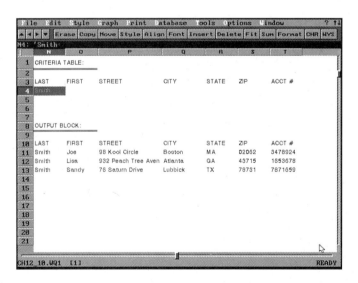

In this example, Quattro Pro has copied to the output block all records in the LAST field that correspond to the search criteria *Smith*.

5. To return to READY mode, press Ⓠ to select Quit .

To accelerate what seems to be a time-consuming setup process, you can establish a standard data block, criteria table, and output block, and then store the block names for these locations. Keeping in mind the limit of 32 criteria fields, you can establish a single criteria table that encompasses all the key fields on which you might search. By establishing such a block, you save the time required to respecify a criteria table for each extract on different field names.

When Quattro Pro is in READY mode, you can press the Query (F7) key to repeat the most recent query operation (**E**xtract, in this example), thereby eliminating the need to select /**D**atabase **Q**uery **E**xtract after modifying the criteria table. Use this shortcut method only when you do not want to change the locations of the data block, criteria table, and output block.

Copying Extracted Records to a New File

If you want to copy extracted records to their own special file, follow these steps:

1. Press / to access the Quattro Pro menu.
2. Press T to select **T**ools.
3. Press X to select **X**tract.
4. Press F to select **F**ormulas or V to select **V**alues, depending on whether the data contains formulas or values you want retained in the new file.
5. Enter a name for the new file and press ↵Enter .
6. Highlight the block or type the block address of the records you want to copy to the new file; then press ↵Enter .

    For example, highlight the block N10..W13 and press ↵Enter .

Quattro Pro creates a new file that contains the data from your extract block. To access this file, you must issue the /**F**ile **R**etrieve command and specify the new file name.

Printing the Extracted Records

To print the extracted records, follow these steps:

1. Press / to access the Quattro Pro menu.
2. Press P to select **P**rint.
3. Press B to select **B**lock; then specify the output block with the extracted records.
4. Press S to select **S**preadsheet Print.

Quattro Pro prints the records in the output block.

Creating More Complex Criteria Tables

In addition to searching for an "exact match" of a specified label within a field of labels (such as *Smith* within the LAST field), Quattro Pro performs a wide variety of other types of record searches. For example, you can search for an exact match in numeric fields. In addition, you can choose a search criteria that only partially matches the contents of specified fields. You also can include formulas in your search criteria, as well as use multiple criteria that involve searching for specified conditions in more than one field.

Using Wild Cards in Criteria Tables

Depending on the complexity of your database operations, you may need to be a bit more creative when specifying criteria tables in Quattro Pro. For that reason, Quattro Pro enables you to use wild cards and formulas in criteria tables. The following examples will help you understand how you can use wild cards in search operations:

Enter	To find
N?	NC, NJ, and NY
BO?L?	BOWLE, but not BOWL
BO?L*	BOWLE, BOWL, BOLLESON, and BOELING
SAN*	SANTA BARBARA and SAN FRANCISCO
SAN *	SAN FRANCISCO and SAN DIEGO, but not SANTA BARBARA
~N*	Strings (in specified fields) that do not begin with the letter *N*

You can use Quattro Pro's wild cards for matching labels in database operations. The characters ?, *, and ~ have special meanings when you use them in the criteria table. The ? character instructs Quattro Pro to accept any single character in that specific position; you can use ? only to find fields of the same length. You can use the * character, which tells Quattro Pro to accept any and all characters that follow, on field contents of unequal length meeting the specified criteria. By placing a tilde (~) at the beginning of a search condition, you tell Quattro Pro to accept all values except those that follow.

12

In this example, the criteria ~N? in the STATE field of the criteria table will exclude all records containing a STATE beginning with *N*.

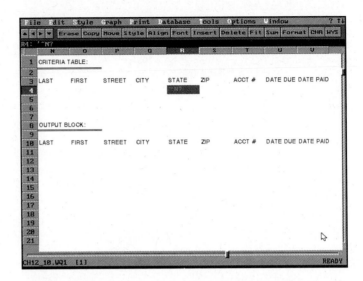

With ~N? as the criteria, the output block after you use the Extract command includes all records that do not match NY or NJ.

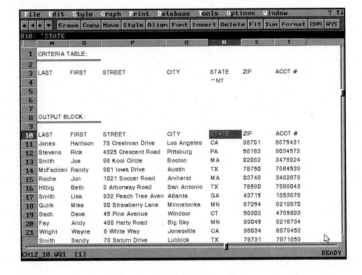

Use the ? and * wild-card characters when you are unsure of the spelling used in field contents. When using a wild card to perform an extract operation, be sure that the results are what you need. Be extremely careful when you use wild cards with a Delete command (discussed later in this chapter). If you are not careful, you may remove more records than you intend.

Entering Formulas in Criteria Tables

To set up formulas that query numeric fields in the database, you can use the following relational (or logical) operators:

Operator	Description
>	Greater than
<	Less than
=	Equal to
>=	Greater than or equal to
<=	Less than or equal to
<>	Not equal to

Create a formula that references the first field entry in the numeric column you want to search. Quattro Pro tests the formula on each cell down the column until the program reaches the end of the database. If you want to reference cells outside the data block of the database, use formulas that include absolute cell addressing rather than relative cell addressing.

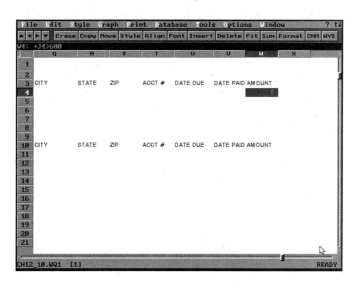

In this example, the criteria is the formula +J4>600 in the AMOUNT field. The formula evaluates to 0 (negative), which indicates that the first record of the database, in row 4, does not match the criteria (the amount is not greater than 600).

If the first record in this example did meet the criteria (the amount is greater than 600), the formula would evaluate to 1 (positive).

12

With the formula +J4>600 specified in the AMOUNT field of the criteria table, the output block after an **Extract** includes all records with an amount due greater than $600.

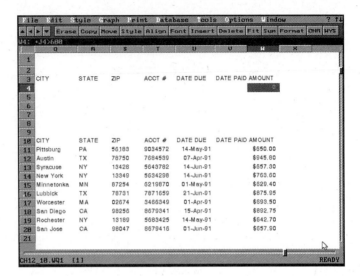

Note: The reference to cell J4 in the formula indicates the location of the first record of the corresponding search field. For example, the first record of the database is in row 4, and the search field is located in column J.

Specifying Multiple Criteria

So far, you have seen how to base a **Locate** or **Extract** operation on only one criterion. In this section, you learn how to use multiple criteria for your queries. When you maintain a criteria table that includes all (or many) field names, you can quickly extract records based on alternative conditions. You also can continue to add more conditions that must be met.

You can set up multiple criteria in which all the criteria must be met or in which any *one* criterion must be met. For example, searching a music department's library for sheet music requiring drums *and* trumpets is likely to produce fewer selections than searching for music appropriate for drums *or* trumpets. You can indicate two or more criteria, all of which must be met, by specifying the conditions in separate fields of the criteria row immediately below the field names.

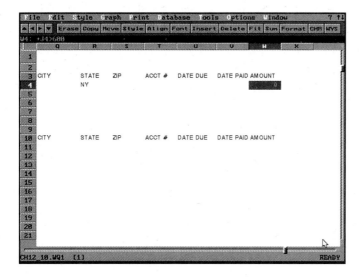

In this example, the criteria are set to extract all records in the data block in which the STATE is NY and the AMOUNT is greater than $600.

12

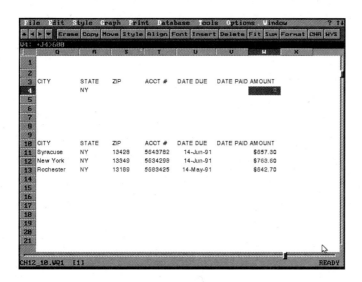

The output block after the Extract displays all customers from NY and who owe at least $600.

Using multiple criteria in a single row of the criteria table tells Quattro Pro to search for the records that meet this criterion *and* that criterion. Notice that the search criteria are listed in a single row immediately below the field-names row.

In contrast, placing criteria on different rows finds or extracts records based on this field condition *or* that field condition. You also can use this type of multiple criteria to *search* on one or more fields.

433

12

Searching a single field for more than one condition is the simplest use of criteria entered on separate rows. For example, you can extract from the overdue accounts database only those records with state abbreviations of NY or TX. To perform this search, under the STATE criteria field, you type one condition immediately below the other. Be sure to use the /Database Query Criteria Table command to expand the definition of the criteria table to include the additional row.

In this example, criteria are in separate rows to find all accounts originating in New York or Texas. Notice that each condition is listed in a separate row under the field-names row.

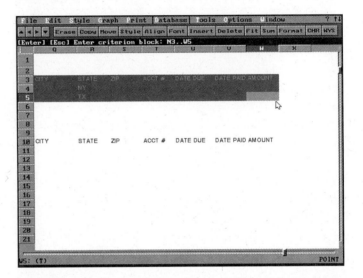

The result of the Extract is shown in the output block.

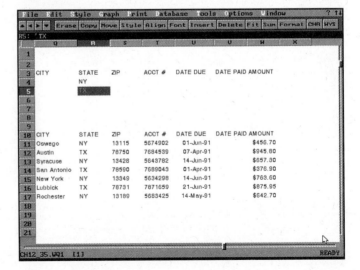

12

You also can specify multiple criteria on different rows with two or more different criteria fields. Building on the preceding example, suppose that you want to find the records with the states NY or TX *and* with overdue amounts of at least $600.

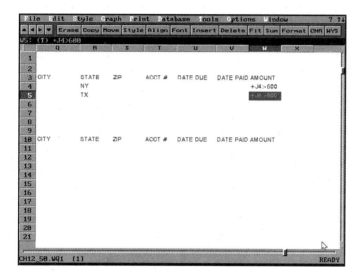

Multiple criteria on different rows are used here to find records that have either NY or TX in the STATE field *and* overdue amounts of at least $600. The formulas under AMOUNT are shown with a Text format so you can easily see the criteria.

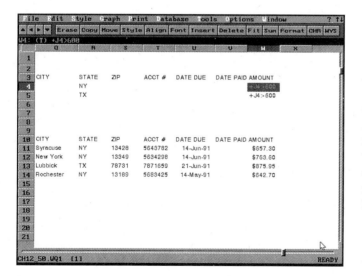

As shown, when the **E**xtract command is issued, the records that meet the specified conditions appear in the output block.

If you are careful when you specify conditions, you can mix both multiple fields and multiple rows within the criteria table. Follow the format of placing

12

records that meet *all* criteria at once in a single row immediately below the criteria field-names row, and placing records that meet *any* of the criteria in a separate row below. Because using multiple criteria may sometimes get confusing, a good practice is to test the logic of your criteria on a small sample of records to verify that the results are what you want. Then you can proceed to search all your records according to the multiple criteria.

Using Special Operators

To combine search conditions within a single field, use the special operators #AND# and #OR#. Use the special operator #NOT# to negate a search condition. Use #AND# or #OR# to search on two or more conditions within the same field. For example, suppose that you want to extract from the overdue accounts database all records with the states New Jersey (NJ) and Massachusetts (MA) in the STATE field.

You use the #AND#, #OR#, and #NOT# operators to enter (in one field) conditions that can be entered some other way (usually in at least two fields). For example, you can enter the following characters in a single cell of the STATE field in the criteria table as an alternative criteria entry to entering each condition on a separate line:

    +E4="NJ"#OR#E4="MA"

Again, the reference to cell E4 in the formula indicates that you are searching the field located in column E, beginning with the first database record located in row 4. Use #NOT# at the beginning of a condition to negate that condition. For example, you can find all records that do not have CA listed in the STATE field by specifying the criteria #NOT#CA in the criteria table.

Here, the formula condition has been entered in cell R4, as shown in the input line. The extracted records are displayed in rows 11 through 14.

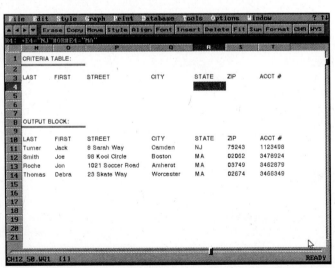

Performing Other Types of Searches

In addition to the Locate and Extract commands, you can use the Database Query menu's Unique and Delete commands for performing searches. By issuing the Unique command, you can produce (in the output block) a copy of only the first occurrence of a record that meets the specified criteria. The Delete command enables you to update the contents of your Quattro Pro database by deleting all records that meet the specified criteria. After entering the search conditions, you need to specify only the data block and criteria table before you issue the Delete command.

Searching for Unique Records

Ordinarily, you use the Unique command to copy into the output area only a small portion of each record that meets the criteria. For example, if you want a list of states represented in the overdue accounts database, set up an output block that includes only the STATE field. To search all records, leave blank the row below the field-names row in the criteria table. Then define the data block, criteria table, and output block and select /Database Query Unique. In the following example, the output block includes only the STATE field, and the row below the field-names row in the criteria table is blank.

To copy to the output block unique records that meet the criteria you have specified, follow these steps:

1. Press ⌐/⌐ to access the Quattro Pro menu.
2. Press ⌐D⌐ to select Database.
3. Press ⌐Q⌐ to select Query.
4. Press ⌐U⌐ to select Unique.

    Quattro Pro copies all records to the output area in the same order of their occurrence in the data block.

12

In this example, the **U**nique command produces a list of the different states represented in the database.

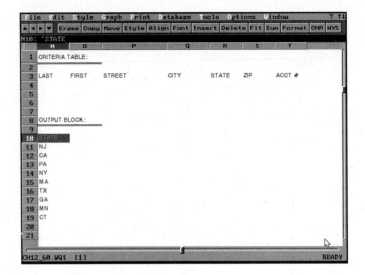

5. To return to READY mode, press ⌷Q⌷ to select **Q**uit.

Deleting Specified Records

As you know, you can use the /**E**dit **D**elete **R**ows command to remove records from a database. An alternative approach is to use the /**D**atabase **Q**uery **D**elete command to remove from the database unwanted records matching a specified criteria. Before you select **D**elete from the **D**atabase **Q**uery menu, specify the block of records you want to search (the data block) and the conditions for the deletion (the criteria).

In this data block, some records contain a date in the DATE PAID column and others do not.

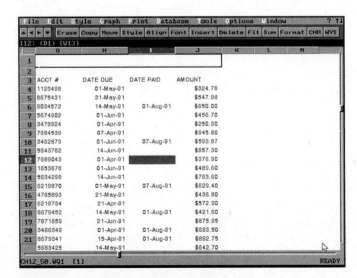

In the following example, you will delete the records from the overdue accounts database that have an entry in the DATE PAID column. The first row of the DATE PAID column in the criteria table contains the following formula that will produce the desired results:

+I4<>" "

12

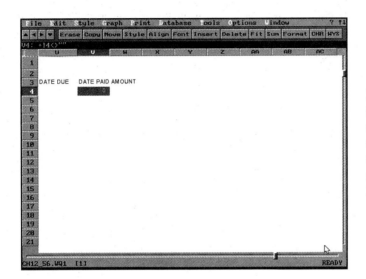

In this example, the criteria (in cell V4) will delete all records that contain a date in the DATE PAID field.

To delete database records that meet the specified criteria, follow these steps:

1. Press ⃞/⃞ to access the Quattro Pro menu.
2. Press ⃞D⃞ to select **D**atabase.
3. Press ⃞Q⃞ to select **Q**uery.
4. Press ⃞D⃞ to select **D**elete.
5. Press ⃞C⃞ to select **C**ancel, or press ⃞D⃞ to select **D**elete and proceed with the command.

12

In this example, press D to select Delete. Quattro Pro acts on the Delete command without displaying the records it deletes.

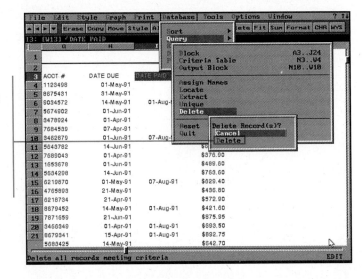

Quattro Pro has deleted all records with an entry in the DATE PAID column of the database.

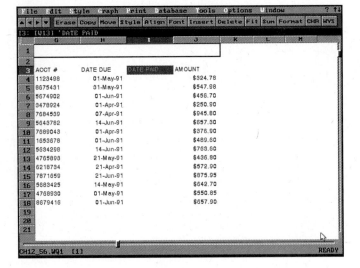

6. To return to READY mode, press Q to select Quit.

Be extremely careful when you issue the Delete command. To give you the opportunity to verify that you indeed want to select the Delete command, Quattro Pro prompts you to select Cancel or Delete. Select Cancel to abort the Delete command. Select Delete to verify that you want to execute the delete operation.

Although you are prompted to verify that you want to delete records, you won't have the opportunity to view the records that match the specified criteria. For this reason, you should use the /File Save As command to make a copy of the database. Alternatively, use the Extract command to copy the records you plan to delete, view them, and then proceed with the delete operation when you are sure that you want to remove those records from the database.

Using the Query (F7) Key

The Query (F7) function key repeats the last /Database Query command you issued. If the Extract command was the last /Database Query command you executed, pressing F7 will perform an extract. Pressing F7 enables you to make changes to the criteria and swiftly search for the new records. For example, if you execute the /Database Query Locate command, you can exit FIND mode, change the criteria, and quickly execute the /Database Query Locate command again simply by pressing F7 .

Summary

Although used frequently for spreadsheet applications, Quattro Pro also is used for many types of database applications. Because a Quattro Pro database is created within the column-row spreadsheet format and uses the same cell selector and direction keys used for other applications, Quattro Pro's database feature is generally faster, and easier to access and use than some programs dedicated solely to database management.

The Database command on Quattro Pro's main menu leads to commands for performing common database applications such as sorting data, searching for records that meet specific criteria, and extracting records from the main database. Fast and easy to use, Quattro Pro's database can sort as many as five fields. When searching for and extracting records, you must create in the spreadsheet a *data block* that contains the field names and all records you want to search, and a *criteria table* to specify the search conditions. When extracting records from a Quattro Pro database, you also must indicate the *output block*, where you want the data copied when extracted.

Search conditions in a Quattro Pro database can be text strings or numbers, but also can be much more complicated. More complicated conditions on which to search a Quattro Pro database can include formulas, as well as conditions that involve multiple criteria.

12

Specifically, you learned the following key information about Quattro Pro:

■ A database consists of records and fields. In Quattro Pro, a record is a row of cells in the database, and a field is one type of information within the record, such as a ZIP code.

■ Quattro Pro's Database menu contains most of the commands commonly used to manage and manipulate databases; however, you can use other options from Quattro Pro's main menu—options often used with spreadsheets—to manage databases.

■ You should carefully plan a database before you create it, determining which categories (fields) of information you want to include and what type of output you want.

■ An ideal location for a database is an area where inserting and deleting rows and columns won't affect other applications above, below, to the right, or to the left of the database.

■ The /Database Restrict Input command restricts input to only unprotected cells in a protected data-input block. The cell selector moves only among the unprotected cells.

■ You can use the /Edit Insert Rows and /Edit Delete Rows commands to add or delete records (rows) in the database. Similarly, you can use the /Edit Insert Columns and /Edit Delete Columns commands to add or delete fields (columns) in the database.

■ The /Database Sort command enables you to change the order of records by sorting them according to the contents of specified key fields. In Quattro Pro, you can sort on as many as five keys, in ascending or descending order, and by rows or columns.

■ Use the /Database Query command to set up a database and search a database for records that match a specified criteria. Before starting a search, you must first specify the *data block* and *criteria table* with the commands /Database Query Block and /Database Query Criteria Table, respectively. When using the Extract and Unique options of the /Database Query command, you also must specify the *output block* with the /Database Query Output command.

■ The /Database Query Locate command positions the cell selector on records matching a given criteria. Records can be modified as you move the cell selector among them.

■ The /Database Query Extract command copies records (or specified portions of records) matching a given criteria to another area of the spreadsheet.

■ To perform complex search operations, you can use the wild-card characters ?, *, and ~; you can enter formulas in criteria tables; and you can enter multiple criteria involving two or more fields.

■ The /Database Query Unique command copies records to an output block, but does not copy duplicate entries based on fields specified in the criteria table.

■ The /Database Query Delete command erases from a database the records that match conditions specified in the criteria table. Quattro Pro asks for confirmation before deleting the records.

■ The Query (F7) key repeats the last /Database Query command issued, which enables you to execute a Query command quickly after you change the criteria.

Now that you have learned about Quattro Pro's spreadsheet, graphics, and data management capabilities, you can go on to the next chapter, which introduces Quattro Pro macros. Macros enable you to perform simple or complex routine operations with the press of a few keystrokes.

12

Understanding Macros

13

Planning macros

Positioning macros in the spreadsheet

Documenting and naming macros

Using the Record feature to record keystrokes

Executing macros

Using an automatic macro

Debugging and editing macros

Creating a macro library

In addition to the capabilities available from the commands in Quattro Pro's main menu, another feature makes Quattro Pro one of the most powerful and popular integrated spreadsheet, graphics, and database programs available today. Quattro Pro macros enable you to automate and customize your Quattro Pro applications. Macros enable you to reduce tasks requiring multiple keystrokes to a two-keystroke operation. Just press two keys and Quattro Pro does the rest, whether you're formatting a block, creating a graph, or printing a spreadsheet. You also can control and customize spreadsheet applications by using Quattro Pro's powerful macro commands—94 built-in commands that give you a greater range of control over your Quattro Pro applications.

You can think of simple keystroke macros as the building blocks for macro command programs. When you begin to add macro commands to simple keystroke macros, you can control and automate many of the actions required to build, modify, and update Quattro Pro spreadsheets. At the most sophisticated level, you can use Quattro Pro's macro commands as a full-fledged programming language for developing custom business applications.

13

Key Terms in This Chapter

Macro	A series of stored keystrokes or commands that you retrieve or replay by pressing two or more keys.
Program	A list of instructions in a computer programming language, such as Quattro Pro's macro commands, that tells the computer what to do.
Macro commands	Quattro Pro's powerful programming language consisting of more than 94 built-in commands that are not accessible through the Quattro Pro menu system.
Tilde (~)	The symbol you use in a macro to indicate the Enter keystroke.
Key names	Representations of keyboard keys used in macros. Key names are enclosed in braces— for example, {EDIT} for the Edit (F2) key.
Documented macro or program	A macro or program that contains information explaining each step in the macro or program.
Bug	An error in a macro or program.
Debugging	The process of identifying and fixing errors in a macro or program.

In this chapter is an introduction to the concept and application of macros. You also learn some simple keystroke macros, which you can include in your own *macro library*, a collection of macros. For more detailed information on macros and macro commands, consult Que's *Using Quattro Pro 4*, Special Edition.

What Is a Macro?

A *macro*, in its most basic form, is a collection of stored keystrokes that you can replay at any time to carry out a particular operation. These keystrokes can be commands or simple text and numeric entries. Macros provide an alternative to typing data and commands from the keyboard. Macros, therefore, can save you time by automating frequently performed tasks.

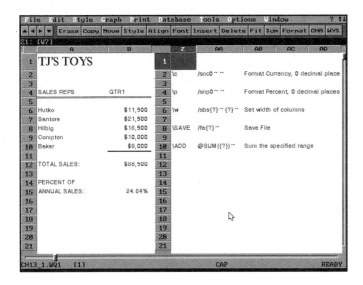

This example shows five simple keystroke macros in the window on the right. The window on the left displays spreadsheet data.

By creating a simple macro, for example, you can automate the sequence of seven keystrokes necessary for formatting a cell in Currency format with zero decimal places.

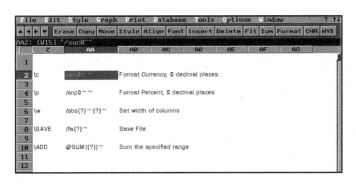

You can execute the seven keystrokes in cell AA2 by pressing two keys, Alt-C.

You can name macros in two ways: with a single letter or with a descriptive name. To identify a macro with a letter, you type a backslash (\) and the letter you want to use to identify the macro. You execute a single-letter macro by holding down Alt and pressing the macro letter you designated. To identify a macro with a descriptive name, you type a macro name of up to 15 characters. You execute this type of macro by pressing /Tools Macro Execute (Alt-F2 E), pressing Choices (F3), highlighting the macro you want to use, and then pressing ↵Enter.

13

447

The Elements of Macros

Quattro Pro macros follow a specific format, whether they are simple keystroke macros or macros that perform complex tasks. A macro is nothing more than a specially named text cell. You create macros by entering the keystrokes (or representations of those keystrokes) you want to store into a spreadsheet cell. Suppose, for example, that you want to create a simple macro that will format the current cell to appear in Currency format with no decimal places. The macro would look like this:

'/snc0~~

The following list explains the elements of this formatting macro, providing descriptions of the actions that result when Quattro Pro executes each element:

Macro Element	Action
'	Tells Quattro Pro that the information that follows is a label.
/	Displays the Quattro Pro menu.
s	Selects Style.
n	Selects Numeric Format.
c	Selects Currency.
0	Tells Quattro Pro to set 0 decimal places.
~~	Functions as two Enter keystrokes (each tilde represents pressing ⏎Enter one time).

You enter this macro into the spreadsheet in exactly the same way you would any other label: type a label prefix, followed by the characters in the label. The label prefix (displayed only in the input line) informs Quattro Pro that what follows should be treated as a label. Every macro that starts with a nontext character (/, \, +, −, or a number) must begin with a label prefix. If you do not use this prefix, Quattro Pro automatically interprets the next character, / in this example, as a command to be executed immediately instead of stored in the cell. Any of the three Quattro Pro label prefixes (', ", or ^) works equally well.

The next four characters in the macro represent the command to create the desired format. After all, *snc* is simply shorthand for /Style Numeric Format Currency. The *0* (zero) tells Quattro Pro that you want no digits displayed to the right of the decimal point. If you were entering this command from the keyboard, you would type **0** in response to a prompt.

At the end of the macro are two characters called *tildes*. When used in a macro, a tilde (~) represents the Enter key. In this case, the two tildes signal that ⏎Enter should be pressed twice—once to accept the number of decimal places, and the second time to select the current cell as the block to format.

Other elements used in macros include block names and cell addresses. Although you can use these two elements interchangeably, you should use block names instead of cell addresses whenever possible. Block names are preferred because if you move data included in specified blocks or if you insert or delete rows and columns, the macro continues to refer to the correct cells and blocks after Quattro Pro adjusts the block names. Cell references you use in macros do not adjust to the changes you make in the spreadsheet; you must modify them manually.

The {?} command included in some of the macro examples in this chapter is a type of macro command. This command pauses the macro so that you can type information, such as a file name, from the keyboard. The macro continues executing after you press ⏎Enter. For example, in a macro that sets column widths, you can include the {?} command to enable you to type the new column width when the macro pauses. Then you press ⏎Enter to complete execution of the macro.

Characters in macro commands are not case-sensitive; you can use capitalization wherever you want. For readability in this book, however, lowercase letters are used in macros to indicate commands; block names and key names are in uppercase letters.

Macro Key Names and Special Keys

In addition to the tilde (~), Quattro Pro uses other symbols to stand for keystrokes. Using the previous formatting example, you can add some key names and special keys to highlight a block of the spreadsheet, just as if you were using the /Style Numeric Format command.

Adding .{END}{RIGHT} to the formatting macro anchors the block and highlights all occupied cells to the right in the current row.

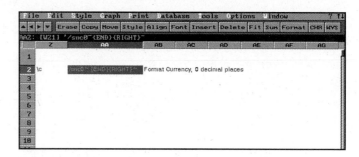

This revised macro is similar to the preceding one, except that the .{END}{RIGHT} command moves the cell selector. You can use this version of the macro to format an entire row instead of just one cell.

Once again, notice the apostrophe (') at the beginning of the macro (displayed in the input line) and the tilde (~) at the end. Notice also the phrase .{END}{RIGHT} in the macro. The period (.) anchors the cell selector. The {END} key name stands for the End key on the keyboard. The {RIGHT} key name represents the right-arrow key. This phrase has the same effect in the macro as these three keys would have if you pressed them in sequence from the keyboard. The cell selector moves to the next boundary between blank and occupied cells in the row.

You use these types of representations to indicate key names and special keys on the keyboard. In every case, you enclose the key name in braces. For example, {UP} represents the up-arrow key, {ESC} stands for the Esc key, and {GRAPH} represents the F10 function key.

Tables 13.1 through 13.4 provide lists of macro key names and special keys, grouped according to how you use them: function keys, direction keys, editing keys, and special keys.

Table 13.1
Macro Key Names for Function Keys

Function Key	Key Name	Action
Help (F1)	{HELP}	Accesses Quattro Pro's on-line Help system.
Edit (F2)	{EDIT}	Edits the contents of the current cell.
Choices (F3)	{CHOICES}	Displays a list of the block names in the current spreadsheet.

Function Key	Key Name	Action
Abs (F4)	{ABS}	Converts a relative reference to absolute, or an absolute reference to relative.
GoTo (F5)	{GOTO}	Moves the cell selector to the specified cell address or block name.
Pane (F6)	{PANE}	Moves the cell selector to the other side of a split screen.
Query (F7)	{QUERY}	Repeats the most recent /Database Query operation.
Table (F8)	{TABLE}	Repeats the most recent table operation.
Calc (F9)	{CALC}	Recalculates the spreadsheet.
Graph (F10)	{GRAPH}	Redraws the current graph on-screen.

Table 13.2
Macro Key Names for Direction Keys

Direction Key	Key Name	Action
↑	{UP} or {U}	Moves the cell selector up one row.
↓	{DOWN} or {D}	Moves the cell selector down one row.
←	{LEFT} or {L}	Moves the cell selector left one column.
→	{RIGHT} or {R}	Moves the cell selector right one column.
Shift-Tab or Ctrl-←	{BIGLEFT} or {BACKTAB}	Moves the cell selector left one screen.
Tab or Ctrl-→	{BIGRIGHT} or {TAB}	Moves the cell selector right one screen.

continues

13

451

13

Table 13.2 *(Continued)*

Direction Key	Key Name	Action
PgUp	{PGUP}	Moves the cell selector up one screen.
PgDn	{PGDN}	Moves the cell selector down one screen.
Home	{HOME}	Moves the cell selector to cell A1 or, if /Window Options Locked Titles is set, to the top left cell outside the titles area.
End	{END}	Used with {UP}, {DOWN}, {LEFT}, or {RIGHT}, moves the cell selector in the indicated direction to the next boundary between blank cells and cells that contain data. Used with {HOME}, moves the cell selector to the lower right corner of the spreadsheet.

Table 13.3
Macro Key Names for Editing Keys

Editing Key	Key Name	Action
Del	{DELETE} or {DEL}	Used with {EDIT}, deletes a single character from a cell entry.
Ins	{INSERT} or {INS}	Toggles between Insert and Overtype modes when you are editing a cell.
Esc	{ESCAPE} or {ESC}	Indicates the Esc key.
◆Backspace	{BACKSPACE} or {BS}	Indicates the Backspace key.

Table 13.4
Macro Key Names for Special Keys

Special Key	Key Name	Action
⏎Enter	~	Indicates the Enter key.
~	{~}	Causes a tilde to appear in the spread-sheet.
{	{{}	Causes an open brace to appear in the spreadsheet.
}	{}}	Causes a close brace to appear in the spreadsheet.

13

Note: A few keys or key combinations do not have a key name to identify them. These include ⇧Shift, PrtSc, Debug (⇧Shift-F2), Macros (⇧Shift-F3), and Undo (Alt-F5). You cannot represent these keys or key combinations within macros.

To specify that you want to use a key name more than once, you can include repetition factors inside the braces. For example, you can use the following statements in macros:

Statement	Action
{PGUP 3}	Press PgUp three times.
{RIGHT JUMP}	Press → the number of times indicated by the value in the cell named JUMP.

Planning Macros

You can think of a simple keystroke macro as a substitute for keyboard commands. The best way to plan a macro, therefore, is to step, one keystroke at a time, through the series of instructions you intend to include in the macro. Perform this exercise before you start creating the macro. Take notes about each step as you proceed with the commands on-screen, and then translate the keystrokes you have written down into a macro that conforms to the rules discussed in this chapter.

Stepping through an operation at the keyboard is an easy way to build simple macros. The more experience you have with Quattro Pro commands, the easier it becomes to "think out" the keystrokes you need to use in a macro and enter them directly into the spreadsheet.

For more complex macros, the best approach is to break them into smaller macros that execute in a series. Each small macro performs one simple operation; the series of simple operations together performs the desired application.

This approach starts with the result of an application. What is the application supposed to do or produce? What form must the results take? If you start with the desired results and work backward, you lower the risk of producing the wrong results with your macro.

Next, consider input. What data do you need? What data is available and in what form? How much work is involved in going from the data to the results?

Finally, look at the process. How do you analyze available data and, using Quattro Pro, produce the desired results? How can you divide necessary calculations into a series of tasks, each of which can have a simple macro?

This "divide-and-conquer" method of breaking a complex task into smaller and simpler pieces is the key to successful development of macros and complex spreadsheets. Although this method entails some initial work, you will be able to detect and correct errors more easily because they will be located in a small section of the macro.

Positioning Macros in the Spreadsheet

In most cases, you should place your macros outside the area that the data on your spreadsheet will occupy. This practice helps you avoid accidentally overwriting or erasing part of a macro as you create your model.

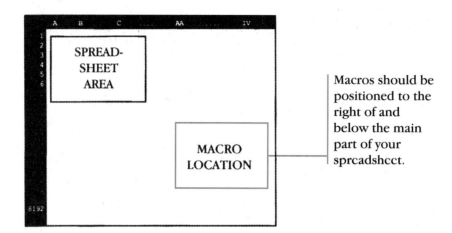

Macros should be positioned to the right of and below the main part of your sprcadshcct.

13

This position lessens the possibility of the macro's block being accidentally included in spreadsheet operations. With this placement, deleting rows or columns in the spreadsheet area will not affect the cells in the macro location.

Quattro Pro has no rule that says you must place your macros in the same place in every spreadsheet. You may, however, want to make a habit of placing your macros in a certain column, such as column AA, so that you always will know where to look in your applications for the macros if you need to modify them. Also, if your spreadsheets rarely require more than 26 columns, you don't have to worry about overwriting the macro area with the spreadsheet data. Positioning the macros as such means that deleting rows or columns from the main part of your spreadsheet will not affect the cells in the macro location.

In small spreadsheets, on the other hand, you may want to put your macros in column I. You can reach the macros from the home screen by pressing `Tab↹` once, if all the columns have a width of nine characters and Quattro Pro is in Text mode.

You can assign the block name MACROS to the area containing the macros. Using a block name enables you to use the GoTo (`F5`) key to move to the macro area quickly.

Documenting Macros

Professional programmers usually write programs that are *documented*. This term means that the program contains comments that help to explain each step in the program. In BASIC, these comments are in REM (for REMark) statements. For example, in the following program, the REM statements explain the actions taken by the other statements:

```
10 REM This program adds two numbers
20 REM Enter first number
30 INPUT A
40 REM Enter second number
50 INPUT B
60 REM Add numbers together
70 C=A+B
80 REM Display result
90 Print C
```

Document your Quattro Pro macros by placing comments in the column to the right of the macro steps.

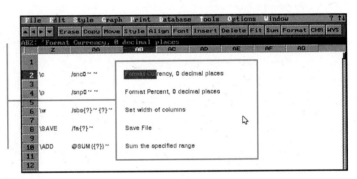

Including comments in your macros makes them far easier to use. Comments are especially useful when you have created complex macros that are important to the spreadsheet's overall design. Suppose that you have created a complex macro but have not looked at it for a month. Then you decide that you want to modify the macro. Without built-in comments, you might have a difficult time remembering what each step of the macro does.

Naming Macros

If you enter a macro into the spreadsheet as a label (or a series of labels), you must assign a name to it before you can execute it.

If you choose to use a letter to name a macro, you should select a letter that in some way helps describe the macro. For example, you might assign the letter *c* to a macro that formats a block as currency.

To assign a name to a macro, follow these steps:

1. Press ⌊/⌋ to access the Quattro Pro menu.

2. Press ⌊E⌋ to select Edit.

3. Press ⌊N⌋ to select Names.

4. Press ⌊C⌋ to select Create.

5. Type \ and a single letter, and then press ⌊↵Enter⌋, or type a descriptive name of up to 15 characters and press ⌊↵Enter⌋.

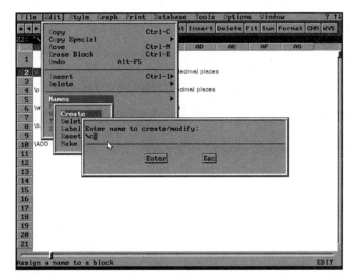

For this example, type \c and press ⌊↵Enter⌋.

6. Highlight, or type the cell address of, the first cell of the macro; then press ⌊↵Enter⌋.

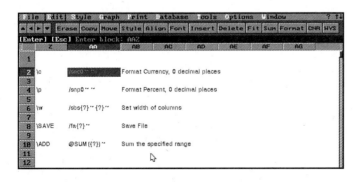

In this example, highlight cell AA2 and press ⌊↵Enter⌋.

457

This book and the Quattro Pro documentation use a format that places the name of the macro in the cell to the immediate left of the macro's first command. If you follow this format, you can use the command /Edit Names Labels and specify the block containing the macro names to assign these names to your macros in the adjacent column. This approach works with descriptive and single-letter macro names and also ensures that you include the name of the macro within the spreadsheet for easy identification. The /Edit Names Labels command also is useful for naming several macros at once, rather than naming them individually with /Edit Names Create.

13

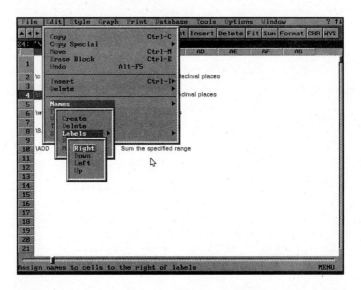

From the /Edit Names Labels menu, select Right to name the macros to the right of the labels.

In this example, highlight the block Z4..Z10 and press ↵Enter) to create the names \p, \w, \SAVE, and \ADD.

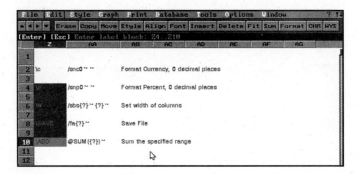

The advantage of using a single letter for a macro name is that you can activate the macro more quickly from the keyboard; a disadvantage is that a single-letter name doesn't offer as much flexibility in describing what the macro does. Remembering the name and purpose of a specific macro may therefore be difficult if you use a single-letter name.

Quattro Pro enables you to assign descriptive names (up to 15 characters in length) to blocks containing macros. To avoid confusing macro names with block names, you can begin descriptive macro names with the backslash (\) character. For example, in this chapter, illustrated macros include one named \SAVE, which you can use to save files, and another named \ADD, which uses the @SUM function to add a specified block of values.

Note: Quattro Pro enables you to assign a third type of name to a macro. You can use the name \0 (backslash zero) to create an *automatic macro*, which is discussed later in this chapter.

Using the Record Feature To Record Keystrokes

Quattro Pro can keep track of every keystroke and command you issue, and then use that information to build a macro. Instead of creating a macro by typing it manually into spreadsheet cells, you can use the Record feature to record all keyboard activity for an indefinite period. Quattro Pro builds the macro for you as you step through the procedures you want to include.

To use the Record feature to record keystrokes, you first must press Alt-F2 R or select /Tools Macro Record to turn on the Record feature and enter REC mode. All your commands and keystrokes are stored in memory as you proceed through the operations you want. You can stop recording at any time by pressing Alt-F2 R again to turn off the Record feature and exit REC mode. You can resume recording by pressing Alt-F2 R once more.

To record keystrokes for a macro with the Record feature, follow these steps:

1. Press / to access the Quattro Pro menu.
2. Press T to select Tools.
3. Press M to select Macro.

13

13

The Record
feature is off
by default.

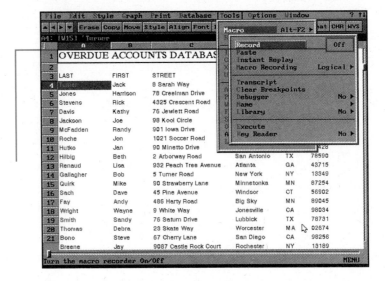

4. Press ⌐R⌐ to select **R**ecord to turn on the Record feature.

   Note: In place of steps 1-4, you can press ⌐Alt⌐-⌐F2⌐ ⌐R⌐ to record
   keystrokes.

The REC indica-
tor, which tells
you that your
keystrokes are
being recorded,
appears at the
bottom of the
screen.

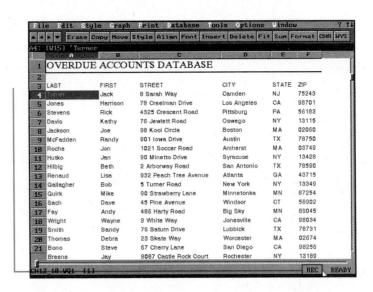

5. Manually type all commands and keystrokes necessary to create your
   macro.

For example, you can build a macro that automatically sorts a database. After you record the keystrokes, Quattro Pro sorts your database, and the Record block (the block into which you paste the command) will contain your keystrokes for future use.

13

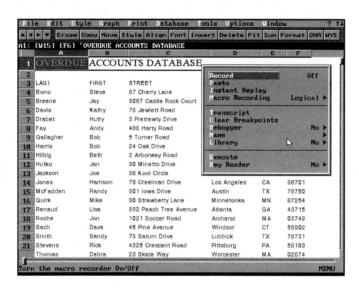

In this example, Quattro Pro has sorted the database alphabetically by last name, and the Alt-F2 (/Tools Macro) menu is displayed.

6. Press Alt-F2 R to stop recording keystrokes.

To see what you have recorded, move the cell selector to a blank area of the spreadsheet, and follow these steps:

1. Press / to access the Quattro Pro menu.
2. Press T to select Tools.
3. Press M to select Macro.
4. Press P to select Paste.

   Note: In place of steps 1-4, you can press Alt-F2 P to enter keystrokes from memory to the spreadsheet.

5. Type the name of the macro at the prompt and press ↵Enter.

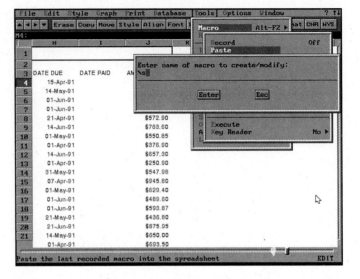

13

In this example, type \s to name the sort macro.

6. Type the address of the cell in which you want to place the first macro instruction, and press ⏎Enter.

In this example, type **N4** as the cell in which you want to paste the sort macro keystrokes, and press ⏎Enter.

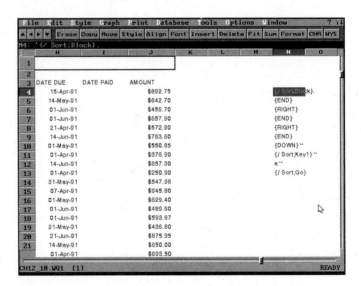

Beginning in cell N4, Quattro Pro pastes the recorded keystrokes and commands, which look like a macro you could have typed manually.

Quattro Pro records the activity of special keys in *macro notation*. For example, if you press the Window (F6) key while in REC mode, the Record block will contain the macro key name {WINDOW}.

13

When you are
satisfied that the
recorded activity
represents what
you want the
macro to do,
name the macro.

Executing Macros

Single-letter macros that you name with a backslash and a single letter are the simplest macros to run. If necessary, move the cell selector to the appropriate position before you execute the macro. For example, before using a macro that will format the current cell, you must move the cell selector to the cell you want to format.

To execute a single-letter macro, follow these steps:

1. Press and hold down Alt .
2. Press the letter in the macro name.
3. Release both keys.

For example, if the macro is named \a, you invoke it by pressing Alt - A . The \ symbol in the name represents the Alt key. Pressing Alt - A plays back the keystrokes recorded in the macro.

Macros you name with a longer descriptive name are not as easy to execute. You must first select /Tools Macro Execute (or press Alt - F2   E) and press Choices (F3) to display a list of block names. Then highlight the macro name you want, and press ↵Enter .

463

To execute a macro with a descriptive name, follow these steps:

1. Press /︎ T M E to select **/Tools Macro Execute** (or press Alt-F2 E).

13

Quattro Pro displays the macro names in a list box. If you don't see the name of the macro you want to run, press F3 (Choices) to display a full-screen listing of names.

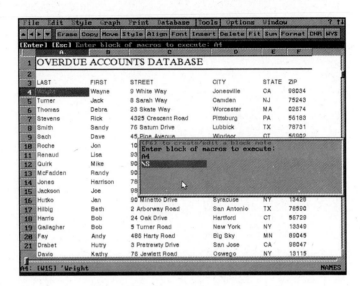

2. Highlight the name of the macro you want to execute, and press ↵Enter.

As soon as you issue the command to execute a macro, Quattro Pro runs the macro. If you have no special instructions built into the macro (such as a pause) and if no bugs are present, the macro continues to run until it is finished. You will be amazed at its speed. The program issues the commands faster than you can see them.

You can store many macro keystrokes or commands in a single cell. If they are especially long or include special commands, you may have to split them into two or more cells. When executing a macro, Quattro Pro begins by executing all the keystrokes stored in the first cell. Next, Quattro Pro moves down one cell to continue execution. If the next cell is blank, the program stops. If that cell contains macro commands, however, Quattro Pro continues reading down the column until it encounters the first blank cell.

Using an Automatic Macro

Quattro Pro enables you to create an *automatic macro* that executes auto-matically when you load your spreadsheet. You create this macro just like any other; the only difference is its name. The macro that you want Quattro Pro to execute automatically must have the name \0 (backslash zero). You can use only one automatic macro in a single spreadsheet.

For example, you can use an automatic macro to position the cell selector at the upper left corner of a block named DATABASE each time you access the spreadsheet file. The macro can then redefine the block DATABASE by anchoring the cell selector and moving it to the right and down to include all contiguous cells.

13

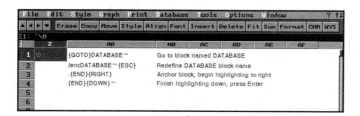

This example shows an automatic (\0) macro, which Quattro Pro executes every time you retrieve this file.

Note that you cannot execute an automatic macro by pressing (Alt)-(0). If you need to execute the macro from the keyboard, you can press (Alt)-(F2) (E), or you can assign the \0 macro an additional name, such as \d. You then have two identical macros on your system: one that executes automatically, and one that you can execute from the keyboard. This tip is especially useful when you want to test new automatic macros.

Debugging and Editing Macros

Almost no program works perfectly the first time. In nearly every case, errors cause programs to malfunction. Programmers call these problems *bugs,* and the process of eliminating such problems in the program is called *debugging.*

Like programs written in other programming languages, Quattro Pro macros usually need to be debugged before you can use them. Quattro Pro has a useful feature—DEBUG mode—that helps make debugging much simpler. When Quattro Pro is in DEBUG mode, the program executes macros one step at a time. Quattro Pro literally pauses between each keystroke stored in the macro. Using this feature means that you can follow along step-by-step with the macro as Quattro Pro executes it.

When Quattro Pro discovers an error, you must press (Ctrl)-(Break) to get out of the macro, and then press (Esc) one or more times to return Quattro Pro to READY mode. You then can edit the macro.

465

13

Common Errors in Macros

Like all computer programs, macros are literal creatures. They have no capability to discern an error in the code. For example, you recognize immediately that {GOTI} is a misspelling of {GOTO}, but a macro cannot make this distinction. The macro tries to interpret the misspelled word and, being unable to, delivers an error message. Here are three reminders to help you avoid some of the most common macro errors:

- Verify all syntax and spelling in your macros.
- Include all required tildes (~) to represent Enter keystrokes in macros.
- Use block names in macros whenever possible to avoid problems with incorrect cell references. Cell references in macros are always absolute; they never change when you make modifications to the spreadsheet.

If a macro is not working correctly, you can use two Quattro Pro features to help you correct spreadsheet or macro errors, or both. Use the Undo (Alt - F5) feature to "undo" spreadsheet damage created by the faulty execution of a macro. (To use this feature, you must enable it with the /Options Other Undo Enable command.) Also, use DEBUG mode to help pinpoint the location of an error in a macro.

Undoing Macros

The Undo feature offers a significant advantage when debugging macros. When a macro not only doesn't work, but also appears to have caused major problems within the spreadsheet, press Undo (Alt - F5) to undo all the steps in the macro. Remember, the Undo feature restores the spreadsheet to the way it was before the last operation. A macro, even though it may contain many steps, is considered one operation.

If you want to undo a macro, make sure that the Undo feature is active before you actually execute the macro. If the macro produces unsatisfactory results, do not perform another operation; use Undo immediately to reverse the effect of the macro.

Note: Certain commands that cannot normally be reversed with Undo (Alt - F5) also cannot be reversed within macros. For example, you cannot reverse a macro that includes the /File Save, /File Save As, or /File Save All command; therefore, you should not rely entirely on Undo when you test macros.

To reverse the results of a macro safely, save the file before you execute the macro. Then, if necessary, you can retrieve the original file after executing the macro.

Using DEBUG Mode To Debug Macros

You need to debug most programs before you can use them. If you cannot locate an error in a macro, your best option is to enter DEBUG mode and rerun the macro one step at a time. After each step, the macro pauses and waits for you to type any keystroke before continuing. Although you can use any key, you should use the space bar to step through a macro. As you step through the macro, each command appears in the input line, and the macro code appears in the Debug Window at the bottom of the screen.

To use DEBUG mode to debug a macro, follow these steps:

1. Select /Tools Macro Debugger or press ⇧Shift-F2 to activate the Debugger.

Select Yes to turn on the Debugger.

13

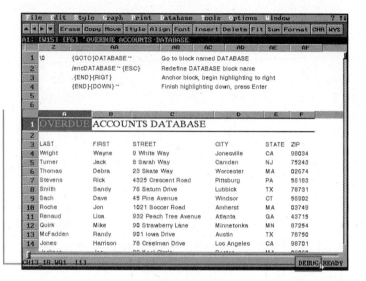

The mode indicator DEBUG appears in the status line.

2. Execute the macro by pressing Alt followed by the letter of the macro name; or press Alt-F2 E F3, highlight the name of the macro, and press ↵Enter to execute the macro.

The Debug Window appears as soon as you execute the macro, Alt-D in this example.

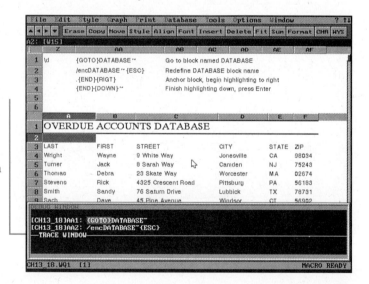

3. Evaluate each step of the macro, pressing space bar after you check each step.

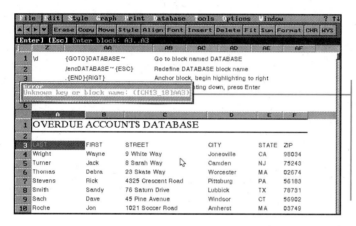

In this example, Quattro Pro displays an error message on-screen. This error is caused by a misspelled key name in cell AA3.

4. When the Debugger discovers an error, press Ctrl-Break to return Quattro Pro to READY mode.

5. Edit the macro. (You can edit the macro while DEBUG is displayed in the status line.)

6. To exit DEBUG mode, press Shift-F2.

Editing Macros

After you identify an error in a macro, you can correct the error. Fixing an error in a macro is as simple as editing the cell that contains the erroneous code. You don't need to rewrite the entire cell contents. You need to change only the element in error. Although editing a complex macro can be much more challenging than editing a simple one, the concept is exactly the same.

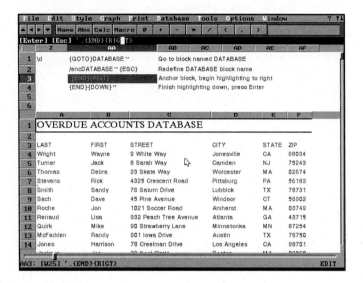

Use the Edit (F2) key to correct the cell that contains the error. In this example, change {RIGT} to {RIGHT}.

Creating a Macro Library

A *macro library* is a group of macros you can use with many different spreadsheet files. These macros can range from simple keystroke macros to more specialized macro command programs. Macro libraries can save you the time required to re-create the same macros in different files. After you create a macro library file, you can copy the macros into the current spreadsheet.

This section introduces five simple keystroke macros you can create in your own macro library—macros called \p, \t, \w, \SAVE, and \ADD. These macros perform common tasks that would require additional keystrokes (and time) if you performed them manually. Each macro is explained in detail in the following sections.

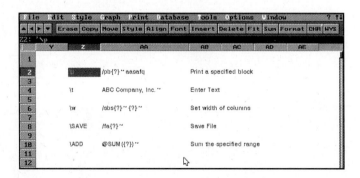

You can include these five simple keystroke macros in a macro library.

To create a macro library file, follow these general steps:

1. Start with a blank spreadsheet, with the cell selector in cell A1.

2. Type the keystrokes exactly as they are displayed in columns Z, AA, and AB of the preceding illustration. Column Z contains the macro names, column AA contains the macros, and column AB contains the documentation for each macro.

   Note: Remember to first type a label prefix (such as ') before entering each of the macros in column AA.

3. Use the /Edit Names Labels command to name the macros by specifying the block containing all macro names in column Z, and then press ⏎Enter.

4. Use the /File Save As command to save the macros in a separate file.

When you are ready to copy the macros from the macro library file to your current spreadsheet, position the cell selector where you want the macros located (such as column AA), and then issue the /Tools Combine Copy File command. Highlight or type the file name containing the macros, and then press ⏎Enter.

Execute one of the single-letter macros (\w, \t, or \p) by pressing and holding down Alt and then pressing the letter key assigned to the macro. Execute one of the macros with descriptive names (\SAVE or \ADD) by pressing Alt-F2 E, and then Choices (F3); then select the desired macro name and press ⏎Enter.

The following sections provide brief explanations of the operation of each macro.

A Macro That Prints a Specified Block

The \p macro in cell AA2 prints a specified block directly to the printer and then advances the paper to the top of the next page. To run this macro, press Alt-P. The macro executes the /Print Block command and then pauses for you to specify the desired print block. After you highlight the block you want to print and press ⏎Enter, the macro executes the following series of commands from the Print menu: Adjust Printer Align, Spreadsheet Print, Adjust Printer Form Feed, and Quit. This series of commands aligns the paper, prints the block, advances the paper to the top of the page, and returns Quattro Pro to READY mode.

If you normally print the same block from a particular spreadsheet, you can name this print block (with /Edit Names Create) and use this name in place of

{?} in the \p macro. For example, to print a block named SALES, use the following macro in place of the macro in cell AA2:

'/pbSALES~aasafq

If you use this form of the print macro, remember to redefine the block named SALES whenever you add new data to the block you want to print.

A Macro That Enters Text

The \t macro in cell AA4 enters a long text label into the current cell. Press Alt-T to execute the macro, which automatically enters the specified label into the highlighted cell. This macro is straightforward but very useful for entering any long label that commonly appears throughout the spreadsheet, such as a company name.

A Macro That Sets the Widths of a Block of Columns

The \w macro in cell AA6 enables you to change the widths of a block of columns. Place the cell pointer in the first column whose width you want to change, and then press Alt-W. The macro begins by executing the /Style Block Size command. Then, as a result of the {?} command, the macro pauses for input. Highlight the columns in which you want to change the width and press Enter. Next, specify the value of the desired width and press Enter.

A Macro That Saves a File

The \SAVE macro in cell AA8 saves a previously saved file with a new name in the current file in the current directory on-disk. To use this macro, press Alt-F2 E, press Choices (F3), select \SAVE from the list of macro names, and then press Enter. This macro executes the /File Save As command and then pauses for you to enter the desired name. After you type the name of the file and press Enter, Quattro Pro saves the file. If the file already exists, the program displays a menu, from which you select Replace to continue saving the file.

A Macro That Sums a Specified Block

The \ADD macro in cell AA10 uses the @SUM function to add values from a specified block. To use this macro, move the cell selector to the cell to contain the result of the formula. Press $\boxed{\text{Alt}}$-$\boxed{\text{F2}}$ $\boxed{\text{E}}$, press Choices ($\boxed{\text{F3}}$), select \ADD from the list of macro names, and then press $\boxed{\text{↵Enter}}$. The macro pauses for you to highlight the block of cells you want to sum. After you select the block and press $\boxed{\text{↵Enter}}$, Quattro Pro displays the formula result on-screen.

Summary

13

This chapter provided the basic information you need to begin creating your own simple keystroke macros—tools you can use to save time, reduce repetition, and automate your spreadsheet applications. The chapter identified each of the steps necessary to create macros and described ways to document, name, and execute macros. The Record feature, which enables you to create macros by recording all keyboard activity, was discussed. You also learned about automatic (\0) macros and about methods to debug and edit your simple keystroke macros.

Specifically, you learned the following key information about Quattro Pro:

- The elements of macros include actual command keystrokes, key names, block names, cell addresses, the tilde (~) to represent the Enter key, and macro commands.

- Macro key names, which represent keyboard keys, are enclosed within braces, such as {EDIT}. Key names are available for the function keys, direction keys, editing keys, and special keys.

- You can specify that you want to use a key name more than once by including repetition factors within the braces, separated by a single space, such as {DOWN 5}.

- Take time to plan your macros. Consider the available input and the desired results. Use the keyboard to proceed through your tasks, jotting down the keystrokes necessary to create simple macros. You can create more complex macros by breaking them into smaller macros consisting of simple operations.

- Position macros outside of the main area of your spreadsheet. To find your macros quickly, place them in the same location in each of your spreadsheets, such as in column AA.

- Always document your Quattro Pro macros. An easy way to document them is to include comments in the cells to the right of the macro steps.

13

- You can name macros in two different ways—with a backslash (\) followed by a single letter, or with a descriptive name of up to 15 characters. Use the /Edit Names Create or /Edit Names Labels command to name your macros.

- The Record feature enables you to create macros automatically by recording your keystrokes in memory, then enables you to store them in a block you specify.

- To execute single-letter macros, press and hold down Alt and then press the letter key assigned to the macro. You execute macros with descriptive names by selecting /Tools Macro Execute (or press Alt- F2 E), pressing Choices (F3), selecting the macro, and pressing ↵Enter.

- Automatic (\0) macros execute whenever you retrieve a file. You can use only one automatic macro in each spreadsheet.

- Quattro Pro's DEBUG mode, accessed by pressing Debug (⇧Shift- F2), enables you to find macro errors by proceeding through a macro one step at a time. Sometimes you can use the Undo (Alt-F5) feature to reverse the effect of a macro if the macro has caused errors in the spreadsheet.

- You edit macros just like you edit any cell entries in the spreadsheet: you correct the cell containing the error. Rewriting the entire contents of these cells is not necessary.

- A macro library is a collection of two or more macros that you save in a separate file and use with several different files. Use the /Tools Combine Copy File command to copy a macro library into the current file.

In the next chapter, you learn how to customize the Quattro Pro SpeedBar— specifically, how to add, delete, and create SpeedBar buttons.

Customizing the SpeedBar

Quattro Pro enables you to customize both the READY mode SpeedBar and the EDIT mode SpeedBar, enabling you to maximize their efficiency for you. You can modify the current default buttons, or you can create new buttons. You decide what buttons appear on the SpeedBar.

In this chapter, you find an introduction to customizing the SpeedBar. You learn how to create a new button, how to modify a button, and how to attach a macro to a button. The power of this feature is that you control what buttons the SpeedBar displays and, in that way, create a SpeedBar that fits your needs.

Customizing the READY mode SpeedBar

Customizing the EDIT mode SpeedBar

14

Key Terms in This Chapter

SpeedBar   The area at the top of or to the right of the Quattro Pro display. The SpeedBar enables you to perform certain Quattro Pro tasks if you have a mouse and mouse driver software loaded in your computer's memory at the beginning of a Quattro Pro session. You can select commands and functions and move around the spreadsheet if you use a mouse with Quattro Pro.

Button   The rectangles that make up the SpeedBar. Each rectangle is titled and corresponds to a Quattro Pro macro or Quattro Pro functionality.

READY mode   The mode in which Quattro Pro is waiting for you to issue a command, enter data, or access the menu. The mode indicator in the lower right hand corner of the spreadsheet displays READY.

EDIT mode   The mode in which Quattro Pro enables you to edit a cell entry. The mode indicator in the lower right corner of the spreadsheet displays EDIT. Press F2 (Edit) to edit the contents of a cell.

Customizing the READY Mode SpeedBar

The READY mode SpeedBar is displayed whenever you are not editing a cell or entering a value or formula. The buttons on the default READY mode SpeedBar are explained in Chapter 2. You can modify the current default buttons or create new ones.

Modifying a Button on the READY Mode SpeedBar

The READY mode SpeedBar has 13 default buttons. You can modify any or all of these buttons by replacing them or simply adjusting them.

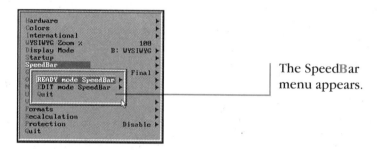

This SpeedBar is the default READY mode SpeedBar.

Replacing a Button

Replacing a button on the SpeedBar involves completely changing the original button. For example, suppose that you want a Save button on the SpeedBar to quickly perform a /File Save operation. You decide that you do not use the Erase button very much and therefore want to replace the Erase button with the Save button.

To replace a READY mode SpeedBar button, follow these steps:

1. Press ⌐/⌐ to access the Quattro Pro menu.
2. Press ⌐O⌐ to select Options.
3. Press ⌐B⌐ to select SpeedBar.

The SpeedBar menu appears.

4. Press ⌐R⌐ to select READY mode SpeedBar.

Quattro Pro displays a list of the current READY mode SpeedBar buttons. You can modify or replace any of these buttons.

By default, buttons A-M are predefined. Each button displays a button title, which is descriptive of the action that button performs when you click it.

5. Press Ⓐ to select **A** Button, which is currently the Erase button.

The dialog box
for the Erase
button appears.

14

Short name specifies the text that will appear on the button in Text mode. **L**ong name specifies the text that will appear on the button in WYSIWYG mode. **M**acro specifies the macro that will accomplish the task when you click the button.

6. Press Ⓢ to select **S**hort name.

Type **SAV** as the
Short name and
press ↵Enter. You
are going to
change this
button so that it
performs a /**F**ile
Save operation
rather than /**E**dit
Erase.

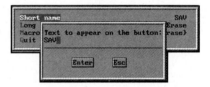

7. Press Ⓛ to select **L**ong name.

Type **Save** as the
Long name and
press ↵Enter.

8. Press Ⓜ to select **M**acro.
9. Enter the macro keystrokes you want Quattro Pro to perform when you click the button, and then press ↵Enter.

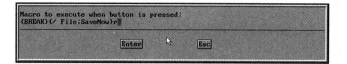

In this example, because you are creating a /File Save macro, the keystrokes to accomplish a /File Save Replace operation are shown.

After you press ⏎Enter), Quattro Pro displays the new definition for the A Button.

10. Press Q to select Quit and return to the list of current READY mode SpeedBar buttons.

The A Button is now defined as Save.

11. Select Quit three times to return to READY mode.

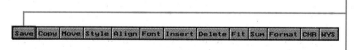

The first button (button A) on the READY mode SpeedBar is now the Save button instead of Erase.

479

Now, when you click the Save button, Quattro Pro performs the /File Save Replace operation.

Adjusting a Button

Rather than replacing a button on the SpeedBar, you can simply adjust one. For example, suppose that you want the Font button to display the /Style FontTable dialog box so that you can use the table to make a font change. By default, the Font button displays the /Style Font dialog box. You want the button to remain a Font button and to perform actions related to changing the font of a block, but you want the button to display the Font Table dialog box rather than the Font dialog box.

To adjust a READY mode SpeedBar button, follow these steps:

1. Press ⌿ to access the Quattro Pro menu.
2. Press Ⓞ to select Options.
3. Press Ⓑ to select SpeedBar.
4. Press Ⓡ to select the READY mode SpeedBar.
5. Press Ⓕ to select F Button, the Font button.

The dialog box for the Font button appears.

```
Short name               FNT
Long name               Font
Macro      {BREAK}{/ Publish;ApplyAnonymo
Quit
```

You are not changing the Short name or the Long name. You are simply adjusting the keystrokes the macro performs when you click the Font button.

6. Press Ⓜ to select Macro.
7. Enter the macro commands to execute the /Style FontTable command when you click the Font button, and then press ⏎Enter.

The macro command to execute the /Style FontTable command is {BREAK}{/ Publish;Font}. See Que's *Using Quattro Pro 4*, Special Edition, for an alphabetical list of macro commands.

This example shows the new macro commands for the Font button.

8. Select Quit four times to return to READY mode.

Now, when you click the Font button, Quattro Pro executes the /Style Font Table command rather than the /Style Font command.

14

Adding a New Button to the READY Mode SpeedBar

Quattro Pro enables you to add new buttons to the SpeedBar. On the default READY mode SpeedBar are two unassigned buttons, N and O.

To add a new button to the READY mode SpeedBar button, follow these steps:

1. Press $\boxed{/}$ to access the Quattro Pro menu.
2. Press $\boxed{O}$ to select Options.
3. Press $\boxed{B}$ to select Speed Bar.
4. Press $\boxed{R}$ to select the READY mode SpeedBar.

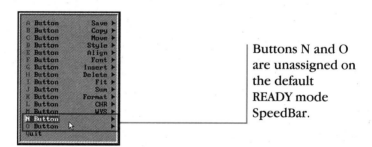

Buttons N and O are unassigned on the default READY mode SpeedBar.

5. Press $\boxed{N}$ to select N Button.

The dialog box for the N Button appears; it is blank.

6. Press ⓢ to select **S**hort name.

    In this example, type **WND** as the **S**hort name. You are going to create a new SpeedBar button to execute the /**W**indows **O**ptions **H**orizontal command.

7. Press ⓛ to select **L**ong name.

    In this example, type **H_WND** as the **L**ong name, because you are setting a horizontal window.

8. Press Ⓜ to select **M**acro.

9. Enter the **M**acro commands for the new button and press ⏎Enter.

    In this example, enter the macro command to execute the /**W**indows **O**ptions **H**orizontal command. The macro command for this procedure is {/ Windows;Horizontal}.

This dialog box shows the completed N Button. When you click the H_WND button, Quattro Pro will execute the /**W**indows **O**ptions **H**orizontal command.

Quattro Pro assigns the **L**ong name H_WND to the N Button.

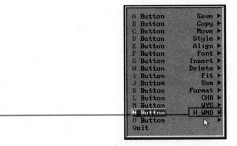

10. Select **Q**uit four times to return to READY mode.

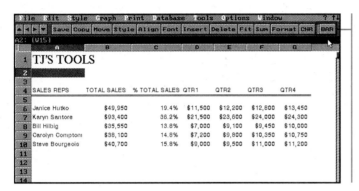

The SpeedBar does not have enough room to display the H_WND button. The BAR button indicates that more buttons are available than you currently can see on-screen.

14

11. Click the BAR button.

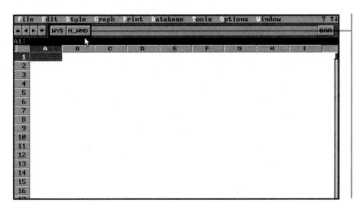

Quattro Pro displays the WYS and H_WND buttons and hides the other buttons. When you click the BAR button again, the other buttons reappear and the WYS and H_WND buttons hide once again.

Note: Any changes you make to a SpeedBar are for only that session, unless you select /Options Update. If you do not select /Options Update, Quattro Pro does not save your changes to the SpeedBar; the SpeedBar reverts to its original form the next time you enter Quattro Pro.

As you can see, each SpeedBar button actually executes a short macro. If you are not sure what macro commands correspond to the keystrokes you need to perform, record the macro and then paste it into the spreadsheet. Unfortunately you cannot use /Edit Copy to copy the macro into the button macro line; however, you can position the spreadsheet so that you can see the pasted macro when you bring up the button macro line and then enter the correct macro. For more information on macros, see Chapter 13, "Understanding Macros."

Customizing the EDIT Mode SpeedBar

The EDIT mode SpeedBar displays whenever you are editing a cell or entering a value or formula. The buttons on the default EDIT mode SpeedBar are explained in Chapter 2. You can modify the current default buttons or create new ones.

This SpeedBar is the default EDIT mode SpeedBar.

Modifying a Button on the EDIT Mode SpeedBar

The EDIT mode SpeedBar has 12 default buttons. Rather than perform short macros, as the READY mode SpeedBar buttons do, the EDIT mode SpeedBar buttons enter operators in the input line, calculate a formula, make a formula cell reference absolute, and display a list of block names that you can use in a formula.

Quattro Pro enables you to modify the buttons on the SpeedBar. For example, suppose that you want to place the exponentiation sign (^) on the SpeedBar, and you want it to replace the comma, which you do not use.

To modify a EDIT mode SpeedBar button, follow these steps:

1. Press / to access the Quattro Pro menu.
2. Press O to select Options.
3. Press B to select SpeedBar.
4. Press E to select the EDIT mode SpeedBar.

By default, buttons A-L are predefined. Each button displays a button title or symbol, which is descriptive of the action the button performs when you click it.

5. Press K to select K Button, which currently is the , (comma) button.

The dialog box for the , (comma) button appears.

Short name specifies the text that will appear on the button in Text mode. Long name specifies the text that will appear on the button in WYSIWYG mode. Macro specifies the macro that will accomplish the task when you click the button.

6. Press S to select Short name.

In this example, type ^ as the Short name and press ↵Enter. You are going to change this button so that it enters an exponentiation sign (^) rather than a comma.

7. Press L to select Long name.

In this example, type ^ as the Long name and press ↵Enter.

8. Press M to select Macro, type the macro command, and press ↵Enter.

In this example, type ^, the simple macro command to enter the exponentiation sign.

Quattro Pro displays the completed K button dialog box.

9. Press Q to select Quit and return to the EDIT mode SpeedBar current button definition dialog box.

The K button is
now defined
as ^.

14

10. Select Quit three times to return to EDIT mode.

The second to last
button on the
EDIT SpeedBar is
now ^.

Now, when you click the ^ button, Quattro Pro displays ^ in the input line.

Adding a New Button to the EDIT Mode SpeedBar

You also can add a new button to the SpeedBar. On the default EDIT mode
SpeedBar, three buttons—M, N and O—are unassigned.

To add a new button to the EDIT mode SpeedBar, follow these steps:

1. Press [/] to access the Quattro Pro menu.
2. Press [O] to select Options.
3. Press [B] to select SpeedBar.
4. Press [E] to select the EDIT mode SpeedBar.

Buttons M, N and
O are unassigned
on the default
EDIT mode
SpeedBar.

5. Press [M] to select **M** Button.

6. Press [S] to select **S**hort name.

   In this example, type \ as the **S**hort name. You are going to create a new SpeedBar button that enters the repeating label character (\).

7. Press [L] to select **L**ong name.

   In this example, type \ as the **L**ong name.

8. Press [M] to select **M**acro.

9. Enter the **M**acro commands for the new button and press [↵Enter].

   In this example, type \, the macro command to execute the repeating label character.

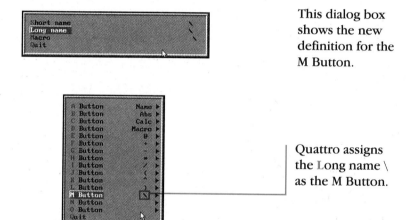

This dialog box shows the new definition for the M Button.

Quattro assigns the **L**ong name \ as the M Button.

10. Select **Q**uit four times to return to EDIT mode.

The EDIT mode SpeedBar now displays the \ button.

Now, when you click the \ button, Quattro Pro types the repeat label character in the input line.

Note: Any changes you make to a SpeedBar are for only that session, unless you select /**O**ptions **U**pdate. If you do not select /**O**ptions **U**pdate, Quattro Pro does not save your changes to the SpeedBar; the SpeedBar reverts to its original form the next time you enter Quattro Pro.

Summary

This chapter provided the basic information you need to customize either the READY mode SpeedBar or the EDIT mode SpeedBar. You can replace a button on a SpeedBar, modify the action taken when you click a button, or add a new button.

Specifically, you learned the following key information about Quattro Pro:

14

- Quattro Pro has two SpeedBars: the READY mode SpeedBar and the EDIT mode SpeedBar.
- The READY mode SpeedBar contains 13 buttons by default. Each button performs a keystroke macro that you can modify.
- You can choose to change a SpeedBar button or to modify the action performed when you click the button.
- The READY mode SpeedBar has two unassigned buttons. If you assign a macro to either of these buttons, the BAR button displays on-screen, indicating that more buttons are available than you can see on-screen.
- The EDIT mode SpeedBar contains 12 buttons by default. The EDIT mode SpeedBar is specific to entering formula related items, such as operators or block names.
- The EDIT mode SpeedBar has three unassigned buttons, which means that you can create three additional buttons for this SpeedBar.

Installing
Quattro Pro 4

Quattro Pro's installation utility is self-explanatory and mostly self-running. Before you begin installing Quattro Pro, review the following checklist to ensure that you have the correct system configuration for using Quattro Pro:

- IBM XT, AT, PS/2, or compatible computer
- 512K of RAM (640K is recommended)
- DOS 2.0 or later (3.1 or later is recommended)
- Hard disk drive with at least 6M of available storage space
- RAM exceeding 1M defined as expanded memory

The first matter to consider when you prepare to install Quattro Pro is how to tailor the program to your particular computer system. You have to let Quattro Pro know what kind of display hardware you have. For example, you must tell the program whether you have a color monitor or a monochrome monitor (green-on-black, amber-on-black, or white-on-black).

The Quattro Pro diskettes

Installing the program

Loading and quitting Quattro Pro

Reconfiguring and enhancing Quattro Pro

Upgrading from Version 3.0 to Version 4.0

Another consideration is the printer configuration, for both the text printer and the graphics printer or plotter. If your text printer is capable of printing graphs or if you have a separate graphics printer or plotter, you can configure the printer for Quattro Pro graphics. If you have special printing needs and use several printers, you need to configure all your printers for Quattro Pro from the Options menu after installation.

The Quattro Pro Diskettes

Quattro Pro 4.0 comes with three diskettes for computers with 5 1/4-inch disk drives and two diskettes for computers with 3 1/2-inch disk drives. The programs contained on the two sets of high-density diskettes are exactly the same, but are divided among the diskettes differently. Each set of diskettes, 5 1/4-inch or 3 1/2-inch, has one diskette designated for installation.

The Program files contain the Quattro Pro spreadsheet, graphics, and database operations. The Help files contain the on-line Help system you can access while using Quattro Pro by pressing the Help (F1) key. The Translate files enable Quattro Pro to quickly retrieve and save files in Lotus 1-2-3 and Symphony format, and compress and decompress SQZ! files. The 1-2-3 and Quattro Pro menu files enable you to choose commands from 1-2-3, Quattro, and Quattro Pro menu tree structures, respectively.

The Install file contains the program that makes the Quattro Pro installation a mostly automatic process. The Sample files contain several examples of Quattro Pro spreadsheet files. Finally, the Character Set and Printer Font files enable you to display data on-screen in WYSIWYG mode and print your spreadsheets, respectively.

Installing the Program

Even though you are installing Quattro Pro on a hard disk system, you should make backup copies of the master diskettes. You need to copy each master diskette onto a blank formatted diskette. For more information about formatting and copying diskettes, see Que's *Using MS-DOS 5*. After you make backup copies of your master diskettes, you can go on to install Quattro Pro on your hard disk.

The following steps are required to copy the Quattro Pro diskettes to your hard disk. The instructions that follow assume that your hard disk is formatted, that DOS is installed on the hard disk, and that drive C is the current drive.

Starting the Installation

During the first part of the installation process, Quattro Pro copies program files to a directory named QPRO. To start the installation, place the Installation diskette—Disk 1—into drive A. Type **A:INSTALL** and press ⏎Enter.

Press ⏎Enter to begin the installation process, or press Esc to quit. Quattro Pro can install itself from any drive you specify. Generally, drive A is the source drive from which you copy the Quattro Pro files, but you can specify *B:* as the source drive. Press ⏎Enter again.

The installation utility ensures that you have enough free storage space on your computer's hard disk drive and displays the directory to which files are copied. If you do not have at least 6M of free storage space, Quattro Pro displays an error message telling you so. If you see this error message, exit the installation program and delete files from your hard disk drive until you free up at least 6M of storage space.

The installation utility copies the Quattro Pro files to the default path, \QPRO. You can change the path by pressing F2 and typing in a new path or by editing the \QPRO path. Press ⏎Enter to continue. During this process, Quattro Pro prompts you to change diskettes and press a key until the files are copied from all diskettes. You see the progress of the installation on-screen as the installation utility reads and writes files. When all the files are transferred, Quattro Pro displays a message telling you that the file transfer is complete.

The next step is to tell Quattro Pro about your computer system. In the second part of the installation process, you select a monitor type, select a printer, and select an operating mode. You also choose whether to install the Bitstream font software.

Selecting a Monitor Type

The installation utility detects whether you have a color graphics display card installed in your computer. You must, however, tell Quattro Pro whether you have a color, black-and-white, or gray-scale monitor.

A

491

To change the default selection, press F2, use the cursor-movement keys to move to your selection, and press ↵Enter. When you are finished, press ↵Enter to continue or press Ctrl-X to quit.

Entering Purchase Information

After you select your monitor type, Quattro Pro prompts you for the name of your company, your name, and the serial number on Disk 1. Press F2, enter the correct information, and press ↵Enter for each prompt.

Selecting To Install on a Server

Quattro Pro next prompts you to specify whether you are installing on a network server. The default is No. Press F2 and select Yes if you are installing Quattro Pro on a server.

Selecting a Printer

Next, select a printer manufacturer and model from the Printer Manufacturer screen. Press F2, use the cursor-movement keys to highlight the appropriate manufacturer, and then press ↵Enter. If your printer manufacturer is not listed, check your printer manual for information on the types of printers your printer can emulate. Many printers emulate EPSON and IBM printers.

After you select a printer manufacturer, Quattro Pro displays the Printer Model screen. To choose a printer model, highlight the appropriate name on the list and press ↵Enter.

After you select a printer model, Quattro Pro asks you to choose an initial mode and resolution at which to print spreadsheets and graphs. You can select a medium or high mode by pressing F2 and selecting a different option. The actual dots-per-inch (dpi) ratings available on this menu depend on the individual printer. If you select an Epson LQ-2500 printer, for example, the dpi rating in high mode is 360 x 180.

Selecting the Display Mode

Quattro Pro operates in either WYSIWYG mode or Text mode. WYSIWYG mode, the default choice, is a graphical interface that creates printouts that match your screen display. Press F2 and select Text mode if you prefer to work in Text mode.

Note that to display Quattro Pro in WYSIWYG mode, your computer system must have an EGA or VGA monitor and a graphics card that supports 640 x 350 display resolution. If you do not have the proper equipment, select No at this point in the installation process. Quattro Pro will display in Text (character) mode.

If you have the proper computer configuration but select No, you can change to WYSIWYG mode later in Quattro Pro, using the /Options Display Mode command. Use the /Options Update command to make WYSIWYG mode the default display for future Quattro Pro sessions.

Selecting To Install for Windows

A

Next, you are asked whether you want to run Quattro Pro under Microsoft Windows. You can automatically set up Quattro Pro in your Windows operating environment by selecting Yes at this prompt. If you select Yes, Quattro Pro creates a QPRO group containing a QPRO 4.0 icon. If you are not operating under Windows, or prefer to set up Quattro Pro under a different Windows group, select No.

Keep in mind, however, that Quattro Pro 4.0 is not a Windows-specific product; therefore, the performance of certain spreadsheet operations may be adversely affected.

Selecting Bitstream Fonts

Quattro Pro prompts you to select Bitstream fonts next. Standard U.S. is the default Bitstream fonts choice. Select Standard European if you will be working with International or Diacritical characters.

When installed, each font file uses 2K to 6K of storage space on your hard disk drive. Larger font files require more space, from 6K to 12K. To install all 150 fonts, Quattro Pro requires 600K.

Completing the Installation

Quattro Pro displays a screen telling you that it has successfully installed the installation utility. If Quattro Pro fails to successfully transfer all configuration files, you must begin the process again. Installation can fail for a number of reasons. The most common reason for failure is because the hard disk drive is full. Make sure that you have 6M on your hard disk before attempting to install Quattro Pro.

After you return to DOS, restart your computer by pressing [Ctrl]-[Alt]-[Del]. This step ensures that changes to your AUTOEXEC.BAT and CONFIG.SYS files will take effect.

Loading and Quitting Quattro Pro

To load Quattro Pro, press [Q] and then press [⏎Enter].

To quit the program, select /File Exit or press [Ctrl]-[X]. Quattro Pro returns you to the operating system.

A

Reconfiguring and Enhancing Quattro Pro

You should never have to install Quattro Pro again, though you can easily reconfigure your copy of Quattro Pro. You can add new printers, customize the mouse palette functions (when you display Quattro Pro in graphics mode), and switch menu trees directly from Quattro Pro's Options menu.

Upgrading from Version 3.0 to Version 4.0

Upgrading from Version 3.0 to Version 4.0 is simple. Be careful when you perform the steps outlined in this section—you will be deleting many Quattro Pro files from at least two directories on your hard disk drive.

The Quattro Pro Version 4.0 installation facility does not automatically upgrade your Version 3.0 files. The only Version 3.0 files that you can use with Version 4.0 are spreadsheet files (.WQ*), workspace files (.WSP), and clip art files (.CLP). Copy these files to another directory (outside of the \QPRO directory) before you install Version 4.0.

The following step-by-step procedure shows you how to prepare a hard disk drive for Version 4.0 installation. The procedure assumes that you have two Quattro Pro directories: \QPRO, where all of the Version 3.0 program files reside, and \QPRO\FONTS, the subdirectory where all of the Version 3.0 font files reside.

1. At the DOS command prompt, type **CD\QPRO\FONTS** and press [⏎Enter] to change to the FONTS subdirectory.

2. Type **DEL *.*** and press [⏎Enter] to delete all Version 3.0 font files from the FONTS subdirectory.

3. Type **CD\QPRO** and press ⏎Enter to change to the QPRO directory.

4. Type **DEL** *.* and press ⏎Enter to delete all Version 3.0 program files from the QPRO directory.

You must remove all Version 3.0 program files and font files from your hard disk drive prior to installing Version 4.0. Do not intermingle program and font files from both versions; this may cause unpredictable results during your Quattro Pro sessions. You are now ready to install Quattro Pro 4.0, as discussed in "Installing the Program," a previous section in this appendix.

A

B

Summary of Quattro Pro Commands

Action	Commands
Moving the Cell Selector	
Move left one column	←
Move right one column	→
Move up one row	↑
Move down one row	↓
Move right one screen	Tab⇄ or Ctrl-→
Move left one screen	⇧Shift-Tab⇄ or Ctrl-←
Move up one screen	PgUp
Move down one screen	PgDn
Return to cell A1	Home

continues

Summary of Quattro Pro Commands

Action	Commands
Move in direction of arrow to next boundary or end of a group of empty or occupied cells	`End`-arrow key
Move to specified cell or block	`F5` (GoTo), type cell address or block name

Editing

Action	Commands
Align block of labels and numbers	/**S**tyle **A**lignment (or `Ctrl`-`A`); **L**eft, **R**ight, or **C**enter; highlight block, `↵Enter`
Align labels in entire spreadsheet	/**O**ptions **F**ormats **A**lign Labels; **L**eft, **R**ight, or **C**enter
Edit cell contents	`F2` (Edit)
Move cursor left one character	`←`
Move cursor right one character	`→`
Move cursor right five characters	`Tab⇄` or `Ctrl`-`→`
Move cursor left five characters	`⇧Shift`-`Tab⇄` or `Ctrl`-`←`
Move cursor to first character in entry	`Home`
Move cursor to right of last character in entry	`End`
Delete character to left of cursor	`⬅Backspace`
Toggle between Insert and Overtype modes	`Ins`
Delete character above cursor	`Del`
Clear input line	`Esc`
Undo last command	`Alt`-`F5` (Undo) when Undo feature is enabled
Temporarily disable Undo	/**O**ptions **O**ther **U**ndo **D**isable

498

Action	*Commands*
Saving and Retrieving Files	
Save new file	/**F**ile **S**ave; type name, ⏎Enter
Save existing file under same name	/**F**ile **S**ave, ⏎Enter, **R**eplace
Save existing file under new name	/**F**ile Save **A**s; type name, ⏎Enter
Retrieve file	/**F**ile **R**etrieve; highlight or type file name, ⏎Enter
Using Blocks	
Designate a block	Type address of upper left cell in block, type one or two periods, type address of lower right cell in block, ⏎Enter
	Or
	In POINT mode, move cell selector to highlight cells in block, ⏎Enter
	Or
	Type existing block name (or press F3 and highlight block name), ⏎Enter
Assign a name to a multicell block	/**E**dit **N**ames **C**reate; type name, ⏎Enter; type cell addresses or highlight block, ⏎Enter
Assign names to a series of one-cell entries with adjacent labels	Position cell selector on first label to use as a block name; /**E**dit **N**ames **L**abels; **R**ight, **L**eft, **A**bove, or **B**elow; highlight cells containing labels to use as block names, ⏎Enter
Delete a single block name	/**E**dit **N**ames **D**elete; highlight or type block name, ⏎Enter
Delete all block names in a spreadsheet	/**E**dit **N**ames **R**eset

continues

B

499

Action	Commands
Erase a block	/**E**dit **B**lock **E**rase (or Ctrl-E); highlight block to erase, ↵Enter
Display a list box of names in current spreadsheet	In POINT mode, press F3 (Choices)
Display a full-screen list of block names in current spreadsheet	In POINT mode, press F3 (Choices) twice
Create a block name table	Move cell selector to spreadsheet location in which you want to display upper left corner of table; /**E**dit **N**ames **M**ake **T**able, ↵Enter
Move cell selector to a named block	F5 (GoTo); F3 (Choices); highlight name, ↵Enter

Building a Spreadsheet

Action	Commands
Set formats that affect entire spreadsheet	/**O**ptions **F**ormats
Set width of single column	/**S**tyle **C**olumn **W**idth (or Ctrl-W); type width or use ← or → to expand or shrink column, ↵Enter
Reset single column to default width	/**S**tyle **R**eset **W**idth
Set widths of all columns at once	/**O**ptions **F**ormats **G**lobal Width; type width or use ← or → to expand or shrink column, ↵Enter
Set widths of contiguous columns	/**S**tyle **B**lock **S**ize **S**et Width; highlight column block; ↵Enter; type width or use ← or → to expand or shrink columns, ↵Enter
Reset contiguous columns to default width	/**S**tyle **B**lock **S**ize **R**eset Width
Split the screen	Position cell selector at location for split; /**W**indow **O**ptions; **H**orizontal or **V**ertical; ↵Enter
Return to single window	/**W**indow **O**ptions **C**lear

500

Action	Commands
Lock titles on-screen	Position cell selector below and to the right of rows and/or columns to be locked; /Window Options Locked Titles; Both, Horizontal, or Vertical
Unlock titles	/Window Options Locked Titles Clear
Insert columns and rows	Position cell selector where you want to insert column(s) or row(s); /Edit Insert (or Ctrl-I); Columns or Rows; highlight block to insert multiple columns or rows, ↵Enter
Delete columns and rows	Position cell selector in first column or row to be deleted; /Edit Delete; Columns or Rows; highlight block of column(s) or row(s) to be deleted, ↵Enter
Hide columns	/Style Hide Column Hide; highlight columns to be hidden, ↵Enter
Redisplay hidden columns	/Style Hide Column Display; specify columns to redisplay, ↵Enter
Suppress display of zeros	/Options Other Hide Zeros Yes
Redisplay zeros	/Options Other Hide Zeros No
Modify spreadsheet recalculation settings	/Options Recalculation
Protect entire spreadsheet	/Options Protection Enable
Unprotect entire spreadsheet	/Options Protection Disable
Turn off protection in a block	/Style Protection Unprotection; specify block, ↵Enter
Reprotect cells in a block	/Style Protection Protect; specify block, ↵Enter
Enter a page-break character	Position cell selector in first column at row where new page should begin, /Style Insert Break

continues

B

501

Action	Commands
Modifying a Spreadsheet	
Move contents of cells	/Edit Move (or `Ctrl`-`M`); specify block to move from, `↵Enter`; specify block to move to, `↵Enter`
Copy contents and formats of cells	/Edit Copy (or `Ctrl`-`C`); specify source block, `↵Enter`; specify destination block, `↵Enter`
Copy format of cells	/Edit Copy Special Format; specify source block, `↵Enter`; specify destination block, `↵Enter`
Copy contents of cells	/Edit Copy Special Contents; specify source block, `↵Enter`; specify destination block, `↵Enter`
Convert cell addresses to absolute or mixed cell addresses	Highlight cell containing formula; `F4` (Edit); move cursor to cell address; press `F4` (Abs) to specify types of cell addresses
Transpose rows and columns	/Edit Transpose; specify source block, `↵Enter`; specify destination block, `↵Enter`
Convert formulas to values	/Edit Values; specify source block of formulas, `↵Enter`; specify destination block, `↵Enter`
Search for occurrence of string	/Edit Search & Replace Block; highlight block, `↵Enter`; Search String; define string to search for, `↵Enter`; Next or Quit
Replace one string with another	/Edit Search & Replace Block; highlight block, `↵Enter`; Search String; define string to search for, `↵Enter`; Replace String; define replacement string, `↵Enter`; Next or Quit

B

Action	*Commands*
Formatting a Spreadsheet	
Change format of a cell or block of cells	/**S**tyle **N**umeric Format (or Ctrl-F); **F**ixed, **S**cientific, **C**urrency, , (Comma), **G**eneral, +/–, **P**ercent, **D**ate, **T**ime, **T**ext, or **H**idden (if prompted, enter number of decimal places or accept default number, Enter); highlight block to format, Enter
Return format of block to global default setting	/**S**tyle **N**umeric Format **R**eset; highlight block to reset, Enter
Set format for date, time, currency symbols, negative values, and punctuation	/**O**ptions **I**nternational
Change font of a cell or block of cells	/**S**tyle **F**ont; highlight block, Enter; **T**ypeface; highlight a typeface, Enter; **P**oint Size; highlight a point size, Enter; **C**olor; highlight a color, Enter; **B**old to boldface; **I**talic to italicize; **U**nderline to underline
Return font of block to global default setting	/**S**tyle **F**ont; highlight block to reset; **R**eset
Apply preset font to a cell or block of cells	/**S**tyle **F**ont**T**able; highlight block, Enter; select a preset font
Change shading of a cell or block of cells	/**S**tyle **S**hading; **N**one, **G**rey, or **B**lack; highlight block, Enter
Change borders of a cell or block of cells	/**S**tyle **L**ine Drawing; highlight block, Enter; **A**ll, **O**utside, **T**op, **B**ottom, **L**eft, **R**ight, **I**nside, **H**orizontal, or **V**ertical; **N**one, **S**ingle, **D**ouble, or **T**hick

B

continues

503

Action	*Commands*
Using @Functions	
Enter a Quattro Pro @function	Type @, type function name, ↵Enter
	Or
	To include arguments, type @, type function name, type (*arguments*), ↵Enter
Printing Reports	
Print text directly to printer	/**Print** **D**estination **P**rinter
Print spreadsheets with fonts and inserted graphs	/**Print** **D**estination **G**raphics Printer
Create a print file on-disk	/**Print** **D**estination **F**ile; type file name, ↵Enter
Print draft of full screen of data	In Text mode, ⇧Shift-PrtSc or PrtSc
Print one-page report	/**Print** **D**estination **P**rinter **B**lock; highlight block to be printed, ↵Enter; **A**djust Printer **A**lign, **S**preadsheet Print, **A**djust Printer, **F**orm Feed; **Q**uit
Print two or more pages with border	/**Print** **H**eadings; **L**eft Heading or **T**op Heading; highlight columns or rows, ↵Enter; **B**lock; highlight block to be printed, ↵Enter; **A**djust Printer, **A**lign, **S**preadsheet Print, **A**djust Printer, **F**orm Feed; **Q**uit
Exclude columns within print block	/**S**tyle **H**ide Column **H**ide; highlight column(s), ↵Enter; /**P**rint **D**estination **P**rinter **B**lock; highlight block to be printed, ↵Enter; **A**djust Printer, **A**lign, **S**preadsheet Print, **A**djust Printer, **F**orm Feed; **Q**uit

Action	*Commands*
Exclude row within print block	Highlight row to be suppressed in first column of print block; type ¦¦, ⏎Enter); /**Print** **D**estination **P**rinter **B**lock; highlight block to be printed, ⏎Enter); **Adjust Printer**, **Align**, **Spread-sheet Print**, **Adjust Printer**, **Form Feed**; **Quit**
Exclude block from printout	/**Style** **N**umeric **Format** **Hidden**; highlight block to be hidden, ⏎Enter); /**Print** **D**estination **P**rinter **Block**; highlight block to be printed, ⏎Enter); **Adjust Printer**, **Align**, **Spreadsheet Print**, **Adjust Printer**, **Form Feed**; **Quit**
Advance paper one line at a time	/**Print Adjust Printer Skip Line**
Advance to new page after printing less than full page	/**Print Adjust Printer Form Feed**
Align printer and set beginning of page	/**Print Adjust Printer Align**
Insert page break automatically	/**Style Insert Break**
Insert page break manually	Insert blank row at location for page break; type ¦:: into blank cell in first column of print block in that row, ⏎Enter)
Add header or footer	/**Print** **D**estination **P**rinter **Block**; highlight print block, ⏎Enter); **Layout**; **Header** or **Footer**; type header or footer—including text or codes for date and page number (if used), ⏎Enter); **Quit**; **Adjust Printer**, **Align**, **Spreadsheet Print**, **Adjust Printer**, **Form Feed**; **Quit**
Change page layout	/**Print Layout Margins**; **Page Length**, **Left**, **Right**, **Top**, or **Bottom**; **Quit**; type a value, ⏎Enter)

continues

B

505

Action	Commands
Print listing of cell contents	/**Print** **D**estination **P**rinter **F**ormat **C**ell-Formulas **B**lock; highlight block to be printed, ⏎Enter; **A**djust Printer, **A**lign, **S**preadsheet Print, **A**djust Printer, **F**orm Feed; **Q**uit
Clear print options	/**Print** **L**ayout **R**eset; **A**ll, **P**rint Block, **H**eadings, or **L**ayout
Prepare output for other programs	/**Print** **D**estination **F**ile; type file name, ⏎Enter; **B**lock; specify block, ⏎Enter; **A**djust Printer, **A**lign, **S**preadsheet Print, **F**orm Feed, **Q**uit; follow instructions of other software program

Managing Files

Action	Commands
Erase the spreadsheet from memory	/**File** **E**rase **Y**es
Create a password	/**File**; **S**ave or Save **A**s; type file name, leave a space, type **P**, ⏎Enter; type password, ⏎Enter; retype password, ⏎Enter
Retrieve a password-protected file	/**File** **R**etrieve; highlight file name, ⏎Enter; type password, ⏎Enter
Delete a password	/**File** **S**ave; press Esc or ←Backspace to erase [Password protected], ⏎Enter
Change a password	/**File** Save **A**s, press Esc or ←Backspace to erase [Password protected]; type file name, leave a space, type **P**, ⏎Enter; type new password, ⏎Enter; retype new password, ⏎Enter
Copy partial spreadsheet to separate file	/**Tools** **X**tract; **F**ormulas or **V**alues; type file name to hold extracted data, ⏎Enter; highlight block to be extracted, ⏎Enter

Action	Commands
Combine files	Position cell selector on block to receive data; /**T**ools **C**ombine; **C**opy, **A**dd, or **S**ubtract; **F**ile or **B**lock; indicate data file or location of incoming block, ⏎Enter
Refresh links	/**T**ools **U**pdate Links **R**efresh
Change default directory	/**O**ptions **S**tartup **D**irectory; Esc or ⬅Backspace ; type new default directory name, ⏎Enter ; **Q**uit; **U**pdate, **Q**uit
Temporarily change directory	/**F**ile **D**irectory; type new directory name, ⏎Enter
Import ASCII text file into Quattro Pro	/**T**ools **I**mport; **A**SCII Text File; highlight name of text file to be imported, ⏎Enter
Translate Quattro Pro files to other program formats	/**F**ile Save **A**s; type file name and other program's three-character file extension

Creating Graphs

Action	Commands
Create a basic graph	Select graph type; specify data blocks; select block for labeling x-axis; display graph on-screen
Select graph type	/**G**raph **G**raph Type; **L**ine, **B**ar, **X**Y, **S**tacked Bar, **P**ie, **A**rea, **R**otated Bar, **C**olumn, **H**igh-Low, **T**ext, **B**ubble or **3**-D Graphs
Specify a data series block	/**G**raph **S**eries, select a block (1st-6th Series); highlight a block, ⏎Enter
Indicate x-axis data block	/**G**raph **S**eries **X**-Axis Series; highlight block, ⏎Enter
Define all data blocks at once	/**G**raph **S**eries **G**roup; highlight a single block that contains **X** and 1st-6th data block, ⏎Enter ; **C**olumns or **R**ows

continues

507

Action	Commands
Display graph on-screen	/Graph View or [F10] (Graph)
Zoom and pan a graph	/Graph View or [F10] (Graph); simultaneously press the left and right mouse buttons.
Insert a graph in a spreadsheet	/Graph Insert; select the graph name, [↵Enter]
Add titles to a graph	/Graph Text; 1st Line, 2nd Line, X-Title, Y-Title, or Secondary Y-Axis
Enter labels within a graph	/Graph Customize Series Interior Labels; specify data series (1st-6th or Group); highlight block to be used as labels, [↵Enter]; indicate location of labels (Center, Left, Above, Right, or Below)
Add a legend to a graph	/Graph Text Legends; select block (1st-6th); type label or press [\]; type cell address containing the label, [↵Enter]; repeat for each label to be included in legend
Add connecting lines and/or symbols	/Graph Customize Series Markers and Lines; assign lines or symbols to whole graph or to individual blocks; Lines, Symbols, or Both
Set background grid	/Graph Overall Grid; Horizontal, Vertical, or Both
Change upper and lower limits	/Graph; X-Axis or Y-Axis; Scale Manual Low; type value, [↵Enter]; High; type value, [↵Enter]
Change format of x- or y-axis values	/Graph; X-Axis or Y-Axis; Format of Ticks; select format option
Suppress x- or y-axis scale	/Graph; X-Axis or Y-Axis; Display Scaling No

B

508

Action	Commands
Space the display of x- or y-axis labels	/**G**raph; **X**-Axis or **Y**-Axis; **N**o. of Minor Ticks; type number, ⏎Enter
Store settings for graph to allow later modification	/**G**raph **N**ame; **D**isplay, **C**reate, **E**rase, **R**eset, **S**lide, or **G**raph Copy
Print a graph	/**P**rint **G**raph Print **N**ame; select name of graph to print; **D**estination **G**raph Printer **G**o; **Q**uit

Managing Data

Action	Commands
Build a database	Choose area for database; enter field names across a single row; set column widths and cell display formats; add records
Add a record	/**E**dit **I**nsert **R**ows; move cell selector to location for new record, ⏎Enter; enter data for new record
Restrict movement to a particular block	/**D**atabase **R**estrict Input; specify block that includes the unprotected cells, ⏎Enter
Delete a record	/**E**dit **D**elete **R**ows; move cell selector to record to be deleted, ⏎Enter
Add a field	/**E**dit **I**nsert **C**olumns; move cell selector to location for new field, ⏎Enter; enter data for new field
Delete a field	/**E**dit **D**elete **C**olumns; move cell selector to field to be deleted, ⏎Enter
Edit a field	Highlight cell to be edited; F2 (Edit)
Sort a database rowwise	/**D**atabase **S**ort **B**lock; designate block, ⏎Enter; specify key field(s), ⏎Enter; choose ascending or descending order for each key field, ⏎Enter; **G**o

continues

Action	Commands
Sort a database columnwise	/Database Sort Block; designate block, ⏎Enter; specify key field(s), ⏎Enter; choose ascending or descending order for each key field, ⏎Enter; select Sort Rules Sort Rows/Columns Columns Quit Go
Perform a one-key sort	/Database Sort Block; highlight block, ⏎Enter; 1st Key; highlight cell in column containing 1st Key field, ⏎Enter; type A for ascending or D for descending, ⏎Enter; Go
Perform a multiple-key sort	/Database Sort Block, highlight block, ⏎Enter; 1st Key; highlight cell in column containing 1st Key field, ⏎Enter; type A for ascending or D for descending, ⏎Enter; 2nd-5th Key(s); highlight cell in column containing 2nd-5th Key field(s), ⏎Enter; type A for ascending or D for descending, ⏎Enter; Go
Create a "counter" column	Insert blank column (/Edit Insert Columns); reduce column width of new column (/Style Column Width); /Edit Fill; highlight rows in new column, ⏎Enter; type 1 and press ⏎Enter for Start; type 1 and press ⏎Enter for Step; press ⏎Enter to accept default Stop value
Define input block	/Database Query Block; highlight block, ⏎Enter; Quit
Define criteria table	Type the label CRITERIA TABLE, ⏎Enter; copy exact field names to section of spreadsheet where criteria table is to be located; type search criteria just below a field name, ⏎Enter; /Database Query Criteria Table; highlight block (include only field names and criteria), ⏎Enter; Quit

510

Action	Commands
Reset input, criteria, and output blocks	/Database Query Reset
Find records that meet criteria	/Database Query Locate; press ⏎Enter to move highlight bar to next record that meets criteria
End a search	⏎Enter or Esc; Quit
Edit records during search	/Database Query Locate; press →] or ←] until cursor is in cell to be edited; F2 (Edit); modify cell contents, ⏎Enter
Define output block	Type the label **OUTPUT BLOCK**, ⏎Enter; copy exact field names to section of spreadsheet where output block is to be located; /Database Query Output Block; highlight block, ⏎Enter; Quit
List all specified records to output block	/Database Query Extract; Quit
Copy extracted records to new file	/Tools Xtract; Formulas or Values; type new file name, ⏎Enter; highlight block of records to copy, ⏎Enter
Copy unique records that meet criteria to output block	/Database Query Unique; Quit
Delete specified records	/Database Query Delete; Quit
Using Macros	
Assign a single-letter name to a macro	/Edit Names Create; type \ and a single letter, ⏎Enter; highlight first cell in block where macro commands are stored, ⏎Enter
Assign a descriptive name to a macro	/Edit Names Create (or /Tools Macro Name Create); type a descriptive name of up to 15 characters, ⏎Enter; highlight first cell in block where macro commands are stored, ⏎Enter

continues

B

Summary of Quattro Pro Commands

Action	Commands
Assign a name to an automatic macro	/Edit Names Create; type \0 (backslash zero), ↵Enter; highlight first cell in block where macro commands are stored, ↵Enter
Assign names to a group of macros	/Edit Names Labels Right; highlight names to be assigned to macros, ↵Enter
Record keystrokes for a macro	/Tools Macro Record (or Alt-F2 R); type all commands and keystrokes to be included in macro; /Tools Macro Record (or Alt-F2 R) to turn off the recorder; /Tools Macro Paste (or Alt-F2 P); type macro name, ↵Enter; type cell or block address for location, ↵Enter
Execute a single-letter macro	Press Alt-*letter*
Execute a macro with a descriptive name	/Tools Macro Execute (or Alt-F2 E); F3 (Choices); highlight macro name, ↵Enter
Undo a macro	With Undo feature enabled, press Alt-F5 (Undo)
Use the Debugger to debug a macro	⇧Shift-F2 (Debug); execute macro; evaluate each step of macro and press space bar after checking each step; when error is found, press Ctrl-Break Esc F2 (Edit); edit macro; ⇧Shift-F2 (Debug)
Edit a macro	Highlight cell to be modified; F2 (Edit)

B

Action	Commands
Customizing the SpeedBar	
Replace a SpeedBar button	/Options SpeedBar; READY mode SpeedBar or EDIT mode SpeedBar; select the predefined button you want to replace (buttons A-M are defined by default); Short Name, change the name; Long Name, change the name; Macro, change the macro
Adjust a SpeedBar button	/Options SpeedBar; READY mode SpeedBar or EDIT mode SpeedBar; select the button you want to adjust (buttons A-M are defined by default); Short Name or Long Name, adjust the name; Macro, adjust the macro
Add a SpeedBar button	/Options SpeedBar; READY mode SpeedBar or EDIT mode SpeedBar; select the button you want to add (buttons N and O are available on the READY mode SpeedBar and M-O on the EDIT mode SpeedBar); Short Name, type the short name; Long Name, type the long name; Macro, enter the macro to perform the desired task

B

Index

Symbols

#AND# complex operator, 245
#NOT# complex operators, 245
#OR# complex operator, 245
% format, 208
+/– format, 207
{?} macro command, 449
' (apostrophe), 450
* (asterisk) wild card, 97, 322
\ (backslash), 447
\0 (backslash zero), 465
, (Comma format), 207
/ (division) operator, 79
== (double-equal sign), 373
–– (double minus sign), 373
++ (double plus sign), 373
= (equal to) operator, 244, 431
^ (exponentiation) mathematical
  operator, 79
> (greater than) operator, 244, 431
>= (greater than or equal to)
  operator, 244, 431
< (less than) operator, 244, 431

<= (less than or equal to) operator,
  245, 431
* (multiplication) mathematical
  operator, 79
– (negative/subtraction)
  mathematical operator, 79
< > (not equal to) operator, 245,
  431
¦:: (page break) symbol, 276
. (period), 37, 450
+ (plus sign), 312
+ (positive/addition) mathematical
  operator, 79
? (question mark) wild card, 97, 322
~ (tilde), 446, 449
/ (slash) key, 19
¦¦ (vertical bars) nonprinting
  symbol, 269
3-D graphs, 345-347

A

@ABS (absolute value) function, 83
absolute cell addresses, 160,
  174-178

formulas, copying, 176-179
referencing with block name,
178, 181
adding
buttons, SpeedBar, 481-487
fields, 386
records, 386
addresses, 174
absolute, 160, 174-178, 181
blocks, 104-106, 114
cells
blocks, 114
macros, 449
changing, 185-186
macros, 449
mixed, 160, 174, 181, 184
relative, 160, 174-176
alignment
labels, 72
blocks, 74
entire spreadsheet, 75
paper, printers, 276
spreadsheets, 75
alphanumeric keys, 37
anchored cells, 106
#AND# search operator, 436
annotating graphs, 368, 372
apostrophe ('), 450
applying styles, 221
area graphs, 342
arguments, 226
arrows, graphs, 356
ASCII files, 296, 322, 325
asterisk (*) wild card, 97, 322
automatic macros, 464-465
automatic recalculation, 148
averages, 238-239
@AVG function, 83, 238-239

axes
origin, 330, 347
scaling, adjusting, 357
tick marks, 330, 347
x-axis, 330, 347-348
y-axis, 330, 347-348

B

background grid, 366-368
background recalculation, 148
backslash (\), 447
backslash zero (\0), 465
bar graphs, 339, 342
Bitstream fonts, 493
blank cells, formatting, 205
block addresses, 104
block names, macros, 449
blocks, 103-104
addresses, 105-106, 114
borders, 215-219
cells, highlighting, 106
commands, 499-500
copying to block, 166-167
databases
output, 384
restricting data entry, 393-395
default, 106
designating, 108
destination, 160
erasing, 105, 116-117
font
changing, 210-215
color, 212-214
formatting, 204-209
highlighting, 58, 106
cell selector, expanding, 162
End key, 162
mouse, 106

labels, alignment, 74
moving, 160-162
names, 56, 104, 108-109
   deleting, 89, 114-115
   listing, 117-118
   notes, 120-122
   referencing absolute
    addresses, 178, 181
   resetting, 89
   selecting, 118
   tables, 104, 119-120
naming, 108-114
notes, 104
output
   databases, 424-426
   limiting size, 426
   open ended, 424
printing, 257, 260
   excluding, 272, 274
   macro, 471, 472
protecting, 151-153
segments, excluding from
   printing, 266-274
shading, 218-219
source, 160
specifying, 118, 348-356
totalling, macro, 472
transposing, 188
borders, blocks, 215-219
bubble graph, 344
bugs, 446
buttons, SpeedBar, 476-486

C

calculating
   averages, 238-239
   loan payments, 236
   spreadsheets, 126, 148-150

see also recalculating
values
   future, 237
   present, 237
calculation
   columnwise, 148
   natural order, 148
   rowwise, 148
case, strings, converting, 248
@CELL function, 83
cell selector, 8, 16, 56
   expanding, 58, 162
   movement keys, 106
   moving, 118, 497, 498
   restricting, 393
@CELLPOINTER function, 83
cells, 8, 16
   addresses, *see* addresses
   anchored, 106
   blank, formatting, 205
   blocks, 104, 385
    destination, 160
    moving, 160-162
    name, 56
    source, 160
   contents
    copying, 163-169
    editing, 86-87
    listings, 286-288
    moving, 160-163
    searching and replacing,
     191-198
   copying
    contents, 169-171
    to another cell, 164
    to block, 165
   cutting and pasting, 160
   entries, counting, 239-240

formats
+/–, 207
changing, 205
Comma (,), 207
copying, 171, 174
Currency, 207
date and time, 208
default, 203
Fixed, 207
General, 206
Hidden, 209
Percent, 208
Scientific, 207
Text, 208
formatting contents, 202-209
formulas, 8
highlighting, 106-108
labels, 56
linking between files, 312-316
primary, 312
references, adjusting, 188
see also addresses
series, naming, 112-114
single, naming, 111
supporting, 312
values, 56
characters
macro commands, 449
repeating, 73, 74
CHKDSK DOS command, 94
clearing spreadsheets from screen,
296
color, fonts, 212-214
column graph, 343
column letters, 10
columns, 10
copying to row format, 188

databases
inserting, 412
one-key sort, 408, 411
width, 391, 412
deleting, 143-145
headings, 256
printing, 262, 266
repeating, 262
hiding, 131-133, 267
displaying, 132
redisplaying, 132
restoring, 269
inserting, 141-143
printing, excluding, 267-269
titles, locked, 137-140
transposing, 186-188
width, 126-131
changing, 127-128
contiguous, 129-131
macro, 472
setting all, 128-129
columnwise calculation, 148
combining files, 305-306, 310-311
Comma (,) format, 207
commands, 8
/ (slash) key, 19
/Data Query Extract, 426
/Database Query, 241, 386
/Database Query Block, 417
/Database Query Criteria Table,
418
/Database Query Delete, 438
/Database Query Extract, 427
/Database Query Locate, 420
/Database Query Output, 425
/Database Query Unique, 437
/Database Restrict Input, 393

/Database Sort, 401

/Database Sort Block, 402-408

/Edit Copy, 160, 163, 179

/Edit Copy Special, 169

/Edit Delete, 143

/Edit Delete Columns, 145

/Edit Delete Rows, 145, 396

/Edit Erase Block, 105-106, 116-117, 296

/Edit Fill, 412

/Edit Insert, 141, 386

/Edit Insert Columns, 143, 412

/Edit Insert Rows, 143, 396

/Edit Names, 108

/Edit Names Create, 108-114, 457

/Edit Names Delete, 89, 114

/Edit Names Labels, 110-112, 458

/Edit Names Make Table, 104, 119

/Edit Names Reset, 89, 114

/Edit Search & Replace, 191

/Edit Search & Replace Block, 191

/Edit Transpose, 186

/Edit Undo, 88

/Edit Values, 186-189

/File Directory, 317

/File Erase, 296

/File Exit, 30, 34

/File Open, 97

/File Retrieve, 95, 98, 300

/File Save, 93, 298

/File Save As, 93

/File Utilities DOS Shell, 33, 94, 320

/Graph Annotate, 369

/Graph Customize Series, 357-360

/Graph Fast Graph, 336-338

/Graph Graph Type, 333, 349

/Graph Insert, 377

/Graph Legend, 363

/Graph Overall, 366

/Graph Overall Grid, 357

/Graph Series Group, 335, 354

/Graph Text, 357

/Graph Text Legends, 363

/Graph View, 373

/Graph X-Axis No, 357

/Options Display Mode, 30

/Options Format Global Width, 128

/Options Formats Align Labels, 75

/Options Formats Global Width, 128

/Options Formats Hide Zeros, 146

/Options Formats Numeric Format, 204

/Options Formats Numeric Formats, 202

/Options Hardware Printers, 291

/Options International, 209

/Options Protection Enable, 150

/Options Protection Formulas, 153

/Options Recalculation, 148

/Options SpeedBar, 477

/Options Startup Directory, 317

/Options Update, 90

/Print Adjust Printer, 275

/Print Adjust Printer Align, 276

/Print Adjust Printer Skip Line, 275

/Print Block, 110, 428

/Print Block Layout Header, 279

/Print Destination File, 255-256, 289

/Print Destination Printer, 255-256
/Print Destination Screen Preview, 284-285
/Print Format As Displayed, 286
/Print Format Cell-Formulas, 82, 286
/Print Graph Print, 379
/Print Headings, 262-264
/Print Layout, 283
/Print Layout Reset, 259, 288-289
/Style Alignment, 74
/Style Block Size, 126, 129
/Style Column Width, 126-128, 391
/Style Define Style, 220
/Style Font, 210
/Style FontTable, 214
/Style Hide Column, 131, 209
/Style Hide Column Expose, 132, 269
/Style Hide Column Hide, 267, 268
/Style Insert Break, 276-277
/Style Line Drawing, 215-216
/Style Numeric Format, 82, 202-204
/Style Numeric Format Hidden, 272
/Style Protection Protect, 153
/Style Protection Unprotect, 153
/Style Reset Width, 128
/Style Shading, 219
/Style Use Style, 221
/Tools Combine, 302, 305
/Tools Combine Copy, 309
/Tools Import, 257
/Tools Macro Debugger, 467
/Tools Macro Execute, 447, 463

/Tools Macro Paste, 461
/Tools Macro Record, 459
/Tools Update Links Refresh, 315
/Tools What-If, 208
/Tools Xtract, 302
/Tools Xtract Formula, 428
/Tools Xtract Formulas, 305
/Tools Xtract Values, 305
/Window Options Clear, 137
/Window Options Grid Lines Display, 215
/Window Options Horizontal, 134
/Window Options Locked Titles, 137
/Window Options Sync, 136
/Window Options Unsync, 136
blocks, 499-500
databases, 386, 509-511
DOS
    CHKDSK, 94
    FORMAT, 95
editing, 498
file management, 506-507
file manipulation, 499
graphs, 507-509
macro, see macro commands
moving cell selector, 497-498
printing, 504-506
Screen Previewer, 284-285
selecting, 67-70
SpeedBar customization, 513
spreadsheets, 500-503
complex operators
    #AND#, 245
    #NOT#, 245
    #OR#, 245
conditional tests, 244-245
configuring printers, 490
continous-feed paper, 275

converting
    date strings to serial numbers, 83,
        231-232
    decimal numbers to integers, 228
    strings, case, 248
    times to serial numbers, 83
copying, 190
    cells
        block to block, 166-167
        contents, 163-171
        formats, 164, 171, 174
        to block of cells, 165
        to cell, 165
    columns to row format, 188
    formats, cells, 164, 171, 174
    formulas
        absolute addresses, 176
        block name absolute address,
            179
        mixed cell addresses, 182
    records, extracted to new file,
        428
    rows to column format, 188
@COS (cosine) function, 83
@COUNT function, 239-240
counting cell entries, 239-240
creating
    criteria tables, 429-433, 436-441
    files
        macro library, 471
        print, 256
    graphs, 330-331
    passwords, 298
    tables, block names, 119-120
criteria, 241, 418
    records, searching, 420-422
    specifying, multiple, 432-433, 436
criteria tables, 384
    creating, 429-433, 436-441
    databases, searching, 418-420

formulas, 431-432
    wild cards, 429
Ctrl-key shortcuts, 41
Currency format, 207
current directory
    changing, 318
    graph, viewing, 357
    date and time, 233
cursor, 56-57
custom styles, 222
customizing SpeedBar, 476-487
cutting and pasting, 160

D

data, 56
    editing, 86-88
    entering, 57, 71-86
    extracting, spreadsheets, 302-305
data blocks, 384, 416-418
data series, *see* series
database functions, 83
    @DAVG, 83
    @DSUM, 83
Database menu, 387-388
/Database Query Unique command,
    437
/Database Query command, 241,
    386
/Database Query Block command,
    417
/Database Query Criteria Table
    command, 418
/Database Query Delete command,
    438
/Database Query Extract command,
    426-427
/Database Query Locate command,
    420
/Database Query Output command,
    425

/Database Restrict Input command, 393
/Database Sort command, 401
/Database Sort Block command, 402-408
database statistical functions, 241-243
databases, 23-24, 383-385
  @functions, 387
  blocks, output, 384
  columns
    inserting, 412
    width, 391, 412
  commands, 386, 509-511
  criteria tables, 384
  data blocks, 384
  entering data, 390-395
  extract area, open ended, 426
  fields, 384-385
    adding, 386
    inserting/deleting, 398-400
    key field, 384-385
  input, restricting, 393
  modifying, 395-400
  output blocks, 424-426
  planning, 388-389
  records, 384-385
    adding, 386
    extracting, 427
    inserting/deleting, 396-398
    searching for, 414-441
    sorting, 400-414
  search requirements, 415-416
  searching
    criteria tables, 418-420
    data blocks, 416-418
  sorting, 386
    one-key, 402-404, 408, 411
    two-key, 405-407

spreadsheets, positioning, 390
@DATE function, 83, 231
date and time
  current, finding, 233
  format, 208
date and time functions, 83, 230-233
  @DATE, 83, 231
  @DATEVALUE, 232
  @NOW, 233
  @TIME, 83
date strings, converting to serial numbers, 232
dates, converting to serial numbers, 83, 231
@DATEVALUE function, 232
@DAVG function, 83
DEBUG mode, 467-469
debugging, 446, 465-470
decimals, 207
default
  block, 106
  directory, changing, 317
  formats, cells, 203
  settings, printing, 256
defining styles, 220-222
deleting
  columns, 143-145
  fields, databases, 398-400
  filcs, 320-322
  names, blocks, 89, 114-115
  passwords, 300-301
  records
    databases, 396-398
    searched for, 438-441
  rows, 143-145
designating blocks, 108
destination block, 160
direction keys, 8, 39, 58-60

directories
 current, changing, 318
 default, changing, 317
 specifying, 317, 320
diskettes, Quattro Pro, 490
disks
 floppy, saving to, 93-94
 hard, saving to, 93-94
 space, 94-95
displaying
 columns, hidden, 132
 graphs
  grid lines, 357
  titles, 358-360
 labels, 72
 zeros, suppressing, 146-148
division (/) operator, 79
documented macros, 446, 455-456
DOS commands
 CHKDSK, 94
 FORMAT, 95
double-equal sign (==), 373
double-minus sign (– –), 373
double-plus sign (++), 373
draft-quality printing, 258-266
drives
 files, retrieving, 99
 specifying, 317, 320
@DSUM function, 83

E

/Edit Erase Block command, 105,
 116-117
/Edit Names command, 108
/Edit Names Create command,
 108-111
/Edit Names Delete command, 114

/Edit Names Labels command,
 110-112
/Edit Names Make Table command,
 104, 119
/Edit Names Reset command, 114
/Edit Copy command, 160-163, 179
/Edit Copy Special command, 169
/Edit Delete command, 143
/Edit Delete Columns command,
 145
/Edit Delete Rows command, 145,
 396
/Edit Erase Block command, 106,
 296
/Edit Fill command, 412
/Edit Insert command, 141, 386
/Edit Insert Columns command,
 143, 412
/Edit Insert Rows command, 143,
 396
EDIT mode, 476
 direction keys, 58-59
 invoking, 86
 key actions, 87-88
 SpeedBar, 475, 484-487
/Edit Names Create command, 114,
 457
/Edit Names Delete command, 89
/Edit Names Labels command, 458
/Edit Names Reset command, 89
/Edit Search & Replace command,
 191
/Edit Search & Replace Block
 command, 191
/Edit Transpose command, 186
/Edit Undo command, 88
/Edit Values command, 186-189

editing
  cells, contents, 86-87
  data, spreadsheets, 86-88
  labels, interior, 363
  legends, 366
  macros, 465-470
  records, during search, 422-423
  titles, graphs, 360
editing commands, 498
electronic spreadsheet, *see*
 spreadsheets
End key, 63-65, 107, 162
entries, cells, counting, 239-240
entries, tables, finding, 251-252
equal to (=) operator, 244, 431
erasing
  blocks, 105, 116-117
  files, 296-297
@ERR function, 251
error checking, 246
error trapping, 251
errors
  acknowledging, 81
  formulas, correcting, 83
  macros, 466
excluding from printing
  blocks, 272-274
  columns, 267-269
  rows, 269-272
executing macros, 463-464
exiting Quattro Pro, 30-35
exponential (^) mathematical
 operator, 79
exponential numbers, 207
exporting files, 289-291, 325-326
extract area, open ended, 426
extracting records, 427-428

F

F1 (Help) key, 39
F2 (Edit) key, 39
F3 (Choices) key, 40
F4 (Abs) key, 40
F5 (GoTo) key, 40, 66
F6 (Pane) key, 40
F7 (Query) key, 40, 441
F8 (Table) key, 40
F9 (Calc) key, 40
F10 (Graph) key, 40
@FALSE function, 83, 246
Fast Graph, 336-338
fields, 384-385
  adding, 386
  inserting/deleting, 398-400
  key field, 384-385
/File Directory command, 317
/File Erase command, 296
/File Exit command, 30, 34
/File Open command, 97
/File Retrieve command, 95, 98, 300
/File Save command, 93, 298
/File Save As command, 93
/File Utilities DOS Shell command,
 33, 94, 320
files
  ASCII, 296
  combining, 305-306, 310-311
  commands, 499, 506-507
  copying, extracted records, 428
  deleting, 320-322
  erasing, 296-297
  exporting, 289-291, 325-326
  importing, 322-326
  linking, 296, 312-316
  macro library, creating, 471

naming, 90-92
opening, 97
passwords, 296-301
print, creating, 256
printing to disk, 255
PRN, 91, 257
retrieving, 95-99
    different drive, 99
    from subdirectories, 98
    partial, 302-311
    password-protected, 300
    wild cards, 97
saving, 92-95
    macro, 472
    new name, 93
    partial, 302-311
saving values, 305
templates, 305
updating, 93
financial functions, 234-237
    @FVAL, 237
    @FVAL (future value), 83
    @IRATE, 83
    @IRR, 83
    @NPV (present value), 83
    @PAYMT, 236
    @PAYMT (loan payment), 83
    @PVAL, 237
    @PVAL (present value), 83
Fixed format, 207
floppy disks, saving to, 93-94
fonts
    Bitstream, selecting, 493
    blocks, 210-215
    prearranged, 214
footers, 256, 278-283
    printing, 281
    repeating, 281
    text, positioning, 278

FORMAT DOS command, 95
formats
    +/−, 207
    blocks, 204-209
    cells
        blank, 205
        changing, 205
        contents, 202-209
        copying, 164, 171, 174
    Comma (,), 207
    Currency, 207
    date and time, 208
    default, cells, 203
    Fixed, 207
    General, 206
    Hidden, 209
    International, 209
    Percent, 208
    resetting, 209
    Scientific, 207
    spreadsheets, 204-209
    Text, 208
formulas, 8-10, 16-17
    @functions, 83-84
    arguments, 226
    built-in, 226
        see also @functions
    converting to values, 188-190
    copying
        absolute addresses, 176
        block name absolute address,
          179
        mixed cell addresses, 182
    criteria tables, 431-432
    entering, 76-79
    errors, correcting, 83
    operators, 56, 79-86
    protecting, 153-155
    recalculating, 160
    spaces, 82

function keys, 28, 39-41
@functions, 8, 19, 83-84, 226, 387, 504
  database statistical, 83, 241-243
    @DAVG, 83
    @DSUM, 83
  date and time, 83, 230-233
    @DATE, 83, 231
    @DATEVALUE, 232
    @NOW, 233
    @TIME, 83
  financial, 83, 234-237
    @FVAL, 237
    @FVAL (future value), 83
    @IRATE, 83
    @IRR, 83
    @NPV (present value), 83
    @PAYMT, 236
    @PAYMT (loan payment), 83
    @PVAL, 237
    @PVAL (present value), 83
  formulas, 84
  logical, 83, 243-246
    @FALSE, 83, 246
    @IF, 83, 244-245
    @TRUE, 83, 246
  mathematical, 83, 227-228
    @ABS (absolute value), 83
    @COS (cosine), 83
    @INT, 228-229
    @ROUND, 229
    @ROUND (rounding), 83
    @SIN (sine), 83
    @SQRT (square root), 83
    @TAN (tangent), 83
  miscellaneous
    @CELL, 83
    @CELLPOINTER, 83

  special, 249-251
    @ERR, 251
    @HLOOKUP, 251-252
    @NA, 251
    @VLOOKUP, 251-252
  statistical, 83, 237-241
    @AVG, 83, 238-239
    @COUNT, 239-240
    @MAX, 83, 240
    @MIN, 83
    @STD, 83
    @SUM, 83
    @VAR, 83
  string, 246-249
    @LOWER, 83, 248
    @REPEAT, 83, 249
    @STRING, 83
    @UPPER, 83, 248
    @VALUE, 83
    @PROPER, 248
functions, 225
future values, calculating, 237
@FVAL (future value) function, 83
@FVAL function, 237

G

General format, 206
GoTo (F5) key, 66
/Graph Annotate command, 369
/Graph Customize Series command, 357-360
/Graph Fast Graph command, 336, 338
/Graph Graph Type command, 333, 349
/Graph Insert command, 377
/Graph Legend command, 363

/Graph Overall command, 366
/Graph Overall Grid command, 357
/Graph Series Group command, 335, 354
/Graph Text command, 357
/Graph Text Legends command, 363
/Graph View command, 373
/Graph X-Axis No command, 357
Graph menu, options, 332
graphics monitors, 331
graphics printers, 331
graphs, 12, 20-22, 330
    3-D, 345-347
    annotating, 368, 372
    area, 342
    arrows, 356
    axes, *see* axes
    background grid, 366-368
    bar, 339, 342
    bubble, 344
    column, 343
    commands, 507-509
    creating, 330-331
    enhancing appearance, 356-372
    grid lines, displaying, 357
    hardware requirements, 331
    high-low, 343
    labels, 356, 360-363
    legends, 330, 363-366
    line, 339
    panning, 373-375
    pie, 341
    printing, 331, 379-380
    series, 334
    settings, saving, 375-376
    spreadsheets, inserting, 377-378
    stacked-bar, 341
    text, 344

text notes, 356
tick marks, 330, 347-348
titles, 358
    displaying, 358-360
    editing, 360
types, selecting, 339-342, 346-348
viewing
    current, 357
    on-screen, 331
XY, 340
zooming, 373-375
    (– –) double minus sign, 373
    (+ +) double-plus sign, 373
    (= =) double-equal sign, 373
greater than (>) operator, 244, 431
greater than or equal to (>=) operator, 244, 431
grid lines
    background, 366-368
    displaying, 357

H

hard disks, saving to, 93-94
hardware requirements, 331
headers, 256, 278-283
    repeating, 281
    text, positioning, 278
headings, 256
    printing, 262, 266
    repeating, 262
help, accessing, 50, 53
Hidden format, 209
hiding
    columns, 131-133, 267-269
    zeros, 146-148
high-low graph, 343

highlighting
    blocks, 58, 106
        cell selector, expanding, 162
        End key, 162
        mouse, 106
    cells, 106-108
    commands, 68
@HLOOKUP function, 251-252
Home key, 63-65

I-J

@IF function, 83, 244-245
importing files, 322-326
indicators
    keys, 49-50
    mode, 48-49
    status, 49
input line, 44
Insert mode, 86
inserting
    columns, 141-143, 412
    fields, databases, 398-400
    graphs, spreadsheets, 377-378
    records, databases, 396-398
    rows, 141-143
installing
    fonts, Bitstream, 493
    monitors, 491-492
    printers, 492
    Quattro Pro, 489-494
        network server, 492
        Windows, 493
@INT function, 228-229
integers, 228
interior labels, 363
    editing, position, 363
    eliminating, 363

international formats, 209
@IRATE function, 83
@IRR function, 83

K

key field, 384-385
key indicators, 49-50
key names, 446-453
keyboard, 28, 35
    alphanumeric keys, 37
    Ctrl-key shortcuts, 41
    direction keys, 8, 39, 58-60
    End key, 63-65, 107
    function keys, 28, 39-41
    GoTo (F5) key, 66
    Home key, 63-65
    key actions, 87-88
    macros, 449-453
    movement keys
        cell selector, 106
        Screen Previewer, 285
    numeric keypad, 28, 39
    special keys, 37-38
keystrokes, recording, macros,
    459-463

L

labels, 56, 71
    aligning, 72, 75
    blocks, alignment, 74
    displaying, 72
    graphs, 356, 360-363
    interior, 363
    prefixes, 56, 72-75, 448
    repeating characters, 73-74

layout, 282-283
   margins, 283
   page length, 283
legends, 330, 363, 366
   editing, 366
   location, 365
less than (<) operator, 244, 431
less than or equal to (<=) operator, 245, 431
letters, columns, 10
libraries, macros, 446, 470-473
line graphs, 339
linking
   cells between files, 312-316
   files, 296
links, 312-314
   primary cell, 312
   refreshing, 315-316
   supporting cell, 312
listings
   cell contents, printing, 286-288
   names, blocks, 117-118
   records, specified for search, 423-428
loading Quattro Pro, 494
loan payments, 236
locking titles, 126, 137-140
logical functions, 243-246
   @FALSE, 83, 246
   @IF, 83, 244-245
   @TRUE, 83, 246
logical operators
   < (less than), 244
   < > (not equal to), 245
   <= (less than or equal to), 245
   = (equal to), 244
   > (greater than), 244
   >= (greater than or equal to), 244
@LOWER function, 83, 248

M

macro commands, 24-25, 446, 449, 511-512
macro library, 446, 470-473
macros, 24-25, 446-450
   (') apostrophe, 450
   (.) period, 450
   (\0) backslash zero, 465
   (~) tilde, 449
   automatic, 464-465
   backslash (\), 447
   block names, 449
   block-printing, 471-472
   block-totalling, 472
   bugs, 446
   cell addresses, 449
   column-width, 472
   debugging, 446, 465-470
   documented, 446, 455-456
   editing, 465-470
   elements, 448
   errors, 466
   executing, 463-464
   file-saving, 472
   key names, 446, 449-453
   keystrokes, recording, 459-463
   labels, prefixes, 448
   naming, 447, 456-459
   notation, 463
   planning, 453-454
   special keys, 449-453
   spreadsheets, positioning, 454-455
   text-entering, 472
   Undo, 466
manual recalculation, 148
margins, 283
mathematical functions, 83, 227-228
   @ABS (absolute value), 83

@COS (cosine), 83
@INT, 228-229
@ROUND, 229
@ROUND (rounding), 83
@SIN (sine), 83
@SQRT (square root), 83
@TAN (tangent), 83
mathematical operators, 79-86
   * (multiplication), 79
   + (positive/addition), 79
   – (negative/subtraction), 79
   / (division), 79
   ^ (exponentiation), 79
@MAX function, 83, 240
maximum/minimum values, 240
menu selector, 56, 67
menus
   commands, selecting, 67-70
   Database, 387-388
   Graph, options, 332
   Print, options, 257
   pull-down bar, 43
@MIN function, 83
mixed cell addresses, 160, 174,
   181-184
mode indicators, 48-49
modes
   DEBUG, 467-469
   EDIT, 476
      direction keys, 58-59
      invoking, 86
      key actions, 87-88
      SpeedBar, 475
   Insert, 86
   Overtype, 86
   POINT, 106, 117
   READY, 475-483

recalculation, 148
Sync, 136
Text, 29-30, 118
WYSIWYG, 29-30
modifying databases, 395-400
monitors
   graphics, 331
   installing, 491-492
mouse, 8
   highlighting blocks, 106
   selecting commands, 69-70
moving
   cell selector, 118, 497-498
   cells, 160-163
multiplication (*) operator, 79

N

@NA function, 251
names
   blocks, 56, 104, 108-114
      deleting, 89, 114-115
      listing, 117-118
      notes, 120-122
      resetting, 89
      selecting, 118
      tables, 104, 119-120
   cell groups, 111
   cell series, 112, 114
   files, 90-93
   keys, 446
   macros, 447, 456, 459
   single cells, 111
natural order calculation, 148
negative values, 207
network servers, 492
nonprinting (¦¦) symbol, 269

#NOT# search operator, 436

not equal to (< >) operator, 245, 431

notes, blocks, 104, 120-122

@NOW function, 233

@NPV (present value) function, 83

numbers

  converting decimals to integers, 228

  decimal places, 207

  entering, 76

  exponential, 207

  rounding, 229

  rows, 10

  see also values

numeric keypad, 28-39

O

one-key column sort, 408, 411

one-key row sort, 402, 404

open-ended extract area, 426

open-ended output blocks, 424

opening files, 97

operators, 56

  < (less than), 431

  <= (less than or equal to), 431

  <> (not equal to), 431

  = (equal to), 431

  > (greater than), 431

  >= (greater than or equal to), 431

  complex

    #AND#, 245

    #NOT#, 245

    #OR#, 245

  logical

    < (less than), 244

    < > (not equal to), 245

    <= (less than or equal to), 245

    = (equal to), 244

    > (greater than), 244

    >= (greater than or equal to), 244

  mathematical, 79-86

    * (multiplication), 79

    + (positive/addition), 79

    – (negative/subtraction), 79

    / (division), 79

    ^ (exponentiation), 79

  order of precedence, 79

  search

    #AND#, 436

    #NOT#, 436

    #OR#, 436

/Options SpeedBar command, 477

options

  Graph menu, 332

  Print menu, 257

  printing, resetting, 288-289

/Options Display Mode command, 30

/Options Format Global Width command, 128

/Options Formats Align Labels command, 75

/Options Formats Hide Zeros command, 146

/Options Formats Numeric Format command, 202-204

/Options Hardware Printers command, 291

/Options International command, 209

/Options Protection Enable command, 150

/Options Protection Formulas command, 153

/Options Recalculation command, 148

/Options Startup Directory command, 317

/Options Update command, 90

#OR# search operator, 436

order of precedence, 56, 79-80

origin, axes, 330, 347

output blocks
databases, 424, 426
limiting size, 426
open-ended, 424

Overtype mode, 86

P

page breaks
establishing, 276
spreadsheet, 276-278

page length, 283

page numbers, controlling, 278

page-break symbol (¦ ::), 276

panning graphs, 373-375

paper
advancing, 275-276
continous-feed, 275
movement, 274-278

parentheses, 80, 207

passwords, 296
changing, 301
creating, 298
deleting, 300-301
files, 297-301
spreadsheets, 298

@PAYMT (loan payment) function, 83

@PAYMT function, 236

Percent format, 208

period (.), 37, 450

pie graph, 341

plotting, 347

plus sign (+), 312

POINT mode, 106, 117

pointers, mouse
Text mode, 30
WYSIWYG mode, 30

points, data, 347

position
databases, spreadsheets, 390
macros, spreadsheets, 454-455

PostScript printer, 291

prearranged fonts, 214

prefixes, labels, 56, 72-75, 448

present values, calculating, 237

previewing printed documents, 284-285

primary cell, 312

/Print Adjust Printer command, 275

/Print Adjust Printer Align command, 276

/Print Adjust Printer Skip Line command, 275

/Print Block command, 110, 428

/Print Block Layout Header command, 279

/Print Destination File command, 255-256, 289

/Print Destination Printer command, 255-256

/Print Destination Screen Preview command, 284-285

print files, creating, 256

/Print Format Cell-Formulas command, 286, 82

/Print Graph Print command, 379
/Print Headings command, 262-264
/Print Layout command, 283
/Print Layout Reset command, 259,
   288-289
Print menu, options, 257
printers
   advancing paper, 275-276
   aligning paper, 276
   configuring, 490
   graphics, 331
   paper movement, 274-278
   PostScript, 291
   printing directly to, 256
   selecting, installation, 492
printing, 255-256
   blocks, 257, 260
      excluding, 272, 274
      macro, 471-472
      segments, excluding, 266-274
   columns, excluding, 267-269
   defaults, 256
   draft-quality, 258-266
   files to disk, 255
   footers, 278-281
   graphs, 331, 379-380
   headers, 278-281
   headings, 262-266
   layout, *see* layout
   listings, cell contents, 286-288
   options, resetting, 288-289
   previewing, 284-285
   rows, excluding, 269, 272
   screens, full, 258-259
   single-page document, 259, 262
   snapshot printout, 259
   spreadsheets, portions, 110
printing commands, 504-506
PRN file, 91, 256-257

program (Quattro Pro) diskettes,
   490
programs, 446
@PROPER function, 248
protecting, 126
   formulas, 153-155
   spreadsheets, 150-155
pull-down menu bar, 43
@PVAL (present value) function, 83
@PVAL function, 237

Q

Quattro Pro
   diskettes, 490
   exiting, 30-35
   installing, 489-494
   loading, 494
   quitting, 494
   reconfiguring, 494
   starting, 28
   suspending, 30-35
   upgrading, 494-495
Query (F7) key, 441
question mark (?) wild card, 97, 322
quitting Quattro Pro, 494

R

READY mode, 475-483
recalculation
   columnwise, 148
   modes, 148
   natural order, 148
   rowwise, 148
   spreadsheets, 148-150, 160
   see also calculating
recording keystrokes, macros,
   459-463

records, 384-385
  adding, 386
  editing during search, 422-423
  extracted, printing, 428
  extracting, 427-428
  inserting/deleting, 396-398
  searching
    criteria, 420-422
    deleting, 438-441
    listing, 423-428
  searching for, 414-441
  sorting, 400-414
  unique, searching for, 437-438
refreshing links, 315-316
relative cell addresses, 160, 174-176
@REPEAT function, 83, 249
repeating
  footers, 281
  headers, 281
  headings, 262
  strings, 249
replacing, 197-198
  cells, contents, 191, 194-198
  strings with strings, 194-197
resetting
  formats, 209
  options, printing, 288-289
restoring, columns, hidden, 269
retrieving files, 95-99
  different drive, 99
  from subdirectories, 98
  partial, 302-311
  password-protected, 300
  wild cards, 97
reverse video, 106
rotated bar graphs, 342
@ROUND (rounding) function, 83, 229

rounding, 229
row numbers, 10
rows, 10
  copying to column format, 188
  databases, 402-407
  deleting, 143-145
  headings, 256
    printing, 262, 266
    repeating, 262
  inserting, 141-143
  printing, excluding, 269, 272
  titles, locked, 137-140
  transposing, 186-188
rowwise calculation, 148

S

saving
  files, 92-95
    macro, 472
    new name, 93
    partial, 302-311
  settings, graphs, 375-376
scaling, axes, 347, 357
Scientific format, 207
screen
  clearing, spreadsheets, 296
  graphs, viewing, 331
  input line, 44
  printing, full, 258-259
  pull-down menu bar, 43
  SpeedBar, 42-47
  splitting, 133-137
  spreadsheet area, 42-44
  status line, 42, 45
Screen Previewer
  commands, 284-285
  movement keys, 285

scrolling, 60-62, 136
search operators
   #AND#, 436
   #NOT#, 436
   #OR#, 436
search requirements, 415-416
search string, 160
searching, 197-198, 437
  databases
     criteria tables, 418-420
     data blocks, 416-418
  for records, 414-441
  for strings, 191, 194
  records
     criteria, 420-422
     deleting, 438-441
     editing, 422-423
     listing, 423-428
searching/replacing, 191-198
segments, blocks, excluding from
  printing, 266-274
selecting
  block names, 118
  cells, 8
  commands from menus, 67-70
  graphs, types, 339-348
  printers, installation, 492
serial numbers, converting, 83,
  231-232
series
  blocks, specifying, 348-356
  cells, naming, 112-114
  graphs, 334
settings, graphs, saving, 375-376
shading
  blocks, 218-219
  borders, blocks, 215-219

@SIN (sine) function, 83
single cells, naming, 111
slash (/) key, 19
snapshot printout, 259
sorting databases, 386
  one-key, 402-411
  records, 400-414
  two-key, 405-407
source block, 160
spaces
  file names, 91
  formulas, 82
special functions
  @ERR, 251
  @HLOOKUP, 251-252
  @NA, 251
  @VLOOKUP, 251-252
specifying
  blocks, 118, 348-356
  criteria, multiple, 432-436
  directories, 317-320
  drives, 317-320
SpeedBar, 20, 28, 42-47, 476
  buttons, 476-486
  customizing commands, 513
  EDIT mode, 475, 484-487
  READY mode, 475
split screen, 133, 136-137
spreadsheet area, 42, 44
spreadsheets, 8-11
  calculating/recalculating, 10, 126,
   148-150
  clearing from screen, 296
  commands, 500-503
  data
     editing, 86-88
     entering, 71-86

databases, positioning, 390
electronic, 11-22
extracting data, 302-305
formats, 204-209
graphs, inserting, 377-378
macros, positioning, 454-455
navigating, 56-66
page breaks, 276-278
passwords, 298
printing, portions, 110
protecting, 150-155
    blocks, 151-153
    formulas, 153-155
recalculating, 160
size, 13-14
SpeedBar, 45-47
values, saving to file, 305
windows, 15
@SQRT (square root) function, 83
stacked-bar graph, 341
starting Quattro Pro, 28
statistical functions, 83, 237-241
    @AVG, 83, 238-239
    @COUNT, 239-240
    @MAX, 83, 240
    @MIN, 83
    @STD, 83
    @SUM, 83
    @VAR, 83
status indicators, 49
status line, 42-45
@STD function, 83
@STRING function, 83
string functions, 246-249
    @LOWER, 83, 248
    @PROPER, 248
    @REPEAT, 83, 249

@STRING, 83
@UPPER, 83, 248
@VALUE, 83
strings
    case, converting, 248
    repeating, 249
    replacing with strings, 194, 197
    search, 160
    searching for, 191, 194
/Style Alignment command, 74
/Style Block Size command, 126, 129
/Style Column Width command, 126-128, 391
/Style Define Style command, 220
/Style Font command, 210
/Style FontTable command, 214
/Style Hide Column command, 131, 209
/Style Hide Column Expose command, 132, 269
/Style Hide Column Hide command, 267, 268
/Style Insert Break command, 276-277
/Style Line Drawing command, 215-216
/Style Numeric Format command, 82, 202-204, 272
/Style Protection Protect command, 153
/Style Protection Unprotect command, 153
/Style Reset Width command, 128
/Style Shading command, 219
/Style Use Style command, 221

styles
   applying, 221
   custom, 222
   defining, 220-222
subdirectories, 98
   see also directories, 98
@SUM function, 83
supporting cell, 312
suppressing zeros, 146-148
suspending Quattro Pro, 30-35
Sync mode, 136
syntax, 226
system prompt, 28

T

tables
   blocks, names, 104, 119-120
   entries, finding, 251-252
@TAN (tangents) function, 83
templates, 296, 305
text
   entering, macro, 472
   footers, positioning, 278
   graphs, notes, 356
   headers, 278
Text format, 208
text graph, 344
Text mode, 29-30, 118
tick marks, 330, 347
tilde (~), 446, 449
@TIME function, 83
times, converting to serial numbers, 83
titles, 358
   graphs
      displaying, 358-360
      editing, 360
   locking, 126, 137-140

/Tools Combine command, 302-305
/Tools Combine Copy command, 309
/Tools Import command, 257
/Tools Macro Debugger command, 467
/Tools Macro Execute command, 447, 463
/Tools Macro Paste command, 461
/Tools Macro Record command, 459
/Tools Update Links Refresh command, 315
/Tools What-If command, 208
/Tools Xtract Formulas command, 302, 305, 428
/Tools Xtract Values command, 305
transposing
   blocks, 188
   columns, 186, 188
   rows, 186, 188
@TRUE function, 83, 246
two-key sort, 405-407

U

Undo, 88-90
   activating, 89
   macros, 466
unique records, 437-438
updating files, 93
upgrading, 494-495
@UPPER function, 83, 248

V

@VALUE function, 83
values, 56
   converting from formulas, 188-190

dates, converting to serial
   numbers, 231
future, calculating, 237
maximum/minimum, 240
negative, 207
present, calculating, 237
rounding, 229
spreadsheets, saving to file, 305
@VAR function, 83
viewing graphs
   current, 357
   on-screen, 331
@VLOOKUP function, 251-252

W

"what-if" analyses, 17-19, 330
wild cards, 56, 97
   * (asterisk), 97, 322
   ? (question mark), 97, 322
   criteria tables, 429
/Window Options Clear command,
   137
/Window Options Grid Lines Display
   command, 215
/Window Options Horizontal
   command, 134
/Window Options Locked Titles
   command, 137

/Window Options Sync command,
   136
/Window Options Unsync
   command, 136
Windows, installing Quattro Pro,
   493
windows, 15, 126
   scrolling, split screen, 136
worksheets, *see* spreadsheets
WYSIWYG (What You See Is What
   You Get), 29-30

X

x-axis, 330, 347, 348
XY graphs, 340

Y

y-axis, 330, 347-348

Z

zeros, suppressing, 146-148
zooming, 373-375
   (– –) double minus sign, 373
   (+ +) double-plus sign, 373
   (= =) double-equal sign, 373

Computer Books from Que Mean PC Performance!

Que—The Leader in Spreadsheet Information!

Using Quattro Pro 4, Special Edition

Patrick T. Burns

This complete, easy-to-follow introduction to Quattro Pro includes in-depth tutorials, tips, and a tear-out Menu Map.

Versions 3 & 4

$27.95 USA
0-88022-931-4, 1,000 pp., 7³/₈ x 9¹/₄

More Spreadsheet Titles From Que

Excel 4 for Windows QuickStart

Version 4 for Windows

$21.95 USA
0-88022-925-X, 400 pp., 7³/₈ x 9¹/₄

Excel 4 for Windows Quick Reference

Version 4

$9.95 USA
0-88022-958-6, 160 pp., 4³/₄ x 8

Quattro Pro 4 Quick Reference

Version 4

$9.95 USA
0-88022-939-X, 160pp., 4³/₄ x 8

Quattro Pro 4 QuickStart

Versions 3 & 4

$21.95 USA
0-88022-938-1, 500 pp., 7³/₈ x 9¹/₄

Using Excel 4 for Windows, Special Edition

Through Latest Version

$29.95 USA
0-88022-916-0, 1,034 pp., 7³/₈ x 9¹/₄

Easy Excel

Shelley O'Hara

This revolutionary text provides ideal coverage for beginners. 4-color illustrations, step-by-step instructions, and before-and-after screen shots make learning easy.

Version 3

$19.95 USA
0-88022-820-2, 200 pp., 8 x 10

Using SuperCalc5, 2nd Edition

SuperCalc4 & SuperCalc5

$29.95 USA
0-88022-404-5, 575 pp., 7³/₈ x 9¹/₄

que

To Order, Call: (800) 428-5331 OR (317) 573-2500

Teach Yourself
with QuickStarts from Que!

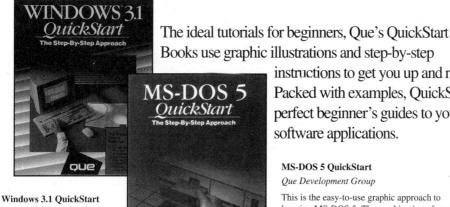

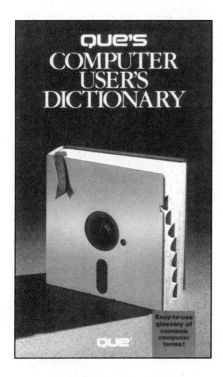